T4-ADM-411

SONG OF THE SKYLARK II
Meditation—
Teachings and Practices

Gabriel Gomes

UNIVERSITY
PRESS OF
AMERICA

LANHAM • NEW YORK • LONDON

Copyright © 1991 by
University Press of America®, Inc.
4720 Boston Way
Lanham, Maryland 20706

3 Henrietta Street
London WC2E 8LU England

All rights reserved
Printed in the United States of America
British Cataloging in Publication Information Available

Library of Congress Cataloging-in-Publication Data

Gomes, Gabriel, 1946-
Song of the skylark / Gabriel Gomes.
p. cm.
Includes bibliographical references and indexes.
Contents: 1. Foundations of experiential religion.
— 2. Meditation : teachings and practices.
1. Spiritual life. 2. Experience (Religion) 3. Meditation.
4. Buddhism—Docttines. I. Title.
BL624.G645   1991
291.4—dc20   91-7893 CIP

ISBN 0–8191–8222–2 (v. 1)
ISBN 0–8191–8223–0 (v. 1 : pbk.)

ISBN 0–8191–8224–9 (v. 2)
ISBN 0–8191–8225–7 (v. 2 : pbk.)

The paper used in this publication meets the minimum requirements of American National Standard for Information Sciences—Permanence of Paper for Printed Library Materials, ANSI Z39.48–1984.

For my mother,
Veronica Maharani Gomes,
who taught me compassion

Copyright Acknowledgements

Grateful acknowledgement is made for permission to reprint excerpts from the following works:

Specific excerpts from *The Practice of Zen* by Garma Chen Chi Chang. Copyright © 1959 by Garma Chen Chi Chang. Reprinted by permission of Harper & Row, Publishers, Inc.

The Three Pillars of Zen, by Philip Kapleau, *Doubleday,* a division of Bantam, Doubleday, Dell Publishing Company, copyright © 1972.

Zen Flesh, Zen Bones, compiled by Paul Reps. Reprinted by permission of Charles E. Tuttle Co., Inc., Tokyo, Japan.

All Biblical citations are from *The New English Bible with the Apocrypha.* New York: Oxford University Press, 1971.

Contents

Preface ix
Introduction xi
1. The Nature, Aims, and Forms of Meditation 1
2. Informal Awareness Meditation 17
3. The Process of Formal Meditation 31
4. Ground Rules for Formal Meditation 51
5. Meaning of the Term *Yoga* 63
6. The *Yoga Sutras* of Patanjali .69
7. Glimpses of *Jnana, Bhakti,* and *Mantra Yoga* 99
8. The Tantric Journey 113
9. The Theravada Path: Concentration and Insight 131
10. The Path of Zen 153
11. The Vajrayana Path: Tibetan Tantras 175
12. The Path of Power: Taoist Meditation 207
13. The Way of Kabbalah 217
14. Christian Meditation: The Eastern Church 229
15. Christian Meditation: The Western (Catholic) Church 237
16. The Way of the Sufi 255
17. Conclusion 269
    Bibliography 271
    Index 283

Preface

This book (together with its companion volume, *Song of the Skylark I: Foundations of Experiential Religion*), has been over a decade in the making. I started getting the initial ideas as early as 1974. But it was not until the fall of 1979, when Marymount College gave me a sabbatical, that I wrote the bulk of the work in the idyllic setting of a solitary house nestled in the woods of Vermont. Every summer thereafter I returned to that house, graciously made available by the owner, my friend Carol-Rae Hoffmann of Philadelphia, to add further refinements. By the end of the summer of 1986 the work was completed. But it required a great deal of revision. Marymount again came to the rescue with another sabbatical in 1987-88.

A work such as this, written over such a long time, needed the help and encouragement (in addition to that of Marymount College) of many friends and colleagues. Sue Bowen, Sr. Ellen Marie Keane, John Lawry, Richard Stojda, and Frederick Strath gave me much encouragement. Julius Vande Kopple, Jeff Gold, and Father Joachim Snyder helped me with the computer. Patrick and Sonya Munroe provided much assistance and encouragement. Patrick also graciously proofread several chapters. Karen Honeycutt, of Berkeley, California, did a splendid job in preparing the camera-ready copy. I am grateful to them all for their assistance and encouragement. I am also indebted to the teachers of insight meditation at the Insight Meditation Society, Barre, Massachusetts—Ruth Denison, Larry Rosenberg, Christopher Titmuss, and Jack Kornfield. I have incorporated their insights and meditation methods in the chapter on the Theravada Buddhist meditation. Above all, I am grateful to Caroline Whiting for her expert editing and proofreading. This book might not have seen the light of day without her felicitous improvement of my English and her deft deletion of unnecessary repetitions.

Introduction

Originally, this volume was planned as an integral part of *Song of the Skylark I*. In conception and method they are one work, but for various practical considerations (I did not wish to force today's overtaxed reader to wade through the theoretical discussions found in *Song of the Skylark I*), I have decided to make them two independent volumes. The two works are not only related; the serious reader will find it essential to read and digest *Song of the Skylark I* in order to fully understand the content of *Song of the Skylark II*. In a real sense the former is a fruit of and illuminates the latter which, in turn, verifies the content of the former. Thus they are complementary and ideally should be read together to gain full understanding and maximum benefit. Still, each is self-contained and can be read independently without any damage to clarity or completeness.

In this volume I have included, virtually unchanged, two of the general chapters on meditation from *Song of the Skylark I*. They form a logical framework for the chapters devoted to the particular meditative traditions representing the sources of what I have called "experiential religion." The individual chapters on meditation break fresh ground, providing details on how each tradition envisions the goal(s) of meditation and carves out the steps toward its realization. In these chapters I have presented a theoretical discussion of these paths and a step-by-step outline of the meditative practices designed to lead the practitioner to the goal. I have included only those representative meditative exercises that provide both a theoretical understanding and an opportunity for the reader to practice on his/her own. Because these chapters are only introductory guides, the reader who wants to become a serious practitioner of a particular path will need to find a qualified teacher and continue under his/her guidance. And s/he will find guidelines on finding a teacher in *Song of the Skylark I*.

In the chapters on particular meditative traditions, I have tried to be representative rather than exhaustive. To represent Hinduism, I have included somewhat lengthy treatments of Patanjali's *Yoga Sutras* and *Tantra*, but shorter ones of *Jnana, Bhakti,* and *Mantra Yogas*. Since Hinduism enfolds many paths, for the sake of brevity I have stayed with these classical and universally recognized paths and away from their offshoots. Similarly, I have included only Theravada Buddhist meditation, Zen, and Tibetan Yoga to represent Buddhism. For lack of available texts in translation at the time of writing, I had to limit the treatment of Taoist Yoga. The same was true of Jewish meditation when I began this study about a decade ago. Now, however, Jewish meditative practices are more openly discussed. For lack of time or space, I could not undertake a full-scale study of all of them here.

The situation is somewhat different with Christian meditative practices. Eastern Orthodox Christianity seems to practice only one type of meditation — "the Jesus Prayer." But Western Christianity, particularly the Roman Catholic tradition, seems to have various meditative schools. Moreover, while Western literature on spirituality and mysticism is enormous, actual descriptions of specific meditative methods are not numerous. Thus I had to limit myself to describing the Jesus Prayer on the one hand and a few meditative exercises culled from classical and contemporary treatments on the other.

Since Sufi initiates vow to keep their meditative practices secret (this is true also of many other traditions), I had to rely on partial descriptions by various authors to piece together the Sufi meditative methods. In attempting to gather information from various translations and secondary sources, I have found that a lack of knowledge of the original languages is truly a hindrance. The works of those authorities who are not themselves practitioners usually show only a partial, erroneous, or confused grasp of meditation. I have tried not to become a victim of the same pitfalls.

The aim of *Song of the Skylark II* is to provide the reader/practitioner a way beyond the oblivion of time, beyond conditioned existence and the problems inherent in it, beyond the present constructions of reality, consciousness, and self; and a realization of that Reality and Awareness that alone brings a full blossoming of humanity by fully incarnating the eternal and the unconditioned in the particularity of time and conditioned existence.

Chapter 1
The Nature, Aims and Forms of Meditation

The Nature and Aims of Meditation

The term *meditation* is currently in vogue in the West. Over the past two decades, an influx of teachers from the East has made it a familiar, if not a household, word. Yet these teachers of diverse methods, each claiming to have the only true or effective path, have often created confusion about the nature and goals of meditation. The general bewilderment many people feel about the subject is compounded by the fact that teachers representing various traditions and methods use the same terms with different meanings. Furthermore, the meanings of words may vary from East to West and according to the specific context of their use. To avoid such pitfalls, I shall approach this discussion on the nature of meditation in terms of its aims.

Although there may be as many reasons to meditate as there are meditators, there appears to be a direct correlation between the intentions of meditators and the three levels of the meditative path: the physiological level, the psychological level, and the spiritual level. Most definitions of meditation include one or more of these levels.

The Physiological Level

Many people begin to practice meditation merely as a technique for relaxation. In a high-pressure, technological society, meditation has become a means of obtaining various physiological benefits. Newspapers frequently report that management training centers are teaching meditative techniques for relaxation and stress reduction. As Daniel Goleman reports, many psychotherapists use it as a method "for patients to manage anxiety without drugs" (1: 169). He says that in 1984 the National Institute of Health issued a report that recommended meditation "above prescription drugs in the first treatment of mild hypertension" (1: 168). Many medical centers throughout the country are undertaking meditation research and teaching patients how to relax in order to reduce stress, tension, and anxiety. Goleman observes that the evidence for the effectiveness of meditation, through relaxation, in treating stress disorders has become compelling (1: 169).[1]

In addition, by inducing relaxation, meditation has been found to lower blood pressure and cholesterol levels, improve blood flow to the heart, and increase circulation. Thus it can help prevent heart disease and stroke.

Research has shown that meditation and relaxation can strengthen the immune system by improving the levels of natural killer cells and antibody titers, thus warding off disease, making people less susceptible to viruses, and helping patients with their own healing (Goleman 1: 170). Attempting to explain this improvement of the immune system, researchers in a new discipline, called psychoneuroimmunology (PNI), have stated, as reported by Rob Wechsler, that "the brain can send signals along nerves to enhance defenses against infection and pump out chemicals that make the body fight more aggressively against disease. And since the pathways can be turned on and off by thoughts and emotions... mental states can alter the course of an illness" (52). Thus the brain and the immune system make a closed circuit and work through feeding and feedback (52-61).

In many cases of diabetes, relaxation has been shown to improve the body's ability to regulate glucose. By reducing emotional upsets and constriction of air passages, meditation also seems to relieve asthma. It can lessen the severity of angina attacks and alleviate chronic, severe pain, migraine headaches, gastrointestinal problems, insomnia, emphysema, and skin disorders (Goleman 1: 168-171). In addition, meditation can cure psychosomatic illnesses, reduce various mental and physical malfunctionings, and increase energy and efficiency in everyday living.

As a result of the demonstrated effectiveness of meditative practice, many people have concluded that meditation is primarily a powerful relaxation technique. As impressive as the stress reduction results are (and each day an increasing number are being reported in medical journals and other periodicals), we must not likewise conclude that meditation is merely a method of attaining physiological benefits. Traditionally, such benefits have been perceived as consequences of meditation, not as goals. In the words of Roger Walsh, the goals of meditation are: to become "conscious of and familiar with our inner life;" to develop "deep insight into the nature of mental processes, consciousness, identity, and reality;" and to attain "optimal states of psychological well-being and consciousness;" and, ultimately, to reach "the source of life and consciousness" (1: 18-19).

Thus meditation is ultimately concerned with bringing about a state of being that not only frees the mind from all existing programming but also does not give rise to new programming. The ultimate state realized in meditation is a state beyond ordinary consciousness. As consciousness is formed by and functions through programming, construct, content, object, and thought, and reacts to stimuli, it is subject to disturbance. Only what is programmed and reacts accordingly can be disturbed. Where there is no programming or content and no functioning through any medium, nothing can act as a stimulus for disturbance. Since only a state beyond programming can free the mind of programmings, traditionally meditation has sought to bring the mind to the state beyond conditioning (to the "source of life and consciousness," as Walsh put it). The following Zen story illustrates how one is relaxed at all times and under all circumstances in this state:

> Buddha told a parable in a Sutra: A man travelling across a field encountered a tiger. He fled, the tiger after him. Coming to a precipice, he caught hold of a wild vine and swung himself down over the edge. The tiger sniffed at him from above. Trembling, the man looked down to where, far below, another tiger was waiting to eat him. Only the vine sustained him. Two mice, one white and one black, little by little started to gnaw away the vine. The man saw a luscious strawberry near him. Grasping the vine with one hand, he plucked the strawberry with the other. How sweet it tasted. (Reps 22-23)

The Psychological Level

To arrive at such a state of continuous mental relaxation that no external event can trigger panic, anxiety, tension, or stress is the goal of the second level of meditation. Additionally, this level is concerned with letting go of control, striving, and the effort to maintain and enhance yourself and your world, which frees you to live continuously in the open space of pure awareness and free being.

This state is not easily arrived at. Suppose you enter an elevator and a woman steps on your toe, cutting a nice slice of skin with the sharp spike of her heel. Do you feel relaxed? Do you smile and thank her for stepping on your toe? Or suppose you have an important job interview, and you are at the station waiting for the train. The station master announces that the train will be delayed an hour, and you cannot get to a phone because they are all tied up. Are you relaxed? If you have just been fired, if your son has just wrecked your car, if your wife has just announced that she is leaving you, do you feel very relaxed?

You may begin a meditation practice in order to relax, and you may feel tranquil during meditation. But as you enter your round of daily activities, you soon discover that your negative programming pulls you out of your relaxed, alert state and plunges you back into a whirlpool of anger, fear, frustration, stress, tension, or anxiety. You realize that in order to remain in relaxed awareness, you need to develop a discipline to keep your awareness free of entrapment in negative programs that create mental turmoil and emotional roller coasters. The development of such a discipline is the task of the second level of meditation. The first-level goal of relaxation is not enough. You must move beyond the physiological to the psychological level so you can free your mind of all programs that trap awareness and fill your world with tension.

At this level you begin by facing yourself and seeing yourself as you actually are. You discover that your mind is constructed with systems of programming, hemming you in, restricting you in every direction, and depriving you of a direct contact with anything. It dawns on you that your task is to free the mind of this programming by dissolving old fixations and habits, removing limits and distortions caused by dualistic constructs, clearing emotional blockages, and freeing awareness from entrapment in thoughts, objects, and mental contents. Eventually you realize that, since your consciousness is constructed of programmings, unless it is completely deconstructed your awareness cannot become fully free. Working on this task enables your attention to stop darting habitually in different directions and to gather and unify around the object of meditation. This allows awareness to begin to expand, eventually transcending the personal stage and venturing out into the transpersonal, spiritual realm. It is at this second, psychological level, that you begin the process of deconstructing and transforming your consciousness, identity, and reality.

These essential tasks of the second level are clearly reflected in many discussions of meditation. For example, Tarthang Tulku has said, "Meditation is the process of self-discovery. On one level the meditation experience shows us the pattern of our lives—how we have carried on our emotional characteristics since childhood. But on another level it frees us from these patterns, making it easier for us to see our inner potential" (1: 97). Thus Tulku clearly recognizes not only the first step of the psychological level, i.e., facing yourself and seeing how your mind has been programmed; but also the second step, i.e., freeing your mind of programming and contents.

Chogyam Trungpa has observed, "Meditation is not a matter of trying to achieve ecstasy, spiritual bliss or tranquility, nor is it attempting to become a better person. It is simply the creation of a space in which we are able to expose and undo our neurotic games, our self-deceptions, our hidden fears and hopes" (4: 2). And Claudio Naranjo has defined meditation as "a persistent effort to detect and become free of all conditioning, compulsive functioning of mind and body, habitual emotional responses that may contaminate the utterly simple situation required by the participant" (Naranjo & Ornstein 9).

The process of becoming free starts with noticing and identifying your programmings. Ordinarily, they not only go unnoticed, remaining beyond your control, but they even control ordinary consciousness. Once you detect and bring them to consciousness, the next step is to become free by dissolving the negative programs and by removing the programs that limit the positive qualities. In this way meditation helps clear the mind of the fixations, distortions, filters, selective attention, limitations, and interpretations that consciousness habitually imposes on things. Void of this imposition, we can directly experience and deal with each situation without interference from conditioning. Arthur Deikman calls this destructuring process "deautomatization" and says that the very nature of meditation involves "an undoing of a psychic structure, permitting the experience of increased detail and sensation at the price of requiring more attention" (Ornstein 2: 229).

Whereas habituation makes us unaware, deautomatization destructures consciousness and frees awareness by dissolving conditioning and habituation. To the extent that consciousness is deautomatized, awareness becomes free, to be invested in whatever is at hand. You start to see things clearly and directly; you notice what is going on in and around you.

Perceiving the centrality of the destructuring process, Robert Ornstein defines meditation as "a set of techniques designed to produce an alteration in consciousness by shifting attention away from the active, object-oriented, linear mode toward the receptive mode, and often, from an external focus of attention to an internal one" (1: 158). When understood not as a regression to the prepersonal stage but as a transcendence of the personal, this destructuring is characteristic not only of the second level of meditation, but also all its phases. Without deconstruction, neither the continuous state of relaxation, nor freedom from negative programming and enhancement of positive states, nor attainment of higher states, nor realization of the ultimate goal of meditation is possible. So long as the mind remains fixated and operates from fixations, it will maintain the present construction, experience separation from Reality, and prevent the emergence of transpersonal states. Thus deconstruction constitutes the very heart of the second level and is the key to meditation as a whole.

Essential to this deconstruction is a reversal of the process by which ordinary consciousness is constructed, reinforced, and maintained. And essential to the reversal are disidentification with and nonattachment to external objects and mental contents. Disidentification and nonattachment are thus essential to transcendence of the personal and realization of the transpersonal states. Indeed, they are so central that meditation can be said to consist of their sustained and continuous practice until complete transcendence of all constructs and programs has been attained. At the point of complete nonattachment, you realize your identity with Reality as Such.

A recognition of this essential point has led Ken Wilber to say that meditation is nothing but a "sustained instrumental path of transcendence. And since transcendence and development are synonymous, it follows that meditation is simply *sustained development* or growth" (3: 93-99; 5: 103-117; italics his). And for Wilber, differentiation or disidentification is the principle by which an individual grows through the successive stages, from prepersonal to transpersonal, until one reaches the ultimate state of Consciousness as Such, which is the final goal of meditation.

Outside the period of formal meditation, in the daily activities of life, the process of deconstruction occurs through the continuous practice of disidentification and nonattachment, especially toward objects of identification, attachment, and desire. Such practice enables you to break free of fixations resulting from habitual ways of thinking, feeling, and acting. As you break free, your scattered attention becomes unified and present-centered, and awareness begins to expand and overcome its distance from things.

During the period of formal meditation itself, consciousness is deconstructed by shifting its orientation from the outside world inward, toward itself. This shift is achieved by stopping its usual mode of functioning. This cessation requires the essential step of cutting off the operations by which consciousness reinforces and maintains itself. The entire mechanism that reinforces and maintains consciousness is deactivated by cutting off external sensory stimuli and internal dialogue, and by keeping attention focused directly on the object of meditation or on the sensory stimuli or mental contents.

Ordinarily, consciousness keeps its attention focused on sensory stimuli, which prompts it to constantly scan the environment, darting from one object to another in order to stabilize and maintain itself and its separation from the world. Moreover, as we have seen, in being focused on the world, attention invariably becomes fixated, trapped, and lost. Unless the external orientation is reversed and attention is directed toward itself, toward its root and source, even a single object to which it is tied will maintain the object orientation, the existing constructions of reality, consciousness and self, and prevent the emergence of higher states. One aim of keeping attention focused on the meditation object is to stop outside stimuli from reinforcing consciousness by triggering thoughts and the information-processing activities.

In addition, consciousness maintains itself and its separation from the world by triggering an incessant flow of thoughts and keeping a running commentary on everything, creating an illusion of continuity, identity, and permanence. Without stopping thoughts, programmed reactions, and the internal dialogue, the ordinary construction of consciousness will continue to be reinforced, and the crucial shift necessary for deconstruction and transcendence will be prevented. Moreover, so long as thoughts persist, attention will also remain trapped in dualistic thinking, and the shift will not occur.

In order to achieve the external and the internal shift, then, it is absolutely crucial that you keep your attention riveted directly on the primary stimulus or the first moment of impact of the meditation object and directly experience it prior to the triggering of thoughts, mental reactions, or any information-processing activities. When you are able to sustain the focus of attention for prolonged periods of time without letting your attention wander or without becoming lost in thought, the siege of the object-world upon your consciousness will begin to lift and your orientation will start to shift. As nothing intervenes at the point of immediate contact between the primary stimulus and attention, nothing will remain to reinforce or maintain the existing construction of consciousness. As a result, the latter will begin to lose its hold and awareness will begin to unify and transcend the ordinary constructions and rise to the trans-conscious states.

This inward shift and deconstruction, which will be explained later, proceeds from the outer to the inner, from the surface structure to the deep, inward structure, from the gross, perceptual to the symbolic, conceptual, or generalized structure. This deconstruction process is largely a reversal of the construction process. At each step of the shift, your attention breaks through yet another restriction, arriving at a more expanded and encompassing structure. A corresponding bridging of the distance between consciousness and reality also occurs. As all structures and forms become deconstructed and transcended, the separation between consciousness and reality disappears. Stopping or transcending thought is, therefore, essential to this inward turn. As Lama Govinda has observed, "In order to get to the hub of existence, into the center of our being, we must reverse the direction of our mental outlook and turn inward. This turning about in the depth of our consciousness is called *paravritti*, and is the main purpose of meditation" (2:106).

It follows that meditation cannot be equated with thinking, which can only trap awareness and reinforce the present construction. It cannot liberate the mind from itself. There is, however, a difference on this point between Eastern and Western approaches to meditation. In the West, particularly in the Catholic tradition, meditation is regarded as a discursive, sustained thought or a reflective inquiry into a subject. As a result, this tradition considers meditation as a stage preliminary to the more advanced stage of contemplation. In the East, on the other hand, essential to meditation is cutting through discursive thought and arriving at the state of awareness beyond thought. So in the East meditation is an advanced practice.

These differences arise from different goals. The East regards the ultimate aim of meditation to be a realization of the Unconditioned State. This state can be reached only by going beyond duality and discursive thought, which maintains duality. Thus the East defines meditation as a stage beyond thought. Working within the dualistic framework, however, the West does not consider discursive thought a hindrance to reaching the final goal of meditation. For the West this goal is not generally considered a realization of *identity* with God but a state of permanent *union* with "him." So the West is not adverse to viewing meditation in terms of thinking.

Nevertheless, meditation does not consist in thinking or trying not to think. Even in Christian meditation, at the advanced stage of infused contemplation, thinking falls away. The contemplative simply rests in a state of loving awareness of God's presence. So central is the need to stop thought that the ancient Indian sage Patanjali defined meditation as *chitta vritti nirodha*, that is, stopping mind-waves or deconstruction of the programmed mind (Prabhavananda and Isherwood 2: 11). For in order to bring about a complete shift in the orientation of consciousness — from the object-world toward itself — it is necessary to stop the entire range of its activities. Both the discursive thinking process of the conscious level and the constant churning of the unconscious, which produces the thoughts, must cease, which will result in deconstruction.

Essentially agreeing with Patanjali, from the perspective of shamanism, Carlos Castaneda's don Juan says that stopping the internal dialogue is the key to transcending our view of the world, for the dialogue perpetuates that view and prevents transcendence. Unless attention turns away from the active face and its view of the world, its receptive face cannot be directed toward Reality. When the dialogue stops, the orientation of consciousness shifts as it pivots around and "faces" itself. As it pivots on itself, as Chuang Tzu intimated, the mind becomes empty, silent, and still; it sheds its identification with objects and consequent limitations and conditions; it experiences itself purely as itself. This process is like closing the door on the active and opening it to the receptive mode of the Janus-faced mind, with the shifts or pivoting taking place at critical junctures. Each one of these shifts consists of deconstructing a layer of programming until all layers are transcended.

The Nature, Aims and Forms of Meditation

In meditation, the mind is like a swinging door, swinging from doing, striving, and grasping to letting go and just Being. In this way, it transcends its fixation on things, on the limits of the objective mode, and becomes pure, limitless Awareness without contents or objects. This shift of the mind toward its essential nature is the essence of the inward turn, which is at the same time its turning directly toward Reality.

This shift from the active to the receptive mode seems to create a paradoxical situation for meditation. As Rajneesh states, "Meditation is always passive; the very essence of it is passive. It cannot be active because the very nature of it is non-doing. If you are doing something, your very doing disturbs the whole thing" (1: 16). Christian infused contemplation is likewise purely passive, as it depends solely on the action of God or All-embracing Awareness. This is true also of the advanced stages of other paths. And yet in meditation you are told to *do* something: to count or follow or observe the breath, to concentrate on an internal or external object, to chant or silently repeat a mantra, to visualize a *mandala*, to whirl *(dhikr)*, and so on. Is this not contradictory? How can you arrive at a state in which there is nowhere to go or nothing to do or to achieve—which means that there is really no arriving or going anywhere—by trying to get there? How can you arrive at not-doing *(wu wei)* by doing?

This seeming paradox can be explained by noting that meditation is an active way of deactivating the mind, of making it totally still, void of doing, so that it can purely BE. In this state there is no activity in the mind that is distinct from its being, so that doing becomes a manifestation of what is. In other words, the aim of meditation is to bring the mind to a state in which its being is its doing, and in which doing is nothing other than pure Awareness, identical with Reality as Such.

However, since our consciousness is so programmed to act, since it has been on automatic pilot for so long, it cannot simply cease doing, striving, controlling, managing, and fixing things; it cannot purely BE. Even its attempts to stop itself are expressions of striving; you cannot just take out the key of a car that has been running and make it stop instantly. As Rajneesh points out, if you have been continuously in an active mode, you cannot instantaneously stop and be nonactive (1: 18-22). If you could at will instantly stop your mind dead in its tracks, open it completely to itself, and directly experience what is, meditation would not be necessary. Since you cannot do that, at the initial phase of meditation your mind is given something to occupy itself with, to play its own game. But the nature of this activity is to undo the action mode by bringing it to a point at which all its activities cease and it becomes silent and still. This process uses doing to stop doing, arriving at not-doing through doing. The nature and aim of all meditative techniques is to use the same process by which the mind becomes programmed and fixated, and awareness trapped and lost, to unhook itself from all contents and objects, to destructure consciousness, and to arrive at absolutely free Awareness and Being.

The way the mind unhooks is by keeping its attention focused directly on the meditation object, not to create another programming, but to break free of automatic or programmed responses, habituation, and unawareness altogether. It is for this reason that you are instructed to hold your attention on the level of the primary stimulus before anything arises in the mind. This will bring the action mode to an impasse, and eventually it will cease its operation. Like a car without fuel, a mind without stimuli will stop running; its thoughts will subside, and its awareness will correspondingly increases, becoming free of conditioning and constructs. *The Lankavatara Sutra* describes this pivotal shift and deconstruction as a turning about in the deepest seat of consciousness, whereby awareness disengages from every content, object, construct, and conditioned state. Like the transformation of the caterpillar into a butterfly, this metamorphosis brings a transcendence of consciousness, and what emerges is pure, All-embracing Awareness. You cannot actively strive for or realize this transformation through any programming or construct (in fact by any means whatsoever), for it is the realm of the Unconditioned to which nothing conditioned has access.

You can see now why meditation is said to be a path without a goal, for the path is the goal. Because the programmed mind is tethered to obtaining results and pursuing goals, we seldom do anything except for the sake of some extrinsic reward that endows our action with value. Since a goal implies duality, a separation from what we desire, and striving only maintains it, all goal-oriented activities reinforce ordinary consciousness. As the ultimate aim of meditation is to deconstruct this consciousness and to arrive at the state beyond all duality or separation, it cannot have a goal external to itself. That is why the core of meditation does not consist in attaining any goal, but in erasing the separation from Reality created by our dualistic, goal-seeking activities. Meditation peels off all artificiality, removing all additives and preservatives deposited on us through years of conditioning, socialization, and training so that we can arrive at our natural, spontaneous, pure Self or nature.

The Spiritual Level

To arrive at this true nature or Self is the aim of the third or spiritual level of meditation. An intensification of the final phase of the psychological level naturally leads you to this third level. As attention stays focused on the meditation object for prolonged periods, awareness becomes unified; it penetrates and becomes one with the object, and, as it reverses its orientation and faces its ultimate nature, it becomes free of thought and the object-world. Thus it finally comes to experience its true nature in enlightenment.

While the second level of awakening, integration, unification, and expansion through the personal stage is concerned primarily with psychological growth, the third, spiritual, level involves growth through the transpersonal stages. While the initial steps of the second level have affinities with various psychologies and psychotherapies, at the third level these affinities are left behind. The cleaning out of negative programmings, habits, and psychic debris, and karmic residue continues, however. The third level is the spirit's return journey to itself, which requires a transcendence of every barrier, limitation, and condition until only pure, Unconditioned Spirit remains as the identity of all that is.

Recognizing this ultimate aim, many experts define meditation as the path toward a realization of the Spirit, the Self, God, or Reality as Such. The classical yogas, Buddhism, Taoism, Kabbalah, Christian mysticism, Sufism, and many of their offshoots embrace this definition. As Swami Muktananda has stated, "We do not meditate to relax a little and experience some peace. We meditate to unfold our inner being...Through meditation, our inner awareness expands and our understanding of inner and outer things becomes steadily deeper...Ultimately, meditation makes us aware of our own true nature. It is this awareness which removes all suffering and delusion, and this awareness comes when we see face to face our own inner Self" (20-24).

Buddhism calls this ultimate goal a realization of Nirvana or Buddha-nature. As Yasutani Roshi states in the context of Zen, the highest aim of Zen meditation is "the actualization of the Supreme Way throughout our entire being and in our daily life" (Kapleau 1: 48). The aim of Taoist meditation is returning to the Source, Tao, and realizing one's oneness with it. And in the traditions of Jewish, Christian and Islamic mysticism, the ultimate aim of meditation or contemplation is union with God. Sheikh Javad Nurbakhsh may well speak on behalf of all three Western traditions when he states:

> Meditation is one of the basic conditions for the attainment of voluntary death which is the aim of the Spiritual Path. As a result of meditation, the Sufi gradually becomes estranged from the world of 'I' and 'you.' He loses even the sense of meditation with its lingering quality of duality, God causing him to die to himself and bringing him to life in Himself. (1: 80-81)

In order to realize this voluntary death, you have to transcend the personal and successively pass through the transpersonal stages. On this spiritual path awareness steadily sheds conditioning, constructs, and limitations, expanding to include more reality in its sweep while at the same time overcoming its separation from Reality.

One of the most cogent characterizations of the transpersonal stages is that of Ken Wilber. According to him, the first of these stages is the psychic, which operates beyond the ordinary causal mode, in terms of what Jung called "synchronicity." It is more intuitive, holistic, integral, inclusive, and panoramic than previous stages. Beyond the psychic is what Wilber calls the subtle level, which is characterized by the experience of union with the object of meditation, universe, or deity. The apex of the subtle stage is union with the personal God or God-as-object. The Transcendent Other is now experienced as the immanent presence at the highest point or deepest level of one's psyche or spirit — the archetypal self. Beyond the subtle is the causal, which is marked by the experience of identity with the Godhead or Reality as Such (6: 27-31). To be permanently established in this state and to live and act from it is the final goal of meditation.

As we have previously said, there is a difference between dualist and nondualist traditions on the final goal of the meditative path. Believing Ultimate Reality to be dualistic, traditions that conceive God to be a personal Being regard the final stage of the path as a state of permanent union between God and the individual. These dualistic traditions often describe this union in terms of the relationship between lover and beloved. On the other hand, experiencing God or Ultimate Reality to be transpersonal (and thus nondualistic), nondualist traditions, such as Vedanta Hinduism, Buddhism, and Taoism (as well as many individuals within the dualist traditions), proclaim the final goal of meditation to be identity with Ultimate Reality. In this view, meditation is essentially a process of waking up from a dream — that you are separate from all things and God — and experiencing yourself as that which IS, absolutely and unconditionally. To arrive at this identity as your permanent state is the end of the path and goal of human existence.

Which of these views represents the final goal of meditation, the final stage of the path, the ultimate state of things?

If we follow the dualist tradition, the answer is clear: Union with God is the ultimate goal of the path. As personal God is the highest or the only form of God, so the highest relationship with "him" is the final end of the path. The claim of identity is either a sacrilege or a regression to the prepersonal stage.

Another viewpoint, that of Lawrence LeShan and others, holds that such ultimate questions pertain to models or systems of reality. Since these systems are relative to each other and our statements about them are made from within a model or system, it is impossible to stand outside all systems and adjudicate their relative truth, validity, adequacy, or finality. Since both dualism and nondualism represent alternate versions of reality, it is not possible to stand outside them and decide which is the ultimate, for any such standpoint would be another version of reality, not a neutral or transcendent ground. For LeShan, all versions are relative to one another and have equal status. Each is ultimate within its own construct. Each does something well while falling short in other respects. None is wholly useful in all matters (LeShan 2: 1-84). So all you can do is to decide pragmatically which one is ultimate for you.

According to a third view, advocated by Ken Wilber, Bernadette Roberts and others, union with God is on the relative plane, whereas identity with God represents the absolute beyond the relativity of planes and states. Thus union with God cannot be the ultimate end of the path; it must rest with identity. As Ken Wilber explains, while communion with God takes place on the subtle plane, which is the stage of "saintly religion," identity with the Godhead is experienced at the causal level, which is the stage of "sagely religion." In this state consciousness reaches Ultimate Reality as it completely transcends all relative planes and totally awakens in its original state of Consciousness as Such. In this state, "saintly communion with Spirit is transcended by sagely identity with Spirit," as "saintly revelation of God as Absolute Other is transcended by sagely revelation of God as radical and transcendental Consciousness as Such." This is the Ultimate Ground and goal of all things and of the meditative path where reigns, "asymptotic to infinity, the absolute identity of Consciousness as Such with all its manifestations" (6:33).

Which of these points of view signifies the ultimate truth? If we follow the first, the answer is clear. On the basis of the second, we cannot answer this question. Since each claim is a point of view, each is relative. So no point of view can represent the ultimate truth. Now, if nonduality is a model of reality alongside duality, then LeShan's view is inescapable. There is no way that you can stand outside either view to decide which is the ultimate. However, the claim of nonduality is that it is not a model of reality, point of view, or a conceptual scheme of any kind but is a term that connotes a transcendence of all models, concepts, constructs, and frameworks, and a direct experience of reality in its Unconditioned State. As long as anything operates within a framework or construct, through models or concepts, or from a point of view, which is the case with dualism, it is on the relative plane. But if a state or experience is beyond them all, so that it cannot take place through anything but is itself the Unconditioned, then it cannot be placed alongside or be equated with relative viewpoints. As nonduality signifies this experience, it must represent the ultimate truth and the final goal of the meditative path.

Kinds of Meditation

In the broadest sense, meditation may be said to be of two kinds: spontaneous and intentional. The former is experienced when the mind suddenly stops its usual internal chatter and preoccupations with things past and future and becomes open to experiencing what is, here and now. At such moments, the distance between you and the object, be it a starry sky, a flower, a sunset, or the stillness of a forest at dawn, is lost and you experience yourself to be one with it.

Intentional meditation itself can be broadly divided into formal and informal meditation. The former requires a specific time, place, and method, while the latter does not require a special setting but can be practiced anywhere and at any time, its context being the daily activities of life.

Formal meditation itself can be divided in several ways. One is in terms of methods, such as various types of meditation based on breathing or mantra repetition. Other common types are: meditation based on sound, either chanted aloud or silently listened to; visualization; movement; focusing attention or observing various senses or parts of the body; observation of mental contents, sensations; and various permutations or combinations of several of these types of meditation.

Others, such as Ornstein, divide formal meditation into two types: concentrative and awareness or insight. He defines the first as "an attempt to restrict awareness to a single, unchanging source of stimulation for a definite period of time" (1: 160). It involves shutting down awareness by keeping focused attention only on the object of meditation to the exclusion of all else. As attention is focused on one object, it stops its usual flitting about from one thing to another, becoming unified around the object.

Ornstein defines the second type as an attempt to open up awareness to what is, here and now, by investing attention in the ongoing stream and content of consciousness and watching it (1: 176-177). This type of meditation can be practiced either in a formal setting, as is done in Buddhism and other traditions, or carried out informally in the midst of daily activities and experiences. In the latter case, positive and negative programmed reactions and the ongoing flux of moment-to-moment experiences can serve as the focus of attention and observation. In formal meditation, as in *vipassana* or insight meditation, you are simply and directly aware of your bodily sensations and mental processes, cutting through their programmed configurations and attempting to arrive at a direct experience of what is. In informal meditation, on the other hand, attention is focused directly on programmed reactions so as to break free of them and arrive at a moment-to-moment awakening to what is.

Although this distinction is important, these two types of meditation are not mutually exclusive. Most fully developed paths of meditation employ both concentrative and insight meditation to arrive at enlightenment. Thus, Patanjali's *Yoga Sutras,* which is usually categorized as concentrative meditation, acknowledges and employs insight at advanced stages. This fact is also true of meditative methods in other traditions. On the other hand, paths that are considered primarily awareness meditation, such as *jnana* yoga, *vipassana,* and Zen, employ concentrative exercises at an early stage of practice. Both types are necessary to attain enlightenment. As Achaan Chah has pointed out: "Meditation is like a single log of wood. Insight and investigation is one end of the log; calm and concentration is the other end." Like a light and its switch, the two go together: "To concentrate the mind is like turning on the switch, and wisdom is the resulting light. Without the switch, there is no light. Concentration must be firmly established for wisdom to arise" (15, 90).

The generalized descriptions of informal awareness meditation and formal meditation that follow in the next two chapters precede a discussion of various meditative paths found in Hinduism, Buddhism, Taoism, Judaism, Christianity, and Islam.

---

[1]Departing from the MLA method of citation, otherwise used throughout, in citing multiple works by the same author, I have adopted a modified course. Accord to this method, the first number in the entry after the name of the author and before the colon refers to the number of the work included in the bibliography, while the number(s) following the colon refer(s) to the page number(s) in the work.

Chapter 2
Informal Awareness Meditation

Almost every tradition of formal meditation enjoins some form of Informal Awareness Meditation (IAM). Its aim is to enable students to break free of their negative programmings and habits, to develop and enhance positive mental states, and to invest awareness in the daily activities that ordinarily pass in unawareness. Thus, Hinduism speaks of self-observation, in which you are instructed purely to observe your programmed states and activities without interpreting, evaluating, judging, approving or disapproving what you discover. You observe yourself and your activities neutrally, as if you were another person simply and directly seeing the nature of what arises in the mind — witnessing what you are thinking, feeling, and doing. Similarly, Krishnamurti teaches nothing but a method of self-observation, which consists in "just watching how you behave, your reactions; seeing without any choice; just observing so that during the day the hidden, the unconscious, is exposed" (4: 28). *Karma Yoga*, that is, acting without expecting anything in return, has the same aim.

The Buddha taught right or complete mindfulness, which can be practiced both formally and informally. In the Tibetan tradition, Chogyam Trungpa used to instruct his students to develop a feeling of space and a general acknowledgment of openness in whatever they do during the day (4: 47). The Vietnamese master Thich Nhat Hahn teaches a number of IAMs in his book *The Miracle of Mindfulness*. In one of them, called "A Day of Mindfulness," he advises the meditator to devote a day in each week to doing everything with full awareness — watching and experiencing everything with complete attention (27-31). Tarthang Tulku instructs the beginner to develop a quality of openness in each situation by maintaining continuous awareness. Even when you forget, as a beginner invariably does, you are to bring the attention back and focus it on the present moment. And, for the ordinary person, who does not engage in formal meditation for prolonged periods, Tulku rightly considers this form of meditation more important than the formal type (1: 87, 132).

In order to correct deficiencies in personality, before initiating the student into formal meditation, the Kabbalah teaches specific methods of self-development. One such exercise, designed for both self-discovery and moment-to-moment awakening, consists of keeping attention focused on the present moment as completely as possible. This is similar to Buddhist mindfulness meditation. Another exercise, among others, involves meditating on one negative program at a time and then ruthlessly confronting it through self-examination until it loses its control over the practitioner (Hoffman 96-111).

In a real sense, all the teachings of Jesus are nothing but forms of IAM, designed to free the mind of all conditioning, positive and negative. Void of conditioning, you can experience the natural state of unconditional love, which opens the way to realizing your oneness with God. In this realization, you attain that Perfection of Being which is God "himself." "Be perfect as your Heavenly Father is perfect," sums up the goal of this path. Since God is the perfection of each thing just as it is, to touch this perfection within yourself is to touch God.

In order that we may realize this perfection, which lies beyond the ordinary state, Jesus taught two basic approaches. The first consists in freeing ourselves from negative and positive programmings by ceasing to react according to their dictates and doing their polar opposite or acting according to the promptings of our true Self. This procedure shifts the action to an altogether different plane and helps us break free of the programming. The second consists in ceaselessly practicing present-centered consciousness. By so doing we become awakened from moment to moment and see perfection as the ever-present nature of our true Self. His teachings on turning the other cheek and loving our enemies aim to free us from negative and positive programmings, respectively; and his counsel on developing a nonjudgmental mind and present- centered consciousness are intended for moment-to-moment awakening.

The Sufis practice various IAMs that have similar aims. Thus, Sheikh Javad Nurbakhsh quotes Abu Osman Maghrebi as saying that the noblest action on the path is self-examination designed to eliminate negative programmings. Since actions that are selfish and contrary to the path are considered vicious and must be eliminated, the initiates are taught first to know what they are. They must constantly examine their mental states and their actions by continuously observing whatever arises in the mind, positive or negative. Next, the initiates must analyze weaknesses or negative programmings and strive to eliminate them; they must assess positive qualities and try to develop them. At the end of each day they must examine themselves and take account of their positive and negative behavior, resolving to rectify the imbalance the next day if the negative outnumbers the positive. If the positive outnumbers the negative, they must redouble their efforts to eliminate the negative programs. Thus they should undertake to resolve psychological conflicts and lessen the control of the self until they reach a state of psychological balance, harmony, and peace of mind (1: 18, 56-97).

Omar Michael Burke reports another Sufi practice, called *"Quiff,"* in which the master, appearing at intervals while the Sufis are doing their assigned tasks, shouts the command, *"Quiff!"* At this everyone freezes in their tracks until the word *"Hu!"* is spoken. During the interval they are to focus attention on their present mental states, discover what they are thinking and feeling, gain insight into themselves, and invest awareness in their daily activities, which were ordinarily performed in unawareness (20).

Learning from the Sufis, Gurdjieff adopted the practice of assigning his students similar exercises. In order to develop moment-to-moment awareness, he instructed them to maintain a continuous awareness of a part of the body. For the same purpose, he taught them to remember "I am" by focusing attention on and being aware of the "I am" in whatever they were doing (Rajneesh 2: 144-149).

Don Juan taught Carlos Castaneda a number of such exercises designed to extend awareness to ordinary activity of his life: disrupting the routines of life, erasing personal history, losing self-importance, acting without expecting anything in return, walking the right way, living like a warrior, assuming responsibility, using death as an adviser, becoming inaccessible, and, in general, not-doing. All such exercises were intended to make him cultivate moment-to-moment awareness of routine activities, to observe automatic responses that normally went unnoticed, to cut through ordinary constructs, to see things as they are, and to arrive at the totality of himself (2: 27-240; 3: 231-236).

Instead of further describing such exercises and outlining their methods, in the rest of this chapter I shall describe the essence of Informal Awareness Meditation in eight steps. Before doing so I shall discuss the differences between formal meditation and IAM in terms of their content, subject matter, method, focus, and aims.

While formal meditation requires you to set aside a specific time and place, IAM can be practiced only in the midst of daily activities, since it is in them that your programmed states, mental fixations, emotional blocks, and habitual patterns manifest themselves.

The material you work on in formal meditation is the method itself. In formal meditation you directly work with attention to bring it into unity with the method and the material, cut through all conditioning and constructs, and arrive at the Unconditioned. From there you proceed to dissolve the residues of positive and negative programmings, and integrate your transformed personality within this new identity and center. The assumption here is that with the mind centered on Reality as Such, you are able to work to penetrate every aspect of your personality until it is transformed and you become totally free of programmings and constructs.

On the other hand, the material IAM works on consists in the programmed reactions of the mind. It, too, works with attention, but instead of proceeding to a direct experience of Reality as Such, attention is kept focused on the programmed reactions themselves. The essence of this method is to observe mental and emotional reactions directly, exactly as they enter awareness, without selection, elaboration, evaluation, judgment, or interpretation. Such observation disidentifies and frees the mind from the grip of reactions. The assumption is that when the programmings are dissolved, the restrictions to your natural qualities are removed, and a pathway to the Unconditioned is opened.

So, while the ultimate aim of both types of meditation is the same, their immediate aim, procedures, approaches, and focus are different. They work from opposite ends toward the same goal. Such differences should not blind us to seeing similarities between the two types of meditation, however. Formal meditation is also concerned with pure, noninterpretative, nonjudgmental observation without interference from the thought process. In many forms of formal meditation, especially the insight type, you are instructed to observe bodily processes, sensations, and mental states and contents just at the moment they register in consciousness — prior to the usual information processing that occurs. Thus formal meditation, too, leads to a dissolution of programmings.

Since these two types of meditation are, in fact, complementary, they should be practiced concurrently in their own contexts — formal meditation at specifically designated times; IAM during the rest of the day. One method should not be practiced to the exclusion of the other. Unless IAM is practiced concurrently with formal meditation, progress in the latter will be slow; you will find it harder to concentrate; and your programmings will remain firmly in control of your mind and personality, constantly invading the mind during meditation. It will be difficult to unify attention and cut through programming and constructs, freeing awareness. On the other hand, unless IAM is accompanied by formal meditation, progress in it will be slow; moment-to-moment awakening will be difficult to achieve; and it will be hard to make dents in your programmings, especially in the deep-seated negative ones. You will tend to feel overwhelmed and discouraged and be tempted to give up your practice.

Before mapping out the eight steps, it may be useful to say what IAM is not. First, it does not consist in repressing or controlling emotions, thoughts, or behavior. Both repression and control prevent growth. They involve fixation on and attachment to responses programmed in the past, responses that keep you from being in touch with the flow of life, that create blockages in your emotional life and prevent it from expanding, deepening, and becoming transformed and integrated into ever higher states. Since growth requires you to be in touch with and experience whatever goes on within you, from the point of view of IAM it is better to express exactly what you experience than to repress or control it, especially when your programming dictates repression. For full growth, however, mere expression is not enough. Expression of fear, anger, anxiety, or stress, for instance, does not make these emotions go away. It relieves the pressure, but it does not release you from the programming. So long as you experience them, you are still stuck in your programmings, which will prevent you from successively breaking free of limited identities and attaining ever higher and more inclusive ones. Since programmings are programmed to maintain themselves, only by directly working to dissolve them can you be free of them and progress toward the ultimate goal. Neither repression nor expression, but IAM, is the suitable avenue toward that goal.

It follows that IAM is not the same as reprogramming. Many systems, such as Ken Keyes' "Living Love" and EST, have been based on reprogramming. IAM is not one of them. It does not give the mind new scripts to tape over the old ones but frees it of all scripts. For IAM consists in focusing attention on the mind's reactions—stress, upset, depression, tension, or whatever—exactly as they occur at the level of the primary stimulus prior to any programmed reaction. Such neutral observation brings no interference with the process and is not itself a reprogramming, since it does not involve any activity of perceptual information-processing, such as selective attention, model-forming, interpretation, evaluation, or judgment. Thus it does not consist of any kind of training, learning, or scripting over the old programs.

Nor is IAM a method of thinking. Thinking splits you from reality and reinforces programming as your mind, working through a model, category, or idea of the event which led to its formation, plays back the programmed tape and judges, approves or disapproves. What happens when, in an effort to control a situation, you think about it? You may, for instance, say to yourself, "I am now getting upset." As you begin to get upset, you stop being in direct contact with the upset. Judging it to be bad, something which lowers your self-esteem or prevents you from getting what you want, the mind disapproves. It reacts to the original programming and says, "Don't get upset, it's all right. You can handle it." Or "I must not get upset." Or "Think of something else, the upset will go away." In the midst of this mental chatter and your attempt to control it, you have reacted with upset and have failed to observe it. Thought has intervened and prevented you from seeing the situation exactly as it is, from experiencing how your programmed mind works and what makes it upset. Thought may even have made you upset for not being able to prevent yourself from being upset, and it certainly has not freed you from being upset.

Third, IAM is not the same as psychotherapy. Admittedly, there are similarities between the two. Both deal with the reactive mind. But, as Daniel Goleman observes, the therapist works to change the impact of the past conditionings on the present behavior; IAM ignores the content and seeks to change the context and the way in which they register in awareness. Assuming programmings to be part of the human condition, the therapist shows how they cause neuroses, and brings the patient round to observing the workings of his/her programmed mind. S/he then helps the patient to break "the hold of past conditioning on present behavior" and to reconcile him/her to the human condition (1: 172-174). On the other hand, assuming the conditioned states not to be any part of one's purely natural condition, IAM helps one to transcend the human condition by dissolving the underlying causes and the programmed states themselves, thus bringing about a transformation of consciousness, identity, and reality (Goleman 1: 172-174).

The essence of IAM, then, consists in focusing your pure, unmediated attention directly on your programmed states and mental reactions in whatever situation and whenever they occur. The observation must be bare or pure, that is, prior to and without becoming mixed up in emotional reactions, thoughts, or inner dialogue; and prior to perceptual information-processing activities, such as selective attention, schematization, interpretation, evaluation, interference, or attempts to change or reprogram the reaction. The mind must watch its activity without labeling, judging, commenting, excusing, blaming or condemning. Like neutrally watching a parade or the flow of a river, you must impartially watch the mental process and see it in total awareness, exactly as it unfolds, without trying to stem the tide, divert the flow, change the direction, or run away in horror or disgust.

Moreover, complete attention must be wholly focused directly on the experience for the entire duration of the reaction. Nothing must intervene between the watching and the unrolling of mental reaction. Cutting through fantasies, illusions, self-deceptions, defenses, preoccupations, and other filtering mechanisms that usually hide the truth of what actually happens, the mind must directly notice the first moment of the reaction, move into and experience it directly as it unfolds. Like a scientist bringing to clear focus what is placed under a microscope, the mind must keep its undivided attention on the entire cycle of reaction from beginning to end so as to discover its source, nature, condition, and consequences. Like a movie director keeping the camera focused on the action unfolding before him, you must move in on the reaction in full awareness. Like a laser beam penetrating darkness, or strong sunlight dissipating a patch of fog, you must penetrate the programming and move through it. Like the TV commercial in which liquid soap dissolves a spot of grease, the clear awareness must act as a catalyst and break up the links that bind the programming so that the emotional coatings and additives that make up the mental reaction can dissolve and disappear, never to reappear in similar situations. The core assumption here is that when the mind is able to experience directly and in full awareness the sources, nature, condition, and consequences of its programmed states and reactions, it can disidentify and become free.

Essentially, then, IAM entails a shift of attention whereby awareness, free of entrapment and focused on the subjective part of the mind, frees itself of this entanglement while dealing with the objective world. Ordinarily, when a reaction to a situation is habitual and ingrained, it completely fills the mental screen, like a camera zooming in on a situation, absorbing the attention and preventing the mind from seeing itself and its reaction. The mind needs to wake up from this slumber if it is to become free of programming. The central task of IAM is to open up this closed side of the mind by shifting attention toward itself and observing in full awareness how it actually is and what it does.

In thus opening itself to itself and becoming aware of its reactive patterns, the subjective part of the mind, which watches the reaction, becomes free. Inasmuch as the awareness that watches is pure, it is free of the reaction. So as long as the awareness is maintained, the subjective part remains free. As the subjective side opens up, the programmed reaction zooms out, clearing that part of the mind which is usually filled up by the reaction. Reduced to its true proportion and no longer inflated by emotional coatings that fill the entire mental screen, the cleared part of the screen is able to watch the other part. Then the situation appears in its true light and takes on a factual character. Regaining control over the clear part of the mind, awareness assumes its mastery over the situation and begins to free the mind of that programming. As awareness cuts through and clears an increasingly larger territory of the mind, the programming proportionately diminishes. To the extent awareness becomes stronger and occupies more of the mental screen, to that extent programming becomes weaker and occupies less of the mind. In time it dissolves and disappears.

Just as there are three spheres in which programming causes unawareness, accordingly, there are three goals of IAM. The first is to dissolve your negative programmings, bringing growth, openness, peace, joy, freedom, and tranquility to life. The second is to free your natural qualities from both positive and negative programming, from being constricted, distorted, or inflated by various illusions, delusions, defenses, and deceptions of ego. When these are removed, your natural qualities expand and assume their unrestricted state. New, positive qualities arise or become manifest — qualities you never thought you had. The third aim is to develop moment-to-moment awareness, so that you can live in the awakened state every moment of your life. Thus you become fully awakened, experiencing every moment as new, fresh, and original, as the first moment of creation.

Dissolving Negative Programming

The eight steps below are intended to enable you to dissolve your negative programmings, such as stress, tension, anxiety, upset, frustration, restlessness, anger, fear, shyness, depression, boredom, greed, jealousy, possessiveness, attachment, defensiveness, self-deception, self-rejection, negative or destructive self-image, and a host of other problems, difficulties, and conflicts.

1. Choose a specific pattern of programming that bothers you, that *you* consider a problem, and that *you* want to eliminate.

It is important that you choose a pattern that you experience frequently. For example, if you experience stress at work almost every day, it would be a great benefit to you to work on and dissolve your stress programming.

Choose a specific pattern, rather than a vague or general one. Thus, instead of working on tension in general, work on a specific pattern of tension that you frequently experience in a specific situation, such as in your work place or in relationship to a specific person. For instance, if you cause yourself to become tense at your job in relationship to your supervisor or a co-worker, then that pattern could be worked on more effectively than could a vague feeling of tension. It is usually something specific that causes problems and prevents us from growing. Its presence is a signal that we are in a rut, trapped in a vicious circle, doomed to repeat the same reaction over and over again. Choosing a specific sequence gives you a handle to work on. Of course, vague feelings do have specific causes that need to be ferreted out and pinpointed, if you choose to work on them.

Choose a programming that you, and not someone else, consider to be a problem. You must personally recognize and accept it as *your* problem, not someone else's. If someone else thinks that you have a problem and you do not, or if you think that the problem is someone else's, not yours, you will not do anything about it.

Moreover, in order for this method to be effective, you must be convinced that you, not anyone or anything else, has caused and maintained this problem, that all problems are in, and caused and maintained by, the programmed mind. Since it is you who causes and maintains your programmed reactions, you alone, and no outside agency—no God, savior, teacher, or society—can free you.

Finally, you must come to a firm resolve that you do not want to live with this problem any more, that you want to be free of it. Just being conscious of a problem is not enough. You must come to see the pain and futility of your present course of programmed reaction and arrive at the decision not to continue behaving this way. You must come to believe that you can change, that you can dissolve the programming, and you must decide to do so. And you must decide to work on it now, rather than putting it off to some indefinite future. Unless you are decisive, no matter how much you may recognize it as a problem, you will not begin to work on it. Instead, you will believe that you cannot dissolve it, that you are helpless; that some outside agency alone can bring it about and hope for a magical change; that somehow it will disappear without your having to do anything about it; or that your fear of change makes it impossible to dissolve the problem.

2. Mentally survey the past and the entire sequence of the programming you have decided to work on—in this case your experience of job-related tension with your boss or a specific co-worker. Try to see as clearly as possible the entire situation or relationship in detail—the personalities, the behavior, the demands, the work itself, your feelings about the work, and the experience of tension. Pinpoint what specifically in the situation, the work, the behavior, or the demands of your boss or co-worker becomes the occasion for your making yourself tense. What do you feel, think, and do at the onset of tension? Carefully examine the pattern and what your mind does after your reaction.

Such a dry run, while you are not in the grip of the tension, should give you valuable insights into how you cause yourself to become tense, the nature of the stimulus, the experience, and the aftermath. Once you see the entire pattern as clearly as possible, you will be ready for the next step.

3. Now in the actual situation, focus your bare attention on the stimulus or situation itself, on the boss or co-worker and what s/he says or does, on your own job, and on whatever is likely to trigger your tension-reaction. Keep your attention pure, sharp and clear; focus it on the whole scene as it unfolds, observing it exactly without your attention's getting caught up in it. Don't let your attention waver or wander off. Keep watching and follow the entire sequence with complete attention.

4. With the tension key being struck by the stimulus, watch how the reaction builds up in your mind like a coiled spring ready to pounce. Each demand, word, action, or gesture of the boss or co-worker strikes the programmed key like a hammer blow and brings the programmed reaction to the point of retrieving and playing it back. The process may be quick or slow. Whatever it is, observe the entire build-up. Keep your entire attention on it and just watch in full awareness. Do not try to stop, repress, deny, or change it. Just experience it exactly as it occurs. Allow it to unfold and take its own course. Do not interpret, evaluate, or think that feeling tension is horrible. Do not keep saying to yourself, "I must not feel tense." But if your mind does keep saying these things as part of its coping mechanism, observe that also. Do not let your attention get caught in either process. Just keep observing by keeping attention riveted on the space of awareness prior to thought or before mental reaction arises.

5. Observe the experience of the tension itself. Watch how your mind reacts both internally and externally in thought, feeling, word, and action. This is the boiling point after the build-up; and it may be gradual or instantaneous. Observe in bare awareness what you think and feel, mentally and physically, and how you characteristically express the tension in word and action. Watch how your mind supplies the emotional coating to form the tension-reaction which the stimulus itself does not create. For the boss's or co-worker's demands, words, actions, or gestures do not themselves have the power to cause the reaction. Keep your attention focused directly on the stimulus at the primary level, at the very moment it contacts your mind, and directly experience the moment the mind reacts, without getting involved in the reaction or becoming sidetracked. Move into and follow the tension-reaction all the way through to the end while staying at the immediate moment of direct contact. Do not let your mind try to stop, fight, change, or run away. Let your awareness burn through and burn up.

6. Observe the aftermath. Watch what your mind does after it reacts and the tension subsides. Observe what you think and feel after you mentally and physically express the tension. Do you feel bad or guilty? Do you blame or condemn yourself for being tense? Do you blame others or your job for creating the tension, when in fact it is you who causes it? What does your mind think? Do you keep repeatedly saying to yourself, "I should not have become tense?" Do you fantasize how you would triumph over the other, so you would not have to become tense? Do you get tense, upset, frustrated or disgusted for becoming tense? Or do you try to rationalize the situation or excuse yourself by repeating, "It's not my fault; the other person is being unreasonable?" The mind will keep playing an endless variety of such preprogrammed tapes as a result of its original

tension-reaction. Since you do not find the situation and your reaction acceptable, you will try to smooth things over as a part of your coping mechanism. You must watch this second level of negative programming with as much clear attention as the first.

7. Watch for any change in the pattern of your tension as a result of this observation. Does watching make you more or less tense? Do other factors enter into your reaction to make it more complicated, or are you getting to the bottom of it?

Of course, in the beginning you will not be able to observe your mental reaction at the time it occurs, but you will do so after the event. If that happens, do not become discouraged, frustrated, annoyed, or upset; do not blame or tell yourself that you cannot follow the method or that it is useless to try. Your mind is programmed to react in this way as a result of your inability to get instant or intended results and the consequent judgment that you are a failure or that the method is useless. However, if you do get caught in this second level of programming, make it the object of IAM until your mind becomes sufficiently calm to return to observing the first level of reaction. Whatever happens, do not give up the practice. The more you succeed in watching your reaction, the more you will be able to observe the exact moment it is triggered. The more sustained your observation becomes, the more awareness will open up in your mind, right in the middle of the reaction itself. And you will feel as if you have some breathing space in a suffocating situation.

If, as a result of watching, you feel at first that you are becoming more tense, do not be discouraged or alarmed. The tension is not increasing; it only feels that way because you are noticing for the first time how strong it is and what confusion and havoc it creates in your mind and nervous system, like slamming on the brakes of your car every five minutes while driving it at sixty miles an hour. However, if you persist in watching, you will soon notice that the intensity of the tension lessens. You will find a direct correlation between the strength and clarity of your observation and the decrease in your tension: the stronger the former becomes the weaker the latter will be. Gradually the tension will decrease until the reaction is reduced from the physical to the emotional and then to the thought level. Finally, when it is dissolved, you will experience the entire situation clearly — your job, the boss's demands, words, actions, etc. — as it occurs without triggering any tension. Thus, your mental reaction will gradually become inactive and in time will disappear.

8. Observe whether you are getting any insight as a result of IAM. When your practice becomes strong and your awareness clear, sometimes you will suddenly

see very clearly how initially, perhaps through some incident in childhood, your mind programmed the tension-reaction. Seeing it, as well as how you maintain the programming, you will come to realize that its cause is not anything outside yourself; that you are not your programming, that the tension is not any part of your identity, nor do you have to continue to trigger it in order to be yourself or function in your work situation or in the world. You existed and functioned well before the programming and will continue to do so after it is dissolved. Your well-being, your self-worth, your job do not depend on your continuing to cause yourself to become tense. You will discover that being tense does not make you function more efficiently; on the contrary, it makes you less efficient, although hitherto you had believed otherwise. You will come to recognize that it is not your programmed reaction but your awareness that is a better guide to efficiency, mental health, and well-being. Seeing this, you will come to disidentify and let go of the tension.

Free of the burden you have been carrying, you will experience a lightness, buoyancy, freshness, freedom, and joy. As you gain the ability to see your situation clearly, instead of reacting with tension, you will respond to your situation, your boss or your co-worker matter-of-factly. You will begin to see his/her programming, that which makes him/her do what s/he does. Instead of responding to his/her programmed reactions, you will be able to respond to him/her as a person and to his/her real needs. Rather than your tension-reaction confirming his/her programming, your change of response may provide him/her an opportunity to see his/her own programming and take steps to overcome it. Beyond insight into this particular programming, you may come to have insight into the entire human condition itself — seeing it as nothing but systems of conditionings caused and maintained by ourselves. This insight into the bondage we have created for ourselves will awaken your compassion.

Freeing Natural Qualities from Positive Programming

The aim of this part of IAM is to free our natural qualities, such as sensitivity, kindness, generosity, openness, acceptance, trust, love, compassion, courage, honesty, fearlessness, and truthfulness, from limitations. These limitations arise from three sources: positive programming, negative programming, and fantasies, projections, defenses, illusions, delusions, and deceptions of the ego. Once freed, our natural qualities can return to their boundless, original state.

When you begin practicing this part of IAM, you may notice at first that your positive qualities appear negative. Do not be discouraged, dismayed, or alarmed at this discovery. Do not stop meditating. As you discover the actual state of these qualities in yourself, be alert, for you have reached a critical stage in which ego will try to step in and disavow your discoveries, trying to bury them under defenses, denials, or fantasies. Your ego will insist that you are the opposite of what you have found. It may argue that if it were not for other people or extenuating circumstances, you could show the world how just, kind, truthful, honest, and marvelous you really are! But if that argument rings hollow, ego may try the opposite ploy – of condemning you and making you reject, hate or blame yourself or others for your condition. You may then try to repress, deny, or avoid; you may get into a cycle of defending, justifying, or rationalizing your situation; or you may feel sorry for yourself. You may feel helpless, depressed, discouraged, or disappointed with yourself or with your meditation. Feeling that your "faults" are so monumental that you can never break free, you may want to give up your meditation practice. Again, these are all programmed reactions designed to make you stop meditating so that your ego can get on with its usual way of running your life. You must be very careful; observe your mind, do not give in to ego's tactics and give up your practice.

Actually, what you have discovered is normal, and your situation is good, wonderful even! You are discovering layers of conditioning, which have chocked off your natural qualities. You are discovering how you want to hide the negative self-image under a positive one in order to gain acceptance, approval, or confirmation. Unable to accept your natural qualities in this limited form, your ego has coated them with illusions, fantasies, and overblown images. Then it has identified with them in an effort to create an oversized self-image which, it believes, will be acceptable to the world, confirm itself, and make life livable.

Your discoveries indicate that, perhaps for the first time, you have come into contact with the reality of your present condition and found that your natural qualities are like specks of gold mixed with sand. Unable to accept your condition, in your illusion you had hitherto thought that all the sand was gold. This belief prevented you from seeing your qualities as they were. As you discover their conditioned state, your ego is bound to be deflated and find the truth hard to accept. But if you can cut through your ego's games, you will have a chance to free your natural qualities and allow them to expand or transform the sand into real gold.

Now, how do you cut through ego's games and programmings and allow your qualities to assume their boundless, natural state? The first step is acceptance of what you have discovered. Acceptance is neither a positive, nor a negative, nor a resigned, stoical, or heroic attitude. It is simply a recognition of what is, as it is. It is only by accepting what you discover that you can be in touch with reality again. As you acknowledge your situation, you are like someone who finds himself at the base of a mountain. Instead of fantasizing that you are close to the top, by discovering where you actually are, you can accurately determine what you need for the climb, take a deep breath, and begin the journey.

Next, you need to keep your attention sharp at all times, lest you fall into dualistic chasms and crevices, false paths of programmings, and ego's traps, which can make you lose your way, perhaps even your life. As you continue to work on your natural qualities by following the eight steps and stop responding to your reactive patterns, your qualities will gradually expand, encompassing more people and situations within their parameters. Finally, they will become free of all limits and conditions and assume their true place in the limitless state of your nature. You will then be able to use your qualities in the service of others.

Moment-to-Moment Awareness

Moment-to-moment awareness, infusing every thought, feeling, and action with awareness at every moment of life until all become transformed into and manifestations of pure Awareness, is the ultimate goal of all meditation. The successful practice of the first two steps of IAM will help you to infuse with awareness those activities and aspects of life that usually pass in unawareness. The third step of IAM consists of exercises, enjoined by various meditative paths, to be practiced every moment throughout the day. I have already described many of these at the beginning of this chapter.

Whatever the suggested task, the aim of the method is to pull your attention out of its outward orientation and unawareness and bring it back to the present; and to keep it focused on the mind itself while you are engaged in various activities throughout the day. This practice will enable the mind to directly perceive its nature, states, and activities, and to become present-centered. Because a specific technique is required to bring your attention back to itself, you are instructed to keep your attention focused directly on the primary stimulus level of one or more acts throughout the day or on some part of the body or internal states, such as the breath, thoughts or mental contents; to repeat some expression while carrying on various activities; or to perform some other task. When awareness stays continuously in the present and completely penetrates, infuses, and transforms every moment so that it becomes identical with and a manifestation of pure Awareness, you become a sage — a fully awakened human being.

Chapter 3
The Process of Formal Meditation

Preliminary Stages

Although each type of meditation has its own sequence, method, experiences, mental terrain, and order of progression, nevertheless a careful examination reveals a basic unity of fundamental structures and stages across meditative traditions. Such a unity strongly supports an attempt to present a generalized picture of the meditative path. Accordingly, in this chapter I shall sketch an outline of formal meditation based on this basic unity. The structures and experiences peculiar to each path or tradition will be treated in a separate volume.

For many traditions, the formal meditative path begins with the experience of what is called "conversion." It is the first step in self-awareness, in which you come to see your condition as it actually is. You see the insufficiency of your present form of life, the futility of continuing your present course, and the need for a fundamental change. You then make a decision to enter a spiritual path to bring about self-transformation. Al-Ghazali describes such an experience of conversion (his own), beginning with awareness of and dissatisfaction with the present condition; the need to break free of its repetitive, meaningless patterns; and the decision to do so (Arberry 1: 80). Other paths post a similar need. Jesus issued a call to repentance. And, following him, the Eastern Orthodox Church, according to John Chirban (Wilber, Engler & Brown 298), regards conversion, or conscious commitment to a path, as the starting point of the journey. Eastern traditions emphasize similar steps in choosing a path.

The Stage of Purification

Once you make your choice and formally enter a path, the next step begins with ethical and body-mind training. The aim of ethical practice is not merely to do good and avoid evil, but to bring about a thoroughgoing inner and outer change. Concerned with the life setting of the meditator, these injunctions are designed, together with other meditative practices, in the words of Roger Walsh, to bring about "a shift in attitudes, thought, speech, and behavior aimed at the deepest possible transformation of mind, awareness, identity, lifestyle, and relationship to the world" (1: 29). Ethical injunctions are prescribed by meditative paths in all traditions. They form the backbone of meditation. They intend not only to eliminate evil behavior but deeper still, they aim at uprooting the desire and intention from which evil springs and which disturb the mind. Thus, not only violence but anger, aggression, and the desire to harm others must be uprooted and to be replaced by positive states.

Similarly, body-mind training, which includes devotional practices and Informal Awareness Meditation (IAM), aims to purify and unify consciousness; rearrange your life according to new, ultimate priorities; help you to gain mastery over your bodily and mental powers, free them from external control, and shift your attention inward. To this end, many traditions enjoin simplicity, silence, solitude, purity, devotional practices, and, of course, IAM. Such training awakens, strengthens, and unifies motivation toward the ultimate goal. Thus you are prepared for the arduous journey ahead. Such aims have led meditative traditions to regard these steps as part of the stage of purification.

Some writers regard mastery of these ethical practices and body-mind training as preliminary to formal meditation (cf. Brown 1: 226). Were this the case, no one could begin formal meditation, since such a mastery would require at least a lifetime. Actually, these practices encompass the entire life of the meditator and are meant to be carried out into the daily activities outside the period of formal meditation.

The Stage of Concentration

After learning the preliminaries of posture, breathing, and directing the attention inward by cutting off external stimuli, you begin formal meditation with concentration. By whatever name it is called and whatever method or object is used, concentration is essential for all forms of formal meditation. You cannot make progress in meditation without developing it. This is obviously true of concentrative meditation, in which it serves as the point of entry into the meditative states. It is no less true, as already stated, of insight meditation. Without developing the calmness and clarity that concentration provides, you will not be able to observe physical sensations and mental phenomena at their immediate point of contact with attention. Only when your mind is, as master Achaan Chah puts it, "like a clear forest pool," which is the result of the advanced state of concentration, will the nature of conditioned existence be reflected in it. You will then be able to gain the insights that blossom into enlightenment. As Achaan Chah has said, "Concentration must be firmly established for wisdom to rise" (Kornfield and Breiter 90).

Essential to concentration is shifting the orientation of consciousness by directing the attention inward and away from the world and your programmed responses to it. This shift toward its source frees and unifies attention, or makes the mind "one-pointed." The key to achieving these steps is to hold attention focused directly on one object prior to triggering the perceptual information-processing activity or any movement in the mind. For this reason, in concentrative meditation you are instructed to hold the attention on one object and become unified with it. The object may be chanting or repeating a mantra; watching, counting, or following the breath; gazing at a flame, a *yantra*, a picture of the guru, or an icon; visualizing a deity or a *mandala;* whirling or walking. In awareness meditation, you may be instructed to observe the sensation of the breath, slowly scan your body from head to foot, and observe your sensations with bare attention and clear comprehension of their nature. Or you may observe each mental event at the exact moment it arises, watch its duration, and notice the exact moment it ceases.

As you begin concentrating, you may start where you are, with a consciousness that experiences itself as separate from everything, including the object of concentration. Scattered among a multitude of objects of identification, attachment, and desire, your attention gets constantly trapped and lost as it restlessly pursues one thing, then another. Or, like a butterfly going from flower to flower, your attention flits from one thing to another, never resting anywhere nor becoming occupied with anything for long, but ever preoccupied with what your programming dictates.

At other times your attention takes a dive and completely disappears from view, only to reemerge minutes, perhaps hours, later. Moreover, as it gets trapped and lost, the mind automatically responds to familiar things, people, and situations without being aware of them. And then, like a radar antenna, it searches for new, different, important, or exciting things to make it feel alive, to give pleasure; or it avoids those things that pose a threat to survival or become potential sources of pain. As a result, not only does your mind exhibit these same characteristics toward the object of concentration, but because it is not an object of identification, attachment, or desire, you find it extremely hard to stay focused. Finding the object of concentration dry, abstract, dull, unfamiliar, and unappealing, your mind runs away and plunges into its habitual preoccupations.

Moreover, in focusing attention on the object of concentration, you have shifted your mind's habitual orientation from the outside inward. Because of a change in its structural orientation and its habitual, constantly shifting field of attention, the mind will not and cannot keep its attention focused on the object for long.

Cut off from external stimuli and turned away from its orientation toward the object world, the mind triggers the only other source of stimuli with which it can maintain itself. It opens up the seemingly inexhaustible reservoir of programmings and impressions, stored up as a result of identification, attachment, and desire. These stimuli now crowd upon the brow of consciousness demanding attention and release. The fountain of inner dialogue now opens up and the stream gushes out in the form of fantasies, arguments, plans, exhortations, admonitions. In the words of Swami Vivekananda, like "a drunken monkey," the mind jumps from one thing to another. Or one thought triggers a chain reaction, and, through association, builds up a fantasy world. Images seen on TV or movies; images of people, places, and things; memories, opportunities, hurts, or pleasures missed, enjoyed, desired, or anticipated leap into view.

Thus, as you begin to meditate, everything floats up into view, clamoring for attention and absorbing it like parched earth soaking up spring rain. When external stimuli are turned off, the mind turns on its internal juices to keep itself going. The programmed tapes begin to play over and over again like a broken record. Unable to find satisfaction in the unreality of its inner circuitry, the mind keeps repeatedly playing its programmed tapes to create an illusion of reality, permanence, continuity, and satisfaction in order to assure itself of its existence or self-worth. But as unreality and dissatisfaction continue, the mind keeps running them along the habitual grooves of its inner circuitry, as if the frequency of their occurrence will overcome the lack. A thousand and one things pull it away from the present and plunge it into the merry-go-round of existence. In the process, attention keeps drifting in and out, resulting in the scattering and entrapment of awareness and loss of concentration. Such is the infinite distractibility of the programmed mind with which you have to deal as you begin to concentrate.

Faced with this situation, your immediate reaction may be to become frustrated, agitated, distracted, or discouraged. You want the mind to stop wandering, but it does not cooperate. So what do you do? You may try to force your mind to stop thinking and become quiet. But as soon as you try this approach, you find that it doesn't work. In fact, the opposite happens. Instead of quieting down, your mind gets more disturbed, giving rise to more thoughts. By forcing the mind to do your bidding, you only add conflict, confusion, or tension to a volatile situation. The effect is like first putting a tiger in a cage and then, wanting it to stop pacing up and down, you place it in a smaller cage, which disturbs it even more. The tension caused by the struggle may even give you a headache. Frustrated, disturbed, discouraged or exhausted, you may be tempted to give up meditating.

If you want to progress in meditation, you must remember never to force your mind to stop thinking or wandering. The mind does what it has been programmed to do. None of the usual tactics will work to quiet it; they will only reinforce its programmed behavior, thus giving rise to more thoughts and wanderings, with added complications.

Rather, essential to making the mind stop is doing something that does not reinforce it, but cuts through its programmed reaction and brings it to a direct contact with the primary stimulus of the object. In the absence of reinforcement, the mind will wind down by itself, just as when the electric current is turned off, the record player comes to a stop by itself. You must never forcibly try to stop your mind from thinking; nor must you allow your attention to be carried off by the wind of every thought that pops into your head. Either action will give rise to more thoughts and trap your awareness further. When you do not choose either alternative but hold your attention focused directly on the primary stimulus, you stop reinforcing your consciousness and begin destructuring it. In addition, you must never pay any attention to whatever arises in your mind, unless, of course, that is the object of concentration. Your attitude toward thoughts must be one of noninvolvement or nonattachment. Simply leave them alone. Allow them to rise and disappear. When the attention slips away, as it invariably will in the beginning, simply bring it back and refocus it on the object of concentration. This nonattachment is to be practiced even when the contents of consciousness are the object of meditation.

The initial stage of concentration, then, consists of constantly bringing attention back to the object of concentration, back to the present, back to itself from its endless wanderings, from its habitual tendency to get immersed and lost in the objects of desire and preoccupation, much like a child let loose in a toy store. Since the mind will not become still overnight, you must be patient and gentle toward it as a loving mother is toward her child. As the mind has been programmed to behave in this way since infancy, its programming is not going to disappear overnight. When you stop trying to control or manage your mind and, instead, stop reinforcing it by practicing ceaseless and unflagging disidentification and nonattachment toward its contents, you will discover that it gradually becomes still by itself.

Your mind may also trigger all kinds of defensive maneuvers. It may tell you that you are too busy to meditate, or that right now you are not in the mood. It may point out that you could meditate if only others would not disturb you, if there were no distractions. Giving in to these promptings will only reinforce and strengthen your programming, confirming your belief that meditation does not work, is too difficult, or that you cannot do it. So it is imperative that you not give in to the frustration or discouragement you may feel. Again, by seeing these frustrations as part of the programmed reactions of your mind, you can begin to break free of the programming and quiet your restless mind.

Another problem may crop up at this stage: unable to find its usual reinforcement, your mind may start triggering all kinds of expectation-reactions. You probably began meditating with all kinds of expectations: You wanted meditation to make all your problems magically disappear; you expected it to be fun, exciting, or exotic. You thought you would see all kinds of images, colors, lights, visions; you thought you would gain paranormal powers. You may even have anticipated world-shattering insights, instant enlightenment, or immediate tranquility. But when you discover that meditation does not reinforce any of your expectations, that nothing spectacular happens, or that for all your efforts you have only pain in your ankles, legs, knees and thighs, you may be tempted to lose interest, feeling cheated, bored, disgusted, angry, or frustrated. Your hopes and expectations are dashed to pieces, doubts creep into your mind, and you begin to think that meditation is a waste of time.

Not finding any of its expectations met, within a few seconds after you begin to concentrate, the mind may drift off into fantasies or reveries. It may run after sensory stimuli, thoughts or experiences, or may become preoccupied with self-therapy. Or it may take a dive into the turbid sea of unawareness, becoming dull, languid, and murky. When it resurfaces, your mind appears heavy, unclear, and disoriented. As you struggle to refocus, your meditation period comes to an end in a state of frustration or confusion.

Progress in meditation does not take place until the mind becomes disenchanted with a forest of illusory desires, goals, hopes, dreams, and expectations for fulfillment and happiness. Again, the paradox is that when you give up your desires, goals, and expectations, what you wanted begins to happen. So, sit in meditation with no expectation of anything happening, of gaining anything, or getting somewhere, but with the firm intention of being nowhere other than the present. Begin with the conviction that since there is only the present and you are already in it, there is nowhere else to go and nothing to do, attain, gain or lose. The only thing lacking in you is the awakening that brings the realization that you lack nothing. When you are able to just sit and be here now, you will have overcome the initial difficulties, and your progress on the path will be assured. You will discover that real progress is slow, subtle, and cumulative.

At the initial stage, especially of insight meditation, as you begin to focus attention on your mental contents, you will come to experience what makes you tick. You will discover discontinuities in your stream of consciousness, and you will see that what was continuous and automatic is made up of thousands of momentary stimuli rapidly succeeding one another. As you directly observe the inner workings of your mind and watch the tangles of your thoughts, fantasies, emotions, desires, and attachments, you will discover how they spin out of your mind and create your world.

In concentrative as well as insight meditation, as you get involved in a process of constantly bringing your attention back from its wanderings, you will begin to become aware of how unaware you are of your unawareness. Thus you discover what the Buddha meant when he said, "Ignorance is the condition of all conditioned things." You see how unawareness envelops the states and activities of the programmed mind and the entire span of conditioned existence as your mind dives into thoughts and fantasies, and is carried along by a current of unawareness, sweeping over your life and carrying you into oblivion. Suddenly your mind pops its head into the fresh air of awareness and sees what it has been doing, only to plunge and get lost again. How different is this unawareness, this wandering of the mind, from that of sleep and dream states? Not much, according to Roger Walsh, who points out how, as we become identified with and lost in mental contents, awareness becomes reduced and distorted, so that we spend much of our life in a hypnotic, trance state or *maya*. And he observes what every meditator has discovered, that even in meditation, at the initial stage, well over ninety percent of our time is spent lost in fantasies (1: 23-38). If this is the case when we try to wake up, what can we say of our *normal* waking hours?

Along with unawareness and unreality or illusoriness, you also gain insights into other characteristics of your present condition. For instance, as you focus attention on the primary stimulus, you discover how in its usual state, consciousness perceives things through such filters as emotions, wants, desires, attachments, judgments, and so on, which are projected onto the primary stimulus. As the stimulus becomes coated with layers of these filters, you discover that what you perceive as objects or things are largely a product of your own mind. You discover how from moment to moment you are constantly evaluating and making judgments and thus distorting the primary process. This brings insight into the illusory character of what you believe to be real.

As you find how little control you have over your mental process, you come to see how, as Ram Dass puts it, you are a prisoner of your own mind. You come to experience how your life is a product of programming, which reduces it to a state of bondage. You see how the framework of your consciousness is fashioned largely out of these programmed states, which cause it to function automatically, putting out repetitive patterns of thought, feeling, and behavior. These patterns make you blindly respond to stimuli, obey their commands, and willingly or helplessly subject yourself to their tyranny.

You discover that what you thought to be yourself, your identity, consists mostly of patterns of learned responses that were programmed as a result of past experiences. Like alien intruders, these patterns came to occupy the vacant territory called "you." Other insights follow as the mind keeps exposing the web it spins to create your world and self.

Such insights and torrential release of thoughts, fantasies, and images must not be thought to be negative or detrimental. On the contrary, they are a necessary part of meditation. Unless they are released, you cannot wake up. Their release means that many of the defenses, blinders, and filters that restrict, distort, interpret, and create your distance from reality are beginning to be removed, deconstructing consciousness.

At this stage people usually experience release of negative emotional fixations or blockages, tensions, and energies, releases that may have physiological manifestations. As Patricia Carrington observes, some people experience a sudden lightness or weightlessness, as if floating in air; others may feel a heaviness of the body, like sinking through the floor; yet others may feel that their body has disappeared. During deep relaxation, some feel intense heat, icy cold, or a burning or tingling sensation, a sudden itch, a temporary numbness in some part of the body, or even a pulsation throughout the body or on top of the head. Sometimes people perspire profusely, tremble, shiver, or if the energy release is particularly intense, they may experience a pounding heart or rapid breathing. Sometimes the body or some part of it may feel enlarged. At other times it may seem very tiny. Some may experience momentary discomfort, pain or a headache; others may sigh, yawn, or make automatic sucking sounds, experience muscle twitches, jerks, or involuntary movements. Some people experience all kinds of smells; others hear various sounds, such as humming, rushing, or ringing; yet others see different images, such as sparks, spirals, whirls, vivid colors, or bright lights. It is not uncommon to experience periods of restlessness or to have strong emotional reactions. Some people burst into laughter or tears, some feel intense rage, sexual sensations, or even experience orgasm (93-95).

During the first few weeks of practice, you may experience one or more of these phenomena; others may experience none at all, depending on the intensity of the meditation practice and the psychological state of each individual.

Carrington observes that each person's pattern of stress release may vary, paralleling their preoccupations, their mental fixations, emotional blockages, conflicts, or, in unusually intense cases, traumatic or unusual experiences. It is not necessary to have such side effects to benefit from meditation. You should neither expect them nor be surprised or disturbed if they occur.

When the repressed contents of the unconscious begin to come to the surface of consciousness, one tendency among many meditators, especially in the West, is to do self-therapy. As Jack Engler observes, many meditators in the West, upon discovering the hidden motives, fears, neurotic tendencies, emotionally charged thoughts, and other mental contents, become fascinated by them, give up meditating, and proceed to analyze them and figure out their causes (1: 27-290). Such self-analysis not only fixates one on the "psychodynamic level of experience" (Engler 1: 27), it derails him/her from meditation. That is the reason all traditions consider this preoccupation a hindrance to meditation. As Abbot Thomas Keating observes, the nature of unloading the unconscious is such that it does not focus on any particular content but loosens up all the psychological rubbish. The best thing to do in this situation is "to throw everything out together in one big garbage bag" (97), that is, practice nonattachment. Just acknowledge them and let them be or simply observe them. They will clear up when all tensions and energies are released.

If they do not disappear, however, Patricia Carrington suggests various strategies to clear them up. If you suddenly feel restless during meditation, for instance, she suggests that you recognize it as normal, continue to meditate, and periodically make it the focus of attention until it disappears. If you have a pain that will not go away, make it the focus of attention, move into it, and keep the focus on it until it dissolves and disappears. Anxiety can be handled by deep abdominal breathing. If none of these strategies works, reduce meditation time or suspend meditation for several days until the anxiety disappears, and then return to your regular practice (98-106).

The more tension and energy are released, the more the mind quiets down, the more attention remains focused on the object of concentration. Instead of scattering attention among a multitude of objects and becoming fragmented as it darts from one thing to another, such an undivided, prolonged focus on one object enables attention to shift its focus, and gather and unify around it. This unification is sometimes called "one-pointedness of mind." The longer it remains thus focused, the less scattered, and more unified it will become, and the more it will shift its focus from the external world to the internal object. This one-pointedness cannot be attained without the shift and unification of attention, which are key steps in the development of formal meditation.

This unification is expansion of awareness. The more awareness is freed, the more it will lose its ordinary, narrow, constricted, and distorted focus, its distance from things. It will begin to include within its embrace more events of the day, mental states, and activities that we usually pass in unawareness. It will become more inclusive, wide-ranging, stable, and present-centered. In terms of the object of concentration, the mind will be able to stay directly on it or on the primary stimulus without being side-tracked by outside goings-on, inside thought processes, or blankness of mind.

This does not mean that thoughts disappear at this stage. Rather, as you stop reinforcing the action mode and begin to disidentify, the object-world begins to lift its siege and the mind cuts loose from it. Cut off at their roots, thoughts at first decrease in frequency and intensity, and gradually drift off. As the clamor of thoughts begins to subside, the mind slows down, jumps around less, and becomes very calm. Fewer thoughts arise, and those that do, do not easily disturb or break concentration. You are able to notice them arising and sailing by without sticking in your mind. Being aware of your thoughts as they arise, you are usually able to let them come and go without getting trapped and lost in them.

As you keep attention focused on the object, you will notice subtler levels of thought and subliminal mental chatter. They represent the mind's tendency to label, categorize, or conceptualize experience. In spite of their presence, your mind will now settle down and remain calm. Occasionally it will become completely calm. More and more gaps will appear in which no thought is present. Your breath will become very gentle, regular, rhythmic, sometimes imperceptible. However, you will need to keep your attention sharp and clear by holding it focused directly on the object or the primary stimulus. Otherwise your mind, without being fed by thoughts or external stimuli, may go blank or play dead (i.e., experience sensory deprivation), a phenomenon the Tibetans call "the sinking mind," as a kind of ultimate protest.

Meditation/Contemplation: Penetration of Duality

At this stage of meditation or initial contemplation, the flow of attention toward the object of concentration or observation becomes fairly uniform and uninterrupted. If concentration was begun with an external object, the focus now shifts to an internal representation. As you continue to make the representation the focus of meditation for prolonged periods, various processes of transformation and deconstruction begin to occur both in the object and in consciousness.

One of these may be called "the displacement effect." A prolonged focus of attention will cause the object of meditation to begin to displace all other thoughts and contents, which were still present during concentration, and begin to flood and occupy the mind during meditation. Assuming center stage, the object will push everything else to the periphery. Increasingly, even throughout the day, the meditation object will break through the barrier of ordinary preoccupations, activities, automatic responses, defenses, and unawareness, and erupt into and occupy your mind, as if the meditation proceeded uninterruptedly during waking hours.

This phenomenon occurs especially when the object of concentration is simultaneously experienced on various sensory levels and becomes, in effect, a condensation of the entire perceptual field. Reduced to one point, which the Hindu and Buddhist traditions call "the seed" ("synesthesia" in psychology), it emits sensory information pertaining to various fields, such as light, sound, patterns of vibration, and images (Brown 1: 237). In Western traditions, such as Christian mysticism, Sufism and Kabbalah, this stage is known as the stage of illumination. In its advanced form it also covers what Christian writers call "acquired contemplation."

As you carry the focus of attention on primary stimuli or objects of perception outside the meditation period, which is an essential feature of every path of formal meditation, you will experience the same clarity and immediacy. You will be aware of and respond to things, people, and situations at the primary level of stimuli. As you do so, it will appear that you are perceiving things with new sensory awareness, as if for the first time. For instance, as you focus attention on the sound of crickets, you will notice discrete tones or sounds succeeding one another and creating the continuity which we ordinarily perceive. The same thing will happen with other sensory awareness. Things will just be there for you in all their nakedness and truth. You will be aware of other people's motivation and subtle behavior, together with your programmed affective or mental reactions as they arise.

And you will be aware of similar processes in yourself. Your hidden thoughts, motivations, drives, and compulsions will now surface and come to focus in the clarity of your awareness. In walking meditation, for instance, you will notice how the continuous process of walking is composed of innumerable discrete moments of decision the brain makes in rapid succession. This is true of everything we do automatically, usually in unawareness. Thus you will be aware from moment to moment how your mind continuously makes judgments and decisions in terms of likes, dislikes, desires, fears, etc. You will also notice more things in your environment. Things in nature, especially things for which hitherto you had no time or which did not hold your interest, will now appear before you in their immediacy, bathed in delight.

Furthermore, as the first phase of the shift of attention away from outer objects and toward inner thoughts and programmings occurs, you will begin to disidentify and become nonattached to the outer realms of things, people, situations, and familiar constructs. As the mind begins to become free of the control exercised by desire, attachment, and identification, you will be less driven to seek identity outside yourself and will correspondingly experience less need to wander among the world of objects, trying to make ego Real. The need to go galloping after possessions, achievements, power, success, or relationships to give you identity or self-worth, to find acceptance or approval in order to be yourself or be happy will diminish. You will be less compelled to seek others' company in order to overcome loneliness or your inability to be by yourself. Instead, a sense of self-confirmation and a feeling of well-being will rise up from within and will be supported by your environment.

In the same measure, the compulsion to fulfill others' or society's expectations will lose its hold over you. You will become increasingly disenchanted with the merry-go-round of life and disensnared by things, thoughts, situations, and relationships that are not growth-producing. Disillusioned with the illusions, fantasies, or deceptions surrounding life, your mind will begin to become reality-based, responding to people and situations directly, rather than in socially accepted ways, imposed categories, or value judgments. Increasingly finding satisfaction in being in the present, your mind will begin to be present-centered. As you become more relaxed and at peace with yourself, you will increasingly discover that just being is enough. Lightness and buoyancy will increase as the feeling of separation from people and things begins to decrease.

Union or *Samadhi:* Oneness with the Object

Beyond the meditative is the state of union or *samadhi*. At this stage, like a laser beam, unified attention cuts through the object-construction and experiences unity with the reality it ordinarily symbolizes or represents. As attention penetrates its construction, the object begins to dissolve into the primary process of the reality. At the same time it cuts through the programming and construction of consciousness and arrives at the primary process of awareness beyond. As both boundaries dissolve, there remains no medium, framework, form, construction, or limitation to keep them separate. The object expands, as does awareness. The two become one process of reality and awareness at the same time. As the construction of a separate subject and a separate object is transcended, the gap dividing them is simultaneously bridged. There remains no mind separate from the object and no object separate from the mind. Rather, what you experience is the reality manifesting itself in the form of the object. So the mind's journey toward the reality of the object is at the same time its journey toward its own reality, leading to their convergence, whereupon they are experienced as one.

This process happens in several stages. The first phase in the deconstruction of ordinary consciousness occurs as attention remains fixed directly on the object for prolonged periods. This deconstruction concerns the outer layers of programming and object-construction. Exclusively focused on the object, like a sperm encircling and penetrating an ovum, attention begins to penetrate and cut through the outer layers of programming: cultural associations, emotional reactions, the verbal layer, categorization or linguistic codification, and interpretation, evaluation, and judgment. Next it penetrates the symbolic construction, the model formed in the brain from single or repeated experiences. As this happens, the ordinary distance between attention and object is bridged. As the outer construction falls away, the object is no longer experienced as a solid, fixed, separate entity but a process of constant change in which no specific perceptual pattern is discerned. Things pass in and out of each other and appear as a mass of light (Brown 1: 237-238).

This movement of attention toward the center of the object is at the same time its journey toward its own center. The core of the journey is this simultaneous penetration and destructuring of reality and consciousness. As the deconstruction of verbal (or category) and symbolic layers (which are the layers of meaning) takes place at this stage and the onset of the next stage of meditation, many meditators report that they experience the world in its nakedness, void of meaning. Speaking of his own experience, Roger Walsh says, "I could be looking at something completely familiar, such as a tree, a building, or the sky, and yet without an accompanying internal dialogue to label and categorize it, it felt totally strange and devoid of meaning. It seems that what made something familiar, and hence secure, was not simply its recognition, but the actual cognitive process of matching, categorizing, and labeling it, and that once this was done, more attention and reactivity was focused on the label and labeling process than on the stimulus itself" (1: 42).

Since the focus of attention now is not on the reaction but the primary process of the stimulus itself, the world no longer appears as familiar or meaning-laden. For instance, if you focus attention on music, it is not music that you hear, but one discrete sound succeeding another. In your daily activities, you will experience people and situations without the normal restrictions, defenses, labels, or value judgments. You will feel as though layers of defenses, limits, and familiar associations that create or give meaning to things in the ordinary world have been peeled off. Instead of responding to programmed reactions, you will relate to people and things in terms of the immediate point of contact between awareness and stimulus. Pointing this out and speaking of his own experience, Roger Walsh says, "The experience feels like having a faint but discernible veil removed from my eyes, and that veil is made up of hundreds of subtle thoughts and feelings" (1: 43).

Such an experience may appear painful and cause anxiety or disorientation at first, as Walsh, Bernadette Roberts and others report. But it is something you have to experience and pass through at this transitional stage in which the old reality-construct is being dismantled and the new Reality has not yet emerged. In terms of the Christian stage-differentiation, this contemplative journey is part of the process of passing though "the dark night of the senses."

On the positive side, it is part of the removal of ordinary restrictions imposed by programming and our habitual way of dealing with the world, which creates what Roger Walsh calls "an unseen prison" (1: 42). Its removal ushers in an expansion of reality and awareness and brings clarity to life and immediate contact with things.

Penetrating further, attention arrives at the first major transpersonal stage — at what Ken Wilber calls the psychic level. At this stage, staying continuously on the object, attention penetrates and deconstructs or transcends the inner stages of the perceptual process and the construction of the ordinary perceptual world (Brown 1: 240). This is the first stage of emptying the mind and stopping the world. As the inner dialogue stops, attention transcends the ordinary perceptual object-construction. Such deconstruction takes awareness beyond the ordinary world where causality operates. Events are perceived more in terms of simultaneity or "synchronicity" than discreteness. As a result, awareness is predominantly intuitive, holistic, integral, inclusive, and panoramic (Wilber 6: 27-29).

At the next major transpersonal stage, called "subtle" by Ken Wilber, the object of meditation retains only the subtle form or the primary process in which solidity is replaced by fluidity. As no thought, concept, idea, or perceptual model is present, the separate self is deactivated. Meditation continues without any effort, activity, or interference on your part. Thus you enter into a passive or purely receptive state, in which the object appears as a constantly changing process. As meditation proceeds and you learn to balance the flow, the construction of focal attention and the sense of separation generated by it are transcended; and you come to experience union with the object, which alone remains in awareness (Brown 1: 241-245).

This stage of *samadhi*, in which you reach the first phase of oneness, may be called "subjective oneness." As primary duality still remains, this relative oneness is achieved with the object and remains limited to its subtle form and to the framework of meditation. Hence in many Eastern traditions it is called "*samadhi* with support" or "seed *samadhi.*" At this stage, there remains only the primary duality or polar principles that constitute the universe as well as the individual. Because both awareness and object arrive at their primary level of construction, both are experienced in their universal, archetypal form. As only the object remains in awareness, it is at this stage that you experience the universal or "cosmic consciousness."

In Christian stage-differentiation, this stage of *samadhi* is the stage of infused contemplation in which all activity on your part ceases and God or the object of contemplation becomes active and dominant. It spans what is called "the prayer of simple union" and full union with God.

At this stage, not only do you experience oneness with the object during meditation, but you carry this absorption over into everything throughout the day. The object's eruption into and assumption of the center stage of consciousness and displacement of everything else now becomes continuous. Remaining at the center, the object now does everything in you, as you. Whatever you do, you experience it as the object doing. Thus, reflecting the Zen experience, Yasutani Roshi says that when you become absorbed in the object of the koan, whatever you experience, it is the object experiencing it: Your hearing, seeing, touching, tasting, smelling, thinking and being are nothing but the object experiencing itself in and as you (Kapleau 1: 110). Similarly, Koryu Osaka Roshi observes, "At this point there is no distinction between inside and outside. You totally become one with the object, from morning to night, even in sleep or dreams. At this stage the object becomes your whole universe" (Maezumi and Glassman 1: 86-87). Confirming this, the author of *The Cloud of Unknowing* says that in this state the object is continuously present in your consciousness (Colledge 180).

According to Ken Wilber, this stage is the seat of archetypal or divine forms, subtle sounds, audible illuminations, transcendent insight, and absorption into or union with the divine forms or the object of meditation. In Hinduism this state is known as *savikapla samadhi;* in Theravada Buddhism it spans the end of the fourth and the beginning of the sixth *jhana* or state of absorption; in insight meditation this is the pseudo-nirvana of subtle-form; in Zen it is experienced as absorption in the koan; and in Tibetan Buddhism it constitutes the experience of identity with the deity of the meditation or with the meditative Buddhas (5: 91-97; 6: 29-30). In the Eastern traditions, this is the god realm. Western traditions speak of it as the angelic (lower subtle) and divine (higher subtle) realms. The lower subtle is also the realm of prophetic vision and revelation, biblical and quranic, as is evidenced by prophetic visions, illumination and clairaudience, such as those experienced by Moses, Isaiah, Muhammad, and Jesus at his baptism.

Thus, because of this unitive mode, various psychic phenomena are likely to manifest themselves at this stage. Not everyone who reaches this stage experiences these paranormal or psychic powers, but they tend to be characteristics of this stage, although some of them may appear earlier or later. Such powers include: telepathy, clairvoyance, clairaudience, out-of-the-body experiences or astral travel, foreknowledge, reading other people's minds, healing, levitation, rapture, ecstasy, visions of God, Christ, the Buddha, etc.

In most cases, these experiences appear spontaneously. Blofeld reports that telepathy is common among advanced Tibetan yogis. Ram Dass intimates that his teacher, Guru Maharaj-ji, was able to perceive events from a distance without being there. And we have stories of Christian saints, such as Teresa of Avila and John of the Cross, experiencing ecstasy and levitation. Some authorities, such as Patanjali in his *Yoga Sutras,* claim that you can even consciously strive to attain such powers.

All major traditions agree, however, that you should not be deceived that attaining such powers is the goal of meditation, or that they constitute enlightenment. In fact, these powers can become obstacles if you get caught in pursuing them for themselves, for gaining power over others, or for recognition and self-enhancement. That is why these traditions warn you to stay clear of them. Thus, after describing how to attain these powers, Patanjali advises avoidance of them since they are obstacles to *nirvikalpa samadhi.* Zen calls them *makyo,* or illusions, and admonishes you not to pay attention to them if they arise. This admonition is the source of the famous Zen saying, "If you see the Buddha on the road, kill him." Similar warnings are issued by other traditions. So, if you happen to experience any paranormal power, do not attach importance to it, but set your sight on the next stage of the path.

According to both Eastern and Western traditions, the subtle stage culminates in union with the personal God of theism. The self with which this union takes place is the archetypal self, described by many Western mystics as the highest or deepest point in ourselves. Beyond the psyche, it is the realm of the spirit, sometimes spoken of as the "divine spark" in us. Thus union takes place between two primal or ultimate forms: the ultimate form in the individual and in reality or God as the ultimate form, as the Transcendent Other. These forms constitute the primary polarity of the primal duality, which are the ultimate forms in which Reality as Such or the Unconditioned State manifests itself. Most Jewish, Christian, and Islamic mystics describe their experience of union with this ultimate divine form. A realization of this union in its permanent form is considered the highest state of consciousness attainable in this life.

Absolute Oneness or Identity: Enlightenment

In many traditions, the onset of the next major stage begins with insight meditation or infused contemplation. Its aim is to cut through the subtle form, the residual contents, programming, and form of consciousness. Using various perspectives, you first cut through the "seed" or subtle form and arrive at what Patanjali calls "seedless *samadhi,*" in which no content, only impressions, remain in awareness. Further refinement leads to a transcendence of the method, object, and framework of the meditation, that is, transcendence of the path itself. From this perspective you are first able to observe and then transcend the structure of space and time. This enables you to experience the simultaneous origin, cessation, and interdependence of all phenomena in the universe as movements in absolute Oneness. You are able to observe the very process whereby forms, objects, and events—or the phenomena of the world—are constructed and maintained, and pass out of existence. From this Oneness you are able to experience the undivided wholeness of the universe in which each thing is seen to interconnect, interpenetrate, and inhere in all and all in each (Brown 1: 246-256).

As attention cuts through even this universal process and the corresponding residual patterns on the unconscious level, it experiences a pivotal shift away from contents and turns toward itself and its Source. Thereby it becomes empty, silent, and still. In this void state, only the original, natural activity of the primordial state, to which even the ordinary meditation becomes a hindrance, remains. Everything else drops off. There is now only the elemental state of awareness itself (Brown 1: 260).

When this state matures or reaches a critical mass, the final breakthrough occurs as absorption in the void is broken up. Thereupon the structural limits of consciousness and object, forms, and events are broken through and transcended; and Awareness emerges in the pure state of itself beyond programming, content, and construct. With nothing other than itself left to create a separation or distance from anything, Awareness experiences its true nature to be pure, unconditioned, undifferentiated, and formless, identical with Reality in its Unconditioned State of itself. Thus it experiences its nature to be the nature and reality of all things in their Unconditioned State. We see then that as the mind comes to experience itself in its ultimate state beyond any form, content, condition, or construct, it experiences nothing to be excluded from it (all-embracing), nothing to be separate from it (nondual), nothing to be other than it (absolutely one or identical). This is enlightenment—the experience of the Supreme Identity: the identity of Awareness and Reality, which is the identity of each thing just as it is, and consequently your own true identity. The paradox is that only when you disidentify, become empty of, and transcend all contents, objects, programming, conditions, and constructs—everything you believe to be real but which in fact separates your from Reality—do you discover yourself to be no other than that very Reality.

This experience of enlightenment is described differently by different traditions. But every tradition that is a witness to it speaks of it in ontological terms as the experience of identity beyond union. This is the ontological revelation in which is laid bare not any form of God, but the very nature of God beyond form, spoken of as *Brahman, Nirvana* or Buddha-nature, Tao, and Godhead by the sources of experiential religion. And the stage in which it occurs is variously described by these sources: for Hinduism it is *nirvikalpa samadhi;* for Theravada Buddhism "path-enlightenment;" for Zen the eighth of the Ten Ox-herding Stages; for Taoism returning to the Source; for Eckhart, Roberts, and other Christian mystics, it is the experience of God's "isness" or essence and identity beyond union; and for Kabbalah and Sufism as passing away into the being of God, which alone remains and is revealed everywhere to be That other than which nothing exists.

Realization of the Unconditioned State

Although enlightenment is the direct experience of the Ultimate as itself, it is not its ultimate realization. To arrive at the latter, you have to pass through progressive stages of enlightenment, which are mapped out in greater or lesser detail by the various sources of experiential religion.

Those who depict these stages agree that your supreme life-journey begins with enlightenment, which is both an end and a beginning of the meditative path. It is the end of the process of arriving at Self-realization and the beginning of the realized life. Enlightenment opens up the boundless, eternal life, but it does not give you a permanent hold on it. Being a transitory experience, it provides a glimpse into your real identity and center but not a realization of it as the permanent, natural, and only state in which you continuously and effortlessly dwell. For this to occur, as we already said, you need to burn up all traces, roots, residues, and consequences of conditionings and constructs from your conscious and unconscious mind. This is the integrative process, the stages of transcendence following the experience of enlightenment.

Finally, in the ultimate state of transcendence, there is a permanent shift of the center of your being and consciousness to the Unconditioned State, which then emerges as the new identity and permanent center from which you think, feel, live, and act. Any trace of duality between ordinary consciousness and All-embracing Awareness is then completely transcended; no distinction between enlightenment and nonenlightenment, between conditioned and unconditioned, remains in your consciousness. All-embracing Awareness alone remains as your normal, ordinary, natural, and permanent state, in which all conditioned things and states appear as its manifestation, so that everywhere and everything you encounter is revealed as its embodiment.

As we have said, the sources of experiential religion describe this end-state in various ways from their own perspectives. Hinduism calls it *sahaja samadhi* and *Turiya;* to Theravada Buddhism it is final enlightenment or *Nirvana;* Zen calls it Buddhahood, attained at the ninth and tenth of the Ox-herding Stages. A similar view is presented by Tibetan Buddhism, which considers it the ultimate end of the path, beyond the Nine Stages of Tranquility. Taoism calls it becoming the Source, Tao. This is the divine state in which all things are at all times, because beyond or other than it there literally is nothing. It is the incarnational state in which the individual is revealed to be a full embodiment of the Unconditioned in conditioned existence, as exemplified by the Buddha, the great sages of the Upanishads, Jesus, and the great sages manifested throughout history, East and West. This is the fullest dimension of humanity and the complete realization of what we truly are.

After discussing the preliminaries of formal meditation, in the subsequent chapters I shall describe at some length some of the classical meditative practices of Hinduism, Buddhism, Taoism, Kabbalah, Christian mysticism, and Sufism.

Chapter 4
Ground Rules for
Formal Meditation

Without adequate preparation nothing worthwhile can be accomplished. This is especially true if what you are about to do is difficult to master and takes a long time or a great deal of effort. No one can just walk into an operating room and perform brain surgery without years of study, residency, and practical experience. Similarly, unless you work hard, discipline yourself, practice, and become the best in your specialty, you cannot hope to compete in the Olympic Games. The same thing is true of meditation, the Olympics of the mind.

Before proceeding with formal meditation, then, you need to make adequate body-mind preparation and establish a proper context. Most monasteries and meditation or retreat centers have already created a meditative context. But for the solitary individual meditating on his/her own, or for one who has a family, this preparation is most important if s/he is serious about meditation or if the meditation is going to bear fruit. Such preparation requires the establishment of a proper time and place. Required body-mind training includes relaxation, posture, breathing, handling distractions, and effort. Since I shall discuss breathing in the context of instructions on how to meditate, I shall not repeat it here.

Place

For someone just beginning to meditate, it is important to set aside a space solely for meditation. This will give you the sense that meditation is not just another habitual activity, but is something special. In the meditative space, you leave your regular activities behind and enter a sacred dimension.

For this reason, you should not meditate in bed or in a cluttered, disorganized room. We usually set aside space for specific purposes. We do not usually sleep in the office or go to school to have dinner. Nor does a doctor perform surgery at home. Even in our homes we have separate places for sleeping, eating, studying, watching television, or enjoying recreation. So it should be with meditation.

Setting aside a room for meditation is ideal, but most people can set aside only part of a room. The space should be free of clutter or things that might distract your mind. A simple space, with bare white walls, is fine. Or you may keep images of Christ, Buddha, or your favorite guru to inspire you. You may want to keep a plant, some flowers, or a candle. And, of course, there should be a meditation mat and a cushion or chair.

For a beginner whose mind can be easily set off by any sound, it is advisable to find a quiet place, free of sudden noises, human voices, and slamming doors. You may have to alter your routine to find a quiet space. On the other hand, natural sounds, such as, a running stream, humming insects, chirping birds, do not usually cause any disturbance.

As you advance in meditation, you will find that you can meditate almost anywhere – in a crowded subway, going to and from work, in a busy train station, in a bar, or at a party. When the mind is still and at peace, it does not require a quiet physical space in order to become still. But for a beginner, a quiet place is most helpful. Just being there will put you in an open and receptive frame of mind conducive to meditation.

Time

When should you meditate, how often, and for how long? Answering this question satisfactorily for yourself is even more important than establishing a place for meditation. For time is at the heart of practice.

Perhaps I should start by indicating when you should *not* meditate. Many meditative traditions say that you should not meditate on a full stomach or when you are very hungry. Just after you eat, your blood supply is routed through your digestive system. Since less blood is available to the brain, you tend to get drowsy. The same thing may happen when you are too tired. On the other hand, if you meditate just before going off to bed, you may be so wide awake that you find it hard to fall asleep. (If, however, you have difficulty falling asleep, when you go to bed, relax, focus your attention on your breath, and let the attention flow with it. You will be asleep in no time). Likewise, if you meditate when you are very hungry, you may find it hard to keep your attention focused on the meditation object. You will be distracted by thoughts of food.

It is hard to state a general rule for the best time to meditate. Some people claim that they are "morning persons," others that they are "evening persons." Most of these claims are, however, derived from habituation rather than from a knowledge of one's biological rhythm. I used to think that I was a hopeless case in the morning. But I could stay up till two or three in the morning studying. So I thought I was an "evening person," until I started meditating. Now I find early morning, just before breakfast, the best time to meditate. On the other hand, some people's biological clocks really seem to make them more alert at certain times of the day than at others. If you really know what your biological clock is, follow it.

Most serious meditators find that early morning, before breakfast, is the best time to meditate. The mind is then relatively fresh and clear. And meditation puts you in a relaxed state so that you are able to face the day with calmness, attentiveness, and purpose. Most people find the end of the workday, before supper, also a good time to meditate. The mind can relax and unwind, refreshed for the evening. But you need to discover what is the best time for you. Meditation is experimental, not subject to rigid rules.

Establishing regularity is most important. Just as you cannot expect to boil a pot of water by applying low heat for a few seconds every few days, so you cannot progress in meditation if you meditate only occasionally or when the mood strikes you. And you might as well forget about meditation if you are going to leave it to chance. If you give in to moods, likes, and dislikes, you will continue to be ruled by your habits, never breaking free.

In this respect, it is important to confront the excuses and defensive maneuvers your mind is programmed to make to head off changes about which it is apprehensive. One excuse is that you are too busy to meditate. Another is that you are too tired — or that there's too much on your mind — or that you are too upset or disturbed to meditate.

Establishing a regular schedule and meditating each day at the same time will help you cut through your mental deceptions. If you wake up at seven every day to go to work, wake up at 6:30 so you can incorporate morning meditation into your schedule. This may require you to go to bed half an hour earlier. In time you will find that the less your mind gets disturbed, upset, anxious, or stressed during the day, the less sleep you need and the more energy you have. You will find that if you currently need seven or eight hours of sleep, as you progress in meditation you can function well with five or six hours of sleep. And you will probably find that you sleep more deeply and soundly every night.

If you meditate only when you feel calm, you will miss a precious opportunity to overcome your avoidance pattern, discover why your mind gets so disturbed, and dissolve the negative programming that causes the disturbance. Then you can achieve real calm, peace, and joy in your life. You may well find that one of the most useful times to meditate is when your mind is disturbed or upset. Rather than running away from and carrying such programmings with you wherever you go, you will welcome them to gain insight into yourself and become free.

As for the frequency of meditation, as you set out, you should meditate at least twice a day. After a while you will discover that your body wants to meditate. And you will come to realize that meditation is one of the most important things you do each day. As you advance and reach a plateau in your meditation, you will realize that just meditating twice a day is not enough. You need intensive periods of meditation in order to make further advances and experience deeper changes in your life, for which your mind will begin to yearn. You will then need to find some meditation centers and participate in a meditation intensive or retreat that lasts several days.

How long should you meditate? Generally speaking, begin with what you find comfortable and then add a few minutes to stretch yourself. Some push is needed in the beginning. As you continue meditating for some time, you will find a spontaneous need to extend the time period. Thus, if you begin meditating for fifteen minutes each session, you will gradually increase it to half an hour. You may even extend it to forty-five minutes or an hour, which is the usual time period at meditation centers. But do not overdo it. It is better to meditate more frequently each day than to unduly extend each session. Half an hour to forty-five minutes is a good time period for each session.

To keep track of time, you may use a kitchen timer or a watch with an alarm. Do not look at a watch to determine when your meditation period is over. Both looking at your watch and wondering when the time will be up will distract you and make you lose concentration. This distraction can be avoided if you set the time before sitting to meditate. As you end a session of meditation, instead of getting up abruptly, sit quietly for a minute or two, then rise slowly and mindfully. Try to do everything mindfully after meditation, instead of immediately plunging into your habitual unawareness. Carry the meditative awareness and attentiveness into everything you do throughout the day.

Relaxation

One of the preconditions for success in meditation is being in a relaxed state of body and mind. Without being in such a state, it will be impossible to keep your mind focused on the meditation object for long. If there are a lot of tensions in your body or your mind is in knots or is foggy, lethargic, and unfocused, you will need to do some exercises that will relax your body and mind, make them come alive, become alert, poised, and focused. Thus, before you sit down to meditate, you need to do some relaxation exercises.

There are a number of options available for relaxation. You may do yoga exercises, take a vigorous walk for a few minutes, jog a mile or two, do body/mind relaxation exercises, or do mental relaxation. I shall not describe yoga exercises here, and walking or jogging you can do on your own. So I shall set down a few simple exercises as aids to meditation.

Relaxation Exercise I

a. Remove your shoes and lie down. Inhale, stretch your legs and toes as far as you can, and then exhale and relax. Mentally tell the muscles to relax and go limp. Do this five times.
b. Rotate each ankle five times, stretching the muscles as far as you comfortably can.
c. Inhale and draw your knees to your chest. Pause, exhale, and straighten and stretch them out as far as you can. Do this five times.
d. Inhale and draw up your stomach muscles; then exhale and relax them. Do this five times.
e. Stand up. Inhale, extend and stretch your arms; spread and stretch your fingers. Then relax and slowly lower your arms. Do this five times.
f. Bend your body from the waist up and lower it as far down as possible. Let your arms relax and go limp. Then slowly move your torso from left to right as far as you can. Next, move from right to left. Do this five times in each direction.
g. Now slowly straighten out your body, beginning with the waist. Put your hands on your hips, hunch your shoulders up toward your ears, and then relax and rotate them forward, down, back, and up toward your ears again. Do this five times on each side.
h. With hands still on your hips, close your eyes, bend your neck over toward your left shoulder as far as it will go, and slowly rotate your neck down the front to your right shoulder as far as you can and continue through the back to the

original position. Do this three times and then reverse and do the same in the other direction.
i. Shake your hands, then your legs; jump up and down. Do this five times.

Relaxation Exercise II

a. Stand. Make fists. Inhale and raise your arms above your head and stretch them as far as possible. Be aware of the sensation as you do so. Then lower your arms, exhaling as you do so, and become aware of the sensation and movement of your arms.
b. Spread your fingers as far as possible, inhale, and raise your arms over your head; then lower them to the level of your right shoulder, stretching as far as you can. Then exhale and bring them back over your head. Next do the same on the left side.
c. Do the neck squeeze and head roll as in Exercise I g-h.
d. Bend your knees, stretch your arms out in front, and lower your torso until you are in a squatting position. Then lower your arms and slowly rise to a standing position; in a continuous motion, raise your arms to the sides up to the shoulder level, stretching as far as you can; then raise them above your head until your palms join. Next, lower them slowly to your sides.
e. Bend forward at the waist. Let your arms dangle loosely, and, without moving your feet, rock back and forth, left to right. Now place your hands on the floor, squat, and stretch your neck from side to side.
f. Slowly stand up, raise your hands above your head, stand on tiptoe, and then come down to the floor hard on your heels. As you do so, let out a "hah" from the root of your abdomen. Observe the sensation.
g. Rotate your pelvis from side to side and be aware of the motion.
h. Assume a squatting position; then slowly straighten your body to a standing position. Raise your arms over your head in a sweeping arc, join your palms, and lower them over your heart center in a prayerful gesture.

Relaxation Exercise III

a. Sit comfortably. You may keep your eyes open or closed.
b. Take five deep breaths. Then inhale and take the breath down to the pit of your stomach. Slowly exhale and follow the breath out, relaxing your body.
c. Relax your neck and head by rotating in a circular motion as before. Now focus attention on your facial muscles, beginning with the forehead. Smooth out

the lines on your forehead by focusing attention on the muscles and observing the tension. Tell your muscles to become completely relaxed, limp, and supple. Keep your attention focused, until you sense that the muscles have indeed become relaxed before moving to the next set of muscles. Proceed in this way to the muscles around your eyes, your mouth, your lips. Next go to your jaw and relax the muscles. Relax your neck and shoulder muscles. Then slowly go over the entire body. Pause whenever you notice muscle tension. Using this method, relax the tension before you proceed to the next step.
d. Let your breathing become relaxed. Breathe slowly, gently, and deeply. Sense your relaxation each time you breathe out.
e. Sit quietly for a few minutes. Sweep your attention over your entire body. Feel it completely relaxed. If tension is still lingering anywhere, take your attention there; tell your muscles to become completely relaxed. Keep your attention focused there until you feel they are relaxed.

When you feel your entire body/mind relaxed, alert, focused, and in a heightened state of attention, you are ready to sit down and meditate.

Posture

What posture does for the body, meditation does for the mind. As Mircea Eliade has remarked, on the level of the body, posture is concentration on a single point (54). Its aim, the Indian sage Patanjali tells us, is to control the activities of the senses and to bring them to a stop so that the mind can become still. With the body brought to a point of unity and stillness, one of the sources of sensory stimuli is cut off. When the body is immobilized, one of the sources by which consciousness maintains its outward orientation — the incessant movement of the body — is deactivated. As long as the body keeps moving, the sensory stimuli to which it gives rise help maintain the outward orientation. But when the body is stilled through posture, the mind has a chance to direct its attention inward toward itself and become unified. This is also true because the incessant movement of the body helps maintain the stream of consciousness and the inherent distractibility of the mind, which scatters its attention and ensures its wandering among objects of the world. But when the mind is stilled through posture, it has a chance not only to reverse its orientation, but also, by remaining focused on itself or on the object of concentration, to stop thought and the stream of consciousness, and to become present-centered and awakened.

For this objective, the kind of posture necessary for meditation is one in which the body remains still and immobilized, yet allows for maximum alertness and attentiveness for the entire meditation period. Such posture should be relaxing, refreshing, and energizing. And it must free attention to be invested solely on the object of concentration.

Thus your posture must allow you to keep your back or spinal column erect but not stiff for the entire meditation period. This will help you remain maximally alert and attentive. When you slouch, you are not very alert; you are either daydreaming or your attention is elsewhere than where your body is. Such a posture is worse than useless, for it maintains, rather than deconstructs, ordinary consciousness. On the other hand, you will notice that when you are attentive, your back straightens out and you sit up straight.

The preferred posture is the full lotus position. It is true that, as Aryeh Kaplan observes, in the East it is common to sit on the floor or on a mat. So the lotus posture is a normal, comfortable posture for Eastern meditators (59). But it is also true that from their years of experience, yogis have found it to be the best posture for remaining in the maximum state of alertness for the longest time. I myself have found it hard to remain alert and awake sitting on a chair for extended periods of time. (I cannot sit in the full lotus posture; I prefer the cross-legged one.) My advice is to experiment and find the posture in which you can remain maximally awake, alert, and attentive for the entire meditation period.

To assume the full lotus posture, first place a thick mat, rug, or carpet on the floor and then place your meditation pillow on it, if you have one. If not, you could make one by folding a blanket several times over or use a couple of very firm toss pillows. Now, after doing the relaxation exercise, sit on the pillow, spread your legs forward, bring the head, the neck, and the trunk into a straight line; then slowly lift the left foot with your hands and place it on the right thigh. Do the same with the right foot, placing it on the left thigh.

Next, place your hands on your knees. You may either keep your hands on your knees, with palms down and fingers draping them, as is recommended by Tibetan Buddhism; or, with palms up, you may form a circle with the tip of the index finger and the thumb joined together, and keep the other three fingers stretched out and joined together. This is one of the *mudras* or hand gestures recommended by yoga. A third alternative is to assume the Zen posture by placing the right hand in the lap, palm upward, and the left hand on the right, palm upward. Then lightly touch the tips of the thumbs so that a flattened circle is formed by the palms and thumbs. The reason for placing the left on the right is that, since the right side of the body is governed by the left brain (which represents the action mode or ordinary form of consciousness while the left side is governed by the receptive mode), by placing the left on the right, you put yourself in the receptive mode of consciousness, which is the mode to be developed in meditation (Kapleau 1: 31). In any case, I have found that placing the hands on the knees gives me greater balance and does not create tension and pain in the lower back, as the Zen method tends to do.

As for the rest of the posture, it is recommended that you slightly tilt your head forward so that your eyes will be cast about five or six feet ahead of you. You may keep your eyes either closed or open without focusing on anything. Some teachers say that you should not close your eyes if that tends to make you fall asleep or daydream. On the other hand, if closing your eyes is less distracting or you can concentrate better, then by all means do so. Since meditation is not anything magical, but is experimental, you should experiment with eye positions as with postures until you find the one which is most conducive to concentration. If the eyes are kept open, the reason for their not focusing on anything and keeping them lowered is that this cuts down sensory stimuli and thus decreases the production of thought or distraction.

Keep the tongue gently touching the upper palate. This will cut down the production of saliva. The teeth can either touch or remain apart, with the jaw dropped and kept loose. Next, you may sway your trunk around in ever-decreasing circles, until your spine settles into the straight position and you feel centered and ready to meditate.

If you find the full lotus posture difficult, painful, or uncomfortable, try the half lotus posture: Place your left foot on your right thigh and tuck the right foot under the left leg or thigh. The rest of the posture is the same as the full lotus.

If you cannot manage the half lotus, or if you feel unbalanced or uncomfortable in it, try the easy, cross-legged posture: Place your left foot under the right thigh and the right foot beside or just lightly touching the left shin. When seated on a meditation pillow, this posture is easy to maintain for forty-five minutes or an hour without any discomfort or the legs going numb.

If you are going to meditate for a period longer than fifteen minutes at a time, in all the above postures try to keep your knees resting on the floor. Otherwise after about fifteen minutes of sitting you will experience a great deal of bodily tension, especially in your lower back and around the knees and thighs. Obviously, this will disturb your meditation as it will be hard to maintain concentration. The same will happen if you do not use a meditation pillow or its equivalent. In addition, blood circulation will be cut off in your legs, which will become numb. When the pillow gives you the right height and your knees touch the floor, none of these deleterious effects are produced and your posture becomes most comfortable. Once you assume a posture, try to maintain it for the duration of the meditation. Unless absolutely necessary, do not move, shift around, or fidget, as that will contribute to your restlessness of mind, distracting you further, and disturbing the meditation.

If you find even the easy posture difficult, try to sit on a straight-backed chair. In this posture keep your trunk, neck, and head in a straight line. Do not lean against the back of the chair. Keep your feet firmly planted on the floor. Rest your hands on your knees, palms down, fingers draping the knees; or adopt one of the other two alternatives. You should sit as if you are a king, in command of the situation and your own mind, which is the center of attention and concentration.

Handling Distractions

The ordinary mind is inherently distractible, scattered among a multitude of objects, and restless, as it pursues one thing, then another. Distractions come from everywhere — from within and without. From without they come in the form of noises, temperature changes, and movements. From the body they come in the form of pains, itches, stomach grumbles, sneezes, throat tickles, yawns, and countless numbers of sensations and vibrations. From your mind they come in the form of colors, voices, and the incessant flow of thoughts and fantasies.

As you sit in meditation, all of these things become distractions if your mind is not calm and concentrated. In themselves or in insight meditation, especially if the mental contents are the object of attention, there are not distractions. However, especially for the beginner, all of these stimuli float up in the form of distractions. The way to handling them is not to fight or try, forcibly, to keep them out of your mind. Nor should you be so lax as to allow your attention to be carried off by every distraction. Either approach will reinforce the distractibility of your mind and derail your meditation. The best method is to pay no attention to distractions and not to allow them to trap your attention. Just let them appear and disappear. But if they become too disturbing or distracting, make them the focus of attention until your mind calms down sufficiently and you can return to your main practice. But if they do trap your attention, as they invariably will in the beginning, just patiently bring your attention back as often as you notice that it has slipped away and focus it on the object of concentration. Here is where effort proves crucial.

Effort

Effort is one of the necessary conditions for success in meditation. As such it is emphasized by all major meditation traditions. Hinduism speaks of *tapas*. The Buddha taught right or perfect effort. The Eastern Orthodox Church urges unceasing prayer. There are, however, different kinds of effort. Too little effort in the beginning is like applying too little heat to ignite a fire. On the other hand, too much effort in the beginning might cause burnout. When you have to make only a hundred-yard dash, you can pull out all the stops and go for broke. But if you do the same in a marathon, you can be sure that you will never finish, let alone win the race. If your goal in meditating is enlightenment, what you are faced with is a marathon race, not a hundred-yard dash. For this the right kind of effort is crucial. As Suzuki Roshi observes, "The most important point in our practice is to have right or perfect effort" (59).

Ordinary effort is based on a dualistic idea of gaining something. It presupposes a goal from which we are separated, of which we are not in possession. Furthermore, it presupposes a lack in ourselves. Hence effort implies striving to attain an external goal, thus overcoming the lack or deficiency. In meditation, on the other hand, the opposite is true. It does not require you to strive for a goal external to yourself. Since you are already That which you aim to attain, in the deepest sense, in meditation there is nothing to gain or lose outside of what you truly are. So long as you meditate with the idea of attaining something you lack or being something you are not, and striving to attain it, you will never arrive at the ultimate goal of meditation. So, one essential point about perfect effort is that it is the effort to let go of effort. It is the effort necessary to arrive at effortless, pure Being. As Suzuki Roshi again says, this kind of effort is "directed from achievement to non-achievement" (59).

Basically this effort requires us to give up something. We have to let go of our idea of getting something extra. We need to break out of the reward-and-punishment mentality that underlies ordinary striving and even much of conventional religion — the idea of getting a reward in heaven for being good or punished in hell for being bad. You have to come to realize that there is absolutely no one to reward or punish you. And you have to refuse to punish, blame, condemn yourself or others. Unless you do this, you will not make much progress in meditation.

The right effort in meditation is what the Buddha called the Middle Path. It is to steer a middle course between aggression and avoidance. It consists in not charging into meditation and trying to force results when you do not get what you want from meditation or when your mind does not become still as you want it to; and it consists in not giving up meditating in the face of discouragement, lack of progress, distractions, and difficulties. This requires a steady, patient, systematic effort; it requires not listening to a thousand and one clamoring voices that can deflect us from the path. As Gerald May has well stated, "To simply stay there while identity dies a thousand deaths, ego writhes like a snake caught by a forked stick, and self-image rumbles like an earthquake beneath you; this is meditative effort" (89). For this kind of effort the Buddha said that we have to be like elephants who are not bothered by hindrances but steadily proceed to their destination. And on the advanced level, it consists in not being satisfied when you reach a plateau, but in pressing on until you arrive at the Unconditioned State of effortless being. This is perfect effort or effort that leads to complete and perfect Being.

Chapter 5
Meaning of the Term *Yoga*

In its vast expanse, Hinduism enfolds many meditative paths, each suited to the personality and endowment of the would-be practitioner. The term *yoga* is generally used to denote them. In this sense, *yoga* can stand as a synonym for *meditation*. And that is how I shall use it here.

It is not my intention to discuss all types of yogas here. That would be a monumental task, well beyond the compass of the present study. I wish simply to present some of the more accessible classical yogas, tested by yogis over the ages, and, for that very reason, verifiable in and suitable for any age, including our own.

The term *yoga* itself is derived from the Sanskrit root *yuj* and has many meanings, such as to join, bind together, unite, aggregate, sum, and so on. Even in our present context it has many connotations, depending on the meditative tradition that uses it. One such meaning, subscribed to by the nondualist Vedanta tradition, is that it is the act of uniting, the process or method leading to union, and the state of union or identity with God. In this view, yoga is a path that traces your growth beyond the personal, through the transpersonal states until you arrive at the Unconditioned State of Awareness and Being. Hence it is a path of life's return journey to the Godhead. As Swami Rama has observed, yoga is the path of how you can be what you are. It is a way of being in the Unconditioned State of realizing your identity as *Brahman*, the Godhead (1: 1).

Echoing this view, Georg Feuerstein points out that in the Upanishads, *yoga* refers to a path of returning to the Source of all things by realizing Oneness with it (69). Since this Source is *Brahman*, yoga is the path of returning to your natural, Unconditioned State and realizing it as your true identity. As this return is a reuniting, which consists in revealing on the conscious plane what you already are in the transconscious state, it is an awakening and recognition of what you are already. Yoga is the act, the process or method of awakening and recognition that your true identity is the Self. Since you have always been nothing but That, this return is a homecoming from separation and alienation from your Self, from what you are, beyond conditioning and constructs.

As recognition, yoga assumes that in our ordinary state we have no knowledge of what we truly are. Since in this state we are not aware and cannot experience the Self, we need a path that will lead us to the transconscious state in which alone such an experience is possible. Put differently, yoga assumes that our ordinary condition is one of separation from God or true Self and all things in the universe. So long as we remain in this condition, we cannot overcome it by ourselves. Yet, as our natural state is assumed to be one of identity with God and all that is, this reuniting consists in a recognition that in reality we have never been parted — the separation being a mental creation due to programming and identification with our triple constructs. The reuniting is nothing other than getting rid of the idea that we are separate and stopping our life-long attempt to forge an identity based on this idea. We need a method that will help us in our quest; yoga is such a method.

As Ramana Maharshi points out, this union *(yoga)* is necessary for those in a state of separation *(viyoga)*. However, since in reality there is no separation, all that is required is that we give up the thought that we are separate (Osborne 58). Thus, yoga is a process of eliminating from yourself all that is not your Self. Since there is nothing other than the Self, what needs to be removed are the things in your mind that create the separation — the thought that you are separate, the programming and constructs that give rise to and maintain the thought, and the striving that attempts to create an identity based on them. Yoga is the process of disidentifying with the thought, or "stopping mind-waves," which create and maintain the belief that separation is our natural state. This stopping is the key to transcending separation and arriving at union. When we give them up and let go of our belief in a separate identity by stopping mind-waves, suddenly our true identity bursts forth into consciousness. Then we recognize who or what we truly are and have always been.

According to a second meaning, yoga is a method of integrating body, mind, and Spirit. This consists in uniting various emotional and mental states, first on the personal, then on transpersonal levels. We must successively awaken each transpersonal state, identify with and integrate it into ourselves, and then disidentify so as to awaken to the next higher state and achieve integration on that level. In this way, through yoga, we can become successively awakened, identified, and integrated on the higher, transpersonal planes of the spirit, until we become awakened and established in the ultimate state of Self or Spirit. Thus, yoga is a path of reconciliation of all conflicts, opposites, and dualities in their transcendent Ground — *Brahman*. In this sense, yoga is a process of expanding our being. This expansion does not consist in acquiring something new or alien to our nature, but in unfolding what we already are. Since our actual state is all-embracing, the expansion is nothing other than removing or transcending the narrow limits imposed on us by our minds as a result of identification with our programming and constructs. Thus our ordinary state is an abstraction from Reality as Such. The expansion is really adding or restoring or returning to our original, primordial nature. This requires breaking free and going beyond the barriers created by our conditioning and constructs, our thoughts and habitual ways of living, and coming to a full realization of the boundless state of our true nature. Thus, yoga expands our being until all its dimensions of our being are restored to ourselves. Since these dimensions are identical with all the dimensions of all that is (in which lies completeness), yoga is a path to completeness and liberation. This meaning of yoga is especially applicable to *Tantra.*

Neither of the above two meanings is to be found in Patanjali's *Yoga Sutras.* As it will be clear presently, he initially defines *yoga* as "stopping mind-waves," which has to do more with the method than with the goal. Nowhere does he state that the goal of yoga is union; and the word God, or rather Lord, occurs only in the form of "chosen deity," which functions as an aid to meditation. Seeing that the goal of his meditation is total transcendence of the Self from phenomenal reality or conditioned existence, following one ancient commentator, Georg Feuerstein suggests that for Patanjali, yoga is disunion rather than union (3: 26). Although on the surface this interpretation appears correct, nevertheless it betrays a confusion about Patanjali's intent.

Such an interpretation is derived from the fact that the philosophy underlying Patanjali's *Yoga Sutras* is dualistic. According to this view, which is closely associated with Samkhya Yoga, there are two primal principles from which all things in the phenomenal world have originated: *Purusha* or the Self, the nature of which is pure Awareness, and *Prakriti,* which is the material or energy principle, the primal stuff from which all things in the phenomenal world are made. Although the Self is our true nature or identity, because of our mistaken identification with constructed reality, consciousness, and self, we become separated and alienated from what we truly are and become bound to the material world. All our suffering results from our attempt to satisfy the desires of ego and thus become who we are not. The aim of Patanjali's yoga is to reverse this process, to retrieve the authentic life of the Self by disidentifying with the triple constructs (reality, consciousness, and self) and attaining the absolute state of effortless Being.

This process of disidentification and transcendence of *Purusha* from *Prakriti* appears like isolating the former from the latter—hence the impression of their disunion. But this impression rests on a mistake. What appears disunion on a cosmic scale is, from the point of view of the yogi, in fact a process of disidentification with and transcendence of the limited identity for the sake of realizing the limitless identity of the transpersonal Self. That, precisely, is the heart of the meditative journey in every tradition—East and West. In this process, what one disidentifies with is not the world as a whole but the constructed world, the consciousness that constructs it, and the ego that makes the identification. It is true that what Patanjali offers us is the absolute transcendence of the Self in which the world is not affirmed or seen because no form remains or appears in Awareness in this state so that what the Self, or the yogi who has realized it, sees everywhere is only itself as that which is. To be sure, in this state a subtle dualism remains; and it may not be the goal to which every form of yoga aspires. But to take this dualism in a literal sense and then to claim that the transcendence envisaged is "the total extinction of man as we know him" (Feuerstein 3:9) represents a serious misunderstanding of Patanjali.

Rather than union or disunion, what Patanjali emphasizes is realization of one's true identity, true Self, by disidentifying with everything that is not it, as the goal of yoga. Thus, for him, yoga is a path of Self-realization. This requires deconstruction and transcendence of constructed reality, consciousness, and self in order to arrive at the transconscious state beyond all phenomenal reality.

There are many forms of yoga to which the above meanings are not fully applicable. Thus *Hatha Yoga,* in which bodily and mental purification and integration are the main focus, seems to fall outside the above meanings. Yet, when you examine it more closely, you realize that it is not without the higher purpose of transcendence of ego and realization of transpersonal states. This is clear from a reading of *Hatha Yoga Pradipika* (one of the texts of *Hatha Yoga),* which includes instructions on *samadhi* and ends with Self-realization, precisely the way Patanjali does. However, its instructions on various bodily techniques to induce *samadhi* make it similar to *Tantra. Laya Yoga* also has a focus similar to that of *Tantra.* The above meanings, therefore, appear to be the primary ones.

Through its various yoga paths, Hinduism recognizes that although the aim of life is the same for all—Self-realization—everyone does not have to walk the same path to realize it. It recognizes that by natural endowment, personality, and temperament we are suited to different things. Hence, to insist that everyone must go down the same road would create unnecessary inner and outer obstacles, resistance, and conflicts. Each person needs a path that is in harmony with his/her capacities, temperaments, and inclinations, enabling him/her to progress on the path more quickly.

Thus, if you are the intellectual type, you may be turned off by something that is suited for practical, active people, and vice versa. People who are very emotional may not be drawn to concentrative exercises, but may want something that engages their emotions, and leads them to ecstasy and union. People of a psychological bent, given to experimentation, may prefer another path.

Imaginative people may want to work with something that fully engages their imagination.

To suit such diverse types of personalities, Hinduism has developed different types of yogas. Since from ancient times it has recognized four basic personality types, it has developed four corresponding types of yogas. Thus, for the predominantly intellectual type, Hinduism has developed *Jnana Yoga,* which is the path of knowledge or direct realization of the Self as one's true identity. This path works on ceaseless disidentification with everything until only the true identity—the Self—remains manifest in Awareness.

Active people, movers who cannot sit still, may at first be given *Karma Yoga.* As discussed in *Song of the Skylark I,* this is the path of selfless, nonattached action, consisting of acting without external goal orientation or attachment to outcome, "renouncing the fruits" and "complete giving up of all actions which are motivated by desire," as the *Gita* puts it (Prabhavananda and Isherwood 1: 40). This "acting without expecting anything in return" (Castaneda 3: 233) severs consciousness from its normal, outward object orientation and directs it, first, toward the action itself. As you engage in this type of action, there is a shift in the orientation of consciousness from the external world toward itself. When attention is focused on the action itself, you become aware, next, of the motives or reasons for your actions. You see why we normally act. You see that much of what we do is motivated by the grasping character of our consciousness, our greed, our attachment, our desire for gain and fear of loss, our drives and compulsions, our automatic and habitual reactions to people, events, and circumstances in our life, and so on. You see the consequences of acting under the spell of these motives. You then can take an active step to purify yourself or dissolve them and develop new, wholesome ones. Gradually you will become free of desires, thoughts, and behavior that reinforce the conditioned state. Eventually this path will lead to disidentification with the ego, a progressive overcoming of your sense of separation from God, and finally to the experience of union. At this stage, a shift will take place in the center of action from the ego to God or the Self. Centered in the Self, all your actions will arise spontaneously as its manifestation. When you act from oneness with God, your every action is prompted by the desire to reveal, and is the revelation of, God. You act as God acts; and your action becomes a saving activity toward others and the world.

The predominantly emotional, devout persons will be assigned *Bhakti Yoga,* the path of devotion and self-surrender, through which to transform their love and their emotions, to awaken ecstasy, and to realize union with God.

For those of a predominantly psychological bent, given to experimentation and working with their minds, there is Patanjali's *Yoga,* sometimes called *Raja*

Yoga, the royal road to realizing the Self through concentrative exercises intended to stop thought and open the mind to All-embracing Awareness.

Since these four types of personality are not exhaustive, other yogas have arisen in response to the needs of other personality types. Thus, those who want to exercise their creative imagination may respond to *Tantra* or *Kundalini Yoga,* which aim to help one realize his/her oneness through working with the polarities of energy and consciousness found in all things in the manifest order.

Although the yogas are described separately and presented as different paths, this is done, as Ramana Maharshi reminds us, in order to introduce the aspirant to the yoga most in accord with his/her personality and endowment. In themselves, they are not mutually exclusive paths. In practice, a fully developed path tends to incorporate the meditative practices of different yogas as appropriate. Thus even *Tantra,* with its very different approach and method, has practices in common with the others. And the very structure of *Yoga Sutras* is integrative. For this reason, I shall first discuss *Yoga Sutras* in detail. Then I shall briefly discuss other yogas, and finally give a somewhat fuller exposition of *Tantra.*

Chapter 6
The *Yoga Sutras* of Patanjali

About 200 A.D. Patanjali organized and systematized his yoga text in the form of aphorisms, calling it *Yoga Sutras*. A composite work that contains practices representing different types of yogas, it is suitable for practitioners with divergent goals and levels of preparation. Possibly going as far back as Vedic times, the *Yoga Sutras* is a distillation of yogas that have been practiced for centuries and passed down by gurus to disciples through oral transmission. (There is some archeological basis for entertaining the hypothesis that yoga was practiced by the people who developed the Indus Valley Civilization that reached its height of development at least as early as 2500 B.C., if not earlier. Indeed, it may well be that yoga was the original form of the religion of India.) Even before being codified by Patanjali, the yogas represented a system of transmission that had been long authenticated in practice, as it continues to be. The yogas constitute a path of Self-discovery and Self-realization for anyone who is resolved to follow it to the very end.

Patanjali begins his exposition by defining yoga as *chitta vritti nirodha*, "stopping mind-waves," or deconstructing the programmed mind. By *chitta* or mind, he means the entire programmed mind. According to yoga psychology, this mind has three levels or states: (i) the conscious, waking state; (ii) the subconscious, which the yogic tradition calls "the dream state"; and (iii) the collective unconscious (both in its individual form, as understood by Jung, and in its universal form, representing the collective experiences of humankind from its emergence to the present, and beyond, including the subtle state), called "deep sleep" [Swami Rama et al. 2: 115-126]). Since the entire human, as well as individual, past has a determining influence on the normal conscious state of the individual, all of it is included in Patanjali's concept of *chitta*, "mind."

It follows that *vritti* ("mind-waves" or mental contents or programmings) includes not only thought and the stream of consciousness, but also undercurrents or impressions, dispositions, and latent tendencies formed in the unconscious, which have their determining influence on various mental activities, five of which Patanjali mentions: knowledge, misconception, imagination, sleep, and memory. Churnings from the unconscious keep these conscious activities going in vortices, filling it with billowing waves of thoughts, emotional reactions, desires, and drives, preventing it from seeing itself. This keeps the lid of programming firmly in place and maintains the internal chaos and confusion that constitutes the human condition.

The third term, *nirodha,* means stopping or stilling, and refers to the central aim of the practice, which is to stop thought and the stream of consciousness so as to deconstruct the programmed mind. By deactivating the impressions and latent tendencies from the unconscious, we can deconstruct the entire programmed mind and stop it from reinforcing itself by producing thoughts and reactivating internal contents and reacting to external stimuli.

This need to deconstruct ordinary consciousness arises for three reasons (already discussed in Chapter One). First, yoga is a method of freeing the mind from the control exercised by the object-world, the environment, society or culture on the one hand, and the internal control exercised by thought, desire, attachment, identification, and the ego on the other. Until these are stopped, their control over the conscious sphere remains complete. You remain bound to your programming and constructs. And the essential shift of attention from external orientation and contents inward, toward the mind itself and the Source, cannot take place. This stopping enables the mind to pivot on itself and become free of its siege by the object-world, shed its fixation on contents and disidentify and become destructured, empty, or void. In the empty space of awareness the Self can emerge to the conscious level, resulting in Self-realization.

Second, yoga is an inward journey of the mind to its Source, *Purusha* — the Self or All-embracing Awareness. Unless attention is able to successively deconstruct both the ordinary perceptual and subtle structures, it cannot arrive at this Formless State. But this deconstruction is impossible so long as ordinary consciousness remains in control. Thus it must be stopped from functioning if attention is to successively pass through the conscious, the subconscious, and the unconscious spheres, break free of conditioning and constructs, and arrive at the transconscious state. Stopping is the key to this ultimate breakthrough. In this sense yoga could be said to be a journey of descent from the conscious, through the unconscious, to the transconscious state. The trajectory of the path is from unawareness to Awareness; the aim is to make the unconscious conscious; and the process consists in infusing with awareness both the conscious and the unconscious by letting attention penetrate and cut through thought and inner dialogue, sinking and settling into the subtler levels, finally transcending them and arriving at the very Source of the mind beyond thought.

Third, stopping is essential for the emergence of insight into the nature of the mind and reality in their Unconditioned State. As strong undercurrents of unconscious tendencies and programmed impressions keep kicking up sediment, it emerges to the surface of consciousness in the form of thought-waves and other objects or contents. As long as these are present, the mind will continue to be disturbed or muddied, lose awareness, and be prevented from seeing its nature, states, activities, and contents. When the waves become still and the sediment settles on the bottom, the mind becomes clear, empty, and still. In this clarity insights arise, and you are able to see the nature of all things just as they are. When night wanes and the darkness dissipates, we can see things in the light of day. Similarly, when ordinary consciousness predominates, All-embracing Awareness cannot rise and shine. But when it is stilled, in the clear space of awareness, we are able to see directly the nature of the mind as All-embracing Awareness. That is why, according to Patanjali, the entire ordinary consciousness must be brought to a stop and deconstructed. This deconstruction of the programmed mind is the key to ultimate transcendence.

For stopping mind-waves, Patanjali offers a two-fold method for working on the mind from both ends, so to speak—one to cut through conditioning and constructs and arrive at the transconscious state; the other to jar loose and break free of the hold they have on the mind and thus lead you toward the final realization. These two methods are practice and nonattachment, respectively (I. 12: Feuerstein 3: 34). He defines the former as "the repeated effort to follow the disciplines which give permanent control over the mind-waves," and the latter as "self-mastery; it is freedom from desire for what is seen and heard" (I. 13, 15: Prabhavananda and Isherwood 2: 19). As we have seen, these two methods form the heart not only of Patanjali's *Yoga,* but of all types of meditation.

The importance of nonattachment for any meditative path should be clear from the definition of meditation. So central is it that meditation can be said to be nothing other than a method of successively breaking free of attachment to every form until you arrive at the Formless, Unconditioned State. Since nonattachment is deconstruction and transcendence, the entire meditative path, from beginning to end, is essentially its systematic application. And since to be fully nonattached is to be fully unconditioned, the goal of meditation is nothing other than to arrive at a state of complete nonattachment. That is why, for Patanjali, nonattachment is one of the two fundamental requirements of *Yoga.* He introduces it at the outset because it is to be practiced at every stage of yoga and is, in fact, the goal of every practice. One side of the Janus-faced goal of yoga is nonattachment and the other is Self-realization.

While practice involves specific exercises of formal meditation, nonattachment has to do with both formal meditation and IAM, and is to be practiced at all times, both inside and outside meditation, and toward everything, especially toward the object-world and mental contents. Without nonattachment you will not be able to cut the mind loose from the bondage of programming, free awareness from entrapment, or shift attention inward. That is why Patanjali defines nonattachment as "self-mastery" and "freedom from desires," since it is desires that create and maintain our world and thus control our programmed mind.

Preliminary Practices

Before outlining the second requirement that constitutes the *Astanga Yoga* or the "eight-limbed yoga," Patanjali speaks of the preliminaries to practice: effort, self-examination, and devotion to the Lord deemed necessary to overcome hindrances and develop concentration. These make up what he calls *Kriya Yoga* or "Yoga of Action." Patanjali repeats them later as the second of the eight limbs. It is here that some commentators see the incorporation, perhaps by another hand or by Patanjali himself, of another type of yoga into the framework of *Astanga Yoga*. Others, however, such as Georg Feuerstein, believe that it was *Kriya Yoga* that Patanjali developed; *Astanga Yoga* was merely incorporated by him or by a copyist into the body of his *Yoga* (3: 59-60). Feuerstein's position is far from convincing. It is curious that *Astanga Yoga* appears nowhere else except in Patanjali's *Yoga Sutras*. The preliminary character of *Kriya Yoga* is not entirely dispelled. In any case, *Kriya Yoga* is for those who have restless minds and active dispositions; it calms them and develops concentration. Here, however, it serves as preparatory body-mind training for yoga proper.

As in any arduous journey, ascent on the yoga path can begin, if you are to successfully reach the peak, only after making adequate preparations. A basic change of attitude and behavior must take place. You cannot progress on the path in your present state of mind, with your habitual, programmed reactions to things. A proper mental attitude is necessary: a toughness of mind, clearheadedness, self-knowledge, effort, dedication, determination, and an active attitude that will enable you to see and face up to the fact that you are about to enter into a life-and-death struggle with yourself and the forces of your environment. Swami Prabhavananda suggests that this mental attitude should be similar to that of one who is about to enter into a battle. Similarly, don Juan tells Carlos

Castaneda: You must be like a warrior and develop personal power if you are to survive the path of knowledge, for what you are about to do is the last battle on earth — the battle with ego, its world, and the forces with which it is identified. Tarthang Tulku has observed that these forces are dangerous unless you are skillful enough to disarm them.

The context of the *Bhagavad Gita,* Kurukshetra, symbolizes the battlefield of the programmed mind in which the warrior Arjuna discovers all the opposing forces within himself. On the one side are the armies of ego, with its habits, attachments, desires, greed, values, ideals, and mental contents and forms — all clamoring for his attention. On the external side are Arjuna's teachers, society and the environmental forces that have shaped him and are demanding his submission so that he can confirm their reality and way of life.

And then there are the promises of the Self, represented by Krishna — the boundless, totally free and complete life, which requires discipline, nonattachment, trust, openness, and self-surrender. When Arjuna sees these forces arrayed against him and realizes that he is faced with nothing less than slaying the very things he considers part of himself and his world, he becomes filled with bewilderment, despondency, and loss of nerve. He refuses to fight, ready to give up the path of enlightenment. It is only the promptings of his guru, Krishna, who urges him to fight, to cut out the dead things from his life, that keep him on course. Such is the situation faced by every aspirant on the yoga path.

The term Patanjali uses to denote the proper attitude and fitness of body and mind as a prerequisite for every aspirant is *tapas,* which literally means "heat" or "energy." When applied to human conduct, as Ernest Wood accurately states, it means "discipline" or "effort" (1: 50). Patanjali himself does not define the term, but as Swami Rama suggests, *tapas* is any act which increases spiritual fervor or heat (1: 20), which, as Swami Prabhavananda points out, requires discipline (Prabhavananda and Isherwood 2: 67-68). According to Swami Ajaya, *tapas* is conserving energy ordinarily dissipated in pursuing diversions and securing comforts; getting rid of the insecurity which is present when we are without them; giving up dependencies and addictions; freeing ourselves from the demands of the senses and habitual responses of the reactive mind, and attaining simplicity (70).

Against our usual distracted, self-indulgent, loose attitude toward ourselves, *tapas* represents a house-cleaning activity: ridding ourselves of years of accumulated bodily and mental habits; toughening and keeping our body and mind fit for the arduous journey ahead. It consists in simplifying and reordering our life — precisely what Thoreau urged in *Walden* and what don Juan called "impeccability" and "cleaning and rearranging the *tonal*" (ordinary consciousness). *Tapas* requires purifying our body and mind so as to render them sensitive, open, alert and attentive, ready to reflect all things, like a prism. *Tapas* concerns developing and strengthening ego so that it can face itself without fear, frustration, despair, dejection, condemnation, or any attempt to evade or avoid what it discovers about itself.

Since no one can progress on the yoga path with an indulgent and passive attitude, Patanjali regards unawareness, ego, attachment, avoidance, and a thirst for life as obstacles on the path of knowledge. Contrary to such ways of avoiding the reality of our present situation, *tapas* requires us to discard our passive attitude and desire for magical answers, and face up to the fact that no guru can save us from ourselves. We must discover answers in our own experience, and travel the path from beginning to end essentially alone, not suffering for company, as St. John of the Cross put it, even of our own kind. *Tapas* weans us out of self-pity or the tendency to play up to our weaknesses, and enables us to develop a center of strength to face the habitual patterns of our self-deception and assume responsibility for our life. For this, we need to develop the discipline, the attitude, and the strength of a long-distance swimmer. For we will be swimming against the current of the past; the habitual patterns of our thought, feeling, behavior, and relationships; the social and cultural patterns that have been programmed into us; and against current cultural fashions, attitudes, and outlooks. Such is the warrior's way. Its development requires self-effort and discipline: *tapas*.

A second prerequisite Patanjali mentions, that is study, is twofold: the study of scripture and yoga texts that will provide you with knowledge of the Self or your true identity; and self-study or self-knowledge, from which you will gain understanding of your present false identification and what you must do to transcend it. Thus study involves both theoretical and practical knowledge. The former includes faith, not in the sense of taking the word of another, but something akin to a scientific hypothesis that needs to be tested and verified in your own experience. In addition, it includes chanting and mantra recitation, which can bring you in contact with the deity chosen by the guru at the time of initiation.

Self-study involves IAM: seeing yourself as you actually are from moment to moment, discovering your negative and positive programmings, and working to dissolve the former and free and enhance the latter. This will enable you to develop balance and harmony in your life (Ajaya 71-74). Study is then directed especially against the obstacles of unawareness, ego, lack of faith in the goal, and doubt, both in your ability and in the effectiveness of the yoga path toward its attainment.

Although the next preliminary—devotion to the Lord—sounds like *Bhakti Yoga*, its intent here is rather two-fold: to arouse your motivation: fervor, devotion, dedication, sincerity, and will or determination; and to use your chosen deity as an object of concentration. The former qualities will help you to throw yourself wholeheartedly into yoga practice. Not only will they raise your energy level and help you concentrate better, but also, as Swami Ajaya observes, will replace self-preoccupation with a sense of direction and rootedness that will enable you to surrender ego more easily to the deity (73-74). Moreover, concentration on your chosen deity is meant for a speedy development of *samadhi*.

Thus fortified against the obstacles, cultivating discipline and ardor, and making the requisite physical and mental preparations, you are ready for the main course. Patanjali proceeds to discuss the practice of *Yoga* in eight steps, some of which form the outer circle and are identical to the ones just discussed, while others form the heart of yoga proper. These steps are: freedom from evil *(yama)*, observances *(niyama)*, posture *(asana)*, breath control *(pranayama)*, sensory withdrawal *(pratyahara)*, concentration *(dharana)*, meditation *(dhyana)*, and absorption or realization of oneness *(samadhi)*. Of these, the first two are ethical injunctions, intended to bring about behavioral and psychological changes; the next three are aimed at shifting attention inward; and the last three form the inner circle of yoga and are concerned with the mind's return journey home. Although the last three form the heart of formal practice, the journey begins with observance of ethical precepts.

Yama: Freedom from Evil

As noted in the previous chapter, the aim of the first two steps *(yama* and *niyama)* is not just doing good and avoiding evil or external behavioral restrictions. These steps are part of a discipline intended to bring about a thoroughgoing change in consciousness and behavior: uprooting from consciousness the unconscious tendencies and programming that lead one to commit evil. As Claudio Naranjo observes, "the real point of *yama* is not at all morality, but the conquest of the Great Illusion" (Naranjo and Ornstein 76). *Yama* and *niyama* aim at mastery over ego through disidentification with its component elements. According to Eliade, their aim is unification of consciousness (56). To Feuerstein, they involve ethical integration and centering, rather than dispersal and confusion, thereby reversing the forces of life from being centrifugal under the dominion of ego to being centripetal and inward (73). Thus these injunctions are designed to bring about a fundamental change in ourselves and a realignment of our consciousness and life according to new, ultimate priorities (Walsh 1: 29). Their assiduous practice will lead to a mastery over our powers of body and mind, free them from external control, and help shift attention inward. As every meditator discovers, without such mastery, progress in meditation is not possible.

To bring about such a complete change, according to Patanjali, you have to begin at the basic level of behavior, ingrained habits and mental tendencies. So he enjoins *yama*, intended to eliminate five types of behavior, their causes and consequences: violence, lying, stealing, sexual indulgence, and greed.

The first, *ahimsa*, does not mean just nonviolence on the external, behavioral level, but total nonviolence in thought, feeling, and behavior. This requires elimination from consciousness the very desire to harm anyone — "utter transcendence of the need to harm," as Naranjo puts it (Naranjo & Ornstein 77). The root meaning of *ahimsa* is not so much nonviolence as freedom from jealousy, envy, hatred, or the desire to cut down anyone which, in India, was seen as the cause of violence. *Ahimsa* is concerned with uprooting such causes through self-awareness and cultivation of opposite tendencies (IAM). When they are eliminated, their effect — violence — also disappears.

Second, *satya*, truthfulness, is concerned with being true to yourself and others in thought, speech, and behavior; and eliminating from consciousness the desire to lie or hide what you know to be true. This eliminates not only lying, but also such behaviors as pretension, misrepresentation, and avoidance; and gives rise to personal integrity and what Carl Rogers called "being real" to yourself and others.

Third, *asteya*, non-stealing, is concerned not only with not taking what belongs to another, but the elimination of the desire to possess, the scheming to appropriate, and the fantasy of having what belongs to another. When you are able to achieve this, says Patanjali, all wealth will come to you — not in the sense that you will get rich magically, but in the sense that you will discover, as Ken Keyes puts it, that life provides you with everything you need in order to be happy (2: 156-157).

Fourth, *Brahmacharya*, does not mean celibacy. As Swami Rama points out, the word literally means "to walk in Brahman or God" and "refers to continence" (1: 18). Similarly, Ramana Maharshi states, "*Brahmacharya* means 'living in Brahman'; it has no connection with celibacy as commonly understood" (Osborne 79). When you attempt to live in God, you find that the pursuit of sensual pleasures distracts the mind and prevents it from being centered. Hence *Brahmacharya* requires that you let go of your attachment to and craving for sensual, especially sexual, pleasure. Further, according to Patanjali, the conservation of sexual energy greatly increases your vitality.

Fifth, *aparigraha*, freedom from greed, possessiveness, or grasping. According to Hinduism, greed or the grasping character of ego and the action mode of consciousness is one of the main sources of suffering and is basic to the human condition. It stems from the dualistic construction, separation from the world and Reality as Such, the consequent sense of emptiness and incompleteness, and the drive to overcome this feeling by appropriating the world. Driven by it, we act like mules with blinders on, treading the crop of incompleteness and getting the same yield of dissatisfaction that characterizes our life and experience. *Aparigraha* is aimed to remove this, open us to all life, and show us the path to completeness that lies within. The inward shift that this nonattachment causes enables you to gain insight into your past programmings.

Niyama: Observances

Although formulated in positive terms, as Naranjo points out, the second step, *niyama* — observances or discipline — has essentially the same intent as *yama*. Its goal is a change in consciousness, attitude, outlook, and lifestyle; enhancement of positive mental and emotional states and elimination of negative ones; a purification, development, and restructuring of ego and its world; and mastery over the mind, bringing it under voluntary control (Walsh 1: 30).

Such is the direct aim of the first observance Patanjali mentions — purity. It does not mean being austere, meticulous, or puritanical, but developing a nonattached attitude toward yourself and avoiding associations that do not lead to spiritual development. A sustained practice of this injunction enables you to achieve clarity of vision, outlook, and wholeness in life. It leads to mastery over the senses and to clarifying life by shedding illusions, pretensions, deceptions, game playing, judgments, artificialities, and fragmentation. When the fog of chaos and confusion that the ordinary whirls of life create are cleared away, we are able to see ourselves, others, and the world with naked eyes. The way is thus prepared for the wisdom eye to open and the ultimate vision to dawn.

Allied to purity, contentment is not fatalism but an antidote to psychological hunger, dissatisfaction, restlessness, and desiringness that arise from a basic feeling of incompleteness. It consists in developing the ability to accept what we discover about ourselves and our situation in life. And it enables us to see our life, in don Juan's phrase, as full "to the brim" (1: 110). This insight brings, Patanjali tells us, supreme happiness.

We have already encountered the other three *niyamas* — effort, self-study, and devotion to the Lord — as preliminaries. Their reappearance here serves to underscore the impression that Patanjali put together different yogas without any attempt at a synthesis. The cumulative effect, however, is to underscore the need for ethical and personal integration, and for psychological and spiritual preparation, through rigorous discipline and practice in awareness. Development of an inwardly poised and focused mind is also necessary if an aspirant is going to succeed in reaching his/her goal.

Asana: Posture

Proceeding from the outer, with the third step, posture, Patanjali moves to the inner circles of yoga. Although the effect of the first two is more than psychological preparation of the aspirant, they are, however, insufficient by themselves to bring about the desired shift of attention and deconstruction of consciousness. For that reason, a direct approach to stilling mind-waves, which begins with posture, is necessary.

Unlike the West, with its body-mind dualism, the East has consistently emphasized a close affinity between the body and states of consciousness. Hence the inclusion of posture, which Patanjali defines as being "seated in a position which is firm but relaxed" (Prabhavananda and Isherwood 2: 110). Beyond this, he does not say anything about posture, presumably because he assumes that the various types of postures are of common knowledge and that whatever instruction may be necessary will be supplied by the guru at initiation.

Patanjali implies that you can assume any standard posture for meditation, so long as you keep your back erect, stable, firm, and relaxed (not stiff or tense), and are able to maintain maximum alertness during meditation. The reason for such a posture, which immobilizes the body, is that it removes tension and discomfort; centers energy; reduces sensory stimuli, which can give rise to thoughts and cause the mind to wander; and renders it calm and alert, ready for concentration. Thus one source of maintaining ordinary consciousness is cut off. Stilling the body precedes and contributes to stilling mind-waves. With the body thus stilled, attention can be directed inward and focused entirely on the mind, which is the theater of *Yoga* practice.

This body-mind correlation seems to be based on sound psychology. If it is true that, as Ornstein states, one of the ways ordinary consciousness maintains itself is by constantly feeding on new stimuli, then by rendering the body immobile we stop one of the processes by which we reinforce and maintain our consciousness and world. Thus disengaged from bodily concern, we can direct our attention inward, toward stopping the second, most difficult, factor—thought and internal dialogue—by which the present construction is maintained. As Eliade observes, on the level of the body, posture is concentration on a single point (54). Moreover, as the gross or external level of the body is stilled, awareness can open up, especially at the stage of insight, to the subtle energy levels (Brown 1: 233-234).

Pranayama: Breath-Control

The word *prana* has a wider connotation than "breath." As Swami Rama points out, it is derived from *pra,* meaning "first unit," and *na,* meaning "energy" (1: 59). Thus it means "primal energy" and refers to the energy-awareness out of which each thing is believed to be formed. As Feuerstein observes, *prana* is "an effluence of the transcendent Being." And he quotes a scriptural passage that says, "Consciousness is connected with *prana* indwelling in all beings" (96-97). In this view, *prana* is the primal energy emanating from formless All-embracing Awareness. The universe and all forms in it are expressions of this primal energy. Thus the universe is a field of energy, the reality of which is Awareness; and all things are forms of this pure energy, which is pure Awareness.

Without making an equation between energy and awareness, some physicists hold a similar view. According to them, quantum and relativity theories have shown that the subatomic particles of matter, the very stuff of the universe, are nothing other than dynamic patterns of energy in process. These energy patterns exist in interrelationship with each other, making the universe a dynamic web of interpenetrating energy patterns (Capra 69, 186-191). An even closer affinity is to be found between *prana* and David Bohm's view of "the implicate" or unmanifest order, which is a primary order of energy, out of which "the explicate" or manifest order takes its form and into which it is enfolded. In viewing energy as the primary stuff out of which all things in the manifest universe take their form, science strikes close to the view experiential religion formulated centuries ago.

In any case, as all forms in the universe are expressions of *prana,* so human beings are its manifestations. In us *prana* is the vital life-force circulating throughout the body and embodied in the breath. That is why the breath is considered to be the vehicle of Brahma, the primal form or creative energy of the universe. As Frederick Spiegelberg states, "Brahma is the primal cause of the world, and manifests itself in the breath." He goes on to point out that in Hindu mythology, the origin and passing away of worlds are "conceived as the breathing of Brahma: in him is produced the force of World-Prana, and through his exhalation the vortex of the universe comes into being." "In the rhythm of man's inhalation and exhalation he experiences a likeness of the process of creation itself" (28-34).

In fact, we could say that this idea of creation, and the corresponding one that the universe is in a cyclic process of expansion and contraction, each lasting over billions of years, is a yogic projection from their meditative experience. At the advanced stage of meditation the entire universe becomes one with the process of inhalation and exhalation. In being identified with this process and experiencing their identity with the universe, yogis came to experience themselves and all things as expressions of the same dynamic process of primal energy in cycles of expansion and contraction, itself a manifestation of pure Awareness or Spirit.

This relationship between the breath, vital energy, and Awareness or Spirit is also found in other traditions. Not only is it the foundation of Hindu *Tantra,* Tibetan Buddhism, and Taoist Yoga, it is also significant in the Jewish, Christian, and Sufi traditions. Thus, in Genesis *Prana* or the Spirit of God is the creative principle of the universe. After creating Adam, God breathes into him and he becomes a living spirit. And in the New Testament, after his resurrection, Jesus transmits the Spirit or *Prana* to the Apostles by breathing into them.

There is, in fact, an intimate connection between the breath and mental and emotional states. Thus, when we are excited, our breathing becomes rapid and heavy; when disturbed, it becomes irregular; when calm and relaxed, it becomes gentle and rhythmic. The opposite is also true: By regulating your breath, you can induce or control mental and emotional states. Next time you get very angry or upset, try this exercise: Breathe very slowly and deeply, filling your lungs and completely emptying them out in regular succession. You will soon calm down and the anger or upset will disappear. By breathing slowly, gently, and rhythmically during meditation, you can cut down distractions and deepen concentration (Rama et al. 2: 34). Referring to this relationship between the breath and states of consciousness, Eliade observes: "By making his breathing rhythmical and successively slower, the yogin can 'penetrate' — that is, he can experience in perfect lucidity — certain states of consciousness that are inaccessible in waking conditions" (56).

Yogis have discovered this deep correlation from hundreds of years of experience. It is a discovery shared by all meditative paths, East and West, and is not confined to yoga alone. That is why all paths consider focusing attention on the breath an ideal method of concentrating the mind. Regulating or stopping the breath, however, appears more a characteristic of yoga and certain tantric practices than of other paths. It is, however, consistent with the main aim of yoga, namely, controlling and regulating the breath in order to control or stop mind-waves and shift attention to the transpersonal states. As Rajneesh suggests, this stopping is a way of breaking up the present patterns of breathing, which enables you to break out of the habitual unawareness and the limits imposed by ordinary consciousness. By reinvesting attention in the automatic process of breathing, you begin the conquest of that unawareness which pervades the ordinary course of life (1: 30). Thus, by bringing respiration under conscious control, by regulating it and slowing it down, you can deepen, intensify, and expand your consciousness. Attention becomes steady and prolonged, and moves toward one-pointedness and the deeper states of meditation.

Another reason for regulating the breath is to bring the two sides of ourselves and the two modes of consciousness into balance and integration. Just as these two polar modes are correlated with the two halves of the brain, so they are said to be associated with right and left nostril breathing. According to the authors of *Yoga and Psychotherapy,* these two modes ordinarily alternate. When the alternation does not work equally, the cycle of breathing is disrupted, and we breathe exclusively through one nostril for longer periods than is normal. This creates an imbalance in our bodily and mental states, making us susceptible to disease. Regulating and making the breath flow equally through both nostrils creates balance and harmony of body and mind. As both sides of the brain and both modes of consciousness work simultaneously, our energy becomes centered and more available for creative work. This is a state most conducive to meditation, as it creates maximum alertness (Rama et al. 2: 32-61).

According to Patanjali, breath control is to be practiced by stopping the inhalation and the exhalation, which may be done externally, internally, or checked in mid-motion, regulating it according to time, place, and a fixed number of moments; and the stoppage can be either brief or prolonged (Prabhavananda & Isherwood 2: 112). Beyond this, no instruction is given on breath-control mainly because traditionally such instructions were given orally by the guru to his disciples at initiation. You are usually advised to do such exercises under the guidance of an experienced instructor, as you may otherwise harm yourself. One possibility is hyperventilation. What follows is a gentle breathing exercise, but if you experience any unusual effect while doing it, stop the exercise immediately or seek the advice of an experienced instructor. As a preparation for meditation, the aim of this exercise is to open both channels, purify the breath and make it calm, slow, and gentle, generate energy, and render the mind relaxed, alert, and centered.

Breath-Control Exercise

a. Sit in a calm, quiet, airy place. Assume an easy, steady posture.
b. Keep the head, the neck, and the trunk straight and the body still.

c. Gently place the index and middle fingers on your forehead between the eyebrows, ring and little fingers on the left nostril near the lower edge, and the thumb on the right nostril near the lower edge.
d. Block the right nostril by pressing with the thumb and inhale slowly, evenly, and completely through the open left nostril only. Next close the left nostril with your ring and little fingers, open the right nostril and exhale slowly, evenly, and completely; then inhale as before. Repeat this procedure three to ten times.
e. Now reverse the process—inhaling through the right, with the left nostril closed, and exhaling through the left, with the right nostril closed. Repeat the cycle three to ten times (Shivananda 50).

Pratyahara: Sensory Withdrawal

This step consists essentially in cutting off external sensory stimuli from feeding the mind and churning up thought waves. For this reason, attention is first brought back to the present from its usual dispersal and lostness among external objects, fantasies, thoughts, and preoccupations. Next, it is centered in the body and then focused on one object. This is the first step in the inward shift whereby you disengage attention from the senses and their objects and focus it on the object of concentration. It is also the first step in shifting the orientation of consciousness from the external object-world to the internal process of consciousness itself.

So, as you sit in a meditative posture, after completing the breath-control exercises and before beginning concentration, you need to become aware of your immediate surroundings; recall what you are about to do; renew your resolve to attain the goal of meditation; determine where your attention is and bring it back from its wanderings to the present. First, focus your attention on your posture and observe whether it is balanced; then withdraw the senses one by one from stimulation: withdraw taste by placing the tongue against the palate, withdraw touch by making the posture immobile, withdraw sight by closing or not focusing the eyes, withdraw hearing and smell by keeping the attention fixed on the object of concentration. This procedure will free your senses from external control, and your attention from control of the senses, making it alert and poised for the inward journey, which begins with concentration.

Dharana: Concentration

Together with meditation and *samadhi*, with which it is continuous, concentration forms the heart of Patanjali's *Yoga* proper. In the inward journey of meditation, concentration is the first direct step in transcending the separation between mind and reality created by programming and constructs. This is achieved by cutting through the latter and arriving at the original unity of the former. This requires disengaging attention from the outside world and focusing it on one form, so that in deconstructing the latter, you can deconstruct both mind and reality and arrive at their formless, Unconditioned State of unity. This focusing and cutting through begins with concentration. Accordingly, Patanjali defines it as "holding the mind on a single object" (III.1: Prabhavananda & Isherwood 2: 121). Essentially, this practice consists in focusing and holding attention on a single object at the level of the primary stimulus until it displaces and pushes to the periphery all other objects. As attention stays focused on the object for increasingly longer periods, it shifts its orientation inward, gathers around the object and becomes unified, which is called one-pointedness of mind.

Although anything can be an object of concentration, your choice should be carefully made, since it is going to be your vehicle for the journey to Self-realization. The best objects are those that symbolize the Unconditioned. Swami Rama suggests that you begin with the external and then proceed to the internal objects as your practice becomes stronger. Although this is not always necessary, it is how concentration proceeds. Patanjali notes that as you progress, many of the external objects become internal. For example, external sound becomes internal sound or mantra. As attention is kept focused on one object, it proceeds from external to internal orientation as it gathers and unifies around the object. Experiment with various objects until you discover the one(s) to which your mind is naturally and calmly drawn without resistance, and with which concentration can develop.

Patanjali suggests that the object of concentration can be external or internal; it can be physical or mental; or it can be nothing at all. Traditional external objects include: a candle flame; a blue, red, or yellow flower or vase; your face in a mirror; any divine form, image, or picture (such as that of Krishna or your guru); any visual image or symbol, such as a *yantra* or a *mandala;* a mantra—word, phrase, or sound; the body and its various parts (such as the tip of the nose), etc. Internal objects include various *chakras* or centers of energy-awareness (such as the spot two or three inches below the navel, the heart, the spot between and behind the eyebrows); the breath, various senses, thoughts, or the stream of consciousness; mental states; dream experiences and deep sleep; the heart of an illuminated person; divine form visualized, etc. Concentration without an object consists in focusing and holding attention on nothing but the mind itself.

Beyond defining and noting the stages of its progression, Patanjali does not provide any instruction for the practice of concentration. To remedy this lack, I shall describe below a few concentrative exercises.

Concentrative Exercise I: The Candle Flame

a. Go to the place you have chosen for meditation at the appointed time when it is relatively free of voices, noises, and distractions. The room should be dark and free of draft. Light a candle and place it about five to ten feet in front of you, that is, at a distance naturally in line with the eye level when your head is slightly tilted forward.
b. Assume one of the postures traditionally prescribed, such as the lotus, the half lotus, or the easy posture. Breathe quietly, gently, slowly, and evenly for a few minutes.
c. Gaze softly, gently, and in a relaxed manner at the candle. Make your gaze as steady as the flame. Do not stare, squint, strain your eyes, or try to avoid blinking.
d. Focus and center your whole attention directly on the flame as the primary stimulus before any thought arises in the mind. Let the attention directly touch, sink, and settle in the center of the flame. Feel yourself inside and become aglow in the flame. As it fills you with its light, let it burn up all your problems, tiredness, tension, stress, anxiety, frustration, restlessness, boredom, depression, or whatever is bothering you right now. Surrender yourself and stay in the flame as long as possible. Let it fill you with its warmth, energy, and light, until you feel clean, refreshed, glowing, and vibrant.
e. You may vary the exercise by alternately gazing at the flame for about two minutes at a time, and then closing your eyes and focusing attention on the after-image. After some practice, as you close your eyes, a bright, clear image of the flame should appear. When that happens, focus your attention on it as detailed above and become one with it.
f. If your attention wanders or becomes trapped by thoughts or fantasies, when you notice it, gently bring it back and refocus it on the flame. If thoughts arise and you are able to notice them, let them appear and disappear without trying to stop them or becoming involved in them. Cast them into the flame and burn them up.

Exercise II: Gazing at a Sacred Image

a-b.   The setting should be the same as above — only this time the room should be well lighted.
c.   Choose a picture of your guru, Krishna, Buddha, Christ, or someone you consider to be the embodiment of truth, someone who evokes an attitude of openness and surrender, a frame of receptivity and response, a letting go of your separateness and a willingness to be filled by the reality s/he represents. Alternately, choose a symbol with the same characteristics — be it a *yantra, mandala,* Cross, Star of David, etc.
d.   Without staring, let your entire gaze softly and gently focus and rest on the object. Keep your eyes relaxed.
e.   Touching and resting on the object, let your attention slowly move to its center, penetrate and sink into, and then expand and merge with the object until you feel you are one with it.
f.   Alternately, gaze for about two or three minutes and then close your eyes and let an internal image arise or float up in your mind. Continue to do this until you develop a clear after-image and it begins to stay for increasingly longer periods, filling your mind, and merging with you.
g.   Your attitude toward thoughts should be the same as in the above exercise.

Exercise III: The Body as Focus

a-b.   The same as in the previous exercise.
c.   Gently gaze at the tip of your nose or at the space between and behind the eyebrows by rolling your eyes. If you find this exercise straining, focus your attention, instead, on the abdominal or heart center.
d.   Without straining, begin gazing, focusing your attention for half a minute at a time, gradually increasing the duration as you are able to keep gazing without straining your eyes. In the beginning, to rest the eyes, alternate between gazing and focusing attention, with eyes open or closed, on the spot chosen for concentration.
e.   As in other exercises, attention should be focused on the spot at which you are gazing and should gradually move to the center, expand, and become one with the object.

Exercise IV: The Breath

NB: The breathing exercise given under breath-control can itself become a concentrative exercise if attention is joined to the breathing. More specifically, you may practice the following methods:
a. Take a few deep breaths and then breathe slowly, deeply and evenly.
b. Focus your attention on the breath. Let it rest on and directly touch the sensation of the breath; then let it penetrate and go inside so that you experience your consciousness as the breath going in and out.
c. Inhale and let your attention-breath go slowly down to the pit of your stomach. Pause, and then slowly exhale and follow the breath out with complete attention. Keep the attention poised and begin to inhale and exhale again.
d. Be especially attentive to the space at the entrance of your nostrils where the breath begins, and where it ends, and do not let attention move away from it. By keeping your attention riveted on the direct sensation of the breath and where it begins and ends, you will be able to cut down mind-wandering.
e. Alternately, focus attention on the abdomen and follow, with complete attention, its rise and fall.
f. Alternately, concentrate your attention on the inhalation and exhalation while repeating a mantra.

Exercise V: External Sound

a-b. The same as before.
c. Take five deep breaths, exhaling slowly and completely. Then breathe slowly, gently, evenly, and rhythmically.
d. Inhale, focus attention on the breath, and follow it down into the abdomen. Then, as you exhale, slowly intone the word *OM*. Begin with a long A...U...U sound and end with M...M...M. Or begin with a long O...O...O sound and end with M...M...M. Coordinate the breath, the sound and the attention, drawing them out together from the abdomen, the primal source of energy in you. Let the vibrations of the sound fill your trunk and resonate throughout the whole body. Inhale, pause briefly, and then repeat.
e. As you focus attention on the sound and coordinate it with the breath, let it sink into, stay inside, and become one with both. Experience yourself, the sound, and the breath as one.
f. An effective way to stop mind-wandering, to keep attention focused in the present, and to stay right inside the sound and the breath is to keep it focused

on the sound-breath just as it leaves your open mouth. As attention hovers there, in time it will become one with the sound-breath. Even if your mind wanders or is trapped by thoughts, it can easily be brought back and held there.

g. Alternately, you may choose to listen to various external sounds: a running stream, a waterfall, waves, crickets, environmental records and tapes, various "new sound" music based on bells and chimes or a zither, and other types of fluid sound or music.

h. Instead of focusing attention in front of your head, keep it stationed in the inner ears and keep it focused on the very first moment the sound contacts your inner ears. Without anything intervening between the attention and the sound, directly concentrate on the physical sensation of the sound until you are able to cut through anything that arises in the mind—emotional reactions, likes and dislikes, ideas, associations, interpretations, judgments, and mental chatter. Concentrate until your mind becomes still, thoughts cease to arise, and only the attention and the sound remain.

Exercise VI: Mental Image or Content

The method of this exercise is the same as above. You may start with an external image, such as in Exercise II, develop an internal one, and then focus attention on it; mentally evoke an image; or form a visualized image. You may choose abstract qualities, such as love, trust, or peace; or mental contents or states. Lawrence LeShan offers the following exercise with thoughts as the object of concentration:

a. Picture yourself sitting quietly and comfortably on the bottom of a clear lake.

b. When a thought, feeling, fantasy, idea, memory, etc. arises, picture it as a bubble rising out of your head into the space above. Follow the bubble with complete attention as it first forms and then slowly rises out of your head on top of the water and pops. Observe it for as long as it remains within your viewing range and then wait for the next one. As you wait, focus attention on the space of awareness between thoughts (1: 60-61).

c. Alternately, focus attention in the center of your forehead, observe whatever arises in the stream of consciousness, and directly experience its nature. When nothing arises, keep the attention focused on itself and in the center of the forehead.

d. Another method is to picture yourself sitting on the bank of a flowing river, which is the stream of your consciousness. When various mental contents appear and disappear like waves, ripples, eddies, whirlpools, currents, logs, twigs, weeds, or leaves, focus attention on them and see them exactly as they are, how they arise and pass, until you gain insight into their nature. When nothing arises, focus attention on the breath or the river itself and let your attention merge with, expand, and become the mighty river of awareness.

The above examples are sufficient to show the nature and range of concentrative exercises and how to practice them. Without concentration no advance toward meditation can be made, for the latter is only an intensification of the former.

As you begin concentrating and are able to go past the initial difficulties of keeping attention focused on the object, various thoughts and associations will arise in your mind. Besides the usual thoughts and fantasies that trap attention, you will be aware of the outer layers of the object-construction and your mental reactions to it, that is, your reactions in terms of labels or categories, cultural associations and meanings, likes and dislikes, desires and fears (rather than being aware of the physical sensation itself on the level of the primary stimulus).

As concentration deepens, you will be able to see the differences between a mental reaction and the primary stimulus of the object and to cut through the former and come to a direct contact with the latter. You stop responding to the object in terms of habitual associations and increasingly observe the process beyond categories.

As this happens, attention becomes progressively unified and one-pointed. As it no longer flits from one object or thought to another but stays focused on the object, your mind increasingly becomes calm and present-centered. Having become one-pointed, the mind withdraws from the pull toward multiplicity. In this unified state, attention is poised to penetrate and become one with the object and deconstruct the dualistic structures of consciousness and reality.

Dhyana: Meditation

Although we ordinarily use the term *meditation* to refer to the path in general, for Patanjali meditation specifically refers to the advanced state of concentration and is equivalent to acquired contemplation in Western traditions. So he defines it as "an unbroken flow of thought toward the object of concentration" (Prabhavananda & Isherwood 2: 121). This means that there is continuity and difference between concentration and meditation. While the former is more active, in the latter the mind is more receptive, open, and drawn toward the object, focusing easily and staying on it without being interrupted by thoughts or disrupted by distractions. Bare attention is now directed solely on the object, where it remains in a steady and uninterrupted fashion. As a result, the mind becomes calm, smooth, and fluid, assuming a depth, clarity, and expansiveness it did not previously have. There is now a steady stream of awareness flowing to a single object, which remains in the center of consciousness and displaces and pushes others to the periphery. From here awareness begins to cut through the constructions of consciousness and object, and expand and progress through transpersonal states. How does this happen?

According to Vyasa, an ancient commentator on Patanjali's work, in meditation the mind assimilates its object; while according to another ancient commentator, Vijnana Bhikshu, meditation consists in the mind's holding itself before itself in the form of the object (Eliade 72). Such statements seem to imply that the process of deconstruction begins at the stage of meditation. However, it does not really happen until the next stage is reached. At the present stage attention penetrates and becomes more directly present to the object, free from interference from mental contents and external stimuli. This appears to be Vijnana Bhikshu's meaning. The assimilation spoken of by Vyasa refers to the process of gradual saturation of the mind by the object prior to union.

Samadhi: Oneness with the Object

Patanjali defines the next major stage of yoga as "that awareness [which], as if empty of its own form, shines forth only in the form of the object" (III.3; Feuerstein 3: 96-97). In *samadhi,* there is "an identity of the knower and the process of knowing with the object to be known" (III.3: Prabhavananda and Isherwood 2: 54). From these statements it is clear that at this stage ordinary consciousness is deconstructed and that, free from the interference, filtering process, limitations, and distance created by thoughts, concepts, mental contents, programming, and constructs, you directly experience the nature of the object by realizing oneness with it. This is the state called "knowledge by identity," in which the knower, the knowing, and the known are experienced as one. The mind becomes, or rather is revealed to be, that which it knows because its nature and what is known are experienced as identical, so that the differentiation, experienced in ordinary consciousness, between itself, the process of knowing, and the object is revealed not to exist. It is at this stage of *samadhi,* then, that the heart of the meditative process — deconstruction of reality, consciousness, and self, and transcendence of all conditioned states — takes place.

This deconstruction and transcendence is not reached in one fell swoop. It is a gradual process. Patanjali describes two major stages: *samadhi* with "seed" *(samprajnata samadhi)* and "seedless" *samadhi.* Some take the word *seed* in the sense of the subliminal impressions, while others think that it refers to the form, word, image, or idea of the object (Feuerstein 3: 55). Others, however, think that it is the object reduced to a seed or point, which contains the essence of the object (Brown 1: 238). The second meaning seems what Patanjali had in mind as it can account for both types of "seed" *samadhi:* with the gross or external form and with the internal or subtle form of the object. The second type of *samadhi* involves no objective support. In its fullest development, it entails a total deconstruction and transcendence of the dualistic structures of reality, consciousness, and self, which leads to the experience of the identity of Awareness and Reality.

The *samadhi* "with seed" itself proceeds in four progressively refined stages or ascending phases, leading to the very limit of form or duality. At the first stage *(savitarka),* the mind identifies with the outward, perceptual form of the object. Since we ordinarily perceive objects through various layers of programming, such as physiological, psychological, cultural, and personal, this unification is accompanied by various associations connected with these layers. Thus, at this stage rational thought, the name of the object, its meaning, memory, and other contents associated with it, and deliberation, which ordinarily follows perception and leads us to differentiate one thing from another, are still present (I.44: Aranya 90-93). But with this identification, the mind is stopped and the external, perceptual construction is destructured.

As the *samadhi* progresses over extended periods, by holding attention on the object and practicing disidentification with the mental contents and associations as they arise, you are able to cut through and deconstruct them, whereupon they cease to arise. Attention becomes one with the bare, pure object, which alone remains in awareness. This stage is known as *nirvitarka samadhi.* As Gaspar Koelman explains, this stage consists in "a direct perception in which there is no intrusion of the modalities proper to the rationalizing mind, no influence of the memory supplying mental appellations, no associative nor constructive phantasmal distortion. In this non-cognitive concentration no words or concepts stand out in consciousness; there remains only the overpowering fascination of the thing-in-itself" (200).

At this stage, unified attention cuts through and goes beyond the symbolic layer of perceptual construction — the level of model construction or perceptual schematization, habituation, and meaning. Since this layer of programming gives permanence, solidity, and stability to the object, when it is transcended, the solidity and stability of the internal object begin to dissolve into the primary process. As the stream of consciousness is correspondingly destructured and rearranged, the perceptual pattern by which we ordinarily recognize objects is transcended. At this stage, then, deconstruction proceeds beyond the physical form, beyond the layer of conditioning, construction, or perceptual synthesis in terms of which a stable world of object and consciousness is formed (Brown 1: 240). As attention transcends the stable, unchanging form of the object, it arrives at the subtle level. Correspondingly going beyond the conscious, it arrives at the subconscious level and makes it conscious. This is the first major phase of emptying the mind and stopping the world or deconstruction of consciousness and reality. Since the separate self operates through a stable consciousness and world, without its stable framework it is likewise deconstructed and transcended (Brown 1: 242).

A similar process of deconstruction and transcendence occurs on the subtle level at the next two stages. At the stage of reflective *(savicara) samadhi,* attention identifies with the subtle form of the object, which assumes its universal, archetypal form, as also does the self. As in the first stage, this union gives rise to various associations of the reflective consciousness connected with the name, idea, category, and memory of the prior knowledge of the object, together with its framework of space, time, and causation. However, only the one object remains in awareness (Aranya 98).

In nonreflective *(nirvicara) samadhi,* attention cuts through the usual reflective and investigative activities of consciousness. Void of thought and other contents and filters, awareness directly experiences or identifies with the archetypal or primary form of the object. Awareness has now arrived at the very limit of object-construction. As a result of this union with the subtle form, without the consciousness of a separate self, the individual in his/her universal or archetypal self is present to the corresponding essential or universal form of the object. This form now dominates awareness; its universalization means that it is what you perceive in every form. As the commentator Vyasa points out, because of this universalization, awareness is unaffected by space, time, and causation. Beyond any particular spatio-temporal position, the object appears as an ever-present reality-awareness, simultaneously present as past, present, and future, and exhibits the properties of all objects under all conditions (Aranya 98-100). As a result, you perceive the object doing everything in and as yourself. Things appear to occur by themselves without any interference on your part. So Patanjali says that at this stage the mind is pure. Only subliminal impressions and unconscious tendencies still remain (Aranya 90-101; Prabhavananda and Isherwood 2: 55-58; Brown 1: 239- 245; Eliade 79-83; Feuerstein 1: 113-122; 3: 52-56).

As I previously noted, upon arriving at the first stage of *samadhi,* you may experience "miraculous" or paranormal powers, many of which Patanjali describes. However, as they are obstacles to enlightenment, he warns you not to go after them or get involved in the heady feeling of their power.

At the advanced stage of nonreflective *samadhi*, with the subconscious mind-waves stilled, the mind becomes like a clear mirror in which the essential or universal nature of the object and outer events can be reflected as they really are, free of the interference patterns of the mind (I. 47). This seeing and the deconstruction and transcendence of the form of the object and the conceptual framework of meditation to which it eventually leads are the crucial functions of the insights that arise in the heel of these *samadhis*.

According to Patanjali, these insights are able to deactivate the impressions created by constructions of consciousness, reality, and self (I. 48-51). As such insights cut down the mental patterning and impressions formed by the object, the meditator arrives at the pure form of the object. A similar process of deconstruction through insight brings awareness to the stage of the archetypal self. This stilling of impressions prepares the way for the dawning of insight into the nature of conditioned existence, consciousness, and reality, and identity.

However, before such liberating insights that bring awareness to its pure state can dawn, a crucial step of deconstruction is necessary. For, while insights deactivate impressions born of ordinary constructions, they and the entire meditative process also give rise to mental patterning and impressions (I. 50). Unless these factors are removed, it is not possible to go beyond the framework of meditation as well as the form of the meditation object and gain insight into the nature of conditioned existence and directly experience pure Awareness. This removal and transcendence is the task of "seedless" *(asamprajnata) samadhi*.

That this is the function of "seedless" *samadhi* is clear from what Patanjali says about its nature. He states that when impressions formed by the insights are also stilled, all impressions are deactivated. When this happens, all mental contents, the form of the object and framework of meditation are deconstructed and transcended, resulting in "seedless" *samadhi* (I. 51; Feuerstein 3: 57-58). It is clear, therefore, as Patanjali also emphasizes later on (IV. 29), that the essence of "seedless" *samadhi* is the deconstruction and transcendence of all objects, contents, forms, and constructs—of consciousness, reality, and self—and realization of pure Awareness, which is revealed to be the true nature of the Self *(Purusha)*.

Accordingly, the first task of insight meditation at this stage is to dissolve or eradicate the programming and subconscious impressions created by meditation theory and practice—the conceptual framework of meditation. This deconstruction in "seedless" *samadhi* occurs gradually. As the framework of Yoga Sutras is dualistic, in which the Self (Purusha) is viewed as eternally unchanging while the universe *(Prakriti)* appears as a process of constant change, the impressions and mental patterning created by this viewpoint must be transcended and brought in line with the viewpoint of the Self. To accomplish this, you need to focus the attention on the object-field under the aspect of sameness. Gradually, as you continue to observe whatever arises in this changing field under the aspect of sameness and see its underlying, unchanging aspect, by continuously practicing disidentification with them, you are able to cut down all impressions. As a result, the mind stops viewing things as changing and arrives at the unchanging state from which it sees the identity of both change and changelessness. Such seeing eliminates the impressions made by the object in samadhi and by the above-mentioned insight. This step is followed by deconstruction and transcendence of the primary or universal form of the object and the conceptual framework of the meditation. Awareness thereby becomes pure and self-transparent (III. 9; Brown 1: 249).

The next stage of insight is to turn awareness to whatever arises. With awareness free of conceptual medium and objective limitation, you are able to be directly aware of the exact moment anything arises before ordinary information-processing activity is triggered and the mind reacts; in other words, before the ordinary consciousness can start functioning. Again, the method that achieves this is constant disidentification and nonattachment toward everything that arises in the mind. As this process continues, you are able to observe the entire sequence of arising and passing of each object or event in the mind-field (III. 11-12).

By practicing this *samadhi* over prolonged periods toward everything, you are able to extend awareness to the very limit of space-time construction. From this vantage point, as you continue to examine the changing and unchanging aspects of observable events and the unchanging field, and search for their cause, you gain insight into their nature and see them as aspects of each other. By disidentifying with the changing aspects that are subject to time, you are able to deconstruct temporality and arrive at the state before anything is constructed (III. 13-15, 52-53; Aranya 265-282; Brown 252-254; Feuerstein 3: 102-103).

From this perspective of witness consciousness, as awareness opens up to the universal state, you are able to observe the nature of conditioning, the nature and process of *karma*-formation and how it can be broken, and the process by which not only mental contents but also all events and conditioned states in the universe are formed and maintained. Seeing the manifest, changing fields as moments of the unmanifest, unchanging reality, you arrive at the state prior to the construction of space and time, subject and object. Established in this primordial state, you experience simultaneous arising and passing away of all things and events. You see everything to be interconnected and to constitute an undivided whole (III. 54). As Georg Feuerstein comments, "At this highest level of enstatic realization consciousness has *become* all things in all times. All objects and all time phases are experienced as one whole. Nothing remains to be known. Now consciousness has become so translucent that its transparency approximates that of the Self" (3: 124; italics his). And Daniel Brown explains the process thus:

> From this now stable and bias-free vantage point, s/he is able to discern the very process by which phenomena seem to come into and go out of existence. Since the same laws governing how mental phenomena pass in and out of existence are operable in the wider universe, the meditator has reached the interface between mind and cosmos.... The ordinary time/space matrix of ordinary perception is transcended and awareness opens up to another order in which all the potential events of the universe and all the fabric of potential connections between these events come forth. Within this undivided interconnectedness of the universe, interactions occur not by causal laws but by relative relationships to everything else. (253-255)

From this point one of the most fundamental shifts takes place in awareness as it pivots on itself, turns away from what arises and toward the Self, and experiences itself as a pure void. This is the final stage of stopping *(nirodha)*. From here awareness experiences the ultimate shift and breaks through the void and transcends all limitations. This ultimate shift is the final transcendence that occurs when the Self completely breaks free of the limitations, conditions, and constituents of nature or conditioned existence, and realizes its true nature as pure All-embracing Awareness. From the point of view of the meditator, this means that at this stage, his/her awareness breaks free and transcends objects, contents, forms, conditioned states, and constructs, and arrives at the pure state of itself as itself, and realizes its identity as the Self. This ultimate shift is the transcendence of all constructs and limitations imposed on the Self by the elemental process of *Prakriti* or nature (IV. 25-30; Aranya 393-395; Brown 1: 260-263; Feuerstein 3: 139-140).

Liberation

According to Patanjali, liberation occurs when the Self completely breaks free of the limitations, conditions, and constructions of nature, and, in Taimini's rendering, "is established in his Real nature which is pure Consciousness" (433).

From the point of view of the meditator, this means that at this stage, his/her Awareness breaks free and transcends forms, conditioned states, and constructs, and s/he becomes permanently established in the state of the Self as his/her true nature or identity. This liberation is a result of absolute nonattachment practiced in insight meditation and of continuous disidentification with not only forms, constructs, conditioned existence, and constituents, but also with "past impressions," residual effects and tendencies in the unconscious, and the illusion and bliss that arise from meditation (IV. 29-30). A continuous and unflagging practice of this insight meditation burns up these "seeds" deposited in the unconscious. This liberation is a result of what Patanjali calls *"dharma-*cloud *samadhi"* (IV. 29).

The meaning of this enigmatic expression is not clear. It cannot mean virtue or duty as some have interpreted it, since it does not have anything to do with morality but certainly refers to a transcendent state. Taimini interprets it to mean that by it "the yogi shakes himself free from the world of Dharmas [relative states] which obscure Reality like a cloud" (433). Rammurti Misra thinks it refers to "Cosmic Consciousness" (357), while Daniel Brown places it in the final stage of enlightenment and says that it means "all forms of knowledge and existence pour forth as if from a raincloud" (1:263). Patanjali, however, places it before the final stage. It follows disidentification and transcendence of subliminal impressions and latent tendencies but does not signify final transcendence of duality. Taimini is more nearly correct in saying that it represents the final removal of the residual effects of conditioning and constructs that tend to create a cloud of obscurity and prevent the yogi from seeing, realizing, and becoming permanently established in the Self as his/her final identity. This is also clear from what Patanjali says about the effects of this *samadhi*.

One of the effects is breaking the chain of *karma* and uprooting the sources of suffering (IV. 30). As this *samadhi* burns up the residue of past impressions and subconscious dispositions, they cease to have any determining influence over your mental or emotional states, behavior, or outlook. As the sources of *karma* are thus burned up, no new *karma* arises. With the causes of unawareness and suffering thus deactivated, you are freed from the determining influence of conditioned existence. Where there is no ego, there is no one left to suffer. And as there is no object in Awareness, no bondage to anything remains.

A second effect is the Self-transparency of Awareness, which shines forth in its own true nature. This implies a total deconstruction of consciousness, whereupon Awareness becomes limitless (*Ananta* IV. 31). This is followed by a corresponding deconstruction of the foundation, frameworks, and constituents of conditioned existence (IV. 32). On the cosmic level, the constituent characteristics of nature are deactivated, and on the level of experience the residual effects of the triple constructs cease. As the natural process terminates for the Self in its natural state of absolute transcendence, so there is a corresponding absolute transcendence for the yogi in which only the Self remains in Awareness.

Thus, for Patanjali, liberation or *kaivalya* is a state in which only pure Awareness, only the Self remains, and it is seen everywhere to be that which IS (IV.34). In terms of the *Heart Sutra,* this stage is comparable to "form is emptiness," which is the first moment of completeness, but not the crucial second moment in which emptiness is seen to be no other than the entire universe of forms.

The liberation thus gained is not magical or imaginary; nor is it antihuman or a denial of human suffering, as Eliade imagines it is; nor does it constitute the cessation of the yogi as a human being and therefore can happen only before death, as Feuerstein believes (3: 142). Rather, it is an utter transcendence of separation, of the suffering inherent in the human condition, and of the ego's attempt to become a separate center. Furthermore, although many so-called Self-realized yogis and "liberated-in-life" *(juvanmukta)* individuals are tempted to isolate themselves, to call their isolation liberation as do Feuerstein, Eliade and others, is a misunderstanding of *moksha.* The term *kaivalya* (aloneness or isolation) used by Patanjali to denote the ultimate state of the Self signifies the state of absolute transcendence, on the cosmic level, of *Purusha* over *Prakriti,* and on the individual level, of the yogi over conditioned existence.

The source of this confusion is that instead of clearly describing what happens to the yogi in this final state of *kaivalya,* Patanjali switches to his cosmic, dualistic philosophy and symbolically expresses the state of the yogi in terms of *Purusha* and *Prakriti* and says that the elements of nature that had until now created the conditioned states dissolve and the Self remains alone in its self-transparent, effulgent, Unconditioned State as that which is. Since commentators take him literally, they fail to grasp that this cosmic language symbolically describes the actual state of absolute transcendence of conditioned existence by the yogi in whose consciousness only All-embracing Awareness remains and is experienced everywhere as that which Is.

Two other misconceptions about liberation to which academics are prone need to be mentioned here. One is that liberation can be gained by following the path of duty. This view is derived from a cursory reading of the *Gita* and an observation of the Indian social structure or caste system, but it has no basis in Hindu scriptures. Nowhere do they state that liberation can be gained by following a path of duty. Rather, all one can hope to do is to gain a better birth in the next life. In fact, Hindu teachings constantly assert that of the four paths of life – pleasure, success, duty, and renunciation or nonattachment – only the last can lead one to liberation. Since the path of nonattachment has been mapped out by the various yogas, it is only by following one of the yogas and coming to a direct experience and realization of the Unconditioned that one can hope to attain liberation in this life, not (unless spontaneously realized) in any other way.

The other misconception is that one can fall from liberation once it has been attained. This misconception is derived from stories about Himalayan ascetics who are said to fall at the first glance of some heavenly nymph, as did Vikram at the sight of the naked Urvasya. These ascetics are not sages at all. In fact, such stories actually represent a putdown of asceticism, which leads not to liberation but to repression, making ascetics easy targets of temptations. This misconception has nothing to do with liberation. It has no support in Hindu scriptures and goes contrary to the very meaning of liberation.

Another source of this view is a confused identification of the first experience of enlightenment, which is transitory, with *moksha*, which is permanent. By definition, *moksha* means release or complete freedom from *karma* or cycles of rebirth or repetitive, programmed states and conditioned existence. It is brought about by their utter transcendence and realization of the Unconditioned as one's permanent identity and center. By its very nature, therefore, this experience cannot be a momentary affair. And were you to fall back from this to conditioned, programmed existence, the very nature and meaning of liberation would be contradicted. Such a fall is a sure sign that the individual was not actually, but only claimed to be, liberated. Regression to prior programmed states is impossible since, for one who is liberated, such a state no longer exists. So *moksha* must be a permanent and irreversible state. Otherwise it is not *moksha* or liberation at all.

According to Hinduism, this *moksha* is deliverance from the arrested development to which we succumb as a result of the belief that human development comes to an end at the personal stage. It is also a deliverance from the consequent settling down to the state of the separate self as the highest to which human beings can aspire. For Hinduism, deliverance from this arrested development is the goal of the human life-journey in time. Thus, the recovery of our true identity, our journey to the heart of who or what we truly are, is at the same time our journey to the heart of Reality as Such — a complete identification with the Godhead and the universe. There are no separate journeys. To arrive at this goal of human existence is to realize everything there is to realize — that we are and have always been free — and to come to the recognition that there is no other way to live fully as human beings.

Chapter 7
Glimpses of *Bhakti, Jnana* and *Mantra Yoga*

Mantra Yoga: Transcendental Meditation

Given the universality of the mantra, its centrality in yoga and other paths, and the fact that meditation based on the mantra has existed from ancient times, not only as part of *Yoga Sutras* but also as a separate form of yoga, there is justification for its separate treatment. In this context, it will also be useful to say something about one version of mantra yoga that has had a widespread appeal in the West: Transcendental Meditation or TM.

The theory of the mantra is based on the experience of the effects of words and sound vibrations on our consciousness. As reactive persons, we respond differently to different words and sounds produced by different persons or objects at different times. We react differently to such statements as, "You are stupid!" "You are the brightest person in the world!" "I love you!" "You are gorgeous!" uttered by various persons at different times. Beethoven's Sixth Symphony may give us a deep sense of peace and tranquility, while punk rock may turn us off or send us into a frenzy, depending on our age. Music may evoke in us a variety of feelings and moods: relaxation, passion, love, desire, longing, exaltation. Thus, in *As You Like It* Shakespeare has Duke Orsino say, as he was pining away for Rosalyn, "If music be the food of love, play on!" Disco music may put us in a mood for dancing. Movie music clues us into the action, the feeling the actors are experiencing, and suggests that we get appropriately involved. We react differently to the sound of a waterfall or the gentle patter of rain than to the honking of horns or screeching car tires. It may be that the loud, jarring, discordant, cacophonous sounds to which the people of a busy metropolis, such as New York City, are subjected make them tense, abrasive, loud, rude, impatient, restless, irritable, aggressive, or hostile. Moreover, research done by Patricia Carrington and Douglas Moltz has shown some correlation between sounds and their specific effects on people who repeat them, whether mentally or out loud (Carrington 161-165).

From practice over millennia, yogis have learned that words and sound vibrations have specific effects on consciousness. From experience, a theory of vibrations was developed. According to it, just as we can speak of all things in the universe as being manifestations of primal energy-awareness, we can also speak of all things as being configurations of primal vibration-awareness. Each form is a configuration of vibrations emitting from the Source, which is *Brahman*. And the sound vibration that represents *Brahman* is expressed by the word *OM*, the primal sound vibration or "seed syllable" from which all others, including human beings, take their form. In the ascent toward *Brahman*, which is the quest of every form for its Source and Suchness, OM embodies the transcendent unity of all vibrations. In the form of descent or manifestation of *Brahman*, it is the primal vibration from which each thing takes its form. As the "seed syllable" or embodiment of *Brahman*, OM can serve as the vehicle or path, as well as the goal, and thus can take humans to that Ultimate Reality.

As farfetched as this view may sound, it has its complement in the so-called "holographic paradigm" put forward by some thinkers. According to Karl Pribram, the universe consists of vibrations; and our reality is constructed by the brain by interpreting frequencies of vibrations from realms transcending space and time (in Wilber 4: 22, 44-104). Thus, every aspect of this universe is an expression of these vibrations. Quantum theory had already revealed that matter consisted of wave-like vibrations, as well as behaving like particles. More recently, the "string theory," as championed by the physicist Edward Witten, holds that the universe consists of tiny loops or closed "strings" that vibrate invisibly in subtle resonances. These vibrations make up everything in the universe. As the loops rotate, twist, and vibrate in ten dimensions — four we ordinarily perceive (height, breadth, width, and time) and six imperceptible ones — they resonate in many different modes. These vibrations determine all the possible particles and forces of the universe (Cole 22-23).

In any case, according to the theory of the mantra, as each thing is a form of vibrations, there are levels of vibrations corresponding to and constituting levels of reality. Since in its primal state vibrations are emanations of *Brahman* and thus expressions of All-embracing Awareness, each form of vibrations is in its very nature an expression of that Awareness. There is, therefore, a correlation between levels of vibrations, reality, states of consciousness, and personality — each state of consciousness, reality, and personality having its level of vibrations. From this it follows that sound vibrations can awaken, evoke, or open up in each person various states of consciousness.

Furthermore, as each person is a form of vibrations, each can experience a whole range of vibrations and their corresponding states of consciousness. However, if your personal vibrations are not developed or open to the highest levels, you cannot be in tune with them and experience the reality and consciousness they represent. Thus, a key is needed to open your mind to the higher, transpersonal levels of vibrations, so that you can experience the corresponding states of reality and consciousness. And that, precisely, is the function of the mantra.

As its etymology suggests, the word *mantra* is derived from the Sanskrit roots *man*, meaning mind or thinking, and *tra*, meaning instrument, vehicle, or that which liberates (Bharati 103). A mantra is therefore an instrument for the liberation of the mind. Consisting of words, phrases, or sounds, a mantra is used as a focus of attention to concentrate the mind and bring it to one-pointedness. It is an instrument for the inward journey, a vehicle whereby the attention can successively pass through the conscious, the unconscious, and various transpersonal states, arriving finally at the ultimate state of Reality-Awareness. Alternately, this journey can be seen as the mind's penetration of ever subtler states, from the conscious through the unconscious, until it settles into the transconscious state of *Turiya*. As attention passes from the gross to the subtle form of the mantra and becomes unified with it, the mantra acts like a luminous sphere, sinking ever deeper into the subtler states until the attention becomes free of even the form of the mantra. Another way of viewing the mantra is to reflect that ordinarily, the pull of programming keeps the mind grounded in the world of objects and prevents it from rising to the gravity-free space of pure Awareness. Acting like a booster rocket, the mantra puts the mind beyond the gravity of programming and into the orbit of the Self. Thus it serves as a vehicle for the mind's journey to its Source — the Self.

A mantra, then, is a connector. By awakening the corresponding vibrations, it connects you with the state of consciousness and reality it represents. Being a medium, it embodies the power and the state of consciousness of which it is the mantra. In general, the various mantras reflect the entire spectrum of vibrations of which the universe is made. More specifically, the subtler levels of vibrations corresponding to the transpersonal states of consciousness, which they are designed to awaken. So, as the mantra of the Godhead, OM, the primal sound-vibration, has the power to awaken in you the Unconditioned State of Reality and Awareness. And since *Soham* is the mantra of the Self, it can awaken the vibrations of the Self and thus lead to Self-realization.

It follows that mantras are not made up of just any sort of words and phrases. Nor do they consist of a meaningless jumble of randomly chosen words, as is sometimes claimed. On the contrary, most traditional mantras are names of or associated with God, or represent aspects of All-embracing Awareness or the transpersonal states (which deities of mantras symbolize). Thus they can be vehicles for realizing the states of consciousness represented by the deities. This is clearly the basis for the initiations at which the initiate is given the mantra of the chosen deity and instructed by the guru to meditate on it so as to attain the corresponding state of consciousness.

Moreover, mantras are chosen for their vibratory quality. For this Sanskrit is eminently suited, as it is a language with lots of words ending in m's, n's, ng's, and vowels, which make up the resonant, sonorous, fluid, vibratory quality of mantras based on it. This is important for calming, stilling and unifying the mind; awakening the vibrations; and raising the corresponding state of consciousness in the meditator.

Finally, there are many mantras that are composed of apparently nonsensical syllables. Their purpose is to break up our usual discursive, conceptual, dualistic thinking and fixation on meaning, and flood consciousness with sounds that have no familiar meaning and cannot be translated into the framework of the present constructions of reality and consciousness. Thus, they are intended to destructure ordinary consciousness and reality. Prolonged focus of attention on such mantras will eventually frustrate and stop conceptual translation, destructure ordinary consciousness, and open you to transpersonal states.

To perform such functions, a proper mantra for each state must be chosen. If the vibrations of the mantra do not symbolize the state to which the meditation is intended to awaken you, or are discordant with your personal vibrations, the mantra may not produce the intended result. So a proper mantra is one which represents and opens the mind to the vibrations of the divinity whose mantra it is and awakens the corresponding state of consciousness. That is why, traditionally, the guru carefully chose a mantra only after knowing the personal characteristics of an aspirant. A harmonious attunement of personality, temperament, and the state of consciousness to which the guru intended to awaken the initiate was a central consideration in the choice of a mantra.

In addition, a proper method of intoning the mantra is necessary. As Patricia Carrington points out, a mantra is given by the guru according to the sound vibrations it produces and the parts of the body the sound is designed to vibrate. The sound frequency determines the energy center it vibrates and the corresponding state of consciousness it awakens. At initiation, the guru must, therefore, be skillful in producing the correct intonation and imparting it to the disciple, who must in turn be able to reproduce it correctly, if the mantra is to produce the intended result (167).

Transcendental Meditation has retained in muted form a semblance of this tradition of the mantra. According to its founder, Maharishi Mahesh Yogi, the ultimate aim of TM is to enable you to come in contact with the unlimited reservoir of energy and "creative intelligence" that lie at the source of thought within the deepest strata of the psyche so that you can realize your "unique potential" (White 3: 87). That potential or destiny of each human being, as well as of the entire cosmos, is "expansion of happiness...The mind naturally seeks happiness. Its constant movement and wanderings spring from its endless search for happiness" (Needleman 1: 129).

However, because it is focused on the world, it seeks happiness in things or relationships outside itself which cannot satisfy it "deeply or for long." So it becomes restless. Like a radar beam, it searches for new and different things in which to find happiness. In so doing, it runs away from the present because it thirsts for greater happiness than it is at the moment experiencing. But nothing it encounters makes it happy because its vibrations and those of the objects of desire are out of harmony with the universal vibrations of Ultimate Reality, which alone can provide the desired happiness. Only a sound having the same vibrations as the mind's search can bring fulfillment by directing it to the Source from which both the quest and its fulfillment spring. A TM mantra is intended to turn "the attention inward toward subtler levels" of thought "until the mind transcends...the subtlest state of thought and arrives at" its source (Needleman 1: 129).

After explaining such theoretical points in initial lectures, the instructor introduces you to TM with an initiation of a sort: You are asked to bring six to twelve fresh flowers, two or three fresh fruits, and a clean, white handkerchief. These symbolize, respectively, life; the seeds of life, growth and fulfillment; and the purity of spirit needed to realize the goal. After you bring these items on the appointed day, the instructor performs the initiation ceremony by himself in Sanskrit. Then he assigns you a mantra, which may not even be correctly formulated, as was the experience of Adam Smith. In any case, after the mantra is imparted, you are instructed to meditate by mentally repeating it, with eyes closed, for a period of twenty minutes at whatever speed you choose. At the end of the session, you are told never to divulge your mantra to anyone, or it will lose its effectiveness (A. Smith 127-128).

Now, while the theory and intent of TM are sound, it gives a rather short shrift to the contextual and practical sides of meditation. For instance, no instructor can know which mantra is suited for whom after only a couple of introductory lectures in a general group session. And, while the intent of the injunction to keep the mantra secret is sound, it is not true, as is claimed, that if you reveal your mantra to someone else, it will not work for him/her, or that something bad will happen to you. Rather, the traditional reasons for secrecy are that since the mantra, together with the method of properly intoning and meditating on it, is given by the guru at the time of initiation, without this instruction on how to practice, the mantra may not be effective. The situation is like instructing a student to play a piano concerto. Without the teacher's skills and the student's preparation, the latter may not learn to play the piano properly. Similarly, without proper instruction, the mantra will be like musical notes on a piece of paper for someone who does not know how to read them and play the instrument.

Moreover, at initiation the power of the mantra is said to be transmitted by the guru to the disciple. Since an enlightened guru, who can properly intone the mantra, embodies the state of consciousness the mantra represents and is a link in the chain of transmission, s/he can effectively transmit its power and, given the disciple's preparation and readiness, can open him/her to receive the power to awaken in him/herself the intended state of consciousness. Without this context of transmission and proper preparation, which will enable the disciple to be open, cut through initial difficulties and resistances, and surrender him/herself to it, the mantra may not be effective in leading him/her to the goal. That is why it is useless to reveal your mantra to someone else. It may not match his/her personality, s/he may not be able to intone it properly, and s/he may lack the necessary preparation. As a result, after trying it on his/her own and finding that it does not work, s/he may become disillusioned with meditation altogether.

It should be noted here that the TM method is essentially the same as other mantra meditations. Besides *SOHAM,* some of the other mantras assigned in TM are: *RAM* (a name of God), *AING* (referring to the Divine Feminine Principle), *KRIM, HRIM, HUM,* and so on. The form of TM meditation is something like the following:

a. Sit comfortably in the meditation posture that suits you.
b. Sit quietly for a few moments without thinking about anything and then close your eyes.
c. For about a minute — count to sixteen breaths — sit quietly without saying anything.
d. Now taking one of the mantras above, say *RAM,* mentally repeat *Raa...ammm* or *Ram, Ram...Ram* with each inhalation and exhalation. You may repeat it at whatever speed you want. Experiment until you find your own appropriate rhythm — one that makes your mind wander less and attention stay

focused on the mantra. Coordinate the attention, the repetition, and the breath, and keep it going for about twenty minutes.

e. If attention wanders and becomes plunged in thoughts or fantasies, just bring it back each time you notice that it has done so, and continue repeating the mantra. Do not try to stop, fight, expel, or in any way get involved in thoughts, feelings, fantasies, etc. Just observe them and let them pass.

f. At the end of the twenty-minute period, stop the repetition, sit quietly for about a minute—sixteen counts of breath again—and then slowly open your eyes (White 1: 50).

This meditation is to be practiced twice a day. Besides the practice, TM involves what is known as "checking," which consists in returning to the instructor to have him examine your progress or lack of it; resolve questions and difficulties you may have; and set you on the road to the goal of TM, which is attaining cosmic consciousness.

Besides *RAM* and *OM*, another great mantra assigned both in TM and other forms of mantra meditation is *SOHAM,* which means "I am That or He [i.e., *Atman* or *Brahman]."* Thus, it is the mantra of the Self.

It is also said that *SOHAM* is the natural sound of the inhalation and the exhalation, and therefore represents *Prana.* When you draw the breath slowly, gently, and evenly through the nostrils, it is said to make the sound *sooo...*and when you similarly exhale, it is said to make the sound *haaa...mmm.* It is interesting that the same claim is made for the reverse, *Hamsa,* by Swami Muktananda and his followers. How do you resolve these conflicting claims, especially since in Sanskrit *hamsa* means "swan"? As noted before, the wild swan is the vehicle of Brahma, who is the creative face of the formless *Brahman* and the embodiment of *Prana* or Primal Energy, which manifests itself in the breath. Thus, as the vehicle of Brahma and consequently of *Prana, hamsa* symbolizes the breath (the swan makes a hissing sound that resembles *hamsa),* and, when joined with it, can serve not only as an instrument for awakening *Prana* but also as a vehicle for the mind's journey to the ultimate Source of all—*Atman,* which is *Brahman.* In either form, therefore, when used in meditation, the mantra can lead to a revelation of the mystery of existence. The following represents such a meditation:

a. Maintain the same posture and breathing as in the concentrative exercises.
b. Take a few deep breaths, filling your lungs completely and exhaling completely. Then breathe slowly, evenly, gently, and rhythmically.
c. Focus your entire attention on the breath and synchronize inhalation and exhalation with the mantra. Keeping attention centered on both the breath and

the mantra, mentally repeat *Sooo...ooo* or *Haaa...mmm* and follow the inhalation from beginning to end. Pause and similarly follow the exhalation as you repeat *haaa...mmm* or *saaa...aaa*. Let your attention flow with the breath and the mantra until they become one or their conscious separation disappears and you experience a unity with the mantra.

Experiment with both *Soham* and *Hamsa* to find out which works better in terms of a smooth, natural flow of the breath and your ability to follow it with complete attention; and which will lead to deepening of concentration.

In general, when correctly intoned or repeated in full awareness, with the appropriate vibrations awakened, mantra meditation works in the same way as any other concentrative meditation — through displacing all other contents and assuming the center of consciousness. As Swami Ajaya observes, at first the mantra is like a tiny seed planted in the mind. In order to grow, it must take hold and sink into its deeper, fertile soil, beyond the conscious sphere (67). As the tiny seed takes hold in the unconscious, it begins gradually to displace the thoughts and preoccupations of the conscious sphere. As attention cuts through both the perceptual object-construction and the programming of ordinary consciousness, the seed assumes its subtle, luminous form, occupying and saturating the entire mind until it alone remains. Then the mind and the mantra become one. Not only during meditation but in every activity in which you engage, the mantra will float up to your consciousness. Having become one with it, you now find that whatever you do, it is the mantra which is doing everything — walking, talking, sitting, working — in and as you. Eventually as this state ripens, you will transcend even the form of the mantra, as well as every other form, and you will directly experience your identity as the Self.

Bhakti Yoga

Bhakti Yoga does not appear to be as structured as *Yoga Sutras*, TM, or other meditative paths. As Ram Dass has noted, it allows too much play of mind. (He was initiated into it by his guru, Neemkaroli Baba.) As a path through the emotions, although the mind is certainly involved, it is especially suited for those of emotional temperament who find the arid world of knowledge or mental focus in concentration difficult to get into. Such persons feel an overwhelming need to express their exuberant, joyous natures in love, devotion, and self-surrender. This makes structuring difficult. Still, *Bhakti Yoga* does have meditative practices similar to other paths.

Another difference from other yogas is the goal. Since the goal espoused by *Bhakti Yoga* is modeled after a union of two persons in love, unlike other yogas, its final realization is not one of identity but relationship with the Self, or God, who is conceived as a personal being. As love requires someone other than oneself to be loved, in this union of two personal beings, the two remain separate and yet become one in love, ecstasy, and self-surrender, which remain the focal point of union. So the framework is dualistic and the union relative. In its goal and framework of meditation, *Bhakti Yoga* most closely resembles Western meditative traditions and theistic meditation in general.

However, as stated before, following *Bhakti Yoga*, it is possible to transcend the dualistic framework and realize absolute oneness with *Brahman*. This can happen, as Daniel Goleman points out, if you reach *nirvikalpa samadhi,* in which state you transcend the divine form and realize oneness with God in the Formless, Unconditioned State (1: 45-47). According to Ramana Maharshi, since all forms are conceptual, created by the mind, all forms of God, including the supreme personal God of theism, are mental projections. When in meditation you transcend these forms, you arrive at the realization of identity with the Formless Essence that is the Godhead. Thus, if the self-surrender of *Bhakti Yoga* is complete, that is, if the self as a separate center is completely disidentified with and transcended, then *Bhakti Yoga* does its job of surrendering even itself and leading the devotee to the ultimate realization (Osborne 160-168).

At the initial and middle stages, however, as Ram Dass explains, the interpersonal quality of this way of the heart allows you to start from your psychological need to love and to be loved, to worship something greater than yourself, and to surrender to the One who completely understands and unconditionally accepts and loves you, in spite of your clinging to your impurities and your inability to love and accept yourself unconditionally. As you begin to love in return, increasingly you begin to lower your defenses, cut through self-rejection, and accept yourself and become open. As you begin to surrender, the negativities to which you were attached begin to clear up. Increasingly, your mind becomes empty and the thought of the Beloved floods in and occupies the open space of your mind. Gradually, you begin to assume and reflect the qualities of the Beloved — love, compassion, wisdom, peace, and stillness (1: 67).

At first, Ram Dass tells us, the path appears romantic. You become absorbed in chanting, worship, meditation. As you advance on the path, the romantic features of devotion give way to seeing everything as the Beloved. At the final stage, as you and the Beloved become one, you discover that what you had seen in all things as perfection is a mirror of your own true being (1: 67-68).

To arrive at this experience, *Bhakti Yoga* meditation may begin with keeping attention focused on the object of devotion at all times, both during and outside actual meditation periods. The object may be any deity or divine form. The aim is to realize the state of consciousness the deity represents. For example, the *Bhagavad Gita*, the foremost scripture of *Bhakti Yoga*, instructs the devotee to see Krishna in all things and all things in him. One who does this "never loses sight of me, nor I of him. He is established in union with me, and worships me devoutly in all things. That yogi abides in me, no matter what his mode of life" (Prabhavananda & Isherwood 1: 67). When the devotee is able to keep Krishna at the center of his consciousness, in time his mind will be transformed into Krishna consciousness which, as some modern exponents of the path, the "Hare Krishnas," will tell you, is the aim of all their meditative practices.

As for the actual meditative practices leading to this goal, the *Gita* and other works of the devotional path reiterate many of the steps and practices of *Yoga Sutras*. However, *Bhakti Yoga* does have its unique practices. One is *kirtan*, which consists of chanting while seated, and singing and dancing. Particularly in the latter form, *kirtan* involves a controlled surrender to the emotions evoked in the ecstatic dance or group movement, and may lead the devotee out of him/herself into trance or ecstasy and to an experience of union.

Another is *japa*, which is a form of mantra repetition, performed audibly, silently verbalized, or mentally repeated, often with the accompaniment of a *mala* or rosary beads. One well-known mantra, used for both *kirtan* and *japa* by the "Hare Krishnas" is: *Hare Krishna, Hare Krishna, Krishna Krishna, Hare hare. Hare Rama, Hare Rama, Rama Rama, Hare Hare.* Another, a favorite of Ram Dass's guru, is: *Sri Ram Jai, Ram Jai, Jai Ram.*

In the practice of the "Hare Krishnas," the devotee is instructed to maintain *japa* with the aid of rosary beads, carried in a pouch wherever s/he goes, in the midst of daily activities. With each bead, s/he is to silently recite the name once, synchronizing each repetition, if s/he so wishes, with each breath or beat of the pulse. When s/he is not doing anything that requires his/her attention, s/he is to immediately return the attention to Krishna. The aim is to keep the practice going at all times so as to flood consciousness with the repetition, making it stronger than other mental habits and bringing it to occupy the central place, displacing all other mental contents. Thus the mind becomes concentrated on God and reaches one-pointedness. From there it goes into *samadhi* as it becomes emptied of all contents. Only God remains. Gradually, it becomes one with God (Goleman 1: 42-43).

The mental as well as the silent and spoken types of repetition take the form of mantra meditation. Following is a description of such a meditation published by the "Hare Krishnas" in their magazine, *Back to Godhead:*

a. The chanting can be done anywhere, at any time. However, the devotee is to set aside specific time periods each day for meditation. Early morning is the best. If you can fit it into your schedule, meditate each morning. You should have two sessions each day. The time period of each session is to be gradually increased to an hour or more.
b. To begin chanting, assume any posture you find comfortable, except slouching or reclining. You can chant while sitting, standing, or walking. You may keep your eyes open, closed, or alternately opened and closed.
c. Repeat the "Hare Krishna" mantra audibly for the entire meditation period. You may chant as loudly or as softly as you like. You may vary your pitch and inflection.
d. While chanting, simply fix your attention on hearing the sound of the mantra. The quality of your meditation will depend on this.
e. When your mind wanders or daydreams, don't fight it. When you notice that it has wandered off, just bring the attention back to hearing the mantra and continue.

Besides such practices, the "Hare Krishnas" observe a discipline and have a lifestyle that require them to carry out the devotional practices several times during the day, which begins with rising at 3:45 A.M., until it is time to retire at 10 P.M. Of their sixty-four rules, a minimum of four are binding on all. They are required to refrain from eating meat, fish, and eggs; from gambling and sexual activities outside marriage; from drugs, intoxicants, and stimulants, such as coffee, tea, and soft drinks; and to recite their mantra on the 108 rosary beads sixteen times a day, repeating the divine names once on each bead. The goal of all these practices—from meditation to chanting to singing and dancing to observing the rules and engaging in the daily round of activities—remains the same: to surrender themselves completely to Krishna and attain spiritual bliss, and, finally, a permanent state of ecstatic union with him (Goleman 42-43).

Jnana Yoga: The Path of Self-Inquiry

Jnana Yoga or the Path of Knowledge is essentially a direct path to the Self. This is not knowledge in the ordinary sense, since it is impossible for the rational mind to know the Self. Rather, it is a path of awareness and direct insight that cuts through the present identifications until only the Supreme Identity is left.

The path begins with a recognition that in our present, conditioned state, whatever we say or do assumes or creates a version of reality, when in Reality there is none. Since every version creates a differentiation from Reality, and the programmed mind always functions within a version or model of reality and through constructs, no one can realize Reality by exercising his/her ordinary mind. That would entail the contradictory task of first creating a separation and then attempting to overcome it within the separate state itself. It is therefore useless to try to realize it through some kind of objective or subjective knowledge, through another or superior version, or in a separate, transcendent, or supernatural realm. That would also be a version of reality, and consequently, would fail to provide us any access to Reality.

Thus the only access to Reality is a direct exposure of the mind in a completely naked, pure state. Only in this state can it directly experience its true identity to be Reality as Such. To arrive at this pure state, attention must cut through the layers of conditioning, conceptual frameworks, filtering mechanisms, constructions of reality, and consciousness — anything that can create a version of reality. The sword of "discrimination" or disidentification in the form of intense self-inquiry is what relentlessly cuts through and deconstructs object, consciousness, and self, transcends all versions and differentiations, and arrives at the undifferentiated state of Reality as Such. Like the soap in the TV commercial, it cuts through the grime of programming, filtering, or perceptual information-processing, through thought and mental contents, and gets to the fabric of Reality cleanly and directly. This self-inquiry consists of questioning and disidentifying with all your present identifications until everything, including the final one — ego or the questioner him/herself and the archetypal self — is disidentified with and let go of. Then only the Supreme Identity, only the Self, remains. And the mind, void of anything other than itself, suddenly experiences its essential nature to be All-embracing Awareness, identical with the Self. Thus you come to recognize your true identity to be this Reality-Awareness and see yourself to be the Self, *Tat tvam asi, Brahman* of the Upanishads.

There is a version of *Jnana Yoga* in the *Chandogya Upanishad* that may be called "the method of identification." It is expressed in the formula, *Tat tvam asi,* "That thou art" or "That's what you are." In the text, the sage Uddalaka seeks to bring his son, Svetaketu, to the realization that his true identity is *Brahman* or the Self. He endeavors to do this by showing him that each thing, just as it is, is pure existence, void of duality, differentiation, or qualification, and that he is nothing other than this pure existence. Consequently, he is identical with all things.

Among modern exponents of *Jnana Yoga,* the foremost is Ramana Maharshi, who designed his method of self-inquiry in order to bring the practitioner to a direct experience of the Ultimate. He considers it superior to other methods because self-inquiry consists in ceaselessly directing thought to its Source until it dissolves and disappears in the radiant luminosity of the Self. He says, "The very purpose of Self-inquiry is to focus the entire mind to its source...it involves an intense activity of the entire mind to keep it steadily poised in pure Self-awareness" (Osborne 123).

The method consists in continuously asking or holding before the mind the question "Who am I?" to the exclusion of all else. If you intend to practice this method, keep your attention focused on this one question and let it sink into and saturate the entire mind, conscious and unconscious. Follow the question to the source from which it arises. As you continue questioning, "Who am I?" keep the focus of attention on the "I." According to Ramana Maharshi, since the "I" or separate self is the source of all thoughts, when you single-mindedly pursue the inquiry to that source and find it to be non-existent, all thoughts will dissolve and disappear in the Self, which alone will remain, resplendent. He says, "The 'I'-thought is therefore the root thought. If the root is pulled out, all the rest is at the same time uprooted. Therefore seek the root 'I'; question yourself: 'Who am I?'; and find out the source of 'I.' Then these problems will vanish and the pure Self alone will remain" (Osborne 117).

It is clear that this is not an eliminative self-inquiry in which you disidentify with every thought that arises until the mind is exhausted and becomes empty. Rather, it is an active inquiry that consists in turning to every thought and asking from what source it arises. Instead of letting the mind pursue its usual tendency to go outward toward the objects of desire, it is constantly turned inward toward its source and made to penetrate and go beyond it. For this to happen, keep your attention fixed on the question, "Who am I?" and, instead of lingering on the various answers that arise, relentlessly try to go past them to their source. In this way, use the question as a vehicle to penetrate and cut through or deconstruct ordinary consciousness and ego. Thus the Maharshi instructs:

> When other thoughts arise, one should not pursue them but should inquire: "To whom did they arise?" It does not matter how many thoughts arise. As each thought arises, one should inquire with diligence, "To whom has this thought arisen?" The answer that would emerge would be "to me." Thereupon if one inquires, "Who am I?" the mind will go back to its source; and the thought that arose will become quiescent. With repeated practice in this manner, the mind will develop the skill to stay in its source...When the mind stays in the Heart [i.e., the Self], the "I" which is the source of all thoughts will go, and the Self which ever exists will shine. (Bercholz 6-7)

Moreover, this inquiry, "Who am I?" is not a mantra and should not be treated as one. Rather, it is similar to a Zen koan used to raise the "great doubt." Hence, instead of mentally repeating the question as if it were a mantra, you should keep it unceasingly before the mind and try to see the nature of its source. Keep the mind continuously focused on the question, not only in formal meditation but, as often as possible, at all times, wherever you are and whatever you do. And whatever and whenever anything arises, immediately ask about the source of what has arisen. Press on until attention gathers and unifies around the question; until the entire consciousness is focused around, gripped, saturated, and encompassed by it so that the mind becomes the question itself. The inquiry will then become a questioning of the source of all existence. Your whole being will become the question, displacing all other thoughts.

In this way, when you continue to press on for the source of thoughts, eventually the mind will become empty, destructured, silent, and still. Unable to answer or maintain itself, the separate self will also be deconstructed. So the Maharshi says, "If one inquires, 'Who am I?' within the mind, the individual 'I' falls down abashed as soon as one reaches the Heart and immediately Reality manifests itself spontaneously as I-I. This is the Infinite, the perfect Being, the Absolute Self" (Osborne 120). Thus, as both are deconstructed, the inquiry will proceed to the unconscious, subtle level. Finally, as it cuts through even this framework, it alone will remain as the pure question without any content or object to which it could be attached or anchored through identification. When you press on further, the question will break through to the transconscious state, where it will resolve in the answer, in the revelation of the One 'I,' the Self, *Brahman*, besides which nothing exists.

Chapter 8
The Tantric Journey

The Meaning and Method of *Tantra*

Misunderstanding has dogged the tantric path from its very inception. Even in the land of its origin, it has never been in the mainstream of the yogas, although it shares with them the same ultimate aim—permanent transformation, realization of completeness, and liberation. One might think that the source of the misunderstanding lies in the methods. Yet *Tantra* uses most of the methods that form the mainstay of other yogas. The source of the misunderstanding, then, must be found in what is peculiar to *Tantra* and in the behavior of some tantrists.

One methodological source of misunderstanding is the veiled or coded language in which the tantric texts are written. However, this practice arose from a need to protect the tantrist from the suspicion and hostility of some segments of society. Such suspicion and hostility continue to persist not only in India, but, judging from people's reaction to Bhajan, Rajneesh, Trungpa, and others, in the West as well.

Another methodological source is the use of intercourse in meditative practices. However, contrary to popular belief, not every method uses sexuality; nor is the practice orgiastic. It is confined to only one type of yoga, the so-called "left-handed path," to which a practitioner is introduced at the advanced stages. It is true that some so-called masters have fallen victims to the lures of the path—sex, power, and money. But such temptations exist on every path. And those who fall victims cannot be called spiritual masters or sages.

In this chapter I hope to clear up some of the misunderstanding surrounding *Tantra* by giving a clear account of its methods and aims. Because the tantric system is very complex, only a sketch of its main features can be presented here.

The word *tantra* means to weave, unfold, or extend. These meanings are a clue to the tantric path. It envisions the universe as a multidimensional field in which polar forms, forces, and energies extend through all levels or dimensions, interpenetrating, interweaving, interconnecting, and making an inseparable, undivided whole. These polarities include: energy and consciousness, time and eternity, the finite and the infinite, the conditioned and the unconditioned, heaven and earth, matter and spirit, male and female, body and mind, reason and emotion, active and receptive modes of consciousness. The same forces that form the whole form each individual, and within each the conscious and the unconscious sphere. Any element can symbolize and reveal the whole. In each human being the body is the axis, the center, and the theater of this intersecting polarity that forms the universe.

The aim of *Tantra* is to unify and transcend polarities, not by repressing or denying them, but by successively rising above their lower, conflict-ridden, and restricted forms into higher, more expanded, and unified ones — until their ultimate unity is reached in the formless, transconscious state of Reality and Awareness. This successive unfoldment begins when you first bring to consciousness the Primal Energy-Awareness that ordinarily lies dormant in the unconscious. This awakening makes you aware of your identification with, attachment to, and fixation on the lower forms of energy that dominate the lower centers and make you subject to their control. You are then able to disidentify and release these energies, become free of or gain control over them, rise to the higher centers, and expand your awareness. As you successively transcend the lower, more limited forms of consciousness and identity and ascend into ever higher states, you are able to transform, assume, and integrate various aspects of yourself trapped in the lower.

This unification of the polarities of energy and states of consciousness within yourself constitutes a simultaneous unification with the energy-awareness that forms the fabric of the universe. The tantric view that the journey to your own center is a journey to the center of the universe is based on the principle that the essence of the whole universe is the essence of each individual. Since your own energies are identical with and hence perfectly mirror those of the universe, by assimilating the former you assimilate and become the universe itself. From this unity you can make the final return to Reality as Such by transcending dualities or polarities, forms and limits. In aiming at the transcendent unity of all polarities within yourself, therefore, you seek to attain a resolution of all problems inherent in the human condition to which the ordinary individual is subject.

This realization of absolute Oneness is not a return to the preconscious state but a return to the transconscious unity by transcending the personal and successively passing through the higher developmental stages. This transpersonal growth does not consist in going back but going forward, for only by transcending the lower, more limited forms and arriving at the higher, more expanded states can unity with and assimilation of the functions of the lower be achieved. However, this conscious development is neither linear nor automatic, but an ever-ascending process that requires an effort to raise consciousness along a trajectory constituting the heart of the tantric journey.

Although this developmental journey is called a return, it is really an ascent of form to its Formless Ground and Source. Beginning with the creation of multiplicity, the ascent traces a trajectory from the inorganic to the organic, the inanimate to the animate, the unconscious to the conscious, and thence to the transconscious state of All-embracing Awareness wherein the original Oneness and Completeness are regained in the Supreme Identity that is *Brahman*. Since at the human level, or what Teilhard de Chardin called "the noosphere," this ascent requires a conscious effort, in essence *Tantra* is a path of conscious development that completes the trajectory of evolution (Swami Narayananda 22-58; Ken Wilber, in many of his works).

Essential to this conscious evolution is the view that our body and mind are pervaded by the Primal Energy or *Prana* that forms the very fabric of the universe. They act like a transmitting station receiving and sending out the heartbeat of Primal Energy. In most people, however, this Primal Energy exists in an unconscious state, so that the channels for its ascent to the conscious and transconscious states remain closed. Moreover, the energy exists in a distorted and restricted form, corresponding to the state of consciousness in which people live. So the energy needs to be awakened and raised from the dormant or unconscious to the conscious state, where it can first be purified or freed from confusion, distortion, programming, and limitations, and then be unified, integrated, and expanded.

To awaken and raise this energy-awareness, one must symbolize and project it into the bodily channels and ascending centers along the spinal column. Following the dualistic Samkhya philosophy, Hindu *Tantra* conceives the primal polarity in religious symbolism: the supreme, conscious principle as the male deity, *Shiva;* and the supreme, primal energy as the female deity, *Shakti*. Thus representing the fundamental polarity of wisdom and energy, the principles of conscious and unconscious forces, Spirit (or the conscious principle) and matter (or the unconscious energy principle) that form the basic fabric of the universe, the yogi aims to bring these forces, both inside and outside himself, to a conscious state and then raise them along the bodily centers and channels.

The tantrist seeks to achieve this union of *Shiva* and *Shakti* in two ways: One is to symbolically represent his own body as a polarity and work with the conscious and unconscious forces within himself to bring about their union. The other is to actually enact the union by symbolically viewing himself and his female partner as *Shiva* and *Shakti*, and, through sexual union, attain the transconscious union. The former is called "the right-handed" and the latter "the left-handed" path.

Both types of *Tantra* have practices in common with Patanjali's *Yoga Sutras:* effort *(tapas),* self-study, chanting and devotional singing, breath-control, and mantra repetition. To these are added, according to Swami Narayananda, the guru's blessing, and *Karma* and *Jnana Yoga* practices. In addition, some of the practices peculiar to *Tantra* are: *mudra* and *bandha, Shakti chalan* (movement and circulation of energy), *yantra, mandala, chakras,* and *nadis.*

A *mudra* is a hand gesture or bodily posture in which breath-control and concentration are practiced in order to evoke or induce certain states of consciousness "by the echo aroused," as Eliade puts it, "in the deepest strata of the human being upon his re-discovering the 'message' hidden in every archetypal gesture" (211).

Two of the main gestures *(mudras)* are: *mahamudra* and *khechari mudra.* To assume the first, carefully press the anus with the left heel, and, extending the right leg, grasp the toes with both hands. Inhale slowly and retain the breath. Press the chin against the chest and contract the throat; then fix your gaze between the eyebrows. Maintain this posture as long as you can and then exhale slowly. Practice this first on the left and then switch to the right leg (Narayananda 87-88).

To assume the *khechari mudra,* inhale slowly and retain the breath; bend the tongue back into the gullet and fix the gaze on the point between the eyebrows. Shake the tongue and produce saliva. Extend the tongue as far as possible, and curl it upward and back to close the meeting place of the nasal passage, the pharynx, and the trachea. Maintain this posture as long as possible and then slowly exhale, gulp down the saliva, and meditate on *Kundalini Shakti* (to be explained later). To extend the tongue further, the yogi has to cut the membrane below it, a hairbreadth at a time, over a period of six months (Rieker 2: 110).

Meaning immobilization, a *bandha* is a bodily position in which the yogi practices control of the nerves and muscles of certain centers, together with breath-control and concentration in order to raise consciousness or immobilize the semen, stop the functioning of ordinary consciousness, and attain transpersonal states (Narayananda 88-89).

Chief among the many immobilizations is the one called *mahabandha*. To assume it, after morning toilet, sit erect, with an empty stomach. Press the left heel against the anus and place the right foot on the left thigh. Inhale and contract the anus or sphincter muscles and those of the perineum, and visualize and draw the energy upward by focusing complete attention on the breath and visualizing and drawing it upward from the anus to the throat. Then hold the breath as long as possible by pressing the chin firmly against the chest. As you draw it up, focus your attention on the central channel *(sushumna)* along and behind the spinal column and follow the attention and the breath, visualized as being inside it. Do this first on the left and then on the right side (Rieker 2: 106-107).

Another practice that accompanies *mahamudra* and *mahabandha* is *mahavedha,* which is formed by the yogi sitting in the *mahabandha* posture, and, with a concentrated mind, slowly inhaling and holding the breath by firmly pressing the chin against the chest. Then, supporting his body with the palms resting on the ground, he raises himself slowly, and then lowers the buttocks and gently hits the ground several times. Then he exhales. This is said to make the energy leave the side channels and enter the central channel, thereby unifying the three channels or the polar states of consciousness. This is said to cure disease, ensure a long life, and help raise energy to higher states of consciousness (Narayananda 88-89).

Important as these practices are, however, the central place of practice in *Tantra* is occupied by mantras. According to Bharati, nearly sixty percent of tantric texts consist of mantras and instructions on their use. Constituting the backbone of tantric practice, they appear everywhere. Each deity has its own *bija-mantra* or seed syllable, which symbolizes the state of consciousness it represents. The *bija-mantra* can awaken this state in the initiate.

Mantras are not only used for concentration and meditation, they are also combined in complex ways with other practices, such as gestures *(mudras)* and visualization. Furthermore, every gesture and action of a complex meditative practice is preceded, accompanied, and followed by a mantra. In addition, phonemes are strung together to form mantra-like *dharanis,* the purpose of which is to awaken the appropriate vibrations and energy-awareness in order to clean out negative programming, awaken positive states, purify the channels for raising consciousness, and dispose the mind toward higher states. By awakening the vibrations and the cosmic forces corresponding to them, *mantras* and *dharanis* enable the yogi to enter into the states of consciousness that their corresponding deities symbolize. Thus they enable the ascent of consciousness and being to that level.

The term *yantra* means "instrument," and is derived from the roots *yam,* which means to sustain, hold, or support, and *tra* meaning "instrument." As the etymology suggests, a *yantra* is an instrument for sustaining, holding, or concentrating the attention on a deity so that the meditator can first awaken, through visualization, and then identify with the energy-awareness it symbolizes, thus realizing the state of consciousness it represents. As Madhu Khana observes, "Yantras function as revelatory symbols of cosmic truths and as instrumental charts of the spiritual aspect of human experience. All the primal shapes of a yantra are psychological symbols corresponding to inner states of human consciousness, through which control and expansion of psychic forces are possible" (11-12).

One such primal form consists of nine triangles, with four apexes pointing upward, representing the male consciousness-principle, and five downward, representing the female energy-principle, symbolized in the primal divine forms of *Shiva* and *Shakti*. At the center of the triangles is a point, called *bindu,* which symbolizes *Brahman,* the undifferentiated unity beyond the duality of forms. The triangles are surrounded by several concentric circles with lotus leaves, framed in a square with four "doors" or openings for entrance or penetration of the object and progression toward its center. Thus, a *yantra* is at once a representation of the transcendent unity of opposite forces in the universe and in the individual, and a method of its realization by the yogi through visualization (Eliade 219-225).

Meaning "circle," a *mandala* is a complex *yantra* and the fullest development of the principle it embodies. As its etymology suggests, a *mandala* is a symbol of completeness. It represents the totality of all that is, both inner and outer; and the ultimate center, perfect interpenetration, and absolute Oneness and integration of all things in their Unconditioned State. It is an image or map of the universe, consciousness, and reality in all their infinite dimensions; a revelation of how things really are; and a way of directly experiencing them through identification. In reference to the individual, as Chogyam Trungpa explains, a *mandala* represents three worlds and his/her relationship with them: the world of perception (outer *mandala),* the world of the body (inner *mandala),* and the world of emotions (secret *mandala).*

According to Trungpa, the first enables you to relate to the world properly, directly, and as a whole — to see the universe as a totality and everything as an interpenetrating whole in which no separation exists. The second enables you to relate to your body properly, which leads to an awakening of the Primal Energy from the unconscious state. You can then proceed to integrate the inner dimensions of things by awakening the higher states (5: 31-36).

The third world is the divine or sacred realm in which, through symbolic or actual enactment of sexual union, you are able to purify consciousness and eliminate mental and emotional fixations and negative programmings; unify and expand consciousness; and realize the union of the primal polarity within yourself. It is at this stage that the pathway to the center of the *mandala*, which is at once the center of the individual and the universe, becomes open. Since this is also the divine realm, here at the center of the *mandala* various deities are represented (5: 36-38). (Although Trungpa's explanation pertains to Buddhist *Tantra*, it is equally applicable to Hindu *Tantra*, since their structures are basically the same.)

Introduced to the mysteries of the *mandala* at initiation, you are led step by step from its periphery to its center. Since the center symbolizes Reality as Such, the object of meditation using the *mandala* is to enable you to experience identity with it, thus realizing your true identity and center. To accomplish this, you must awaken and master the Primal Energy-Awareness that lies dormant within yourself. Since these are the same forces that govern the universal process, their mastery and integration within yourself means a unity and integration with the universe.

To this end the central meditative practice the guru enjoins is visualization, which is central to *Tantra*. Not only at initiation into a *mandala*, but at all initiations, you are given a deity to visualize, together with a *bija mantra* or "seed syllable" (a combination of letters of the Sanskrit alphabet), which symbolizes its essence. First you view the divine form in a painting or other forms of representation placed in front of you; then you close your eyes and allow it to appear on your mental screen. Once you succeed in clearly reproducing the image and are able to hold it in your attention for prolonged periods, you are instructed to become identified with it. Identification will happen only through a progressive deepening of meditation and upon attaining *samadhi*. Since the deity is given according to your personality, the aim of visualization is to awaken from the unconscious the divine forces and states of consciousness the deity symbolizes and become identified with them. This process will also bring about a transformation and integration of the conscious and unconscious aspects of yourself, enabling you to ascend to that higher plane (Eliade 227).

In the center of a complex *mandala* there are inner circles, each of which contains a divine image or its emblem. Each of these deities represents, in archetypal form, an aspect of All-embracing Awareness. After being initiated, you must be able to mentally recreate the entire *mandala* piece by piece. At first you may be given a model of a *mandala* to visualize. But as you are able to construct it mentally and your meditation on it deepens, you must be able to dwell continuously within the *mandala* itself. This requires you to visualize the entire *mandala*, penetrate it in full awareness, travel to and establish yourself at the center and become one with the *mandala*, thus attaining *samadhi* with it (Eliade 225). In so doing, you must simultaneously enter into your own center and that of the universe, bring into unity the polar forces of Energy-Awareness, and finally transcend even the form of the *mandala* itself and directly experience the Reality it represents. Thus you are able to return to the undifferentiated unity of All-embracing Awareness, in which all polarities are reunited, integrated, and completed. This unity of the universe and the individual explains why one purpose of the meditation is to project or locate the *mandala* in your own body and thus work toward a realization of the oneness of polarity, which is the task of *Kundalini Yoga*.

Peculiar to "the left-handed path" (used by "the right-handed path," if at all, only symbolically), is the meditation with the "Five M's": wine, fish, meat, parched kidney beans, or any other grain ritually prepared, and sexual union (Bharati 224). This yoga begins with the disciple rising in the morning and paying homage first to his guru, by repeating various mantras and gestures, and then to his chosen deity. Next he gets out of bed, and, after a morning bath, ablutions, and various invocations, assumes the meditative posture. Taking hemp and performing other preparatory rites, he installs bowls containing four of the M's: wine, fish, meat, and parched kidney beans. Then, drawing a *mandala* with powdered rice, sesamum seeds or cinnabar, and accompanied by various mantras, he pays homage to various deities in the *mandala* and to his chosen deity; he meditates on the *mandala;* repeats its "seed syllable;" offers a mantra to the rosary beads; and then repeats it on the rosary 108 times. Next he surrenders himself to his chosen deity.

After concluding the preparatory rites, for the main part of the meditation the participants sit in a circle, with the female partner *(Shakti)* seated on the left of each yogi. Each participant places a flower in the guru-bowl and offers it to the guru. After meditating on his chosen deity and performing various symbolic purifications, each yogi begins to take the four M's, starting with the wine. While copulating, each repeats a mantra and mentally draws up Primal Energy *(Kundalini Shakti)* from the root center (projected between the anus and the genitals). Then he visualizes Primal Energy as sitting on the tip of his tongue and offers it the drink. While taking the drink and the other three M's, he silently repeats his seed syllable, focuses attention on the thought and visualizes feeding the Energy. Taking the ingredients is, then, a way of awakening and raising Primal Energy.

As the yogi awakens, or attempts to awaken, the Energy in this way, he proceeds to the final part of the meditation by first making a triangle-*mandala* on the couch with an appropriate mantra, and then, visualizing the Energy in the center, he offers mantras both to the Energy and the couch. As he then sits down, his female partner (Energy) is brought in. After bathing her and ritually touching various parts of her body with appropriate mantras, he begins copulation. While copulating, he visualizes his partner as Energy *(Shakti)* and himself as Wisdom *(Shiva),* and repeats the seed syllable of his chosen deity. During the act he keeps mentally repeating the mantra: "Om, thou goddess, resplendent by the oblation of dharma and non-dharma, into the fire of the self, using the mind as a sacrificial ladle, along the path of the central channel, I, who am engaged in harnessing the sense organs, constantly offer this oblation." As he repeats the mantra, he visualizes the oneness of Energy and Wisdom, and repeats his seed syllable, together with the above mantra. In the end he releases his sperm while repeating the mantra: "Om, with light and ether as my two hands, I, the exulting one, relying on the ladle, I, who takes dharma and non-dharma as his sacrificial ingredients, offer this oblation lovingly into the fire, svaha" (Bharati 244-265).

Through this enactment of the union of Wisdom and Energy, the yogi aims to achieve in his own body the primal union of the polarity of Spirit and Matter, Consciousness and Reality, Wisdom and Energy.

The Method of Raising Primal Energy *(Kundalini)*

Like a coiled serpent, in each individual Primal Energy lies in a dormant or unconscious state, at the base of the spine. Hence it is called *Kundalini,* "the coiled one." Since our conditioned state is one of unawareness, we are ordinarily unaware that we are embodiments of archetypal, polar energies and forces. As a result, not only do we not allow them to emerge to the conscious state to effect further development, expansion, and transformation of our life, we repress and deny their existence. This repression and denial cause them to affect us negatively, becoming a source of conflict, confusion, and chaos that pervades our life. As we continue to live a narrow, ego-bound life, we remain unaware of the Energy or the power of self-transformation that lies within us.

In order to resolve conflict, remove chaos and confusion, and bring clarity and wholeness to life, Primal Energy must be awakened and raised to the conscious and transconscious states, where alone the unity beyond polarity and the final resolution can be achieved. That, precisely, is the aim of *Kundalini* or Energy Yoga.

The human body is the axis, center, and path of ascent of Primal Energy. The actual pathway along which this ascent occurs is called the central channel or *sushumna nadi.* The word *nadi* is derived from the Sanskrit root *nad,* which means "motion." A *nadi* is a pathway or channel along which Primal Energy, as manifested in the breath, moves or circulates.

According to Energy Yoga, in its subtle form, the human body contains as many as 350,000 channels, of which three sets are the main ones. Of these the central and most important is the central channel, symbolically projected along the spinal column. It runs from the base of the spine, seat of the lowest center of consciousness, called *muladhara chakra* or "root center," to the brain, where it disappears in the highest center, called *sahasrara*, or "crown center," which is projected on top of the head. In front of the central channel is *megha nadi*, to the left is *ida* or left channel, and to the right is *pingala* or right channel. Corresponding to and in front of the latter two are *sarasvati* and *laksmi nadis*, respectively (Narayananda 33-40).

These channels are not the same as nerves, veins, or any physiological organ or part of the body. They are, rather, part of the "subtle body," connecting us to Primal Energy and thus to the universe. Thus they are mental constructions or symbolic representations of states of consciousness, and as such can be perceived only by the mind.

Situated on the left side of the body, the left channel is characterized as female and symbolized by the moon; while the opposite, right channel, on the right side, is characterized as male and represented by the sun. The former is Energy *(Shakti)*, associated with the breath in the left nostril; and the latter is Wisdom *(Shiva)*, associated with the breath in the right nostril. Thus they represent the active and receptive modes of consciousness, which are sometimes associated with the two halves of the brain.

The right half of the brain, with which some psychologists correlate the receptive, intuitive, holistic mode of consciousness, governs the left side of the body. And the left half of the brain, to which the active, analytical, rational, linear mode is assigned, governs the right side of the body. Thus these channels are not purely imaginary, but represent bimodal consciousness in terms of which we ordinarily function. These modes not only ordinarily operate in alternation (which explains why, as I said before, we breathe alternately from the left and right nostrils and infrequently through both at once); they are also in opposition. This fact accounts for our split mind and for Freud's theory of conflict between the conscious and the unconscious. And it explains the view of Energy Yoga that, in the normal state of consciousness, the entrance to the central channel, the pathway to their integration, is closed or blocked (that is, these two modes are not integrated); and that the breath or Energy circulates only along the left and the right channel (Narayananda 33-40).

In addition to these channels, along the central channels there are also centers, which represent a concentration of various forces, energies, and states of consciousness through which Primal Energy passes. Not only is every center pervaded by Breath-Energy, but there are other subtle energies special to and operative in each center. These centers are called *chakras* or "wheels." There are seven primary ones, which serve as symbolic points at which the forces within the individual and the universe intersect and interact. They represent individual and universal centers of concentration, interpenetration, and diffusion of various energies or forms of Primal Energy. The number of energies in each center corresponds to the number of channels that meet there; and the number of lotus petals in each corresponds to assigned letters of the Sanskrit alphabet. The energies of each center are presided over by a different deity, each of which represents a different state of consciousness. Each center has a "seed syllable," which is the natural name of the deity who presides over that center. Corresponding to the fifty letters of the Sanskrit alphabet there are fifty "seed syllables" and fifty kinds of energy (Narayananda 41-58).

While the central channel is the path of the ascent of consciousness, the seven centers represent seven stations or states of consciousness in an ascending and expanding order. Just as the descent of Energy-Awareness represents narrowing and restriction of consciousness until it disappears in unawareness, so the ascent represents its successive expansion. In the process of this conscious development, as the Energy-Awareness ascends to a higher state or center, it assumes, transforms, and integrates within itself the energies or qualities of the state of consciousness represented by the lower. This frees you from identification with lower forms and the corresponding narrowness, fixation, programming, and negativities. This freedom enables you to unify successively within yourself the positive qualities and energies of the lower, attain progressively more expanded and integrated identities, and finally arrive at the Supreme Identity.

Located between the anus and the genitals, the first or root center *(muladhara chakra)* is the lowest. Since the descent of consciousness is symbolized by a triangle with its apex pointing downward, this center, which is the root of all the channels, represents the farthest point of its descent. It is the lowest, narrowest, and most restricted form of consciousness. It gives one the greatest point of separation and disconnection from everything. The dominant characteristic evoked at this center is a constant preoccupation with security, the feeling of a lack, of not having enough of anything, of having to struggle with everything. For someone in this state of consciousness life becomes a battleground in which s/he is at odds with everyone and everything, which appears to pose a constant threat to his/her security or survival. This is a state dominated by survival mentality. It does not matter whether s/he is a pauper or a millionaire. There is a constant feeling of a threat, of danger lurking at every corner. S/he lives for him/herself alone. This is the life of a solitary individual focused in on him/herself. The expression, "What's in it for me?" typifies his/her every action and decision.

Thus in this state you are involved in a constant struggle to survive and secure your domain against the forces, actual, possible, or imaginary, that could threaten it. As a result, your mind is set in a background of fear, worry, anxiety, or hostility. Afraid of being hurt, you become distrustful and suspicious of everyone and everything. To cope with this feeling, you may become lonely and withdrawn, defensive, reserved, quiet, shy, or develop a conservative cast of mind. Or to counteract it, you may be driven by the need to expand and become acquisitive and possessive. Or, feeling helpless, you may be driven by a need to depend and become a clinging vine. Or, driven by the opposite, you may become aggressive and hostile, developing an attitude of constant struggle expressed by such sayings as, "It's a dog-eat-dog world" and "Everyone is out for themselves." Feeling disconnected and separate from everyone, you feel that this is a "me versus them" world.

In focusing attention on this center and raising Energy-Awareness to this level, you intend to become conscious of, face, and overcome your fear and aggression, paranoia and hostility, insecurity and helplessness, and other characteristics that form the dominant features of your consciousness. The energy thus freed from entrapment in negative programming and destructive behavior toward oneself and others can be assumed and integrated into a higher plane and put to creative use.

Located in the genitals, *(svadhisthana chakra)* the sensation center represents a state of consciousness that hovers over the sensate edge of life and is impelled by the feeling of a need to be constantly entertained. When this state becomes the dominant tendency of consciousness, the mind is preoccupied with the desire for enjoyment and sensual pleasures. Craving new and different sensations and experiences, you run around from one experience, affair, and relationship to another, or look for something new and exciting to do. Since you seek this outside yourself and it is not always available, you become restless, frustrated, dissatisfied, and easily bored. Always on the go, you are unable to commit yourself to anything. You may be driven to find relief from this condition by becoming possessive and greedy, or you may develop an avoidance tendency. You may refuse to face anything, becoming afraid to get involved, especially in anything that is difficult, requires effort or commitment, or is not sensation-laden. You become self-centered, narcissistic, self-absorbed, impatient with other people. Your life becomes hollow, fleeting, and shallow.

The aim of raising Energy-Awareness to this center is to become awakened to its forces and to your own condition in relationship to them, to face and overcome any fixation you may have to this state, to free trapped energies, to raise and integrate them in higher states, and to have them available for creative purposes.

The power center *(manipura chakra),* is located about three inches below the navel. In this state you are preoccupied with manipulating and controlling others, making them do what you want. You are driven to have everything under your control, including yourself. Constantly wanting to change people and the environment to suit you, you become preoccupied with making everything fit your ideas, your self-image, or your image of how others should be. You want everybody to support your self-image. Wanting to gain the upper hand over others, you become competitive, aggressive, and involved in power games. Or, taking the opposite ploy of dependency and submissiveness, you aim to please others and become a nice guy or a clinging vine. As these tactics do not give you a confirmation of your identity, you become filled with anger or resentment toward yourself and others and seek ever greater power and control. In general, you develop the dominant negative characteristics of this state: aggression, resentment, hostility, hatred, irritation, frustration, hunger for power, control, domination, and manipulation.

By raising Energy-Awareness to this center, you are able to become conscious of these forces in yourself, the type of manipulator you are, the power you feel you lack and strive for, and the identity you are trying to fashion through your striving for power and control. You can then work to free the energy trapped in negativity and transform it into psychological and spiritual power that arises from wholeness and a unified self. Thus you can transform yourself from being a manipulator to being, in the words of Everet Shostrom, "an actualizer."

The heart center *(anahata chakra)*, is projected in the center of the chest and along the spine. It represents a state of consciousness dominated by the feelings of love, caring, compassion, generosity, trust, acceptance, openness, warmth, sharing, and nurturance. As the authors of *Yoga and Psychotherapy* observe, because this center integrates more basic impulses and evolved aspirations than the ones below, it is represented by a six-pointed star. Its axial importance to yoga is derived from the fact that it is the meeting point between two different polarities in the body—one between the centers above and below it; the other between right and left sides, representing male and female, active and receptive modes of consciousness, respectively. When a line is drawn between these two polarities, a cross is formed, thus bringing together Christian, Jewish, and Hindu symbolism. The heart center, therefore, represents a locus of integration of these polarities. This integration consists in freeing the emotions from negative programming, the ego's control, and the drives and fixations inherent in the lower centers, allowing them to rise higher and assume their unrestricted state in the Self and become unconditionally available for the service of others (216-280).

People ordinarily live in a state of consciousness in which the characteristics of one of the three lower centers predominate, constituting the main shape of their consciousness and style of personality. Thus, while characteristics of other centers are also present, people are generally either security-, sensation-, or power-minded; and this dominant state shapes and controls the others. One who lives on the plane of the heart center, however, is already beyond them and lives by the characteristics of love, trust, compassion, generosity, and kindness. Such a person is relatively free of the control of outside circumstances.

Next, the throat center *(visuddha chakra),* represents a state of purity, clarity, and wakefulness; a state of consciousness that is awakening from unawareness and delusion and freeing itself from the primal illusion that ordinarily leads us to identify with ego and our constructions of reality and consciousness, and the belief that they represent Reality as Such.

As you raise Energy-Awareness to this center, you wake up from unawareness, illusions, delusions, and self-deceptions; as you move toward disidentifying with ego and your version of how things are, you begin to wake up and see how things really are. As old identifications fall away, a sense that life comes complete with everything you need here and now to be happy begins to suffuse you. You begin to see that every situation is workable. Instead of constantly feeling a lack, you begin to experience the wholeness of life and see wholeness everywhere. At the same time, you see the incompleteness and fragmentation we ordinarily create and in which we live.

The sixth, the wisdom center *(ajna chakra),* also known as the "third eye center," is located between and behind the eyebrows. When Energy-Awareness is raised to this center, the third or wisdom eye is opened and intuitive power is brought to the conscious level. The central characteristic of consciousness in this state is an expansive wakefulness that opens up a panoramic view; you begin to see things exactly as they are. Cutting through programming, constructs and filtering mechanisms that ordinarily create a distance and shield us from things as they are, awareness is now able to be directly present and relate to people and things without imposing mental constructions, interpretations, evaluations, and judgments on them. As a result, at this stage all but the final duality or separation from things falls away. Deconstruction of ordinary consciousness, reality, and ego has now been accomplished on the gross level and awareness has entered the subtle stage. All forms, except the form of the deity or the meditation object, have fallen away from the mind. Only the primal, archetypal duality of Energy and Wisdom, signified by the two lotus petals and the two deities—*Shiva* and *Shakti*—that preside over them, are left. Having become nonjudgmental and noninterpretative, the mind has now become the supreme witness of all phenomena.

The seventh, the crown center *(sahasrara),* located in the crown of the head, is not strictly a center *(chakra).* Symbolizing the highest state of consciousness projected on the body, it represents the development of what was opened and activated at the "third eye" to its universal state. Hence it is sometimes called "cosmic consciousness" and is represented by a thousand-petaled lotus. In this state all the energies and states of consciousness represented by the lower centers are assumed, transformed, unified, and integrated. They exist in it and proceed from it as their source. The primal polarity of Wisdom and Energy, *Shiva* and *Shakti*, unite or exist in the state of union at this stage, so that Primal Energy in the individual unites with universal Primal Energy.

As you reach this universal, integrated state of consciousness, there is an interface between the mind and the universe as you directly experience that the same principles that constitute the individual also constitute the universe, so that each individual is identical with the whole. When Primal Energy reaches the crown center, you enter *samadhi* and experience the oneness of all polarities everywhere: oneness within yourself and oneness with the universe. You experience the universe as an undivided whole, in which all things interweave, intersect, interpenetrate, and interrelate (Narayananda 54-58; Keyes 2: 142-162; Rama et al. 216-280).

Since the pathway to this evolution of consciousness normally remains closed, in order to raise Primal Energy, the central channel must be opened and the Energy made to enter and travel upward through it and the centers. As there is an essential connection between Primal Energy and *Prana* manifested in us through the breath, essential to raising it is the act of drawing the *Prana*-breath up through the central channel. This process requires, according to Eliade, stopping the breath, the sperm, and the mind.

Various techniques are used for controlling and stopping the breath, essential to which is retaining and holding it, accompanied by the use of mantras and visualization, for increasingly longer periods of time. In addition, you need to do breath-control and immobilization *(bandha)* exercises, among which is the *jaladhara bandha*. It consists in contracting the throat and firmly pressing the chin against the chest, thus stopping the breath. You have to do this at the end of inhalation, accompanied by drawing up the abdomen. Then hold the breath and practice *uddyana bandha* by contracting the sphincter muscle and drawing up the intestines above or below the navel in such a way that they touch the back and the diaphragm. This method causes Primal Energy to rise through the central channel (Rieker 2: 120-126).

Of the other gestures and immobilizations described before, the *mahamudra* is said to unite the main currents of energies from their usual upward and downward flow. *Mahabandha* stops them from reverting to their usual course; and *mahavedha* makes the Breath-Energy leave the left and right channels and enter the central channel, thus uniting the three. To make the normally downward flow of Energy rise upward, another immobilization you are instructed to practice is *mula bandha*. It is formed by pressing the scrotum with one heel, contracting the anus and pressing it with the other, and visualizing and mentally drawing the breath upward through the central channel (Rieker 2: 122).

To hasten the ascent of Energy, especially in the "left-handed" path, the yogi is enjoined to practice the yoga of the Five M's and stop or immobilize the semen, the breath, and the mind in sexual union. Assuming one of the yogic postures, with his female partner sitting astride his lap, he visualizes himself as *Shiva* (Wisdom), his partner as *Shakti* (Energy), and intercourse as their union; and repeats the mantras, along with stopping the breath. After discharging the semen and mixing it with the partner's fluid, he is instructed to draw back and reabsorb it into himself. This practice is essentially similar to the one in Taoist Yoga. Although Bharati says that the main difference between the Hindu and the Buddhist *Tantra* is that while the Hindu tantrist ejects his sperm, the Buddhist tantrist does not, Eliade presents evidence to the contrary and Bharati himself cites texts that go contrary to his statement. In any case, this practice is symbolically enacted by the right-handed path (Eliade 248-249; Bharati 265).

Together with bringing the breath and the semen to a stop, the yogi is instructed to stop the mind and enter into *samadhi*. This simultaneous stilling of the three planes of movement is the goal of the practice. The stopping of breath and semen is for the sake of stilling the mind, symbolized by the semen, and entering into *samadhi*, signified by reabsorption. *Samadhi* is reached when the yogi is able to stop, first briefly and then for longer periods, thought and inner dialogue, to destructure and transcend ordinary consciousness, and to attain oneness with Primal Energy-Wisdom (Eliade 249).

One method used by both left- and right-handed *Tantra* to awaken and raise Primal Energy is called *shakti chalan,* or circulation of Energy, performed by stopping the breath and stirring up the *svarasvati nadi* (in front of the left channel). To do this exercise, when the breath flows through the left nostril, assume the lotus posture and breathe in and out slowly and deeply in equal lengths. Mentally bind the *svarasvati nadi* with the breath and hold the ribs near the navel with the thumbs and forefingers of both hands. Then stir up Energy with all your might by repeatedly moving the body from right to left for a period of forty-eight minutes. When you feel that Energy is entering the central channel, slightly draw up the lower abdomen, compress the neck, expand the navel, and shake the *svarasvati nadi*. This will make it rise up above the chest (Narayananda 89).

After you are able to keep Energy in the central channel, among the methods used to raise it from the sensation to the crown center, one is the following described by Swami Narayananda: After rising and completing your morning toilet, with an empty stomach sit up straight in a cross-legged posture in a clean and well-ventilated room. Inhale slowly and evenly through both nostrils; draw the stomach and the lower abdomen toward the spine and upward; close the anus firmly by contracting the sphincter muscles; and very slowly and cautiously draw up the Energy from the tip of the genitals to the crown center by drawing up the breath and visualizing the Breath-Energy rising and mentally tracing the upward movement, through the central channel up to the crown center. Then exhale and relax the stomach, the lower abdomen, and the anus. After inhaling through both nostrils, repeat the exercise again and again, with rest or pause in between for the duration of the meditation period. While doing the exercise, mentally repeat *OM* and have a firm conviction that you are taking the Primal Energy to the crown center. Do this exercise in the morning and the evening five minutes each time and gradually extend the meditation period to half an hour (193-194).

Swami Narayananda observes that from the sensation center the Energy can be raised by three different routes and made to enter the central channel: (a) taking it to the root center and making it to enter the central channel, and thence to higher centers; (b) taking the fully risen Energy to the physical heart center, turning it at right angles and joining it to the spiritual heart, which is on the right side of the chest, then, turning it back to the spine, joining it at the passage of the central channel; and (c) after taking it through *svarasvati nadi* to the heart region, taking it right up to the third eye and joining it with the central channel. However, to awaken, transform, and integrate various energies and states of consciousness so as to transform, unify, and expand your consciousness and identity, the Energy must be awakened and made to rise through the central channel and the centers to the crown center (195-211).

Whatever the method used, according to Swami Narayananda, Primal Energy must be raised through the central channel fully, at least to the throat center, otherwise no permanent transformation and expansion of consciousness will take place. But when it is so raised, it will never go down again. And this will enable you to assume and transform the lower states from that higher center. When the Energy rises to this center, you may see various lights and visions and gain paranormal powers (202-208).

To complete the development of consciousness, the Energy must be raised from the throat to the wisdom center. When you do this, the subtle energies and state of the throat center become merged into the body of the Energy — that is, the mind becomes unified, integrated, and expanded — as it reaches the wisdom center. At this stage the gross perceptual form and ordinary consciousness are deconstructed and you arrive at the subtle form. Mentally you see the universal state but primal duality and mental operations still remain.

When the Energy reaches the crown center, you enter into *samadhi* with Primal Energy. Initially, you experience oneness with Primal Energy. As you advance through various stages of *samadhi,* and following fundamental shifts, you transcend all forms and arrive at *nirvikalpa samadhi.* At this stage, transcending all duality, polarity, multiplicity, and constructs, you experience enlightenment (Narayananda 210-220).

If the yogi presses beyond *nirvikalpa samadhi*, s/he may come to realize *sahaja samadhi,* the Unconditioned State of *Turiya,* which is the transcendent unity of all that is. This final stage would constitute the return to the Primordial Oneness, in which s/he would realize that all things are This only, besides which nothing exists. Becoming established at this Supreme Identity and Center, s/he would see all things as the embodiment and manifestation of this Totality and experience completeness and liberation. This realization would then be the ultimate state of development of consciousness and the final goal of the tantric journey.

Chapter 9
The Theravada Path: Concentration and Insight

Buddha's Eightfold Way

In understanding and finding a way out of the human condition for himself and all human beings, the Buddha manifested the essence of Buddhism in his life, his experience of enlightenment, and his teachings. These are neatly summarized under the Four Noble Truths, the last of which outlines the path that leads to liberation:

> Now this, monks, is the noble truth of the way that leads to the cessation of suffering: this is the noble Eightfold Way, namely, right views, right intention, right speech, right action, right livelihood, right effort, right mindfulness, right *samadhi*. (Burtt 30)

The eightfold character of the path immediately brings to mind Patanjali's eightfold *Yoga Sutras*. This similarity is not coincidental. In fact, Buddhism's link to Hinduism is through the yogas. Just as the first two steps of Patanjali's *Yoga Sutras* form part of the discipline and ethical practices designed to bring about self-transformation, so the first six of Buddha's eightfold path are components of a way that aims to bring about in the practitioner a fundamental shift in outlook and a moral change that will eradicate from consciousness the very tendency to commit evil. Nothing short of a complete mind-change – a change of the way s/he sees him/herself, others and the world – can be an adequate preparation for *Nirvana*. In Castaneda's terms, s/he must clean, shrink, and rearrange his/her consciousness, identity, lifestyle, and relationship to others and the world so as to open up a space in which insight can dawn. This is precisely the reason that each one of the eight steps begins with the word *sama,* which means, as H. Saddhatissa points out, not so much "right" (as opposed to "wrong") as "perfect," "full," or "complete" (47).

To bring about this complete transformation, the eightfold path begins, similar to Patanjali's "study," with "right views" or complete seeing, which consists in both theoretical and practical knowledge of the path, the goal, and the self. It is seeing the actual condition of your life exactly as it is; seeing how you cause and maintain it; and seeing the need for liberation and in what it consists. In other words, this first step consists in thoroughly understanding the first three Noble Truths. Related to this is the second, "right intention" *(sankalpa)* — which is better translated as "resolve" or "determination." Designed to bring about a motivational change, it requires in the aspirant a full and unshakable determination to walk on the path completely, to the very end, so as to attain the goal.

Once we have full understanding and motivation, we can embark on the practical course of reordering our lives in relationship to the goal. Hence the next four injunctions. Similar to Patanjali's *yama* and other *niyamas,* the next three — right speech, behavior, and livelihood — are concerned with a purification of life, thought, speech, and behavior, and elimination of evil tendencies from the unconscious. And "right effort" has the same intent as Patanjali's *tapas* or "effort." Taken together, these are designed, as in the *Yoga Sutras,* to eradicate negative programmings and the evils that ensue from them; eliminate emotional and mental blockages and conflicts; enhance positive states; and in general, bring about a transformation of consciousness, attitudes, and lifestyle, preparatory to meditation proper, which begins with "right" or complete mindfulness.

Complete Mindfulness

As it encompasses every aspect of life and relationship to the world, mindfulness is to be practiced at all times and in every situation. Implying an attentive, watchful, or awakened state of mind, it is the very opposite of the mindless unawareness in which we live most of the time. The initial aim of mindfulness is to free the meditator from programming and his/her habitual, automatic, reactive states. Essentially, this freedom implies your extricating the awareness from being trapped and lost in mental processes and contents, so that you can see each thing exactly as it is, and clearly understand its nature. Thus, outside the period of formal meditation, complete mindfulness has the same goal as IAM: dissolving negative programming, enhancing positive qualities, and developing moment-to-moment awareness. In formal meditation, its aim is to destructure ordinary consciousness. Essential to achieving these goals are bare attention and clear comprehension.

As I have said before, bare attention is pure, unmediated attention focused directly on the stimulus at each moment and directly observing it at the immediate moment of its impact on the senses and the mind without anything intervening or creating a distance between the attention and the stimulus. From moment to moment, you focus your unmediated attention on the physical sensations, feelings, mental contents, or events, directly observing their nature as they arise and disappear, before they are processed, interpreted, and perceived by the mind as objects; before they are evaluated as objects of desire or avoidance, of likes or dislikes; and before triggering any mental or emotional reaction, any addition, restriction, or distortion introduced through past emotional reactions, experiences, and associations. As Joseph Goldstein observes, "Bare attention means observing things as they are, without choosing, without comparing, without evaluating, without laying our projections and expectations on to what is happening; cultivating instead a choiceless and noninterfering awareness" (20). Similarly, according to Jack Engler, bare attention is "registering the mere occurrence of any thought, feeling or sensation exactly as it occurs and enters awareness from moment to moment, without further elaboration . . . without preference, comment, judgment, reflection or interpretation" (1: 20-21).

As bare attention is directly focused on what arises, you clearly notice and precisely understand its exact nature. You directly observe and become aware of the exact moment something arises, its nature for the duration it lasts, and the exact moment it passes away. This clear comprehension is the second aspect of mindfulness. It is what yields insight into the nature of what arises, of all phenomena and mental contents. You see the impermanence of all conditioned things. Without developing clear comprehension, mindfulness cannot be complete and cannot lead to the deepening of practice.

Although clear comprehension is meant to range over whatever arises in the mind throughout the whole of life, Theravada Buddhist tradition singles out four key aspects for intensification of practice and change in motivation: clear comprehension of purpose, suitability, the domain of meditation, and reality (Nyanaponika Thera 45-56).

First, clear comprehension of purpose is intended to clarify life goal and arouse single minded determination and high motivation to take up practice. More specifically, it is aimed at developing a clear understanding of the motivation and purpose behind every action before you embark on it – developing the ability to see from moment to moment why you are doing whatever you are doing. This understanding will prevent aimless, habitual, or automatic activity; prevent falling into the trap of mistaking means for ends; and keep the purpose of mindfulness, meditation, and existence clearly in mind before undertaking any action.

Second, once your goals become clear, you need to clearly understand what kinds of action are suitable to attain them. This understanding will help you eliminate harmful or destructive motives and actions that prevent self-growth and the growth of others; make you lose interest in everyday activities that are not conducive to the path or do not lead to deepening of practice; and motivate you to do those things that will lead to awakening, development, self-growth, and liberation.

Third, you need to clearly comprehend meditation methods and how to practice them; and the need to practice complete mindfulness at all times, in all circumstances and toward everything, until every moment of life is infused with awareness and the boundary between meditation and life disappears. As Nyanaponika Thera states, "Step by step the practice of Right Mindfulness should absorb all activities of body, speech and mind, so that ultimately . . . life becomes one with the spiritual practice, and that the practice becomes full-blooded life" (50).

Fourth, complete mindfulness is intended to penetrate the bare bones of reality and lead to a clear comprehension of all its dimensions. You must perceive that you construct your reality and identify with it; that this identification creates the primary illusion about reality and the delusion that ego is something real, permanent, and your true identity. Such seeing will bring insight into the impermanence *(anicca)* and the not-self nature *(anatta)* of all conditioned things. You will then be able to disidentify with your mental processes and contents.

To inject each aspect of your lives with awareness, to infuse every thought, feeling, and behavior with it, you need a handle. Theravada Buddhist tradition sees such a lever in four pivotal aspects of life: mindfulness of the body, feelings, mind, and the contents of the mind.

Mindfulness of the Body

In mindfulness of the body, awareness is grounded in the body as the base of operation. From there it opens out and embraces others and the world. Since the body is always in the present, as we ground awareness in the body, we are able to develop an inclusive mindfulness and center the mind in the present. Such mindfulness will not only help us face and cut through our fantasies, fears, anxieties, tensions, compulsions, and illusions about our body, and develop a proper attitude and direct relationship to things; but more fundamentally, it will enable us to develop moment-to-moment awareness and gain insight into the nature of all phenomena.

To develop such a comprehensive awareness and present-centered consciousness, the *Satipattana Sutra* recommends practicing mindfulness of breathing both in and outside formal meditation. In formal meditation and throughout the day you are to observe (by focusing your bare attention on the body) and clearly comprehend the nature of the various sensations that arise. Another practice is to observe your body throughout the day in various postures, whether you are lying, sitting, standing, moving, working, eating, playing, resting, etc. An alternate exercise is to observe with bare attention various parts of the body, external and internal, while you engage in various activities. As you observe various parts or changes in posture, you come to see their nature, develop present-centeredness, and disidentify with your present attitudes.

To develop nonattachment, awareness, and acceptance of the body as an ever-changing process, you are instructed to move your attention from its outer to its inner parts—from the skin to the tissues, muscles, bones, skeleton, etc. Alternately, you may visualize your body in various stages of decomposition, or as a skeleton, or meditate sitting in a cemetery. This practice will help you become free of narcissistic self-absorption, the fear of growing old and dying, fixation on likes and dislikes, attachment or repulsion, and negative attitudes toward the body. You will thus become more objective and see your body as it is, without any mental and emotional reaction.

Mindfulness of Feeling

Moving from the outer to the inner dimensions, the next sphere you penetrate and infuse with awareness is that of the emotions. In the tangled web of the emotions, awareness gets invariably trapped and lost. In their grip we react in unawareness like blind creatures making their way through an impenetrable forest. We identify and cling to our emotions as the most intimate part of ourselves. As a result, instead of being their masters, we become their victims, as we come to be controlled and ruled by them, and by our grasping and avoidance, our desires and fears.

Mindfulness of feeling consists in focusing our bare attention on and clearly comprehending the nature of these mental reactions exactly as they occur from moment to moment. With such a focus, we notice immediately the moment of contact or impact of the sense object—whether we are seeing, hearing, tasting, smelling, touching, or thinking—on consciousness. This is the primary order of experience. From this contact arises a pleasant, unpleasant, or neutral sensation that accompanies every experience of an object.

Then the mental reaction sets in. If the sensation is pleasant, the mind reacts with grasping. It attaches or holds onto the sensation; it wants to prolong or repeat it. So desire, greed, and similar mental reactions are born. If the sensation is unpleasant, the mind reacts with dislike and avoidance; and an entire host of negative programmings are born. When the sensation is neutral, it does not register in our consciousness, and we fall into unawareness and delusion. Our mental reaction is what causes fixations, emotional blockages, and *dukkha*. As Goldstein and Kornfield point out, "Being caught by likes and dislikes, we try to perpetuate certain conditions and avoid other conditions, and so continually create the whole samsaric pattern of suffering and duality" (64).

The aim of the mindfulness of feeling is to dissolve mental reactions altogether, thus breaking free of emotional fixations and negative programmings, expanding positive qualities, and becoming aware moment to moment. To this end you need to focus your bare attention on and clearly observe from moment to moment whatever feeling arises in your mind—whether it be pleasant, unpleasant, or neither. When a feeling, say depression, arises, focus your bare attention on it the very first moment it arises. With your pure attention directly focused on it from moment to moment for the whole period it lasts, clearly comprehend its exact nature—noting precisely what it is, how it feels, its intensity, the sadness, the feeling of let down and being left alone or abandoned, and every other component of the feeling without letting your attention getting caught in it, identifying with it, or wallowing in it. You may also mentally note "depression, depression" while it lingers, if it helps you keep the attention clear and to observe its nature without getting caught up in it. Observe the changes the feeling goes through as it fills your mind and as it subsides. Observe also other mental reactions and associations that may accompany it.

As you are able to do this without identifying, attaching, or getting caught up in any of the programmed reactions, you will be able to disidentify with them, and they will begin to lose their hold over you. You will let go of your present attachments, and become free. In time the fixations and blockages will dissolve and disappear (Rahula 73).

Mindfulness of Mind

This mindfulness consists in focusing your bare attention directly on the mind itself and observing its actual states from moment to moment. You are to observe the various programmed states and moods of your mind exactly as they arise, so long as they remain, and as they disappear. You need to observe the nature and variety of your mental states, the various attitudes and outlooks of your mind; how it sees things, people, situations, and itself; and how it works or what triggers each of these states. Finally, observe the state in which your mind primarily abides.

When you are able to observe your mind impartially and see it as it actually is, you will notice that it constantly changes from one thought or state to another. In the roller coaster of its moods, at one time it is joyful or peaceful (god state); at another it is sad or lonely, or tumbles into depression or despondency as its expectations are dashed to pieces (hell state). Sometimes it is sure of itself, at other times it is full of doubt and confusion; at one time it is loving, tender and caring, at another uncaring, insensitive, cold, and selfish (human state). At one time it is full of desires and wants or is restless (hungry ghost state); at another it is dull and listless (animal state). Sometimes it is seized by the desire for security; at other times it craves sensation or entertainment; at yet other times it is on a power trip (giant state). Thus it may traverse the six states that make up *samsara* or conditioned existence. Whatever the state, as you keep your bare attention focused and clearly comprehend its nature without interfering, evaluating, judging, approving, or disapproving, you become aware of your mental process and you begin to cut through its layers of programming and construction.

Mindfulness of the Objects of the Mind

Since all programmings, mental states, objects, constructs, and events are objects of the mind, in one sense the other objects of mindfulness can be reduced to this one. More specifically, however, this mindfulness is concerned with directly seeing the mental contents, such as thoughts, plans, and fantasies, from moment to moment as they arise, take up the center of attention, and then subside. You need to clearly comprehend the nature of all mental contents in terms of their three characteristics, which are also the three characteristics of conditioned existence: their impermanence or constantly changing nature *(anicca)*, their lack of a permanent, substantial reality called "self" *(anatta)*, and their unsatisfactoriness and inability to become the foundation of existence, or to provide completeness and liberation *(dukkha)*. If attachment arises, you observe its nature, causes and consequences; its effects on yourself; why and how it arises and disappears; and how you can free yourself from it. Thus this mindfulness can lead you to discover the range of your consciousness and world;

how they are constructed and maintained through programming, identification, attachment, and desire; and how the ego is nothing but a mental content or construct (Saddhatissa 56; Goleman 1: 23; Conze et al. 59).

Concentration

Besides mindfulness, a second component of Buddhist meditation, which is the last of the Eightfold Path, is complete concentration. As we saw in the case of Yoga, the process of formal meditation begins with concentration, intensifies through meditation, and ripens into *samadhi* in which the mind becomes one with the object. From here you proceed to enlightenment. This holds true also of Buddhist meditation.

As is well-known, *vipassana* or insight meditation ha two main components — concentration and insight. Whereas concentration leads to *samadhi,* insight begins with mindfulness, develops through concentration and *samadhi,* and blossoms into enlightenment and *Nirvana.* Both are necessary. As Achaan Chah has well stated, "Meditation is like a single log of wood. Insight and investigation are one end of the log; calm and concentration are the other end. ... You cannot really separate concentration, inner tranquility, and insight. ... One grows into the other; without the first we would never have the second" (Kornfield and Breiter 15). Thus without stilling the activities of ordinary consciousness, which comes about in the progressive stages of concentration, that is, in *samadhi,* you cannot gain the insights that enable you to directly see the nature of things as they are and become free from conditioned existence. When concentration is firmly established and *samadhi* is reached, and ordinary consciousness is destructured to the stage of gross perceptual construction, insight into the nature, construction, and maintenance of conditioned existence, into the universal process or creation itself, the nature of the universe, and Reality as Such, can follow.

Concentrative *(Samatha)* Meditation

As in other concentrative meditations, in these exercises you keep the attention focused exclusively on one object so that you can bring the mind to one-pointedness, attain the initial stages of *samadhi* and deconstruct perceptual construction, and arrive at the subtle form of the object with which you can attain the more advanced stage of *samadhi.* Following are some concentrative exercises that can lead the mind to this stage.

Meditation I: Mindfulness of Breathing

a. Find a suitable place (as before, one relatively free of noises and voices, clean and uncluttered, etc.).
b. Assume one of the traditional postures, keeping your back, neck, and trunk erect but not stiff. You may keep your eyes open or closed. The mind should be relaxed and alert. Slowly bring your attention from its wanderings to the present. Focus it on your posture and be mindful that you are sitting and to what purpose.
c. Breathe normally and naturally, slowly and evenly. Focus and hold your bare and unmediated attention on the spot in the nostrils where you are most aware of the sensation the breath makes as it enters and leaves. As you inhale, hold the attention riveted on the sensation of the breath from the beginning to the end, and directly observe each sensation at each successive moment at the immediate point of contact between the breath and the nostrils. As you begin to exhale, switch the attention to the exhalation and similarly experience the sensation the passage of air makes each successive moment from the beginning to the end. Then switch the attention to the inhalation and repeat.
d. When you notice that the mind has wandered off, just bring the attention back to the spot, refocus it on the sensation, and continue as before. The attention tends to lose direct contact with the sensation and drift off, especially at the juncture at which the exhalation ends and the inhalation begins. To stop the mind from wandering, then, it is extremely important that you keep the attention fixed on the sensation at the beginning and the end of both inhalation and exhalation, but especially where the exhalation ends and inhalation begins. Keep the attention especially sharp, clear, and fixed directly on the sensation. Do not let it waver for even an instant from the breath as it ends and the new one begins.
e. To aid concentration you may also count to ten and back again or repeat a phrase or word such as *Buddho* or *Dhammo* while you watch the inhalation and exhalation.
f. Observe everything that happens during the meditation as a result of your focusing attention on the breath — whether it speeds up or slows down, becomes jerky or smooth; whether your concentration is sharp and clear, or dull, fitful, restless, etc. Without thinking about anything, keep your attention sharp and clear by holding it directly focused on the first moment of sensation. Let it become one with the breath, so that there remains only this sensation of breathing (Rahula 69-70; Saddhatissa 76, 81; Kornfield and Breiter 81-82).

Meditation II: The Burmese Method of Breathing

a. Sit cross-legged on a chair, or in any position in which you are comfortable and relaxed. Keep your back straight but not stiff. Close your eyes.
b. Take a few deep breaths and then breathe normally. Focus your bare attention directly on the abdomen and precisely observe the exact bodily sensation of pressure caused by the slight rising and falling of the abdomen as you inhale and exhale.
c. While continuing to observe, make a mental note of *rising* for the upward movement and *falling* for the downward movement. Do not verbally repeat the words *rising* and *falling,* but just be aware only of the actual process of the rising and falling movement of the abdomen and clearly note their occurrence.
e. Each time you notice that the attention has wandered off, mentally note it as wandering, and then bring the attention firmly back, and continue as before. If distractions become too persistent and refuse to go away, make them the object of observation until the mind calms down sufficiently; then return to the original practice (Shattock 38-40; Mahasi Sayadaw Center, 1970).

Meditation III: Mindfulness of Walking

a. Find an area ten to thirty feet in length, relatively free of noise or distractions, where you can walk back and forth without being disturbed and where you will not feel embarrassed or self-conscious about doing the meditation. The location could be indoors or outdoors. To prevent the eyes from wandering and to keep the attention concentrated, slightly tilt your head downward and cast your eyes about ten feet ahead of you without focusing on anything in particular.
b. Your hands may be held clasped in such a way that they cause a slight tension. You may also relax them and keep them to your sides.
c. Walk in such a way as to be able to maintain continuous attention on the movement of your feet. Focus attention on your right foot exactly at the moment you are lifting it and keep observing the sensations as you raise, step, and place the foot. While placing it on the ground, hold the attention riveted on the sensation from the heel to the end of the toes. Then transfer it to the left, which is by now partially raised, and similarly experience the sensation of lifting, stepping, and placing, especially as the foot contacts the ground. Then experience every sensation from the heel to the toes. As you lift, step, and place each foot, you may mentally note "lifting," "stepping," and "placing."

d. To stop the mind from wandering, hold the attention on the foot and do not let it move away from it until you contact the ground, experience every sensation in the foot from the heel to the toes, and transfer the attention to the other foot.
e. At the end of the walk slowly turn around in four steps, and again, transfer the attention from one foot to the other, pause for a few moments, bring the attention to the right foot, and resume walking.

Meditation IV: Visualization — The *Kasina* Exercise

a. An object for visualization, a *kasina* is a disk made of light brown earth, about the size of a plate or smaller. Or it may be any red, white, yellow, or blue object, such as a flower, vase, or disk. It may be a bowl filled with water, a candle flame, or the clear blue sky. Or you may construct your own *kasina*. Its size should be according to what is most conducive to concentration. You should construct it mindfully, with full, relaxed attention to every action. After you have made or chosen a *kasina,* set it at a reasonable distance from your meditation seat — about ten to fifteen feet in front of you. The center of the *kasina* should be slightly lower than the horizontal eye level when you are seated.
b. After setting up the *kasina,* go to your seat and assume a convenient meditative posture; then focus your gaze softly on the *kasina*. Do not stare or strain your eyes. Relax the muscles around your eyes, and, keeping them partly open, softly and calmly place your sight on the *kasina,* somewhat as though you were looking at your own face in a mirror. Concentrate your complete attention on the *kasina,* and starting at the outer edge, slowly move your attention to the center.
c. After gazing for a few minutes with concentrated attention, close your eyes while still concentrating on the *kasina* and see if a mental or after-image appears before you. Since the first step is to develop such an internal representation and to concentrate on it, continue opening and closing your eyes until such an image arises in your mental screen.
d. After the image arises and becomes stabilized, instead of concentrating on the external *kasina,* make the internal representation the object of your concentration. It will then serve as the object on which the mind will become one-pointed as it gradually becomes one with it. As meditation deepens, the image will become refined. When the image becomes further refined, it will become a concept, idea, or "seed," which is a perceptual synthesis containing sensory information from various fields (Spiegelberg 44-48; Hewitt 82-87).

Another form of visualization is the *mandala,* which is the same as that discussed in the chapter on *Tantra.* As in the *kasina* exercise, when a mental image of the *mandala* appears, focus attention on it rather than on the external *mandala.* If it floats away from view, focus attention on the spot where it first appeared, and it will float back there again. As the image becomes stabilized and you are able to hold your attention on it for increasingly longer periods, with deepening concentration, in time your mind will enter into *samadhi* with it (Saddhatissa 75-78). A mantra, sound, mental contents, and a variety of other things discussed in the chapter on *Yoga Sutras* may also be used for concentration.

Whatever the object used, the aim of concentrative exercises is the same as in other paths: to bring about a shift of attention away from external objects and toward the internal one; to steady and center the object; to unify, integrate, and make the mind one-pointed, and eventually to enter into *samadhi.*

According to the *Visuddhimagga,* by concentrating beyond the initial stage, you can progressively attain eight stages of *samadhi,* the first four of which are based on forms, while the last four have formless objects. At the first stage, perception and sensory awareness are stilled. By first focusing on the primary object, and then turning away from it and turning toward consciousness itself and what arises in it, at the second stage, attention cuts through the outer, gross construction, the verbal layer. Thereupon you experience rapture. As the mind becomes tranquil and steady at the third stage, it goes beyond rapture and enters into bliss. Going beyond symbolic or model layer of the object construction at the fourth stage, you experience *samadhi* with the subtle form of the object and enter into total stillness (*Visuddhimagga* 144-408; Goleman 1: 13-16). Upon reaching this stage of *samadhi,* the mind becomes limpid and still, "like a clear forest pool" (162), to use Achaan Chah's phrase, in which things can be reflected as they really are.

The stages of formless *samadhi* are experienced by abandoning forms and substituting formless objects for the focus of attention. Thus, at the fifth stage, perception of form is transcended by entering into *samadhi* with infinite space. At the sixth stage, by turning attention away from infinite space and turning toward infinite consciousness, you enter into *samadhi* with it. At the seventh stage, attention is turned away from even infinite consciousness and directed toward the pure void, where no object is present. At the eighth stage, attention is turned away from even the void. *Samadhi* now reaches the state beyond objects and beyond the duality of perception and nonperception (*Visuddhimagga* 354-408; Goleman 1: 16-18).

Stages of Insight: Mindfulness

The stage of insight begins with mindfulness. The four objects of mindfulness serve as the starting point for insight meditation. Unlike concentrative meditation, the aim here is not to develop one-pointedness of mind but to begin with a concentrated mind so that you can directly observe with bare attention the contents of your mind and clearly comprehend the nature of ordinary consciousness, reality, and identity. By directly observing whatever arises in the mind, you need to see how they are constructed and maintained. More specifically, you need to directly observe and clearly comprehend them in terms of the three characteristics of conditioned existence described above.

In formal meditation based on mindfulness of breathing, you observe with bare attention the exact moment each inhalation arises, its entire duration, and end; the beginning, duration, and end of the exhalation; the pause, and the beginning of the next inhalation. You experience your breath-awareness as a process that arises from the void, becomes the present reality, and passes into the void.

Similarly, when anything arises in the mind, you focus your bare attention on it and directly observe it the very first moment it arises and as long as it lasts. You clearly comprehend the nature of all things arising and passing away from moment to moment as a process in the vast, open space of your mind. When you do so, you notice that there is no mental reaction, no continuity, permanence, or solidity, no substantial entity behind or separate from the individual moment of observation which arises and passes, leaving no trace.

With regard to bodily sensation, you may practice either one of the following form of formal meditation:

Formal Meditation on Bodily Sensations

a. First develop concentration by focusing attention on the sensation of the breath at the nostrils. Proceed with insight meditation after your concentration becomes firm and steady.
b. Begin by being mindful of your posture and stabilizing your attention and then observing the sensation of the breath at the tip of your nostrils. Next, take your bare attention to the top of your head, and, using it like a narrow beam of intense light, begin to examine the top of the skull or scalp. Directly observe every sensation by holding attention at the precise point it immediately contacts the skin and the sensation arises. When you notice a sensation pause, pinpoint

it, zoom attention into it, and minutely observe its nature. Proceed very slowly and deliberately, with intense concentration and bare attention, until you are able to cut through unawareness, mental fog, perceptual filters, thoughts, other mental contents, and emotional and other programmed reactions. Once you are in direct contact with and able to observe each moment as it arises, notice its duration, intensity, diminution, and cessation. Then another arises or a gap follows. Observe the gap or discontinuity. Penetrate and move through each sensation, going deeper and deeper, from the surface to the inner dimensions until you are able to observe it on a primary, subtle level as a constant process of change. Observe how, upon contact, the mind reacts, and, if the sensation is pleasant, how the mind grabs it, wants to prolong, repeat, and make it permanent. If the sensation is judged unpleasant, see how the mind resists, pushes away or avoids it. Observe how such reactions render what you experience each moment insufficient unto itself.

Now go inside your head and directly observe the brain's electrical hum. Focus your bare attention on the sound, on any tension, tightness, heaviness, pressure, stress, pain, tingling, or any other sensation in the head. As though you were performing a microscopic surgery, examine your head with your sharp, clear scalpel of attention by resting it on the point of contact where the sensation arises. Penetrate it until you can observe the subtler level of sensations.

Then gradually take your searchlight of attention down to the forehead, the eyes, the nose, the lips, and the sensation the breath makes. Move inside the mouth to the upper palate, the teeth, the gums; slowly scan the tongue from the tip all the way to its roots; the entire face, including the jaws. After you have scanned the throat and the neck, go down the outer part of your right arm all the way to the finger tips and minutely scan every inch, observing the rising and passing of each sensation along the way. Be especially attentive to the vast field of sensation in the finger tips, fingers, and the palm; then very slowly move the attention up the inner side of the wrist, the arm, the elbow, and to the armpit. Then go across the shoulder blades to the left arm and similarly scan it.

Now bring your attention to the chest area and slowly take it down and observe the sensations in the chest, the heart, the thorax, the stomach; the sensation of expansion and contraction of the abdomen from inhalation and exhalation; the front of the pelvis, buttocks, thigh joints, and muscles. Then go down the outer part of the right thigh and directly observe the sensations in the thigh, the knee, the leg, the ankle, the upper part of the foot, the toes, the sole of the foot (a vast field of changing sensations). Then go up the inner part and across to the left leg and scan it similarly.

Next, move the attention up the back, scanning from the lower to the upper part of the back, paying particular attention to the lower back, the spinal column,

the shoulder joints, and to any muscle tension in that region. Move the attention up the back of the neck to the base of the skull and to the top of the head. At the end of every sweep, pause, bring the whole body into the focus of your attention, and observe it as a field of constantly changing sensations in which there is no continuity, permanence, or substantiality. Then repeat the process.
c. Just keep sensations at the center of your attention and keep scanning the entire body until you are aware and clearly comprehend their nature to be impermanent, nonsubstantial, and empty of self or separate, individual entities — only a symphony of sensations in constant change, arising and existing in mutual dependence and interrelationship. Close every meditation session by clearly comprehending or recognizing this primary order.

Meditation V: Sensations — An Alternate Method

a. First develop concentration by using the mindfulness of the breath meditation. Continue to station your attention at the entrance of the nostrils as before.
b. When a sensation arises, shift the focus of your attention from the breath to the sensation and continue to observe it from the moment it arises until it ends and another arises (if nothing arises, go back to observing the breath).
c. Clearly comprehend its exact nature by mentally noting or recognizing what kind it is, such as pain, itching, discomfort, for the entire period it lingers without letting your attention become trapped and lost in it. Observe its exact nature and characteristics as sensation on the primary level and at the immediate moment of contact between the stimulus, and the attention. Observe what happens when it arises, what it feels like, its intensity, the bodily (involuntary) reaction, the mental reaction in terms of desire, attachment, or avoidance, the changes it undergoes. Watch how it subsides. Notice and clearly comprehend its nature as impermanence; see how it is empty of self or substantiality, and how we create suffering through our mental reaction to what arises.
d. Go back to watching the breath after the bodily sensation subsides. When another sensation arises, proceed to observe it as above.

Formal meditation based on mindfulness of feeling, mind, and mental contents or objects proceeds in the same was as mindfulness of breathing and sensation. Thus when a feeling (fear, anger, anxiety, love, joy) arises, turn the focus of your attention to it and observe it exactly as it is from the moment of its contact with attention to the time it subsides. Clearly comprehend its nature on the primary level of stimulus as it arises, fills your mind, and subsides, without getting caught in it, identifying with it, or wallowing in it. Do not become involved in self-therapy or self-pity. Especially at the beginning when the automatic tendency is to identify with it, to prevent entrapment of attention, you may mentally note the nature of the emotion, such as "fear, fear," for the entire period it lasts. Precisely note and clearly comprehend what it feels like, its various characteristics and qualities, its intensity, your bodily and mental reactions to it; its constantly changing nature; your tendency to identify with it and make it permanent and thus build up a substantial self; and how this activity makes life unsatisfactory.

When a mental state, such as restlessness or peacefulness, or a mental content, such as thought, arises, focus your bare attention directly on it and clearly comprehend its nature by following the same steps as above. Do not analyze the content. Just directly see exactly at the immediate point of contact the form, nature, qualities, and characteristics of what arises. Thus, if a thought arises, see it the exact moment it arises; see how it takes on the center stage of attention; see how, through association, it tends to build up a fantasy world; see if it is part of a recurring pattern and what lies behind it, such as anxiety, attachment, avoidance; and see how it seeks and wants to trap your attention, which makes you unaware.

Insights arise when you are able to directly observe discontinuity and impermanence in the stream of consciousness. As you focus your bare attention and directly observe, from moment to moment, your bodily sensations or mental contents exactly at their point of origin or contact, and as you clearly comprehend their nature, you see that they are discontinuous and constantly changing. You notice from moment to moment how each one arises, holds the center stage of attention, and then passes, like an actor on a stage, to make room for the next one. Between one and the other, you notice a gap, a discontinuity in the stream of consciousness. Thus, when you focus attention on the sensation of the breath or a bodily sensation, you notice that each area is a vast field in which one sensation arises and passes, and another follows in a constantly changing field.

In walking meditation, you notice that every step, every turn, is made up of innumerable discontinuous decisions succeeding one another in which the impression of continuity is created by the mind from the rapid succession of decisions and from unawareness. Outside meditation, as you focus attention especially on natural sounds, such as those of crickets, birds, a rushing stream, or a waterfall, you notice how their apparent continuity consists of one sound succeeding another, with gaps between them.

As you also observe the same discontinuity outside meditation, you realize that in the entire world of direct experience, or at the moment of immediate impact of the object on the senses or the mind, there is only discontinuity, only this constant process of change. You also notice that in this process things are interrelated. There is no permanent or isolated event, existing by itself, separate from or behind the process, unrelated to anything else. Rather, things condition one another, arise and exist in mutual dependence and relationship. This makes the universe an undivided whole of limitless dimensions in which things exist in mutual interconnection and interaction. And you come to see the creator not only of the contents but also of continuity. You see how the mind forms the idea of continuity or permanence out of memory, selective attention, unawareness of gaps, and the speed with which the contents succeed one another. You observe how the mind creates and maintains its world out of the contents and imposes permanence on it. Thus you come to realize that impermanence *(anicca)* and mutual dependence constitute the nature of all phenomena, of all conditioned existence.

From observing impermanence and the mind's reaction to it, you also come to see the grasping and avoiding tendency of consciousness. You notice how, in its drive to form a stable world and self, it identifies with and attaches to the sensations or to mental contents and events and creates the impression of permanence, continuity, and solidity. But in this shifting and discontinuous stream, nowhere do you discover a permanent self. As you perceive only a succession of events in the mental and physical phenomena, you come to see that the permanent self is only a thought and that in reality there is no permanent, individual entity called "the self" that remains unchanged and exists as separate from the events unfolding before you. Thus you gain insight into *anatta* — the not-self nature or emptiness of all mental and physical phenomena or conditioned existence. You see that in its drive to overcome this feeling of impermanence, emptiness, and incompleteness by constructing a permanent self, the mind detaches itself from reality and becomes encased in a world of illusions. But, sensing itself to be empty and incomplete, the self is filled with a drive to create a world to overcome the feeling. However, as the world is a materialization of the inner states and remains separate from the self, it becomes equally empty and enveloped in illusions, and so fails to provide the desired completeness.

Thus you come to see how you create *dukkha* through the mind's reaction, its attempt to grasp, lay hold of sensations or mental contents so as to stabilize its world and itself, and find a solid footing in the ever-changing process. You notice this happening when there is a contact with something and a sensation arises. Finding it pleasurable, through identification and attachment the mind wants to make the experience last, wants to hold on to it, repeat it, have more of it. So desire is born. Or, judging it unpleasant, the mind reacts with the opposite emotion, wants none of it, and so resists or avoids it, and reacts with further emotions. You notice how either reaction dissociates you from the primary process and makes your experience of life unsatisfactory. Because the programmed mind wants permanence, wants the pleasurable event or moment to last, and wants to avoid the unpleasurable, it causes *dukkha* and encases us in illusions.

As you continue to directly observe, from moment to moment, the arising and passing away of phenomena, a dissociation begins to develop between the mind's seeing on the one hand, and the mental states and contents on the other; between awareness without contents, and the contents and processes of the mind; between the mental screen and the objects projected on it. These insights blossom when awareness becomes sharp, clear, and direct, and ranges over every aspect of life and the world of experience.

As you gain these insights and clearly comprehend the nature of all things as change and realize that you make yourself unhappy by trying to find permanence in the midst of this ever-changing process, you begin to let go of your identification, attachment, and fixation on the separate self; let go of mental contents, programming, and reality-construct. Thus you lose the entire grasping character of the present life (Saddhatissa 56; Goleman 23; Conze et al. 57-59).

The consequences of mindfulness and the insights that result from it are reversal of the orientation of attention from external objects to the object of meditation, gathering of attention and its unification with the object, *samadhi*, and deconstruction of the external, perceptual form of ordinary consciousness and reality (*Visuddhimagga* 315-317). Upon this deconstruction, you arrive at *samadhi* with the subtle form of the object and experience deconstruction of symbolic layer of object formation.

Stages of Insight or "Direct Knowledge"

The *Visuddhimagga* begins its discussion of the advanced stages of insight with a description of paranormal powers, such as clairaudience, clairvoyance, telepathy, and recollection of past life, that may manifest themselves for the first time when the meditator attains formless *samadhi* (446-487).

To go beyond these phenomena, which are regarded as hindrances, and experience advanced stages of insight that will enable you to "purify" your "views," that is, deconstruct and transcend the form of the object and the conceptual framework of meditation, you need, first, to develop right understanding of the nature of conditioned existence *(anicca)*, identity *(anatta)*, and the human condition *(dukkha)*. You need to correctly understand their nature in terms of their elements, causes, and conditions, the process of their construction, and the method of their maintenance.

Having gained this understanding, you return to *samadhi,* either with the subtle form or formless *samadhi* (but not neither perception nor nonperception form of *samadhi),* and begin the process of deconstruction or "purification of views" by observing whatever arises from the perspectives of "materiality-mentality," or physical *(rupa)* and mental phenomena *(nama)* on the level of their primary construction. "Like following a snake that s/he has seen in his/her house," as you directly observe each moment of awareness and search for the basis of the construction of continuity in the stream of consciousness, that is, for the very foundation of consciousness, you find that it has no basis other than the object or programmed contents that arise. A similar observation of the primary form of the object-construction by investigating whatever arises reveals that the basis for permanence and solidity, that is, object-construction is no other than its concomitant momentary states of awareness. Thus you discern the interdependence and mutually constructive nature of the dualistic structures of consciousness and reality (*Visuddhimagga* 679-680).

Investigating various elements, planes, and states of reality and consciousness in this way, you come to realize that apart from or beyond this mutually constructive primary polarity "there is nothing else that is a being or a person or a deity or a Brahma" (687). This is the direct experience of the not-self *(anatta)* nature of all conditioned states and events, and their interdependence. From this experience, you come to realize that since "mentality-materiality occurs as an interdependent state, each of its components giving the other consolidating support, . . . when one falls owing to death, the other falls too" (689). the eventual outcome of this investigation is the deconstruction and transcendence of the separate self, permanence, the form of the object, and the conceptual framework of meditation.

With your insight thus purified, like a modern physicist attempting to investigate the very first moment of "the big bang" so as to find out how the universe was created, you next turn your awareness to the very first moment anything is created so as to discern the very "cause and condition" of any event or conditioned existence in the universal process itself. First you directly observe the exact moment each content or event arises prior to the information-processing activity of consciousness, each moment of its duration, and the exact moment it passes out of existence. You see that each event is conditioned, discover that all events are interdependent through the twelve chain of causation or "conditioned coarising," and discern that "there is no doer apart from *kamma [karma]"* (693-701). You see that there is no structure of consciousness or object either before the creation of the dualistic structure or after its cessation, and that instant by instant the entire process of rising and passing is governed by the twelve chain.

Continuing to meditate in this way, you come to directly observe and clearly comprehend the dependent coarising of all events in the universe and their characteristics of not-self *(anatta)* and discontinuity. You also discover the law of Conservation—whatever is conditioned is conditioned to maintain itself—and the Law of Rise and Fall—"Only what is subject to fall arises; and to be arisen necessitates fall" (704-738). The *Visuddhimagga* says that upon such realizations, you become a "beginner of insight" (738).

According to the *Visuddhimagga*, upon the attainment of these insights, you again experience various paranormal states, such as brilliant light, rapture, bliss, happiness, tranquility, equanimity, and attachment to the object of contemplation. Since these phenomena are considered "imperfections of insight," you are instructed to disidentify with them. Upon doing so, you again turn to observing the "rise and fall" of whatever arises in order to be directly aware and clearly comprehend the three characteristics of all conditioned existence in the universe, free from any medium, content, conditioning, or attachment in the mind.

Once observation of the construction of reality and consciousness becomes sharp and clear, you switch awareness to the dissolution and cessation of each event. Prolonged observation of this dissolution leads to the perfection of insight into the dualistic construction of consciousness and reality, and into their impermanence, nonsubstantiality, and insufficiency. Seeing the dissolution of all constructs and experiencing nothing beyond cessation, you realize the void nature of all phenomena. According to the *Visuddhimagga*, as you constantly see the dissolution of all forms and your contemplation becomes strong, you disidentify with and transcend these constructs and false views of their origin, and let go of your attachment to and thirst for life (745-753).

Seeing the impermanence and dissolution of all forms without any possibility of holding onto anything, you are gripped by the terror of existence. Because of their emptiness, their inability to provide any meaning, and their insufficiency to be the foundation of existence, all events appear as a terror. Everything that enters your awareness now becomes oppressive. This is the experience of conditioned existence as impasse and the inability of human beings to find completeness and fulfillment within anything in ordinary consciousness and reality. All phenomena then appear to pose nothing but danger. As the *Visuddhimagga* states, "When all formations have appeared as a terror by contemplation of dissolution, this meditator sees them as utterly destitute of any core or any satisfaction and as nothing but danger" (755). It is the most palpable and naked experience of *dukkha* and is comparable to "the dark night of the soul" spoken of by St. John of the Cross and "all is pain" expressed by Bernadette Roberts. Upon this realization, you disidentify with all phenomena, conditioned existence, and states of consciousness, become nonattached, and desire deliverance from them (758-60).

With the desire for liberation thus awakened, you again turn to and observe all phenomena as impermanent, unsatisfactory, and not-self, and again come to discern voidness of all conditioned reality and consciousness. Seeing this void nature, you experience a fundamental shift. Awareness turns away from objects, contents, states, and conditioned existence; turns toward itself and its source; and becomes a pure void. Not a trace of any form, object, content, or construct remains. As you continue this insight meditation, session after session, your awareness becomes purified and transparent. Increasingly, it conforms to the preceding insights and to the primordial state of enlightenment that is to follow (760-783).

When you reach this stage, you have nothing more left to do but to maintain your awareness in this "conformity knowledge." As this knowledge matures, awareness cuts through and deconstructs the residual effects of conditioning and construct that separate it from its identity with reality. Thereupon awareness makes the most fundamental shift whereby it transcends all objects, contents, programmings, forms, conditioned states, and constructs, and arrives at the pure, unconditioned, limitless state of itself in which it is identical with reality. The *Visuddhimagga* calls this "change-of-lineage knowledge" and says that it "takes as its object the signless, no-occurrence, no-formation, cessation, nibbana, which knowledge passes out of the lineage, the category, the plane, of the ordinary man and enters the lineage, the category, the plane, of the Noble Ones" (785). It is the stage of what the *Heart Sutra* calls "form is emptiness." This experience of the objectless, formless, undifferentiated, unconditioned, beginningless, endless state that is utterly unaffected by any phenomena or conditioned existence is the first moment of enlightenment or *Nirvana*.

Stages of Liberation

The Theravada Buddhist tradition recognizes four progressive stages of *Nirvana*, culminating in *arahantship*. They represent the progressive stages in which the residual effects of conditioning, construction, duality, and ego are completely transcended and a shift of identity and center of consciousness and being to the Unconditioned State of Reality and Awareness takes place. At the first stage, called "stream enterer," which is the first moment of enlightenment, you transcend all objects and contents, forms and constructs, enter the stream of the Unconditioned, and become "permanently free from psychological structures... so that no new karma can be generated" (Brown 1: 270). As you enter the stream, the effects of past *karma*—its programmings, unconscious tendencies, habit patterns—begin to dissolve or wash away (Goleman 32).

Comparable to what the *Heart Sutra* calls "emptiness is form," at the next stage, called "once returner," ordinary events reappear. But because Awareness has been permanently freed from or disidentified with them, they in no way limit, bind, program, or control it. So there is no falling back into conditioned existence. Rather, as you see it in the matrix of the Unconditioned, you transcend the dualities between likes and dislikes, cease discriminating, and develop the eye of equality (Goleman 1: 32-33).

The causes of *dukkha* burn down to their very roots and the subconscious tendencies are uprooted at the third, "non-returner," stage. Because the sources of rebirth are thus burned out, you become permanently free from rebirth: from the return of repetitive and programmed states and behavior that had hitherto exercised control over your life, and from rebirth into the next life.

At the final stage of *arahantship,* you fully realize *Nirvana* and your ordinary consciousness is permanently transformed as your identity and center of being and consciousness permanently shift to the Unconditioned State, from which you continuously live. The very causes, reality, and consequences of *dukkha* thereby entirely cease. Nothing remains in you that could provide a foothold for *karma,* conditioned existence, separateness, ego, or suffering to germinate again (Goleman 1:34-36). Having extinguished suffering, "laid down the burden, reached your goal and destroyed the fetters of becoming, you are rightly liberated with [final] knowledge" (792). Freed from past conditioning and habits with no new conditioning sprouting again, although you live in a conditioned world, you live freely, spontaneously, and in the present. Love and compassion become the energizing principles of your actions.

Chapter 10
The Path of Zen

Zen has been described as a revolution against Indian Buddhism. Yet the real point of this revolution is not always clearly indicated. That point lies in its fidelity to the Buddha's Way. For it came to see that the marrow of Buddhism lies in nothing short of realizing what the Buddha had realized – complete enlightenment, liberation, the Unconditioned State of Buddhahood. This is comparable to saying that the core of Christianity lies not in faith, dogmas, belief in Christ's teachings, or worshipping God or Christ, but in realizing what Christ realized – the state of Awareness that declared, "I and the Father are one," not a oneness of relationship, but of identity. Like the Buddha, Zen insists on the absolute primacy of experience, since it alone leads to the transformation necessary for self-transcendence and realization of the Unconditioned. And following the Buddha, it came to see that it is not faith, doctrine, scripture, worship, ritual, or anything usually associated with religion that is essential to this goal. Only that pivotal experience that opens the doorway to the Unconditioned is necessary for the journey.

For this reason Zen appears simple and direct: No cult, code, or creed. No God to believe in and nothing to worship; no dogmas to uphold. No talk of morality, sin, or sacrifice. Only a constant call to humankind to look into the unfathomable depths of its Illimitable Nature. Everything in Zen is geared to its direct realization. To this end Zen dispenses with or pushes to the periphery anything that will not lead to Buddhahood. In this single-minded approach, it is again faithful to the Buddha who said, "I show you *dukkha* and a way to end it." Zen does not aim to be sidetracked. It keeps both eyes fixed on the absolute living center of Buddhism. All that matters is realizing the Unconditioned. Hence the pivotal place Zen gives to enlightenment. That is why it is the direct path. Almost everything is pared down to the essentials for the climb. There is no massaging of ego here. Zen does not brook any criminal negligence of ourselves. It is the warrior's way.

The essentials of the path, Yasutani Roshi tells us, are its precepts, *zazen*, and *satori*-wisdom (Kapleau 1: 125). The precepts are the teachings of the

Buddha as contained especially in the *Sutras,* the teachings of the Yogachara and Madhyamika Schools, of the Patriarchs and Zen masters. But these are secondary. The main focus is practice, not doctrine. And practice begins with *zazen* or sitting meditation. *Zazen* is aimed at *satori*-wisdom, the experience of enlightenment, with which the path of Zen really begins. And *zazen* begins with instructions on its practice.

How to Practice *Zazen*

The preliminaries of the practice, pertaining to the place, the setting, the postures, and breathing were set down by Zen master Dogen in the thirteenth century and are adhered to even today as is shown by Yasutani Roshi's repeating the same instructions (Dogen in Maezumi & Glassman 1: 13-16; Yasutani Roshi in Kapleau 1: 30-32).

Meditation I: Breath-Counting

The aim of the initial practice is the same as in other forms of concentrative meditation. As Yasutani Roshi states, the aim of sitting is to unify attention by allowing it to become one with the breath, to shift the orientation of consciousness from outward objects inward, toward itself and the breath, and to dismantle the gross perceptual construction of consciousness (Kapleau 1: 32). To bring this about, *zazen* begins with breath-counting, to be practiced as follows:

a. Assume one of the traditional, preferably the lotus, postures.
b. Breathe quietly, naturally, evenly, smoothly, and abdominally (to be explained below). As you inhale, fix attention on the breath and count the inhalation as "one." The count should be slow, deliberate, with full attention, and drawn out for the entire length of the inhalation as "wooo...nne." Similarly, as you exhale, keeping the attention entirely on the breath, count it as "twooo...ooo," for the entire duration of the exhalation. In this way count to ten and then go back to one. Keep repeating this for the entire meditation period. Do not count mechanically and lose the attention in thoughts and fantasies; do not be in a hurry to get the count over with so you can do something else. And do not try to control or interfere with your breathing process, which will tend to make it speed up. There is nowhere to go and nothing to do, other than being in the present, for which the exercise is designed. Do not hypnotize yourself with the count. Remember, the aim is not counting, repetition, programming, or

hypnotizing the mind, but waking up from our usual hypnotic trance state; freeing the attention from entrapment in mental contents, objects, and programming; concentrating and unifying attention; and allowing it to become present-centered.

c. If, as a result of counting, your breathing speeds up, you can slow it down by deliberately slowing down the count. Simply breathe very slowly, gently, evenly, with deep abdominal breathing, and count "wooo...nnne" and "t-wooo...ooo" in a prolonged, deliberate fashion.

d. In order to improve your breathing and slow it down even more, Koryu Osaka Roshi recommends that you narrow your breath by holding down the diaphragm and keeping it immobile, and exhaling and inhaling less air than you usually do but keeping their length and frequency normal. He further recommends that you breathe abdominally by keeping the thorax and the diaphragm immobile, pushing the lower abdomen out slightly as you inhale, and, as you exhale, letting it go in as the air goes out (In Maezumi and Glassman 1: 62-64; Sekida 53-59).

e. While breathing abdominally, fix the attention on the abdomen, either about three inches below the navel or on the in-and-out movement of the abdomen. Allow the attention to penetrate and become one with the inhalation, the exhalation, and the count.

These last two steps are very helpful in stopping mind-wandering and cutting down thoughts. You will notice that if you can hold down the diaphragm and keep it immobile, riveting attention directly on the sensation of the in-and-out movement of the abdomen, the mind stops wandering and fewer thoughts arise. Conversely, you will notice that when the mind wanders off, the attention is no longer focused on the abdomen, and the diaphragm is not being held down and kept immobile.

f. When you notice that the mind has wandered and you have lost the count, simply bring the attention back to focus, synchronize it with the breath and the count, and start the count over with "o-n-e" and continue as before. Do not wrestle with your mind and forcibly try to make it stop, nor allow attention to become trapped. Just let thoughts appear and disappear while attention remains focused on the breath, the count, and the abdomen. In time, as concentration deepens, the number of thoughts will decrease. As you reach *samadhi,* they will disappear altogether.

g. An alternate method of breath-counting is to count inhalations only, from one to ten, and then repeat. And a third method is to count exhalations only by mentally repeating "wooo...nnne," drawing out the exhalation, inhaling, and then exhaling and continuing to count as before.

Meditation II: Following the Breath

a. After you practice breath-counting for some time and gain some degree of concentration, you may be assigned the following breath exercise.
b. Follow each breath with complete attention, without counting it. Simply place your attention directly on the inhalation; let it penetrate and become one with it; and then, as the abdomen goes out, follow the sensation all the way to the end of the inhalation, the pressure, and the slight tension it makes against the abdominal skin. Next, pause for a moment, and as you exhale, similarly follow it to the other end of the abdomen as it goes in. Then inhale and continue as before. As you follow the breath, let your attention, the breath, and the movement become one, so that there remains no consciousness of a separation between you and the breath. There remains only this process of breathing, which has become awareness itself. When you arrive at this point of concentration, your mind will have become one-pointed. This meditation is similar to the mindfulness of breathing in insight meditation.

Meditation III: *Kinhin*—Walking Meditation

As in the Theravada Path, Zen has a form of walking meditation called *kinhin*. Walking meditation usually takes place between sessions of sitting meditation. Its aim, besides getting rid of muscle stiffness, is the same as the sitting meditation.

a. As you rise slowly from the meditation cushion and stand up, go to your chosen spot or select a suitable spot for the meditation, pause and stand still for a few moments. Then make a fist with your left hand, with the thumb inside, and place it in the center of your chest. Cover the left with the open right hand; and keep the elbows in the same plane as the hands. The position of the hands may be reversed. Keep your body—trunk, neck, and head—erect. Cast your eyes, unfocused, about six feet ahead of you.
b. Step with the right foot half its length, and then with the left foot half its length. Each step should correspond to and be coordinated with a complete inhalation and exhalation. This is the Soto Zen way of walking. The Rinzai method is to walk fast. Thich Nhat Hahn recommends that you take two or three steps to each inhalation and three or two steps to each exhalation (Kapleau 1: 129; Nishijima and Langdon 39-43; Hahn 2: 45).

c. Fix the attention on the movement of the feet and synchronize your breath with it so that the movement, the breath, and the attention become one. Directly observe the sensation of the movement and let your attention become one with it, so that only the sensation remains in your consciousness.

d. Again, to stop mind-wandering, do not look around as you walk. Keep your attention riveted on the movement, especially where one step begins and the other ends, and deliberately shift the attention from the one to the other. You may vary the speed of your walking in order to keep your attention focused on the movement. You will discover that as your concentration deepens, your walking will correspondingly slow down.

The Meaning of *Koan*

Koan meditation is the most distinctive feature of Rinzai Zen. The word *koan* literally means "public case record" and refers to a legal or public case establishing a precedent whereby other cases are authoritatively settled. In the context of Zen, it refers to a dialogue between a master and his disciple, a problem set up by the master or a question the master had asked the disciple, a situation set up by the master, or an illustrative story that sets up a standard of inquiry intended to lead the disciple to the experience of enlightenment. Koan also serves as a standard method of testing the authenticity or authoritativeness of the disciple's realization. As such, coming from the master, a koan is a direct manifestation of All-embracing Awareness or the enlightened mind. For the disciple, it is a way of opening his/her mind to its direct experience.

For the meditator, then, a koan is a gateway to the Unconditioned State of his/her true or Buddha-nature. As a gateway, it is Janus-faced, double-edged, having two functions: to bring ordinary consciousness to an impasse and stop and destructure it, and to allow awareness to swing open or shift to Reality as Such. Only when this shift occurs, can you find the real answer to a koan. Thus a koan is resolved when you directly experience your true identity as the Unconditioned. That experience is *satori* or enlightenment. As Kapleau Roshi observes, "The complete solution of a koan involves the movement of the mind from a state of ignorance (delusion) to the vibrant inner awareness of living Truth. This implies the emergence into the field of consciousness of the immaculate Bodhi-mind" (1: 65).

As you proceed with the koan meditation, this essentially gateway character of the koan must be kept in mind. It implies a state of Reality and Awareness that is the very opposite of ego and its consciousness of a separation from what is. Just as ego is the guardian of the gate of dualism, so the koan is the gateway to the transcendence of duality and the realization of absolute Oneness. Accordingly, its function is to remove from the mind all barriers that separate it from, and to open it to, Reality as Such. Thus a koan is a gate or barrier that removes all barriers to seeing Reality as Such and one through which you have to pass in order to realize it as your true nature or identity.

From the definition, it should be clear that there are different kinds of koans. According to their origin, some koans are questions put by disciples to their masters and include the latter's responses. As such responses come from the Unconditioned, their aim is to open the disciple's mind to that state. Very often this aim is immediately achieved, depending, of course, on the readiness of the disciple's mind to breaking free of the final barrier of primary duality. That is why many of these koans end with a statement such as, "And the disciple was immediately enlightened." Although the Koan *Mu* is of this type, the text does not indicate whether the disciple was enlightened by Chao Chou's answer. The following, however, is a koan in which the monk does experience enlightenment:

> A monk told Chao Chou: "I have just entered the monastery. Please teach me."
> Chao Chou asked: "Have you eaten your rice porridge?"
> The monk replied: "I have eaten."
> Chao Chou said: "Then you had better wash your bowl."
> At that moment the monk was enlightened. (Reps 96)

Detecting their minds in a state of "ripeness," that is, in a state of what Katsuki Sekida calls "absolute *samadhi*" (12) — a state which, Daniel Brown declares, conforms to the natural, primordial state (1: 260) — and that only a jolt or push was needed to make the limit-barrier of primary duality fall away, many masters asked their disciples such questions or did such things as were needed to pry their minds out of fixation in *samadhi*, transcend the last barrier, and arrive at the experience of *satori*. Many koans are of this sort, including "The Flying Geese Koan." Another koan reads:

> One night Te Shan was attending master Lung Tan, who said, "It is now late. Why don't you go back to your room and retire?" Te Shan then said good night to his master, and went out. But immediately he returned, saying: "It is very dark outside." Lung Tan lit a candle and handed it to Te Shan, then suddenly blew it out. At once Te Shan was awakened. (Chang 1: 27)

Some koans are questions devised or situations set up by masters to test the depth and genuineness of their disciples' understanding and realization. Such a koan is the following:

> Chu, also called Kokushi, the emperor's teacher, called to his attendant, "Oshin!"
> Oshin answered, "Yes!"
> To test his pupil, Chu repeated, "Oshin!" Oshin replied, "Yes!"
> Chu called out again, "Oshin!"
> Oshin answered, "Yes!"
> Chu said, "I have been thinking that I am independent, but now I realize that you, too, are an independent fellow". (Eido Roshi 139)

Other koans are statements or formulas in which the masters expressed a teaching, the direct experience of which would lead their disciples to the Unconditioned. In this category also are koans in the form of questions posed by masters to bring their disciples to Self-realization without indicating to us that they had, in fact, done so. The following two koans are of this type:

> Shuzan held out his short staff and said, "If you call this a short staff, you oppose its reality. If you do not call it a short staff, you ignore the fact. Now what do you wish to call this?" (Reps 124)

> Goso said, "When a buffalo goes out of his enclosure to the edge of the abyss, his horns, head, and hoofs all pass through, but why can't the tail also pass?" (Reps 119)

Some koans are anecdotes from the lives of the masters in which their actions or attitudes illustrate the functioning of All-embracing Awareness. The following koan illustrates this:

> One day, in the monastery of Nan Chuan, the monks of the East and the West wings had a dispute over the possession of a cat. They came to master Nan Chuan for arbitration. Holding a knife in one hand and the cat in the other, Nan Chuan declared, "If any of you can say the right thing, this cat will be saved; otherwise it will be cut to two pieces." None of the monks could say anything. Nan Chuan then cut the cat in two. In the evening, when Chao Chou returned to the monastery, Nan Chuan asked him what he would have said had he been there at the time. Thereupon Chao Chou took off his straw sandals, put

them upon his head and walked out. Then Nan Chuan exclaimed, "Oh, if you had only been here, the cat would have been saved!" (Chang 1: 24)

There are, of course, other kinds of koans illustrating other aspects of the teachings. It is not my intention here to classify koans or explain their meaning. Although it is admirable to try to analyze them, as some have attempted, you must always remember that koans are not directed to the rational mind for analysis and that whatever intellectual understanding you may gain is useless for its main purpose, which is a direct experience of the truth they embody. Making some sense out of a koan is not, of course, difficult. Take, for instance, Fu Ta Shih's famous stanza:

Empty-handed I go, but a spade is in my hands;
I walk on my feet, yet I am riding on the back of a bull;
When I pass over the bridge,
Lo, the bridge, but not the water, flows. (Chang 1: 16)

Although this koan, as do most, appears paradoxical and senseless, it abounds with allusions to various Buddhist teachings, which make it comprehensible. Thus, "empty-handed" refers to the doctrine of emptiness *(Sunyata);* and the entire first line refers to Shih's seeing into the nature of reality as void of programming and construct, thought and object. This seeing is the key to understanding the entire koan. It implies that Shih is speaking of a direct experience of the Unconditioned State in which (since it is completely void of any form or construct, differentiation or condition) being "empty-handed" is not opposed to and in fact is no other than "having a spade in my hand." Since in this state things are not bound by the ordinary, two-valued logic, you can have a spade in your hand, or be under any condition, without being conditioned or restricted by it and, for that very reason, without being cut off from anything. Therefore, being "empty-handed" and having "a spade in your hand," and "walking on your feet" and at the same time "riding on the back of a bull" can both be affirmed without contradicting yourself because this emptiness is the fullness in which their duality is resolved in its transcending Unity. In fact, it is the very condition for the possibility of anything. And riding on the bull, which is a symbol of All-embracing Awareness and signifies your unity with it, you are for the first time walking on your two feet in the freedom of the Absolute.

That this is no ordinary way of seeing is indicated by the expression "riding on the back of a bull." It refers to the sixth of the Ten Ox-herding Stages in which the struggle between All-embracing Awareness and ordinary consciousness is over. The two now exist in interpenetration. The former having integrated the latter into itself, they now flow into each other without obstruction; and a unity and harmony reigns. This implies that Shih is beginning to live effortlessly from the former state, which is becoming the new center of his being and consciousness. In this state he no longer walks with another's feet, sees with another's eyes, or lives with borrowed meaning. He directly experiences ultimate truth, which has become his own "feet" or way of life and being.

Similarly, "passing over the bridge" alludes to Buddha's sermon on crossing over from, or transcending, conditioned existence *(samsara)* to the Unconditioned State *(Nirvana)*. Since the "bridge" is the Path, when you walk over and become one with it, all solidifications in your life due to programmings and constructs dissolve and disappear. You are then no longer stuck on anything. Void of fixation and calcification, life takes on the fluidity of the ever-changing process and primary order of reality itself. Having become one with it, your life becomes as fluid as the Path, the bridge to the Unconditioned. The river of desire now runs dry; the stream of thought and inner dialogue have become silent and still; and the water of life no longer becomes muddied or disturbed. The currents of ego's desires no longer run your life. The struggle between ordinary consciousness and All-embracing Awareness being over and the center having shifted, the bridge and the river have become one, flowing into life everlasting.

Thus, although you can give a reasonable explanation to an apparently nonsensical affair, a koan is not directed to the rational mind so that you can explain or translate it in terms of ordinary categories and reality-construct, and thus confirm yourself and your world. On the contrary, a koan puts up a barrier to ordinary consciousness so as to bring to a stop all its operations and to enable you to see its limitations and the futility of your attempts to make life meaningful by making the ego a separate center of being and consciousness. You see the impasse of life in its inability to solve the koan, thereby solving the paradox of existence and contradiction that is the ego. Upon palpably seeing all this, you are able to give up not only translation, but the ego itself and leap into the state beyond all reason and explanation, categories and constructs — a state at which all reasons and explanations aim but which none can ever reach, because this state can only be directly experienced. That is why an intellectual understanding of a koan is useless, since that would only create another barrier, if you deluded yourself into thinking that such explanations constituted attainment of the truth. To unlock the secret of the koan, therefore, you have to proceed on an entirely different track — the track of the Ox — the koan meditation.

Koan Meditation: Preliminary Steps

In order for the koan to perform its Janus-faced function of closing off or stilling and deconstructing ordinary consciousness and reality, and opening awareness to the Unconditioned, Zen speaks of three conditions necessary in the meditator: great faith, great doubt, and great determination to dispel the doubt (Kapleau 1: 58-59).

By "great faith" Zen does not mean some kind of dogmatic belief or taking the word of another as a substitute for your own experience. Rather, it is the same fourfold faith discussed in *Song of the Skylark I*: an unshakable faith in the Unconditioned State as your true nature and the goal of your life; faith in your ability to realize it and a firm resolution to do so; faith in the Path, more specifically, in the koan as the way to that realization; and faith in the teacher and his ability to help you realize it.

By "great doubt" Zen means the doubt generated by the palpable experience of a contradiction between your present world and identity, and your belief in the Buddha-nature as the true nature and identity of all things, and consequently your own. This experience gives rise to a doubt about the sufficiency of your present world and identity and their ability to resolve the problem of existence. The greater the faith in the Buddha-nature and the experience of the contradiction, the greater is the doubt that your actual condition represents your true nature. The more the Unconditioned appears real, the less real conditioned existence will become, and the greater the question in your mind as to how the former can be revealed in any conditioned state, especially your own.

Thus the core of the great doubt is nothing other than a total questioning, as the Buddha had done, not only of your own, but the very foundation of, conditioned existence, so that in questioning your own, all existence stands questioned. The koan must bring you to the point of seeing your whole life, all conditioned existence, as empty, void, insufficient, and a problem unto itself – as the only problem, which is that of being conditioned – which it cannot itself resolve. It must bring you to see that the human condition, your own life, has no foundation in reality. So long as you remain within its boundary, no revelation of the Unconditioned is possible. Seeing all conditioned existence as an impasse, in questioning your own, all existence as embodied in your life will become the great doubt. Unless this doubt grips you totally on both conscious and unconscious levels, there will be no resolution that transcends conditioned existence altogether, and so no enlightenment will occur.

To raise this universal doubt, the first task of the koan is to bring you to a palpable experience of *dukkha,* which is what the Buddha had experienced and expressed as the First Noble Truth. If you have not yet fully awakened to it, the koan meditation will help you do so. When it grips your whole being, body and mind, it will raise to the conscious level the entire problem of existence that had been present all along but had not been experienced in its actual, naked state in all its depth, breadth, clarity, and intensity.

As the koan seeps into the unconscious and raises the problem of existence to the conscious level, you will become aware of how your life-force craves to be, but is incapable of being, complete. You will also see how your self becomes a contradiction in its very effort to become real in separation from the Real, thereby striving to become the very thing from which it is separated. As Richard DeMartino observes, "The initial function of the koan is to get ego to arouse, crystallize, and become the living contradiction which it actually is" (in Fromm 164). The koan will inevitably lead you to the experience of the human paradox: ego's inability to realize what it most deeply desires, namely, to become Real or sufficient unto itself, in its present consciousness and by identifying with things within its world, created in separation from Reality.

Thus the koan brings the ego face to face with itself and makes it see the utter futility of its striving to resolve the contradiction and the paradox as long as it remains locked within the limits of its consciousness and world, since those limits constitute the core problem. As DeMartino states, "The inability of the koan to be resolved as an object by the ego as the subject is, in fact, precisely the inability of the ego as ego in its subject-object bifurcation to resolve the existential contradiction which is that bifurcation" (In Fromm et al. 159).

Concretely, ego's experience of the inability to find an answer to the koan by thinking or resorting to any operation of the dualistic mind is an expression of its inability to resolve the problem of existence. In Kantian terms, in the struggle to find an answer, the koan drives "pure reason" to the very limits of all constructs and makes it see that the impossibility of realizing the truth of the koan so long as it remains within its own or in any other construction is an expression of ordinary life as a quandary, conditioned existence as an impasse, and ordinary consciousness as a dead end state. Upon realizing this truth, your mind enters into a state of fermentation and crisis, and becomes the "great doubt" or a critical "doubt-mass."

With his insistence that you provide him with an answer, and his refusal to accept any that the rational mind conjures up, the master acts to drive your mind to the dead end state and become a doubt-mass. Thus master Han Shan urges, "Use all your attention and strength patiently to push your mind to the very dead end [of consciousness]; just push it on and on" (Chang 1: 113). The master presses you relentlessly to pursue the question and find an answer by, on the one hand, refusing to accept your answers (that is, in Ken Wilber's words, frustrating your attempt to translate the koan in rational explanatory terms into your construction of reality); and, on the other, by "encouraging [you] to undergo the new transformation" (3: 94-95), that is, by deconstructing and transcending your reality and consciousness. Thus, master Kao-Feng Yuanmiao urges, "Make the inquiry with all the strength that lies in your personality, giving yourself no time to relax in this effort...try to bring about a state of perfect identification by pressing your spirit of inquiry forward, steadily and uninterruptedly...When your search comes to this stage, the time has come for your mental powers to burst out" (D.T. Suzuki 4: Series II, 103-104). To achieve this, he urges you to take the koan down to the *hara*, that is, to the unconscious level, and he does not give you a respite until you reach the limits of the dualistic mind and experience the "great doubt," impasse, and crisis.

Until that happens, there is no breaking through the limits of constructs and conditioned existence. The mind must first be awakened to, then be totally gripped by, the doubt-mass, become the contradiction by identifying with the koan, and reach the critical, explosive stage if the koan is to explode and resolve the contradiction in the deconstruction and transcendence of all constructs and experience *satori*.

That is why Zen masters have insisted on a correlation between the doubt and the experience of enlightenment: no doubt, no enlightenment; great doubt, great enlightenment. If your doubt is as great as the one which gripped the Buddha and drove him from home to find its resolution, your enlightenment will also be as great as his. That is why the doubt has to be thorough, encompassing the entire conditioned existence, penetrating to the core of ego's contradiction and the limit of the human paradox, becoming a critical mass. Otherwise there will be no uprooting of ego, no resolution of the contradiction and the paradox, no breaking through the impasse, no transcendence of reason and duality in the explosive experience of limitlessness. Only when the ego is uprooted can there be an answer to the question of existence or a revelation of the truth of the koan.

To achieve this breakthrough, you must have a strong determination, such as the one Buddha had, to resolve the doubt. This alone can sustain you through the crisis and give you the energy to press forward through the impasse and arrive at the resolution in the experience of the Buddha-nature.

The master's intense questioning and insistence on your coming up with an answer to the koan are also designed to keep the inquiry properly directed and to make you summon every ounce of energy and determination to resolve it. And the master's own example also encourages you to this end. As Kapleau Roshi observes, "Formal Zen training is basically nothing more than the master's effort to stimulate this intense questioning, this doubt-mass, when it does not arise spontaneously. The indispensable pre-conditions of such an inquiry, however, are the unwavering conviction that one can dissolve the doubt-mass, and the grim determination to do so" (2: 50). Such determination will sustain you through to the end.

Now the question is: How does the koan meditation proceed? How do you raise and resolve the doubt-mass?

Koan Meditation: Meditation on the Koan *Mu*

Once you develop some concentration by counting and following the breath, or when the master perceives you to be ready, he assigns a koan and instructs you on how to meditate. According to D.T. Suzuki, the following are among the koans commonly assigned a beginner:

A monk asked Chao Chou (Joshu, in Japanese), "Does a dog have the Buddha-nature?" Chao Chou replied, *"Wu!"* (*"Mu!"* in Japanese).

A monk asked Tung-shan, "Who is the Buddha?" He replied, "Three chin of flax."

When Ming the monk overtook the fugitive Hui-neng and wanted him to disclose the secret of Zen, Hui-neng said, "Not thinking of good, not thinking of no-good, right at this very moment, what is your original face before your parents were born?"

Chao Chou asked Nan Chuan, "What is the Tao?" Nan Chuan replied, "Your everyday mind is the Tao." Chao Chou asked, "How do you approach it?" Nan Chuan replied, "If you try to approach it, you will surely miss it."

A monk asked, "All things return to the One, to what does the One return?" Chao Chou answered, "When I was in the district of Ching, I had a robe made that weighed seven chin."

A monk asked Chao Chou, "What is the meaning of the First Patriarch's coming to China?" Chao Chou replied, "The cypress tree in the garden." (4: Series II, 68-69)

Of these and other koans that are assigned a beginner, the favorite with many Zen masters is the first, which is commonly called the Koan *Mu*. So, I shall take it to illustrate how the beginner is instructed to meditate and raise and resolve the doubt-mass, as follows:

a. Assume one of the traditional postures, preferably the lotus posture. Observe all the preliminary procedures and breathe as described before. Breathe abdominally.

b. Fix your attention in the abdominal center, and, instead of counting or following the breath, concentrate on the koan. To help you do this, some Zen masters recommend that you reduce a koan to a word or phrase and mentally repeat it like a mantra. In your case, this means reduce the entire koan to *Mu*.

c. Focus your total attention on *Mu* and mentally repeat it in a slow, deliberate, prolonged, and yet natural manner, coordinating and unifying it with your breath: *"Mu-u-u...u-u-u."* You may repeat it as you inhale and exhale, as you inhale only, or only as you exhale, whichever you find most suitable for concentration. Bring the attention, *Mu,* and the breath into a focus at the abdominal center, and proceed with the repetition. Breathe abdominally. Hold the attention on *Mu* and the breath, and let it slowly sink into and become one with both, and expand and contract with the abdomen as you inhale and exhale.

To help concentrate better, in the beginning you may visualize *Mu* as a ball of white light slowly descending to the abdominal center and resting there, making your abdomen glow and becoming diaphanous in its light. As you inhale, see it as expanding with your abdomen and filling the universe; and as you exhale, let it contract into nothingness.

Koryu Osaka Roshi recommends that you harmonize *Mu* with your breath by concentrating and holding your attention in your lower abdomen as you inhale and exhale (in Maezumi and Glassman 1: 88).

d. An alternate method of breathing is what Sekida calls "The Bamboo Method": As you exhale, mentally repeat *Mu* either as a series of separate syllables, such as, *"Mu, Mu,...Mu,"* or in a prolonged, wavelike, intermittent exhalations, such as, *"Mu-u-u...Mu-u-u."* In either case, exhale completely in a wavelike, intermittent manner, with force, determination, and persistence, as if you were pushing at a closed door that will not open. Either continuously or with repeated stress, so as to break up a long exhalation, push from your abdomen through a series of pauses and repeat *Mu*. Keeping the thorax as still as possible, tense the respiratory muscles and breathe only with the rhythm of *Mu* (71).

e. Do not repeat *Mu* mechanically, but with a fully concentrated mind, press on and try to penetrate and become one with *Mu*.

At first you will find that you are getting nowhere, that you are, as Yasutani Roshi puts it, like a mosquito attacking an iron bowl. But you will succeed if, as D.T. Suzuki states, you continue to repeat it until the mind is thoroughly saturated with *Mu* and no room is left for any other thought, that is, until it displaces all other thoughts and mental contents, and enters into and becomes the stream of consciousness on all levels. This initial aim of the meditation is described as taking the koan down to and thinking with the abdomen. This is why Zen masters repeatedly emphasize that you must let *Mu* sink into the abdomen which, as Suzuki points out, means taking it down to the unconscious and not letting it remain merely on the conscious level (in Fromm et al. 46, 55). Otherwise, you will not be able to go to the very root of dualism deep in the unconscious, in the "store-house of consciousness," to penetrate and deconstruct it, and break through the final barrier that stands in the way of reaching the transconscious state. As Yasutani Roshi states, "The roots of ego-forming ideas are deep in the unconscious mind, out of reach of ordinary consciousness...Your single-minded concentration on *Mu* will gradually dispel this I-concept from your consciousness. With its complete banishment you suddenly experience Oneness" (Kapleau 1: 109, 137).

f. Once you take it down to the unconscious level, the next step is to become one with *Mu* by letting it occupy, at all times, your whole mind, conscious and unconscious. This is crucial to attaining *samadhi*, without which there is no breakthrough to *satori*. As Osaka Roshi observes, "The whole essence of work on this koan can be summed up like this: you totally become *mu* yourself, from morning to night. Even in dreams, even in sleep you are with *mu* and *mu* becomes yourself" (in Maezumi and Glassman 1: 87).

There are two ways to reach this stage. One is the above, mantra-like approach, which leads to absolute *samadhi*. The other is similar to Ramana Maharshi's method of Self-inquiry or *Jnana Yoga* and Theravada insight Meditation. It is the method of intense and relentless questioning to raise the doubt-mass, drive ordinary consciousness to an impasse, and, in positive *samadhi*, deconstruct it, empty itself out, make it shift toward itself and become void, and break out through it and experience *satori*.

g. The method of questioning should begin after you are able to concentrate and hold *Mu* in your attention. As you continue to mentally repeat *Mu*, keep the question, "What is *Mu?*" continuously in your mind. Do not look for a meaning or rational explanation of *Mu*, which is beyond meaning since it is beyond anything our dualistic mind can conceive or grasp. For *Mu* is the Buddha-nature or Ultimate Reality, which can never be reached by dualistic thinking or the programmed mind or within any construct. So the aim of questioning is to make the question penetrate and occupy your entire consciousness, displacing everything else and becoming its total content as well as a questioning of conditioned existence. You are to achieve this by holding the question continuously in the center of your awareness through fixing all your attention on it, not only in formal meditation, but at all times and in whatever you do until it grips, totally occupies, and absorbs your mind; and your whole self becomes one mass of questioning. Thus your mind, self, and all existence will become the total question.

As stated before, the first aim of the Zen master's relentless questioning is to push your mind to becoming this doubt-mass. Thus Yasutani Roshi instructs: "Let all of you become one mass of doubt and questioning. Concentrate on and penetrate fully into *Mu*. To penetrate into *Mu* means to achieve absolute unity with it. How can you achieve this unity? By holding to *Mu* tenaciously day and night" (Kapleau 1: 79). By "holding," of course, he means keeping *Mu* at the center of your attention and pushing everything else out into the periphery so that, empty of everything but *Mu*, all dimensions of your mind become filled and one with it. Similarly, directing you to hold the question at the center of your attention, master Ku-yin Ching-chin admonishes:

> Apply yourself wholeheartedly to the task of holding on to your koan, never letting it go off the center of your consciousness, whether you are sitting or lying, walking or standing still. Never mind in what condition you are placed, whether pleasing or displeasing, but try all the time to keep the koan in mind, and reflect within yourself who it is that is pursuing the koan so untiringly and asking you this question so unremittingly. (D.T. Suzuki 4: Series II, 102)

Clearly, this "who" is the same "who" that forms the core of Ramana Maharshi's Self-inquiry and it has the same intent of reaching the source beyond the question.

Once the doubt-mass arises, the form of the koan and the question may change. As Yasutani Roshi points out, "What is *Mu?*" becomes simply *"Mu."* And that is sufficient to continue the inquiry. This shortened form, containing the essential point of the question, is called *"Hua Tou"* (Chang 1: 76-77). This distilled form of the inquiry is similar to Patanjali's "seed meditation." Beyond the gross perceptual form, this distillation reduces the koan to a subtle "seed" or synthesis containing information from several perceptual modalities. Consequently it is capable, not merely of engaging attention on several levels, but also of unifying and shifting it inward. It is thus able to deconstruct the outer, perceptual form and arrive at the subtle level, where it becomes unified with the subtle form of the koan.

Once your whole self becomes the question through identification with the koan, the next step, as already discussed, is to drive your mind to the very limit of dualistic constructs and conditioned existence without letting it revert to its usual way of functioning in search of an answer. Your mind will be incapable of functioning as usual in any case, thus arriving at an impasse. In persistently pressing you with his unrelenting demand that you show him what *Mu* is, the master intends to bring you to just this state. As Yasutani Roshi observes, "In the intense asking, 'What is *Mu?*' you bring the reasoning mind to an impasse, void of every thought, even as you gradually destroy the tenacious roots of I and not-I in the unconscious mind" (Kapleau 1: 171).

When kept in this state for prolonged periods without letting it backslide or revert to the old translation, pressed to the limit and yet incapable of providing an answer, ordinary consciousness eventually becomes emptied of all programming, thought, and content. It is destructured, and its orientation shifts wholly to *Mu*. So master Bassui instructs you to question yourself with complete absorption "until the time comes when your mind, unable to answer, exhausts itself, with its thinking mind totally checked. It will reach a cul-de-sac. The dualism of body and mind, self and other will disappear, and your long-held concepts and ideas will perish...Only if you exhaust the questioning will the question burst" (Kapleau 1: 180).

As the mind becomes completely emptied of all contents and becomes one with *Mu* and any sense of a separation disappears, it becomes completely silent and still. The object world collapses or is destructured and transcended as awareness shifts away from content toward itself and its source – pure Awareness. Deprived of the object-pole and pressed by the master to push ahead with the inquiry, unable to maintain itself as the subject-pole, the self also collapses.

In this state the mind, subjectless and objectless, save for *Mu*, enters into "seedless" or absolute *samadhi* and becomes identified with it as the sole content. This is the stage of universal consciousness, in which *Mu* becomes the whole universe and your identity. As D.T. Suzuki points out, in this state you as an individual vanish from the field of consciousness, which is now completely occupied by *Mu*. Any sense of separation between yourself and it disappears, so that it is *Mu* that does everything – eating, talking, reading, thinking, feeling, working, playing, etc. – in and as you. Thus the whole universe becomes nothing but *Mu*. As Yasutani Roshi states, "Absolute unity with *Mu*, unthinking absorption in *Mu* – this is ripeness. Upon your attainment to this stage of purity, both inside and outside naturally fuse...When you fully absorb yourself in *Mu*, the external and internal merge into a single unity" (Kapleau 1: 80).

This is the stage prior to the final breakthrough to *satori*. The only obstacle now remaining is the limit-barrier of primary duality, or absorption in the form of the koan. This limit-barrier prevents the mind from realizing its identity as All-embracing Awareness, identical with Buddha-nature. This state of mind, called "ripeness," is also described as "being immured in a crystal palace" and "the great fixation" (Kapleau 1: 91). Thus Hakuin states:

> When you arrive at this great fixation, you feel as if you are in an empty space open on all sides, extending boundlessly. There is a feeling of extraordinary transparency, as if you were in a great crystal basin, or shut up in an immense mass of solid ice. You feel as if you are devoid of all sense, forgetful of all else, not knowing whether living or dead. Not a thought or emotion is stirred in the mind, which is now entirely and exclusively occupied with the koan itself. (Suzuki 4: Series II, 111-112)

This is a most critical stage in which you are suspended between two worlds — one not yet completely left behind, the other not yet completely opened up. So Bassui admonishes:

> You have now reached a decisive point where you have been emptied of everything else and feel a deep void, without any awareness of anything inner and outer — everything, including your body, having become shining, transparent, and clear like the blue sky on a bright day. (Suzuki 4: Series II, 112)

When the master sees you in this condition (on the verge of a breakthrough), which corresponds to "form is emptiness" of the *Heart Sutra,* he directs all his efforts toward shocking your mind out of the fixation and coming to experience *satori*. Concretely, he urges you not to separate yourself from the koan but, like the silkworm, to work from within in order to cut through the form and arrive at the formless state of *Sunyata*. To bring about such a breakthrough, he may, as does Yasutani Roshi, shoot rapid-fire questions at you, demanding a spontaneous, instantaneous answer: "Show me *Mu*. How old is *Mu?* How do you see *Mu?* Where do you see *Mu?* What is the sound of *Mu?* How much does *Mu* weigh" (Kapleau 1: 227). He may urge you, as does master Hsu Yun, "to penetrate through the barrier and arrive at the state before any thought arises...until you break through it, at which point your dualistic mind will come to an end" (Chang 1: 160). Like Hakuin, he may admonish you to "go resolutely ahead with the koan and eventually arrive at a point when all of a sudden you will experience something akin to an explosion, as if an ice basin were shattered to pieces, or as if a tower of jade had crumbled, and the event will be accompanied with a feeling of immense joy such as you had never before experienced in your life" (Suzuki 4: Series II, 103). Similarly, he may say, as does Bassui:

> If you push forward with the last ounce of strength at the very point where the path of your thinking has been blocked, and then, completely stymied, leap with hands high in the air into the tremendous abyss of fire confronting you — into the ever-burning flame of your own primordial nature — all ego-consciousness, all delusive feelings and thoughts and perceptions will perish with your ego-root and the true source of your Self-nature will appear. (Kapleau 1: 177)

At this stage of absolute *samadhi*, a seemingly insignificant event or action may push you over the edge, bring you out of the state of absorption in *Mu*, break up the dualistic barrier, and break through to the Unconditioned. Thus, a monk attained enlightenment when he heard the sound of a heap of firewood tumbling down; the barrier or mental fixation on *samadhi* came tumbling down likewise. Another experienced the breakthrough from the sound of a pebble striking a bamboo. The sudden sound woke him up from the dream-like absorption of *samadhi* and brought him to a direct experience of Reality as Such. Seeing peach blossoms in full bloom opened the mind of one meditator; while another, hearing the word *unborn*, experienced the uncreated state of the Buddha-nature (Sekida 100-104). In all such cases, the final barrier separating their minds from Reality fell away and they came to a direct experience of their identity.

A second way this breakthrough can occur is through some strategically placed word, action, or gesture of the master. As already explained, many koans are derived from, and therefore depict precisely, this process of enlightenment. This is how the seemingly bizarre actions of many Zen masters, such as Ma-tsu's twisting the nose of Pai-chang and kicking another in the chest, are to be understood. When Ryutan gave Tokusan a lighted candle to find his way in the dark, and, just as the latter received it, blew it out, this sudden action brought about the experience of the extinction of ego and the leap into *Nirvana*.

Thus, when the doubt-block matures in the state of absolute *samadhi*, absorption in the form of the koan (which assumes the universal, archetypal form — the primary construction that creates duality) is broken up, ushered by the most profound shift in awareness, which *The Lankavatara Sutra* calls "the turning-about in the deepest seat of consciousness." In this pivotal shift awareness finally breaks free and transcends all forms, constructs, programming, contents, and objects. This transcendence of duality brings about a dissolution of the contradiction and a solution of the koan in the revelation of the Formless,

Unconditioned Reality of the Buddha-nature, signified by *Mu*, as your true nature and that of all that is.

While the above gives you an indication of how to meditate on a koan and arrive at the experience of enlightenment, there is another form of meditation practiced especially, but not exclusively, by the Soto Zen sect, which leads to absolute *samadhi*, and eventually to enlightenment. It is called *shikan-taza*, which means "just sitting," pure sitting, which itself is intended to be an expression of pure, Unconditioned Being. It goes as follows:

Shikan-Taza Meditation

a. Posture and other preliminaries are the same as in previous exercises.
b. Follow the breath for a few minutes.
c. Without focusing your attention on anything, just sit. Empty your mind of all thoughts, ideas, concepts, and other contents. Push them to the periphery of consciousness and try to hold the attention in the state or space of awareness before mental contents arise or come between them. You have nothing to focus attention on except itself. "Try to cut off the root of consciousness from the beginning," Dogen instructs (in Maezumi and Glassman 1: 14). This means that you are to cut off the root of thought and the stream of consciousness by holding attention at the point where there is no thought, and, if a thought arises, shifting the attention so that it remains in the empty space void of thought. Thus Yasutani Roshi instructs: "Casting all sorts of self-consciousness away and making yourself unconditioned as if a sheet of plain white paper, sit; just firmly sit. Sit with no conditioning, believing in the fact that such sitting itself is nothing but the actualization of Buddhahood" (in Maezumi and Glassman 1: 70).
d. Keeping your attention focused directly on itself and holding itself in the interval between thoughts, maintain bare, pure alertness of mind such that when thoughts arise, they slide off it just as an egg slides off a diamond. The mind must be unhurried, composed, and in a state of absolute stillness or concentrated awareness, without being tense or slack.
e. Sitting in this way, you will gradually enter into absolute *samadhi* which, when it ripens by itself, will fall into enlightenment. Since it is difficult to maintain such concentration for long, you are instructed to meditate for no longer than half an hour, do *kinhin,* and then resume sitting.

Being pure not-doing *(wu-wei)*, *shikan-taza* is difficult. As Suzuki Roshi observes, "To work on something is not difficult, since that is what we are always doing. But not to work on anything is difficult." And in *shikan-taza,* not only do you not work on anything, but you stop absolutely everything and arrive at pure stillness.

Because of its nature, progress in *shikan-taza* is slow. A gradual ripening of the mind takes place, whereas in koan meditation enlightenment is attained more quickly. Suzuki Roshi himself admits, "Even though you try very hard, the progress you make is always little by little" (46). The possibility of drowsiness in meditation is greater. And even when you reach *samadhi,* it may be very difficult to break through to *satori.* It may take years.

Either way, however, enlightenment is a momentary experience. It is not the goal but the beginning of the Path. It is only the third of the Ten Ox-herding Stages. To arrive at the goal of Buddhahood, there must be a progressive deepening of your realization. You must go through seven deepening stages until you are permanently established in the Unconditioned State. Thereupon you become a Buddha, an embodiment of the Supreme Way, of Absolute, Eternal Life. Few reach this peak. In practice, when your realization matures and your master judges you ready, you bid him farewell, shouldering the task of propagating the Buddha's teachings and caring for all beings. You are now a roshi.

Chapter 11
The Vajrayana Path: Tibetan Tantras

While Zen is the very direct path in which, as Blofeld observes, all props and climbing gears are dispensed with, the Tantric Buddhism of Tibet, or the Vajrayana Path, uses all kinds of colorful aids—rites, rituals, symbols, gods, goddesses—to help the climber attain the same goal. Taking a very elaborate and panoramic view, it approaches the goal in stages. Purporting to use everything as skillful means (things other religions would not even dream of using in rituals or worship services), such as human skin to make drums, a human skull as a drinking cup, ritual intercourse, wearing a rosary made of 108 pieces (representing the number of human defilements) of human skull, and the like, it aims to transcend all dualities, distinctions and limitations, forms and constructs, and to realize the ultimate goal of Buddhahood.

For these and other reasons, the Vajrayana or Diamond Vehicle is a vast and complex subject, intending as it does to enable the adept to realize his/her *vajra* or diamond-like, clear, effulgent, and indestructible nature. Even with texts now available in English (thanks to the Dalai Lama), it will not be possible to do justice to the Vajrayana within the scope of the present study. A few etchings will have to suffice.

Preliminaries of the Practice

In general, Tantric paths, be they Hindu, Buddhist, or Chinese (Taoist), hold viewpoints and practices in common. So it is not surprising that, leaving aside the question of dependence, their goals are the same—to awaken the meditator's latent powers, psychic energies or states of consciousness that lie deeply buried in the unconscious; eliminate from the body and mind everything that obstructs the full blossoming and development of these powers and states, and thus enable him/her to attain ever higher unities and expansion of consciousness and being. The ultimate goal is to transcend archetypal duality or polarity of energy-awareness, and arrive at the Unconditioned State. For the Hindu tantrist, this Unconditioned is *Brahman;* for the Buddhist, it is the state opened in *Sunyata* and realized in *Nirvana;* and for the Taoist, it is Tao.

Beyond this unity of aims, there is also some similarity of methods. Like Hindu Tantra discussed earlier, Tibetan Buddhism makes extensive use of *mudras, mantras, yantras, mandalas,* visualization, and various rites and rituals, such as the one with the "Five M's": meat, fish, wine, parched grains, and sexual union. Some of these elements, however, are used more extensively or in a different order and combination in Vajrayana than in Hindu Tantra.

There are, of course, differences of conception and method between the two. For Vajrayana, the differences have to do not only with its Buddhist, particularly Mahayana, setting, especially with its teachings on *Sunyata* (Madhyamika) and Mind (Yogachara), but also with four types of tantras and their methods. Native Tibetan elements, such as wrathful and peaceful deities, *Jinas* or five kinds of energy, *Dakinis* (symbolic form of wisdom-means), *Yidams* (chosen deity), angels and demons, are transformed, to be sure, from their original significance and context of shamanism and Bon religion into psychological and spiritual forces pertaining to the transpersonal realms and archetypal forms in the individual and the universe.

Moreover, while Hindu Tantra symbolizes wisdom or the universal consciousness principle as a male *(Shiva)* and receptive, and the cosmic energy principle as a female *(Shakti)* and active, Vajrayana reverses the order. However, this is not always adhered to. Some *mandalas* depict the five wisdom aspects of the consciousness principle in forms of meditative Buddhas and the energy principle in forms of five corresponding female consorts *(Jinas),* interacting with their wisdom partners. Again, while the *sadhana* or meditation of the Five M's proceeds, in general, along the same line as the Hindu Tantra, there are differences of detail. Thus, while in the climactic act of sexual union, some Hindu tantric texts instruct the tantrist, in Taoist fashion, to release his sperm, and, mixing it with the female's fluid, to draw it back. The Vajrayanist stops the semen, together with the breath and thought, for the purpose of stopping and transcending ordinary consciousness. Another instance of difference is the *mandala* which, in Vajrayana, reflects Buddhist teachings.

Turning to Tibetan Buddhism itself, we notice that its various elements are designed to engage simultaneously three aspects of an individual, called "the three doors of personality": body, speech, and mind. The intent is to awaken, transform, raise or expand, and integrate the various energies and states of consciousness into higher unities until the meditator arrives at the final identity.

The basis for this aim is Vajrayana's perception that each form is a *mandala* that mirrors the universe. As a *mandala* of energy, the body is no other than the universal energy. Because the individual is an embodiment of the universe, in awakening and realizing these states within yourself, you attain your identity with the universal principle and become the universe itself. In its embodied form, the universal energy circulates in the body through fifty channels which correspond, as in Hindu Tantra, to the fifty letters of the Sanskrit alphabet.

Since the body is the *mandala* of the universal energy, while the letters form the *mandala* of the universal sound vibrations, in linking fifty channels of energy with fifty letters, not only does the *mandala* of the body join with the *mandala* of speech, but a corresponding unity is formed with the universe. Herein is an implicit recognition that the universe, viewed as a field of energy, is formed by none other than sound vibrations or waves. As Trungpa observes, the *mandala* of speech views the world as a world of syllables and letters which embody, and, consequently, can awaken and enable the meditator to realize oneness with the world made up of sound vibrations (5: 71-75).

As the *mandala* of mind, the individual mind is a manifestation of All-embracing Awareness. So, when opened to the universal energy and primal sound vibrations, each mind can suddenly experience itself to be the universal Mind.

To awaken in the meditator the primal energy-awareness locked in the body-*mandala*, prostrations, offerings, *mudras* or gestures, postures, and methods of breathing are used. A prostration, considered a preliminary practice, is to be performed, in some sects, before you are initiated into the yogas proper. Prostrations are performed — a hundred thousand of them — by keeping the feet together, joining the palms and raising them over the head and bringing them down to the lips and chest; and then bending down and placing the hands, knees, elbows, and head on the ground, and extending the arms and legs to their maximum length. While doing this, mentally repeat: "I so-and-so, on behalf of all sentient beings, and freely offering my body, speech, and mind, bow to the earth in adoration of the Guru and the Three Precious Ones." Then visualize a host of divine beings from whose luminous bodies rays of light come out and penetrate all ten directions, giving comfort to the six orders of sentient beings, and then entering your own body, transforming it into a shining crystal (Blofeld 2: 150-152).

Among other preliminaries, a prominent place is given to gestures *(mudras)*. Used extensively, not only do they occur in the preliminary stages, in which each activity is accompanied by a gesture and an appropriate mantra, they are also performed in meditations themselves, especially in the lower tantras. All preparatory activities, from rising early in the morning for the first meditation session to the beginning of other sessions, are accompanied by gestures. These activities include: pledge to the lineage, taking refuge, seeking protection, self-surrender, bathing, purifying, removing bodily and mental blockages, creating a protective setting, sitting on the meditation cushion, and creating a sacred context for meditation. During meditation itself, they help evoke and visualize the deities in front of the meditator.

An example of a gesture performed during meditation is the following, called "Offering Oblations": Interlace the little and the ring fingers inside. After aligning and straightening the two middle fingers, bend the forefingers to the third joint of the former. Next join the two thumbs to the sides of the hands (Tsong-ka-pa II-III: 126). This is followed by recitation of a mantra.

More complex gestures combine mantric syllables and visualization. In one such gesture, for instance, each finger is mentally correlated with a color associated with one of the five aspects of the supreme wisdom of Buddhahood, represented by the five meditative Buddhas, and correlated with a mantric syllable associated with the five elements of space, air, earth, fire, and water (Willis 33).

The effect of the gestures used in the preliminary practices is essentially to evoke or create a proper mental attitude for the meditation to follow. The attitude is one of openness, receptivity, attentiveness and alertness of mind; and a realization that you are about to enter into a sacred space and time, and engage in a sacred activity. In the meditation, gestures help visualization. And their overall aim is to dispose, evoke, or awaken certain states of consciousness to be realized in the meditation.

The frequency of its appearance alone is an indication, just as in the case of Hindu Tantra, of the central importance of the *mandala* of speech (mantra) in Tibetan Buddhism. Since a mantra is based on and consequently arouses sound vibrations which, in their primal form, constitute a principle of the universe, it ranges over the entire field of reality and awareness. And since the gods represent archetypal planes of reality and awareness, they can be viewed as forms of primal sound vibrations and so can be said to be embodied in certain primal or seed *(bija)* mantras. A seed-mantra is therefore a manifestation in concrete form of the primal vibration and the deity of which it is the mantra. Being the essence of the deity, a seed-mantra not only awakens primal vibrations, but also enables one to attain the state of consciousness and reality it represents. Such a seed mantra is *OM AH HUM*.

Usually aligned with speech, because of what they symbolize, mantras range over the entire field of meditation. Accordingly, the seed-mantra *OM* is assigned to the body, *AH* to speech, and *HUM* to mind. As Lama Govinda points out, while generally corresponding to the three highest psychic centers and the meditative Buddhas, Vairochana, Amoghasiddhi, and Aksobhya, in this all-encompassing configuration, they go beyond the aspects of wisdom the three Buddhas symbolize and become the embodiment of all aspects of the supreme wisdom of the Buddha-nature represented by the five meditative Buddhas (2: 206-207).

Of central importance to Tibetan Buddhism is another mantra: *OM MANI PADME HUM*. Ordinarily translated as, "Hail to the jewel in the lotus," its meaning, reality, and meditative effects go far beyond this literal significance. It is multidimensional and works on all levels of the meditator's body, speech, and mind. As Lama Govinda observes, "The meaning and the effectiveness of a mantra consists in its multi-dimensionality, its capacity to be valid not only on one, but on all planes of reality, and to reveal on each of these planes a new meaning—until, after having repeatedly gone through the various stages of experience, we are able to grasp the totality of the mantric experience-body" (2: 228). This is especially the case with the present mantra.

On the level of meaning and what it symbolizes, this is evident. Thus, as the seed-mantra of the Unconditioned State, *OM* symbolizes or embodies the Supreme Identity, and, on the part of the meditator, the intention to realize it. The lotus is the symbol of the Mind or All-embracing Awareness, while the jewel symbolizes enlightenment. According to this interpretation, the mantra means: "I identify myself with the Unconditioned State, which is revealed in enlightenment." And since *HUM* stands for integration and completeness, the aim of the mantra is to lead the meditator to a complete integration with all states and planes of reality and awareness, conditioned and unconditioned, in the state of Buddhahood.

On yet another level, jewel symbolizes primal energy and lotus supreme wisdom. Together they stand for the transcendent unity of the primal polarity of Energy and Wisdom. Furthermore, in the context of the *sadhana* of the Five M's, jewel represents the penis and lotus the vagina, and sexual yoga their joining. Since this union symbolizes the union of the archetypal polarity, the mantra is saying that enlightenment is to be found in the transcendent unity of the primal polarity through the yoga of sexual union. The mantra both embodies and serves as a vehicle for this realization.

As a tool for meditation, however, the mantra is incomplete without the bodily centers *(chakras)* on which it is projected and the *mandala* in which its six syllables, with their accompanying deities, are visualized. As the mantra of Avalokitesvara, the Lord of the present age, who vowed to save all beings and whose nature it embodies, *OM MANI PADME UM* can help the meditator to save him/herself and all beings in the six mental states that make up conditioned existence. With each recitation of the mantra, the sound of *OM* is said to penetrate the realm of the gods, offer the blessing of liberation to the beings who dwell there, and, by freeing the meditator from it, close the gate to that state of consciousness. Similar processes occur with the sound of *MA* in the giant or supra-human state; the sound of *NI* in the human, the sound of *PAD* in the animal, the sound of *ME* in the hungry ghost, and of *HUM* in the hell state (Eliade 220-221; Willis 33-35). Thus the mantra can free you from the "Wheel of Birth and Death" or repetitive, compulsive thought, feeling, and behavior, and from fixation in conditioned existence.

In the full realization of what the mantra embodies, you become, through visualization and identification, the embodiment of Avalokitesvara and actualize in yourself the Awareness and Reality of the three bodies: the body or state of Reality as Such *(Dharma-kaya)*, its complete manifestation *(Nirmana-kaya)*, and complete joy *(Sambhoga-kaya)*. For this practice, you also need to visualize the mantra in the appropriate bodily centers and the *mandala*, and become identified with it.

Mandala and Visualization

The *yantra* and the *mandala* are especially used to open the door of the mind. Since it embodies all reality, the *mandala* is most extensively used in the highest Tibetan tantras. To attain the state of awareness and reality it symbolizes, the central method used is visualization and identification with the *mandala* visualized. This is also true of the *yantra*.

Many different *yantras* of deities are used for visualization. In a typical *yantra*, you are instructed to mentally picture, project, or allow the image of the deity, which may be placed in front of you, to appear on the mental screen and then concentrate on it until you experience yourself as the deity. Since each deity is an archetypal form of All-embracing Awareness, by identifying with it you can realize that aspect of it which the deity awakens and thus attain that transpersonal state.

As in Hindu Tantra, while the *yantra* symbolizes only an aspect, the *mandala* represents the whole of Awareness and Reality. Correspondingly, *mandalas* are crystallizations of all the teachings. When you are able to visualize an entire *mandala* and become identified with it, you can attain the truth of all the teachings, and see the *mandala* as the embodiment of all reality and each thing as its aspect.

The all-embracing character of the *mandala* is seen from its very construction. Although there are four types of *mandalas*, they have essentially the same structure. A *mandala* is generally drawn with powdered rice, sand, or two cords:

one white, to trace the outer limits; the other, composed of five different colors, to draw the rest. The colored sand *mandala* is drawn on smooth ground, symbolizing the transcendent state it is to represent.

According to Mircea Eliade and Daniel Odier, a *mandala* has five main spheres. First, the border consists of a circle of fire, drawn in five different colors. It symbolizes the awareness that burns unawareness, constitutes a barrier to the uninitiated, and acts as a reminder to the initiate that s/he must purify him/herself of negative programmings and burn away mental and emotional blockages if s/he is to have access to the inner realms.

Second, there is a ring of diamonds, representing the *vajra* (scepter) and the bell. These two signify a unity of enlightenment and the *Vajra-* or Buddha-nature and empowerment of the initiate toward its realization.

Third, representing wrathful deities, there is a circle with eight cemeteries, signifying eight forms of consciousness—smell, touch, taste, hearing, sight, intelligence, ordinary consciousness, and omniscience. This is a reminder that you must deconstruct and transcend the first seven if you are to have access to the last, which lies at the center of the *mandala*.

The fourth circle, containing ritual implements, such as vases filled with precious or aromatic substances, fillets, flowers, and so on, symbolizes spiritual rebirth. In this sphere, some *mandalas* have lotus crowns and steps leading to the palace, symbolizing purity of consciousness, illumination, and steps or transpersonal stages. These two progressive steps toward the center signify that in order to be reborn or enlightened, you must undergo the death or transcendence of the ego, programmings, and conditioned states, and must successively pass through transpersonal stages in order to gain access to the center of the *mandala* (Eliade 221-227; Odier 126-127).

Next is the inner realm of the *mandala*, called "the palace," where images of the gods are set. Generally, it consists of a square quadrangle with four doors guarded by four dragons. On the one hand, they guard consciousness from being invaded and ruled by unconscious drives, tendencies, and dispositions; on the other hand, these unconscious forces remind you that you must awaken, face, and overcome them (that is, master and integrate them within yourself), as well as transcend the archetypal forms in consciousness and the dualistic barrier (slaying the dragons), if you are to gain access to the center of the *mandala*, where resides the deity chosen by your guru at the time of initiation (Eliade 227).

In the center circle of a grand *mandala*, representing the center of Reality, out of the Void-nature from which arise the primal forms, dwell the central deities or five-fold Energy-Wisdom in the form of meditative Buddhas. Together with their consorts, the Buddhas symbolize Energy-Wisdom—the ultimate, constitutive principles of all things. In the center, representing the Unconditioned State and pure, Absolute Wisdom, is Buddha Vajrasattva (Diamond-Truth). The seed-mantra *OM* and the color white are assigned to him. Being in the center of the *mandala,* Vajrasattva is the Formless Reality *(Sunyata),* the Center, Source, and Identity of all things.

On the left, representing the west, is Buddha Amitabha, symbolizing discriminating wisdom or the ability to differentiate between the real and the illusory and to perceive things directly, just as they are. The seed-mantra *HRIH* and the color red are assigned to him. He is associated with perception. To the right, in the east, symbolizing mirror-like wisdom or the clarity and self-transparency of All-embracing Awareness, which illuminates all and in which all are reflected as they actually are, is Buddha Aksobhya. To him are assigned the seed-mantra *HUM* and the color blue. Consciousness is associated with him. To the north, representing all-accomplishing wisdom or the inner potentiality, creative possibilities and renewal of all things, is Amoghasiddhi. To him are assigned the seed-mantra *AH* and the color green. He is associated with will and unconscious tendencies. In the south is Ratnasambhava, representing equalizing wisdom or the wisdom of perceiving all things with an eye of equality and achieving balance, harmony, and integration in life. He is associated with feeling, and is given the seed-mantra *TRAM* and the color yellow.

The five Buddhas at the center of the *mandala* also correspond to the five forms of energy and the *skandhas* — form, feeling, perception, will or unconscious tendency, and consciousness — in each individual. These are to be transformed, through meditation on the *mandala,* into universal states of wisdom characteristic of Buddhahood. Nothing is to be repressed or denied; everything is to be freed from entrapment in narrow limits and brought to its perfection in the Unconditioned State of Buddha-nature. Thus, form is to be transformed into the Absolute, Formless Reality; perception to be freed from programmings and constructs (thus from delusive existence), and transformed into differentiating wisdom. Consciousness is to be freed from the constraints of present programmings, contents, and constructs so that it can become mirror-like wisdom, reflecting the true nature of all things. Unconscious tendencies, drives, desires, and will are to be brought to the clear light of consciousness and their energies to be released from fixations, compulsions, and habitual patterns, and made available for creative purposes. Finally, the emotions are to be freed from negative and positive programmings and transformed into the wisdom of equality, so that you can see all with an eye of nondiscrimination; integrate your emotions within the totality of yourself, bringing balance, harmony, and completeness in your life; and release your compassion in the service of others without any discrimination of persons (Blofeld 2: 84-87; Eliade 208-209; Govinda 1: 108-122).

Through meditation on the *mandala*, then, bondage is transformed into absolute freedom; separation, limitation, and isolation into oneness with all; and conditioned states into the Unconditioned State of your own true being. The very things that cause *dukkha* are penetrated and transformed by wisdom, integrated into the Unconditioned, and brought to completeness and liberation. The key to achieving this state is visualization and identification with what is visualized.

The crux of Tibetan Tantra is visualization. Its importance is derived from the fact that not only does it simultaneously engage body, speech, and mind on various levels, but also through its highest object — *mandala* — it enables you to attain your identity with all reality, which is the ultimate goal of all meditation.

To attain this highest aim, you must first mentally create the image in every detail until it is very distinct; and then stabilize it so that attention can stay focused on it for prolonged periods. This prolonged focus enables you to simultaneously penetrate and deconstruct the gross perceptual form of the *mandala* and consciousness. As attention becomes relatively free from fixation on the object-world, it shifts toward the symbolic object-construction or the inner image, gathers around and becomes unified with it, and reaches one-pointedness.

In the process of visualizing the image, you awaken the forces and states of consciousness within yourself that had hitherto been dormant. The next step is to realize the state to which you have awakened by identifying with the deity that represents it. As identification becomes prolonged and your own form increasingly dissolves into the deity during meditation, your mind takes on its form and dimensions and you directly experience the reality it represents. As you identify with and assimilate the deities and various aspects of the *mandala*, you become one with the corresponding forces and energies of the universe. With perfect identification, the state becomes a conscious part of your identity, which goes through destructuring, transformation, expansion, and reintegration on this higher plane. Thus, you successively pass from "seed" *samadhi*, or union with the inner image of the deity, in which state solidity dissolves into fluidity — the luminous, energy-form that is interlinked with the energy-aspect of the universe — to "seedless" *samadhi* with the subtle, archetypal form or the primal Energy-Wisdom that constitutes the universe. At this stage, as you reach cosmic or universal consciousness, no other form except this one remains in your awareness.

As this happens and you enter into insight meditation, you are able to transcend even the form of the deity and the conceptual framework of the meditation. From this vantage point you are able to perceive that the gods and powers in the universe are aspects of your own mind, and that your mind and Primal Energy are identical, existing in a state of perfect interpenetration with all things. Thus, as will be discussed later, in the advanced state of *samadhi* and insight meditation, as you gradually penetrate to the center of the *mandala* and experience identity with the five meditative Buddhas, you transcend all forms and constructs, and arrive at the Unconditioned State.

As you can see from this brief description, by meditating on the *mandala* through visualization, you can progress through all the essential stages of meditation and realize its highest aim.

Forms of Tibetan Tantra

To experience enlightenment and realize the goal of Buddhahood, Vajrayana follows essentially two paths: the Path of Forms and the Formless Path, which is also called the Yoga of *Sunyata,* and the Path of Liberation. This path is somewhat similar to Zen, as it directly focuses on the mind and works toward its unfoldment in enlightenment. The Path of Form constitutes the main part of Tibetan tantras, of which there are four or six, depending on how they are divided: *Kriya, Carya, Yoga, Mahayoga, Anuttara,* and *Atiyoga.* Although the methods used in the two paths are different, in their progressively deepening forms, concentration and insight make up the foundation of Tibetan tantras. As in other Buddhist paths, concentration leads to *samadhi,* while insight opens the mind to enlightenment and Buddhahood.

Although *Kriya* and *Carya* tantras are mainly concerned with purification, they are not without higher operations. They have a structure that contains both concentrative and insight meditation. As a result, they have two foci: purification and "deity yoga," or meditation on the deity assigned by the guru at the time of initiation. The former aims to dissolve mental fixations, emotional blockages, and negative programming by disidentifying with the present restrictive form of identity and habits and freeing psychological energy for transformation into spiritual energy. The latter aims to help the initiate to transform consciousness and attain higher states through visualization of his/her body as divine, identification with the deity visualized, and meditation on emptiness. While visualization is the concentrative type, meditation on emptiness is the insight type of meditation.

Accordingly, after the preliminaries in which gestures and mantras are extensively used, in the deity yoga of *Kriya Tantra,* the meditator first visualizes the deity placed in front of him/her and then visualizes him/herself as a deity;

practices mantra repetition, and concentration without repetition. In *Carya Tantra,* on the other hand, s/he first meditates on emptiness; and then, visualizing him/herself as Vairochana, repeats mantras and meditates on emptiness.

Yoga Tantra emphasizes internal bodily activities involving both body and mind with the aim of raising consciousness to the higher states through postures, gestures, breath-control, visualization, and the use of *chakras,* psychic channels, etc. As such, it is the Buddhist form of Energy Yoga and resembles Hindu Kundalini Yoga and Taoist Yoga. Like Kundalini, of the six yogas of Naropa, the Energy Yoga or the Yoga of Inner Fire especially involves awakening Primal Energy from its ordinarily dormant or unconscious state and raising it through the central channel into the ascending centers. In the process consciousness is raised, unified, and expanded. This prepares you for experiencing the final unity of Energy and Wisdom.

The attainment of these higher unities and the expansion of consciousness is especially the aim of *Mahayoga Tantra.* It works by first cleansing body, speech, and mind; then, by raising Energy-Awareness through the channels and centers, it opens up higher states of consciousness. Through visualization of the deities, it aims to lead the yogi to various types of *samadhis* and attainment of *siddhis* or paranormal powers. Because it works essentially with the same methods as *Yoga Tantra,* it is not regarded as a separate form of tantra.

Anuttara Tantra brings together the practices of the lower tantras and leads the practitioner to the highest realization. Using body, speech, and especially mind, it combines breath-control, mantra, *yantra, mandala*, visualization, and sexual union, symbolically or with a real consort, in an attempt to raise, unify, expand, and bring Energy-Awareness to its ultimate unity in the Unconditioned. The key to it lies in first visualizing the deity and then experiencing identity with it (Trungpa 5: 125-130).

Atiyoga Tantra is not so much a separate form of tantra as a continuation of the practices of *Anuttara Tantra* and their highest realization. Its focus is directly on the mind itself. It aims, according to Chogyam Trungpa, to attain "that which transcends coming, that which transcends going, and that which transcends dwelling" (5: 134). In focusing directly on itself, the mind is able to experience itself as pure Awareness without any props, screens, filters, structures, or frameworks that could separate it from Reality as Such. Consequently, as Trungpa points out, the *Atiyoga* practitioner sees a completely naked world. Established in the Unconditioned and experiencing no separation from anything, s/he experiences no becoming or ceasing, no limitation to conditioned existence, no fixation on anything. At this stage, *samadhi* becomes spontaneous and the duality between ordinary and transconscious states, enlightenment and nonenlightenment disappears. It is in this state, then, that the final integration of all states in the unity of the Unconditioned takes place (Trungpa 5: 133-140; Blofeld 2: 219-221).

As Blofeld points out, the tantras (especially the lower ones), begin by creating the proper motivation through taking three refuges—the Buddha or the Awakened Mind, the Dharma or the Teachings or the Way of Awakening, and the Sangha or the Community of luminous beings (in Vajrayana a fourth refuge, the Guru, is added to the traditional list). Thus the first aim is to arouse faith and the desire for enlightenment. Next, you create a proper mental disposition by surrounding yourself in the protective sphere of the deity or deities to be visualized or by putting yourself in sacred space and time, with offerings and confessions to the deity. Next is the main part of the meditation, concerned with purifying the mind and dissolving mental and emotional fixations; developing concentration and one-pointedness of mind by visualizing both the deity in front and yourself as the deity; mantra repetition; and concentration without repetition.

While continuing these practices, in the higher tantras, through different types of meditation already discussed, you seek to identify with the deity through entering into *samadhi* with it. Lastly, after becoming identified with the deity, you contract yourself into a point and become dissolved into the pure Void. This enables you to transcend all forms and constructs and arrive at the formless state of *Sunyata*, thus realizing the absolute Oneness of Energy and Wisdom. Since this realization is the ultimate goal, although practiced in the lower tantras, it is rarely achieved there. In effect, they serve as preparatory exercises and a gradual process of penetrating duality and destructuring consciousness, while the ultimate unity is achieved in the highest tantras.

In addition to these methods, which are forms of concentrative meditation, similar to Theravada and Zen traditions, Tibetan Tantra also has insight meditation, as already mentioned. In the lower tantras, this consists of meditation on mindfulness and emptiness, gaining insight into the body-mind states and, in general, into all phenomena as being empty of permanence, substantiality, or a separate existence of their own. In the advanced stages, after reaching *samadhi*, through insight meditation, you proceed to enlightenment (Blofeld 2: 200-203; Hopkins 19-42).

In what follows, I shall briefly describe the simplest and shortest forms of *Kriya, Carya,* and *Yoga Tantra,* representing the lower tantras, and *Mahamudra* meditation, representing the highest tantra. In so doing I hope to give you some basic understanding of the nature of Tibetan Tantras and how they are practiced. They are not presented here for practice on your own. If by reading my account, you develop a desire to follow this path, you should find a center and an accomplished teacher or lama who can initiate you into Tibetan Tantra. Of course, as a preparatory step, you will need to develop concentration by practicing Theravada and Mahayana types of meditation.

A *Kriya Tantra* Meditation

The following text is from Tsong-ka-pa, the fifteenth-century reformer to whom the Gelugpa sect, of which the Dalai Lama is the head, traces its lineage.

The meditation is preceded by initiation, pledges, vows, and preliminaries that involve extensive use of gestures and mantras. These are intended to create a mental attitude of openness, receptivity, and self-surrender; to arouse the desire to attain the goal of the meditation; and to attune the mind of the meditator to a realization that s/he is about to enter into another dimension, a sacred space and time beyond the world of ordinary events. These factors help direct the attention from its outward orientation inward. The meditation itself has four parts: visualizing the meditator's own body as that of the deity; visualizing the deity in front; mantra repetition; and concentration without repetition. The complete meditation includes much more than what is set down by Tsong-ka-pa or what is summarized below.

Visualizing Your Body as That of the Deity

Initially you are to make offerings to a deity visualized in front of you and then visualize yourself as the deity as follows:
a. Sit up straight and then, from its usual incessant scanning of the object-world, gather the attention together and focus it inward. Making your neck like that of a peacock, inhale and exhale smoothly, gently, evenly. Keeping the eyes slightly open, aim them at the tip of your nose. Lightly press the teeth together, and press the tongue against the upper palate.
b. Arouse compassion for all sentient beings, assuming the burden of freeing them from suffering. Then strive to arouse in yourself the desire for enlightenment while thinking, "For their sake I will attain the highest enlightenment," and then arouse the desire to attain all virtues and omniscient wisdom.
c. After making offerings, etc., as above, to a deity visualized and invited in front of you, reflect and analyze the Ultimate Deity, your own essential formless nature, with the aim of directly experiencing it. Stop differentiating yourself from others, and see the self, all subjects and objects, as being void of duality or separate existence. Continue this exercise until you come to sense the nature of the self and that of the deity as being void of duality, concepts, and constructs.

d. Visualize as arising out of emptiness in resounding and vibrating tones the appropriate mantra of the deity. Visualize the vibrating mantra rising from a moon disc.

e. Picture your mind appearing in the sky in the form of the mantra's letters. See your mind merging with the deity and appearing in the form of a moon disc and the letters on top of the disc appearing like pure mercury studded with grains of gold.

f. Visualize forms of the deity emerging from light emitted by the moon and the mantra and filling all spheres of the sky. Streams of ambrosia descend from great clouds, extinguishing the fires of hell and satisfying the wants of all beings. Make clouds of offerings to the deity. Then see the light and divine forms reverse their direction and enter the moon disc in your mind. Meditate on the moon and the letters of the mantra, transformed into the body of the deity, and become aware of your identity with the deity.

g. Form the gestures of the crown protrusion, hair-treasury, etc. Recite the appropriate mantra and bless the crown of the lineage deity with gestures and mantras.

h. Concentrate on the deity visualized in six forms: emptiness, sound, letter, form, gesture, and concept. Continue to concentrate until your mind becomes one-pointed and stabilized on the deity and you can enter into and stay in *samadhi*, contemplating it. Do this by visualizing the deity in front and then visualizing your own body as the form of the deity. This is to be achieved by stopping the breath, thought, and the stream of consciousness. To stop the breath, hold your breath by pressing the chin against the chest for as long as possible while mentally observing one aspect of the divine body. Then slowly and gently exhale and relax, while viewing yourself transparent as a deity. Then repeat. While doing this, stop thought or your mind by withdrawing attention from the senses and the external world and holding it fixed on the deity. Cut off thoughts and distractions, make attention one-pointed on the deity, and observe your body as that of the deity.

i. Visualize the deity contracting into a point and dissolving into yourself, visualized as the deity. Next confer initiation and the gesture of the lineage on yourself (Tsong-ka-pa 103-114).

Visualizing the Deity in Front

a. In front of you, in the direction where a painting or image of the deity has been set, visualize a field of many precious substances covered with golden sand. Bless it with the mantra *Om chalavi hum svaha*.

b. On top of it picture a great ocean of milk free from anything, such as scum, that could distract the mind. It is adorned with flowers, such as lotus and uptala, with many flocks of precious birds flying overhead. Bless them with the mantra *Om vimala-dhaha hum.*
c. In the center visualize the square Mount Meru, having on all four sides sets of stairs made of gold, silver, sapphire and topaz. Growing all over it are wish-granting trees, adorned with a thousand banners. On top of the mountain visualize a lotus stalk adorned with many precious substances, having petals of various jewels, golden corolla, and anthers of topaz with silver lines surrounding the top of its center. The wise lotus stalk arises from the center of Mount Meru. From it emerge ten million lotus latticeworks.

Joining the palms, with interlaced fingers, and pressing the left thumb with the right, bless the residence of the deity, repeating a hundred times, *Namah sarva tathagatanam sarvatha udgate spharanahimam gaganakham svaha.*

Picture or visualize a canopy appearing in an instant above the residence of the deity.

d. Visualize an inestimable empty palace in the center of the former lotus, either all at once or seeing the syllables *BHRUM* turning into the palace. The deity comes to this palace with his own palace, which fuses into it.
e. Offer an oblation of ground barley and milk, etc., in a vessel of gold, silver, copper, or other substances and ask the deity to sit. Bless the oblation with incense, repeating seven times the appropriate mantra.
f. Facing the direction of the deity, kneel on the ground, and bow down; form the gesture of invitation by intertwining the fingers, turning the palms upward, aligning and straightening the forefingers and beckoning with the thumbs. Then say:

> Due to my faith and your compassionate pledges
> Come here, come here, O Blessed One
> Accept this oblation of mine
> Be pleased with me through this offering.

Next, holding the vessel in line with the head, the chest, and the navel, make offerings and visualize deities coming to receive them.

g. Offer a seat to the deity with the gesture of the lotus, the *vajra*, and the heroic postures, and recite:

Om kamalaya svaha,
Om vajra-asani hum phat,
Om vajraka hum phat.

h. Saying *Samkare samaye svaha*, display the pledge *vajra* or gesture by pressing the nail of the little fingers with the thumb of the right hand and holding the remaining fingers like a gesture. Then form the appropriate lineage gesture, recite the corresponding mantra, and construct the great pledge gesture.

i. Present the offerings by performing the dispelling of obstructions and cleansing the articles of offering while repeating the eight mantras of offering and viewing the articles as magnificent.

j. Next offer oblation, a foot-bath, a bath, clothing, adornment, music, perfume, flowers, incense, food, and lamps with appropriate gestures and mantras.

k. Praise the Three Jewels and the lords of the three lineages, confess, take refuge, admire, make entreaty, supplication, prayer-wishes, and cultivate the Four Immeasurables (wishing all creatures freedom from suffering, happiness, bliss of Buddhahood, and *Nirvana* of a Buddha) with appropriate mantras.

This part of the meditation ends with arousing the desire for enlightenment while thinking, "I will attain Buddhahood in order to liberate stricken migrators" (Tsong-ka-pa 115-138).

Mantra Repetition

Begin by visualizing yourself as a deity and then visualizing the deity in front. Keep the mind focused on it for as long as possible. When this one-pointed meditation becomes tiring, practice mantra repetition with the help of a rosary made of 21, 54, 108, or 1008 beads. Placing the rosary in your cupped palms, bow down to the lamas and gods, and then, in order to empower the rosary, repeat the appropriate mantra of the three lineages 108 times. Next, pay homage to the lamas and gods, repeat the appropriate mantra of the lineage seven times. Now raise the rosary to the heart, extend the middle and little fingers of either the right or the left hand, and, putting the forefinger behind, count with the ring finger and the thumb.

Do this repetition while holding the breath and stopping thought and mind-wandering as before. As you practice this, visualize and hold your undeviating attention on the deity in front with a moon disc in its heart on which stand the letters of the mantra. Visualize the letters as set around the edges of the moon. Perform the repetition while visualizing yourself as a deity. When exhaling, without repeating the mantra, visualize your body as a deity.

When the meditation becomes tiring, in order to rest at the end of the session, stop the concentration and observation in the reverse order, first with the sounds of the mantra, then the letters, the moon disc, the body of the deity, and finally your own body.

To resume the meditation, begin by observing the form of the letters in your heart while softly or audibly inhaling and holding the breath. Then, with the mind fully concentrated and free of distractions, visualize in the heart of the deity a moon disc on which the letters of the mantra are set. Next, visualize yourself as a deity and, as you inhale, move the moon and the letters to your own heart. Concentrate on the visualization and mentally repeat the mantra as long as you can hold the breath. As you exhale, picture the moon disc and the letters going out to the deity's heart and contemplate them there. As you exhale, they again return to your heart, where you hold them in your attention and contemplate them.

Next, concentrate on the sound of the letters. Again, holding the breath and stopping thought, visualize the deity in front, having in its heart a moon disc and the letters of the mantra set around its edge. Mentally or in a whisper repeat the mantra while listening to its tone or sound as you intone it. You may first whisper the repetition and then, as the mind becomes concentrated, free of distractions, do it mentally.

When you come to the first and the last bead of the rosary, mentally pay homage to the deities. When a full count of the beads is finished, look at the image or painting of the deity set in front of you; then with eyes slightly open, continue the repetition. The number of repetitions varies from three to a hundred thousand.

When the repetitions are completed, to conclude the session, form the vase gesture, offer your virtuous act to the deity, ask for forbearance for not doing the repetition perfectly, make offerings, praise, etc., and, forming the gesture of invitation, request departure in this way: Extend the thumbs and form the gesture of requesting departure by intertwining the little, ring, and middle fingers, and opening and extending the index fingers and the thumbs. Repeat your seed-mantra, adding *gaccha,* and asking the deity, along with its mansion, to depart. Then place the right palm on the upturned left palm, join the tips of the crossed fingers at the base, and extend your hands in front of you. Circle this gesture from the left to the right and free the directions as well as the upper and lower gods bound earlier with the mantra *Om hulu hulu chandali-matam givi svaha* (Tsong-ka-pa 139-154).

Concentration Without Repetition

After you have become proficient in the previous meditations, that is, your visualization of the deity has become vivid and concentration has stabilized so that attention stays continuously focused on the vivid appearance, you may proceed with concentration without repetition.

The first part of this exercise is called "abiding in fire." To begin the meditation, contemplate *Sunyata* by stopping to view the self as a substantial entity having a separate existence of its own and keeping the attention focused, as in *shikan-taza,* on the space of awareness before any thought or mental reaction arises.

Next, visualize your own body as that of the deity of your mantra, in the heart of which there is a fire burning like that of the flame of a butter lamp, and visualize the letters of the mantra as arising in a series on the form of their sounds, appearing steadily, uninterruptedly, and without fluctuation, like the continual rising of the sound of a bell. Stop the breath, thought and distractions, and concentrate on the sound of the letters as if you were listening to another person reciting the mantra. Concentrate without believing that the sound truly exists. Your concentration should be such that your own mind appears in the form of the tones of the mantra dwelling in the midst of the flame.

Next, visualize a deity, forming the base of the letters of the mantra, in the previous tongue of the flame, which is set in a subtle stainless moon disc located in the heart. After your concentration becomes focused and steady, leave the rest and hold the attention on only the sounds of the mantra. As you exhale, see your body as that of the deity.

After your concentration deepens and your mind becomes steady and one-pointed while meditating on the sound, shift the focus of attention entirely to *Sunyata*. Then, like Theravada insight meditation, analyze the nature of all phenomena in order to arrive at insight into the Void-nature of all conditioned existence. These two forms of meditation—concentration with visualization and analyzing the nature of phenomena—are to be alternated until the goal of the meditation is attained (Tsong-ka-pa 155-171. For a full account of the meditation, consult the text).

A *Carya Tantra* Meditation

The first part of this meditation, called "Yoga with Signs," begins with meditation on *Sunyata* or emptiness by viewing yourself and the deity to be visualized as not being separate entities or in themselves anything real. View your own nature and that of the deity as void of differentiation. Continue to hold this view in the center of your awareness until a firm conviction develops, and then visualize yourself as a deity.

Next, centering your mind on emptiness, which serves as the context, visualize your mind itself arising as a deity out of emptiness in the form of a moon disc with the seed-syllable *AM* on top of it. Make the light expand from and contract into the syllable. Then see it change into Buddha Vairochana, with one face, a golden body surrounded by an interwoven flame, two hands making the gesture of equipoise, sitting on cushions of white lotus and the moon, head adorned and plaited hair wound up on top, and wearing light upper and lower garments. Then perform the blessing with appropriate gestures and mantras.

After visualizing yourself as one, visualize another Vairochana in front, similar to yourself, and then visualize a moon disc in its heart with the form of the mantra syllables set upright around its edge and facing inward.

After stopping the breath and thought, stabilize the visualizations in your mind and then perform mantra repetition while viewing the letters. If observing the mantra set on the moon disc in the heart of the deity in front gets to be tiring, alternate the exercise with viewing it in your own heart.

Stop the breath and thought or mind-wandering, and repeat the mantra first in a whisper and then mentally. For the mental repetition, first set the visualization within emptiness. See yourself as a deity arising out of *A, AM,* or *AH* set on a very pure and stable moon disc in the heart of the Buddha. Continue the exercise until you see your own body as that of a deity. Next, meditate on Vairochana in the upright moon as if dwelling in a cave, and the mantra syllables set upright and facing inward around the edges of a moon in his heart. Third, contemplate your own mind as the moon; and fourth, contemplate the letters standing around the edges. Continue to meditate in this way – for a month with and a month without offerings – until your concentration becomes one-pointed.

The second part of the meditation, called "Yoga without Signs," is to be undertaken after the above visualization becomes clear, concentration stable, and the mind one-pointed on the fourfold repetition. Again, this part of the meditation is similar to Theravada insight meditation.

It is a meditation on the Void-nature of all conditioned existence, particularly focused on the body, mind, and self. As to the first, view your body as not being affected by the duality of good and bad. Next, hold your attention on and contemplate or become aware of your body as impermanent, nonsubstantial, having no separate, individual existence of its own. Continue to meditate until you come to realize the inherent Void-nature of solidity.

Similarly view the mind until you come to the realization that it is void of separate existence, programming, contents or objects, form, or construct; that it abides nowhere; is neither created nor destroyed. Finally, contemplate the self until you arrive at the realization that it is not a substantial entity, has no inherent existence, separate from the ever-changing phenomena.

The process of this meditation consists in first clearly visualizing and becoming aware of your own body as that of the deity, and then coming to a realization of its emptiness by reflecting that it is neither one nor many; nor does it come into being from self, other, both, or neither. Alternate this reflection with a concentrative meditation on emptiness. Finally, directly observe all phenomena as pure process, void of permanence, substantiality, and separate existence.

Alternate between concentration and observation, analysis and insight, until both concentration and insight develop equally, so that it can prepare you for a direct experience of *Sunyata* (Tsong-ka-pa 183-203; for a full account of the Tantra, consult the text).

As you can see, although they are different, like Theravada and Zen, both *Kriya* and *Carya Tantra* consist of concentrative and insight meditation.

Yoga Tantra: Yoga of Inner Fire

This yoga is concerned with generating psychological and spiritual energy so as to purify body and mind; remove mental and emotional fixations due to positive and negative programmings and habits; awaken and raise Primal Energy through the channels and centers; and in the process unify, integrate, and expand consciousness into the transpersonal states, eventually transcending primal polarity and reaching the ultimate Unity. In conception, method and aim, this yoga is similar to Hindu Kundalini Yoga.

Before engaging in the main practice, you need to practice preliminary meditations on the impermanence of life, *dukkha,* the difficulty of obtaining a favorable birth in which to practice the Teachings, nonattachment, kindness and compassion, and the infinite Bodhi-Mind. Furthermore, four initiations have to be completed before you can practice the yoga, which runs as follows:

1. Visualizing the Void-Nature of Your Body

a. Sit in the lotus posture as in other tantras.
b. Visualize your body as that of your chosen deity, but hollow as a balloon. If visualizing the entire body at once as a hollow balloon proves difficult, try a part at a time until you get the whole, and your visualization becomes stable and extremely clear.
c. Next, visualize your body in different sizes, small as a mustard seed and large as the universe – all empty inside.

2. Visualizing the Main Psychic Channels

a. When the visualization of your body as that of the deity chosen at initiation becomes clear, picture the central channel with its upper end reaching the top of your head and then curving down to the third eye center, and its lower end reaching down to three inches below the navel. It is wide as a whipcord, white outside and red inside. Then visualize the other two channels to its left and right, wide as an arrow shaft. The right channel is red, slightly tinged with white; the left channel is the reverse. They run parallel to the central channel. Their upper ends reach the top of the head and then curve down to the nostrils. Visualize all three channels as hollow, straight, clear, and transparent.
b. When the visualization of the channels becomes clear, visualize the crown, the throat, the heart and the power center — all connected to or sprouting from the central channel like ribs from the stick of an umbrella. Visualize the throat and power centers as red, the heart center as white, and the crown center as green. From the tip of each main channel numerous thin channels spread throughout the body, forming a network for the circulation of Energy. All these channels are hollow; red inside and white outside. Again, if visualizing all this at the same time is difficult, try a part at a time until you are able to visualize the whole. The important thing is to continue to practice until the entire visualization becomes stable and extremely clear.

3. The Vase-Breathing Exercise

a. Since this should be done when the breath is flowing evenly through both nostrils, if it is not doing so at the time of your meditation, lie down on the side through which more air is passing, use the thumb to close that nostril and then force the air through the other nostril until it opens up. Then sit up, use a finger to close the left nostril and draw a long exhalation through the right; inhale and draw a short exhalation and then a long and gentle one. After doing this tree times, switch to the left and do the same; then breathe similarly through both nostrils. While exhaling, visualize all hindrances, emotional blocks, mental fixations, negative programmings or sins, and sickness going out of your body, rendering it clear, fresh, vibrant, alive, full of energy, warmth, and awareness.
b. Next, for the Vase-Breathing Exercise, sit as instructed before; put a pillow or folded blanket under the hips; take a slow, gentle, long breath and press the air down below the navel and, as you do so, press the chin against the chest and swallow the saliva. Now hold the breath, contract the sphincter muscles of the

anus slightly and pull the lower air up while holding down the upper air at the power center and keeping the abdomen distended and immobile for as long as possible. Then exhale, take a very short breath to relieve the tension, roll the belly muscles three times, and hold the breath once more for as long as possible. Next raise the head slightly and release the air as slowly as you can, while holding the attention on the exhalation.

c. When inhaling, visualize the energies of the five elements — earth, water, air, fire, and ether — in five different colors and draw them into the nostrils from a distance of about ten inches from your nose. When pressing them down, together with the inhalation, to the abdomen, visualize the air descending through the left and right channels, meeting at their point of intersection, and entering and remaining in the central channel. When rolling the belly muscle, visualize the breath circulating in the central channel. And when exhaling, visualize a drop or dot, the size of a pea (which symbolizes the oneness of Energy-Wisdom or signifies the mixture or union of male sperm and female fluid, and represents, in the form of a seed, the subtle form of the meditation object containing information from various sensory fields), shooting up through the central channel and going out at the crown center. Except for shooting the drop, which should be done only once at the beginning, do this exercise eight to ten times; rest a while; and then repeat.

4. Manipulating the Drop

At the third eye center, visualize the drop as white, transparent, and sparkling or emitting its own light. Clearly comprehending that the drop is the embodiment of the Buddha-nature, continue to visualize until it becomes extremely clear. Then, while inhaling as above, visualize it as ascending from the third eye to the crown center. Hold the breath and concentrate on it there. As you exhale, see it as flowing down to the third eye center. After doing this several times, inhale deeply and push the breath down to the power center and visualize the drop descending through the central channel like a small iron ball falling through a tube with a rattle. Hold and concentrate on the breath at the power center. As you exhale, let it again return to the third eye center and concentrate on it there.

5. Bodily Exercises

a. Sit on the floor, cross your legs, put a high pillow under the hips, and, in order to steady the body during the meditation, use a cotton belt to fasten the waist and the knees.
b. Breathe and visualize as above. Then visualize a small, almond-shaped flame with a sharp, narrow tongue tapering to a point. It is reddish-brown, intensely hot and undulating, and is capable of producing energy and bliss in all the channels. When inhaling, press the breath down to the abdomen; and as you do so, visualize it flowing down the right and left channels, and, like the air from a bellows, fanning the fire to an intense heat. When rolling the belly muscles and circulating them, visualize all the energies in the body gathering at and dissolving into the fire. During the exhalation visualize the fire rising through the central channel. Continue doing this exercise until the visualization becomes extremely clear, heat is produced, Energy rises to the higher centers, and eventually to the crown center, where you experience the perfect unfoldment of Energy-Wisdom.

6. Advanced Practice

To reach one-pointed concentration and *samadhi* on the one hand, and insight into the Void-nature of all things on the other, the following advanced practices, very briefly summarized, are enjoined:

a. In order to increase the heat or raise the Energy, deepen concentration, and raise or expand consciousness, you may lengthen the tongue of the flame up to five inches while still continuing to concentrate on the original base. Then visualize the tongue of the flame rising to the heart, the throat, or even the crown center. Visualize the fire spreading into all the channels until the entire body becomes a blazing fireball. At the end of the meditation withdraw all the fire to the main base.
b. To increase the bliss, sit on the ground with the heel of the left foot pressed against the sphincter muscle of the anus. Then visualize the pea-size drop as snow-white, round, sparkling with radiance, and embodied in the reversed Tibetan syllable *HAM* and situated in the crown center. In the power center visualize the fire with its upper end thin as a needle but intensely hot. Visualize it as producing penetrating heat within the central channel, causing the drop to melt and drip down. Inhale to fan the heat below the power center and continue to melt and have the drop drip down to the throat center and spread throughout

the channels, thereby producing great heat and bliss. As the flow of the dripping drop reaches down to the power center and spreads throughout the body, it will produce a greater bliss.

c. The aim of this practice is to increase insight into nonduality and the Void-nature of all things. With bare attention, observe the nature of the bliss produced by the fire and of the mind and its manifestations. Try to observe and remain in the primordial, void state before anything arises in the mind for as long as possible by concentrating on and seeing the voidness in all things. Hold your bare attention in the void state before anything arises. Simply and directly observe at the primary level of stimulus how mental contents and states arise from the Void, hold the center of attention, and then pass into the Void. Identify the Void with sound, phenomena, and enlightenment, thus experiencing nonduality. While practicing the Yoga of Bliss, try to merge the bliss with the void.

d. To deepen the Bliss-Void *Samadhi*, when the first bliss arises with the spreading of the melting drop through the crown center, first, throw your mind right into the bliss and make it become identified with and remain in the void state beyond thought. This will stop the surface mind-chatter and the perceptual information processing activity will be deconstructed and transcended. When the drop descends and spreads through the throat center, giving rise to great bliss, and you concentrate on it while being absorbed in the Bliss-Void, the stream of consciousness will be emptied and stilled, and *samadhi* with the subtle form will result. Similar practices with the descent of the drop to the heart and power centers will stop distracting thoughts. As this happens, reverse the process and trace the ascent. At the end of the meditation, practice soft Vase-Breathing several times and concentrate on nonduality and the fire. In daily activities, try to retain the Bliss-Void experience and use everything to attain it.

Although this practice does not ordinarily lead to enlightenment as it aims at the *samadhi* of form and is tinged with subtle subject-object dualistic ideas, its continual practice will maintain and stabilize the Bliss-Void experience and can eventually lead Energy-Awareness to the central channel. When the Energy-Awareness is raised through it into the four highest centers, the four types of bliss will arise. If you can recognize and identify them with the void-nature, you will experience four corresponding types of Bliss-Wisdom. By pushing beyond, you will experience the identity of Energy and Wisdom in the state of universal consciousness. If you continue to push, you may even go beyond the *samadhi* of form and experience formless *samadhi* (Chang 3: 52-64; Evans-Wentz 2: 171-209; Govinda 1: 150-177; Muses 146-199; for a full account of this Yoga, consult these texts).

As you can see from this account of the Yoga of Inner Fire, although some of its practices are different, in general conception, method, and aim, it is the Buddhist version of the Hindu Kundalini Yoga. Of course, there are differences of emphasis. The former emphasizes heat or energy and bliss and works more with the upper centers, while the latter concentrates more on awakening the Energy from the root all the way to the crown center. As we shall see, in this respect the former is akin to Taoist Yoga. Yet some of its methods are identical to Kundalini's methods, such as *bandhas* or stopping the breath and thought so as to deconstruct consciousness and raise awareness to transpersonal states.

The Yoga of Illusory-Body

The purpose of this yoga is to recognize the illusory *(maya)* or constructive nature not only of your gross and subtle bodies, but also of all objects, mental and physical, all forms, and everything that makes up conditioned existence. The method consists in seeing all things on the primary level as ever-changing process, impermanent, nonsubstantial, and void of a separate existence of their own.

After preliminary meditation similar to that of the Yoga of Inner Fire, in a well-lit room place a mirror in front of you and softly gaze at your face in it. With bare attention directly observe the thoughts, feelings, and mental reactions that arise about what you perceive in the mirror—pleasure or displeasure, attachment or aversion, self-satisfaction or fear, and so on. Then, like an actor, arouse various emotions; observe and clearly comprehend the nature of what arises, namely, that they are mental creations. This will give you insight into *maya* or how the mind constructs what it perceives through selective attention, model-construction, interpretation, evaluation, judgment, and reactions to what it experiences on the primary order. Seeing this, disidentification will occur. This exercise can also be done through listening to echoes.

For the pure illusory body exercise, place an image of the Buddha between two mirrors so that the image is reflected in them. Then visualize the entire image until it becomes stable and extremely clear. Next, holding the clear image in your mind, identify it with Voidness *(Sunyata)*. This will bring insight into the impermanence and nonsubstantiality of all phenomena.

In order to realize all things as constructs, to perceive the nonduality of conditioned existence *(samsara)* and the Unconditioned *(Nirvana)*, after the Buddha-image has been stabilized and you are able to hold attention on it for prolonged periods, expand it so that it fills the entire universe; then contract it to the size of a mustard seed; multiply it to countless numbers until they fill the sky, and then withdraw them all back to the one body and meditate on it. In daily activities, identify all human beings as Buddhas, all experiences as the Buddha-realm, all sounds as mantras, all houses and towns as mandalas, all thoughts as manifestations of All-embracing Awareness, all enjoyable things as the Enjoyment-Body of the Buddha *(Sambhoga-kaya)*, and the world as Buddha's Pure Land. Thus you should try to purify conditioned existence and identify it with the Unconditioned.

The two yogas above form the foundation of the other four yogas, making up the Six Yogas of Naropa. These four are: Dream, Clear Light, *Bardo* or After-Death State, and Transference of Consciousness. Basically, the first consists in going into the dream state and recognizing it as such, and then trying to dream with your eyes open, creating your own dreams. The objective is to observe and clearly comprehend the ordinary waking state as a dream state or as a culturally induced, hypnotic trance in which most of us live. When you recognize that our ordinary state is a dream projected by the mind onto phenomena and when you perceive the constructive nature of our reality and consciousness, you have an opportunity to wake up from this trance and experience Reality as Such.

The aim of the fourth yoga is to reach *samadhi* by visualizing in your heart a blue Buddha with consort. First practice the previous yogas; next allow the Buddha to burn all obstructions until the light becomes extremely clear; and then through prolonged concentration, expand awareness and enter into *samadhi*.

The fifth yoga is concerned with your entering into the state of forty-nine days between death and rebirth, recognizing all manifestations and the conditioned existence as this intermediate state, and entering into the intermediate state of *samadhi* in which the ordinary state has not yet been fully deconstructed and the Ultimate State has not been reached in enlightenment. A mastery of this meditation will lead to the experience of rebirth or awakening.

Finally, the last one, which completes the others, is concerned with transferring your consciousness to Buddha's Pure Land or a higher state of birth. In other words, it is concerned with the experience of rebirth through self-transformation (Chang 3: 81-115; Evans-Wentz 2: 209-250; Muses 201-261).

Mahamudra Meditation

The preliminary steps, such as ethical training and motivational, psychological, and behavioral change, prior to formal meditative practice, are similar to those we have encountered in other yogas. Like them, actual meditation practice begins with posture.

a. Sit in the lotus posture with your gaze cast five feet ahead of you, not focusing on anything in particular.
b. Repeat the four refuses and the Bodhisattva vow.
c. Visualize the entire assembly as in other meditations.
d. Keep your breath, senses, and attention calm and quiet without focusing on anything.

e. The Stage of Concentration

Formal meditation begins with concentration and leads, first, to one-pointedness of mind, and then to "seed" and "seedless" *samadhis* through stopping and destructuring ordinary consciousness. This is achieved either through breathing exercises, as in other meditation, or through concentration on various "nonmoving" objects.

1. Place a small ball or a bit of wood in front of you and fix your gaze on it without letting your attention waver. Hold your attention fixed on just the primary stimulus prior to thought, mental reaction, or the triggering of ordinary information-processing, until attention is able to stabilize on the meditation object, shift its orientation solely on it, and become unified and one-pointed.
2. Visualize your guru in the form of the Buddha, sitting on the crown of your head. Pray to him and ask him to help you attain the goal of *Mahamudra* meditation. Having prayed for psychic energy, absorb it in yourself. Visualize your mind as becoming identified with the Buddha/guru mind. Stay in this state of oneness for as long as possible.
3. Concentrate on an image of the Buddha or visualize him in bodily form. Symbolizing his speech, visualize a lunar disc, about the size of a fingernail, and upon it visualize the syllable *HUM*, as fine as a hair. Then concentrate on it. Symbolizing his mind, visualize a seed, shaped like an egg, about the size of a pea, emitting rays of light. Then concentrate on it. This is concentration with the "seed."
4. In a relaxed and calm state of mind, directly focus your attention and wholly concentrate on each inhalation and exhalation, and mentally count up to 21,600 breaths.
5. Holding your bare attention directly on the primary sensation, observe the exact moment your breath begins, enters through the nostrils, passes from the tip of the nose to the bottom of the lungs; note the duration it is retained; follow

it through the entire length of exhalation; then note the exact moment it begins again. Directly observe the increase or decrease, the slowing down or speeding up of your breath. Let your attention become completely one with the breath, so that it is the breath that is happening as yourself.

6. Now visualize each exhalation as a white *OM*, each inhalation as a blue *HUM*, and each retention of the breath as a red *AH*. Concentrate on them and clearly observe the three processes of breathing.

7. Next, employing the Vase-Breathing method described in the Yoga of Inner Fire, empty out your lungs completely through three intermittent exhalations. Then gently inhale through the nostrils, fill your abdomen completely, and retain the breath for as long as possible before exhaling. As you do this, directly focus and hold your attention on the sensation of the breath.

8. In this exercise, which is similar to *shikan-taza,* fix the attention in the space of awareness before anything arises or in the interval between thoughts. Instantly cut it off as soon as anything arises. Prolong the interval between thoughts by maintaining alertness and a heightened state of concentrated awareness without straining your mind or letting it become lax. Then, focusing and holding your attention directly on the primary stimulus, observe the interminable flow of thoughts and mental contents as they arise and pass without letting your attention become trapped in that flow. Prolonged practice of this method will enable attention to remain in direct contact with the primary stimulus, gather around it and become unified and one-pointed.

9. Next, as attention becomes one-pointed, watch the stream of consciousness and observe whatever arises without letting attention get caught in it or without trying to get rid of it. Just hold the attention on and directly observe the first moment of impact of the object before anything arises in the mind. This will lead to the first phase of stilling or emptying the mind, to *samadhi* and deconstruction of the outer form of the object and consciousness.

10. This deconstruction is accomplished by what is called "letting the mind assume its natural condition" (Evans-Wentz 2: 131), which is achieved in four steps: (i) maintaining evenness of mind by alternating cutting down thoughts as soon as they arise, and letting them be, just watching them, so that your awareness of the flow is not lost by involvement in mental contents; (ii) dropping the point of observation and holding the attention in the void-state, thus disidentifying with both mental contents and the self and shifting the focus to the experience itself; (iii) keeping awareness focused on the content and clearly comprehending its nature in a stable and clear fashion; and (iv) bringing awareness to the state of total nonreaction by disidentifying with the observer, the point of observation, and the content or object. Upon mastering these steps, you arrive at the state in which events happen by themselves or take their

"natural course" without any input on your part. All you do is observe both simultaneously. In this state, "the unbroken current of consciousness functions automatically" (Evans-Wentz 2: 134). The net result of these four steps is to empty or deconstruct the mind further by cutting through and transcending the inner symbolic layer of construction. This brings about a disidentification with the object-world, transcendence of ego or the point of observation, and union with the subtle form of the object in *samadhi*.

f. The Stage of Insight

As in other tantras, the second phase is insight meditation through which attention successively penetrates, cuts through, and transcends the primary or archetypal level of subject and objective constructions and the form and framework of meditation through seedless *samadhi* and insight meditation. Going beyond and arriving at the state beyond all object, construct, or form, you perceive the nature of the universe and conditioned existence, make a radical shift toward the Source, and become a pure void. Attainment of these steps is the objective of the following meditation:
1. Holding awareness in the state of *samadhi*, focus attention on your stream of consciousness and observe and actively inquire into the nature of what arises, and into the nature of the mind. Observe whether there is a self behind either. Continue this inquiry until you can see directly that there is no self behind either mental or physical events and that the subject or mind and the object or phenomenon are one. Continuing in this way, the mind will be eventually emptied out, in seedless *samadhi*, of theories, ideas, categories, the form of the object, and the conceptual form and framework of meditation.
2. Holding the attention in the "seedless" or void state of the mind, you are to practice, next, "reverse" *samadhi*. Maintaining complete nonattachment to mental contents and keeping the attention focused on the void state itself, just observe the nature of whatever arises at the exact moment of its contact with attention prior to any mental reaction or information-processing activity of consciousness. Keep the attention on or in the content for the entire duration it remains in the field of awareness and see it pass out of existence. By meditating in this way, you will enter into "arising and passing away *samadhi*," observing the very process by which conditioned states and events in the universe come into being and pass away; and you will attain "cosmic" consciousness or experience an identity with the universe itself.
3. A similar observation and examination of the temporal structure of phenomena will lead to a transcendence of the temporal structure of

consciousness. An observation of the nature of mind and matter will bring about a transcendence of their duality. And an observation and clear comprehension of the nature of the one and the many will enable you to transcend their differentiation. This process is called the "Yoga of the Uncreated" because it leads to insight not only into the nature of conditioned existence, that things are impermanent, nonsubstantial, and have no inherent existence of their own, but also to transcendence of duality and differentiation of anything into existent and nonexistent, material and nonmaterial, one and many. This is called "entrance into the Middle Path," wherein the final framework and spatio-temporal structure of ordinary consciousness is destructed and transcended; and you arrive at the state prior to the creation or construction of any object, form, conditioning, construct, or framework. From this state you are able to observe the simultaneous arising and passing away of all events and phenomena of the universe, and their interpenetration and mutual inherence. As Daniel Brown has well stated, thus you come to see that the same laws that constitute the individual constitute the universe, which appears as an undivided and interconnected whole (Brown 1: 253-258). Such an experience is the basis for the *Avatamsaka Sutra*-Hua Yen teaching on interpenetration, mutual inherence, and identity of all things and events in the universe. As discussed in *Song of the Skylark I,* according to this teaching, all things and events in all universes, actual and possible, simultaneously arise, interpenetrate, and inhere — each in all and all in each — constituting their infinite dimensions and making them an undivided whole.

g. Extraordinary Practice

This part of the meditation consists of the "Yoga of Transforming All Phenomena and Mind into their Primordial State" and the "Yoga of Nonmeditation." These methods are designed to bring the mind to enlightenment. The first consists of the following exercises:
1. In the state of *samadhi,* allow your relaxed mind to rest on whatever arises, external events and internal states, and see their oneness beyond duality. This will lead you to the state of nondifferentiation of all phenomena, physical and mental. Another practice is to recognize all phenomena as All-embracing Awareness; see whatever appears during sleep as no other than this Awareness; and whatever phenomena appear during the waking state as dream contents arising from unawareness.

2. Holding to the oneness of duality continuously in the focus of attention, see all phenomena or conditioned existence as expressions of the Unconditioned. Such seeing will lead to a realization of their oneness or nondifferentiation.
3. Keeping attention in the void state, see all things as the Void *(Sunyata)* and see the Void as manifesting itself as all things. A direct seeing of this will bring realizations of oneness of the manifest and the unmanifest and the Void-nature of all things.

These exercises, particularly the last one, lead to the state before anything becomes manifest. From this vantage point you can directly observe how the links in the chain of *karma* are forged and become manifest as forms and observable events. Upon such a realization, a profound shift takes place in awareness whereby it turns away from objects and turns toward itself and its Source — All-embracing Awareness. As mind pivots on itself, it becomes completely emptied of contents, and the fixation on the object-world even on the unconscious level is broken up. In this void state of itself, but for the final limit-barrier of duality, awareness arrives at the closest proximity to the unmanifest, primordial state of its true nature (Brown 1: 256-260).
h. The Yoga of Nonmeditation is so-called because at this stage, awareness has to be kept closest to its natural, primordial state so that enlightenment can break into the conscious sphere. All activities, even meditative ones, which interfere with this state, are stopped. As the mind stays in this void state, silent and still, it comes to a state of what Zen calls "ripeness," "absolute *samadhi,*" or being immured in a crystal basin, the condition from which awareness breaks through to the Unconditioned.

When awareness makes its final and most profound shift and breaks through the final limit-barrier of contents, objects and forms, conditioning, constructs and frameworks, it transcends all limitation and arrives at the Unconditioned, the Formless Ground of all forms and conditioned states. This experience reveals the identity of the unmanifest and the manifest, the Unconditioned and the conditioned, and your identity as pure, All-embracing Awareness, which is identical with Reality as Such (Evans-Wentz 2: 115-154; Brown 1: 260-262).

Although it may appear that Tibetan Buddhism is very different from the Zen and Theravada paths, a closer examination reveals, beyond undeniable differences, broad and deep similarities: All three have the same basic structure, consisting of concentrative and insight meditation. But within this basic framework, there are differences of method, forms of meditation, and surface structures. While Theravada and Zen tend to play down concentrative and emphasize insight meditation as the direct path to enlightenment, Tibetan *Tantra* seems to strike a greater balance between the two. Although the latter's various *tantras* are spectacular examples of the highest development of concentrative meditation, nevertheless not only the second part of the highest *tantras* but even the lower *tantras* give a prominent place to insight meditation. Again, all three emphasize impermanence and insight as essential to the method and the meditation process, and Buddhahood as the goal. But, whereas Theravada mainly emphasizes breathing meditation to attain *samadhi* and insight meditation as the path to *Nirvana,* and Zen stresses *zazen,* koan study and *shikan-taza* as the path to enlightenment and Buddhahood, Tibetan Buddhism aims at the same goal through its *tantras.* And, like the others, in keeping both eyes and mind fixed on *Sunyata* and Buddhahood, we see it teaching the same true *Dharma* of the Supreme Master of the Middle Way.

Chapter 12
The Path of Power: Taoist Yoga

Like its Hindu and Buddhist counterparts, Taoist Yoga operates on the principle that, beyond the duality imposed by the human mind, reality in its natural, unconditioned state is an identity and interpenetration of each with all and all with each; that the unmanifest is identical with the manifest; that the manifest order is governed by a primal polarity of Energy and Awareness, epitomized by the terms *yin* and *yang*, female and male, respectively; and that each individual is a point of convergence of these forces such that the essence of the universe is the essence of the individual. Taoist Yoga further holds that in the present state, the human individual suffers from a dual separation: a separation from universal forces and hence a separation from the universe and from others, and a separation and fragmentation within so that his/her present state is chaos.

The initial aim of Taoist yoga is to reverse this process of fragmentation and help you achieve a dual unity: a unity within yourself and a unity with the universe. Since each individual is an embodiment of the universe, the same process that leads to unity and integration within yourself brings about unity with the universe, if the continuum of the path is not broken. This unity brings about an "egress" or emergence of "the immortal foetus," that is, a unified, universal consciousness capable of proceeding to the final goal of transcending primal polarity and realizing the primordial Oneness that is Tao, which is called a return to and becoming the Source. In sum, this was the original aim of both Taoist mysticism and yoga. As Blofeld has noted, "Originally the objective of all Taoist forms of contemplation and yoga had probably been identical—the union of opposites within oneself in order that the mysterious light of the indwelling Tao might be made manifest" (3: 126). Later, however, as Taoist yogis became more preoccupied with achieving longevity and physical immortality than pursuing true immortality, there seems to have been a parting of the ways between Taoist mysticism and yoga or inner alchemy. Even when apparently sidetracked, its true aim continued to endure. This aim is clearly discernible as much in a fourth-century text as one composed in the nineteenth century.

Unlike other tantric systems, unique to Taoist yoga is the belief that three primal forces, called "The Three Ones," constitute the universe and the individual alike. In the universe they constitute the first division of the primordial unity of Tao. These forces are vitality, essence, and spirit. As this fundamental trinity, also conceived in early texts as three supreme gods, constitutes all levels of existence, in the individual they manifest as breath or energy *(chi)*, essence *(ching)*, and spirit *(shen)*, and reside in the three governing centers or cinnabar-fields of the human body: the third eye, the heart, and the abdominal center (three inches below the navel and two inches inside the body). The aim of yoga is to return to the Original Oneness, to Primordial Unity, by reversing the process which sundered it and created multiplicity. This consists in restoring unity by uniting the Three Ones within yourself and in the universe. The fundamental sign of such a realization is the emergence of the Child or the Immortal Foetus. That is why the Three Ones are said to look like infants (Andersen 22-27).

The method of achieving this unity is a successive transformation of breath-energy into the subtle essence; the essence into spirit or the unified, subtle state of consciousness; and the latter into the Child, the archetypal self, or universal, cosmic consciousness. Thus the platform is constructed for the final transcendence of form, for realizing oneness with Tao, thereby returning to the Source and attaining true immortality. The first transformation brings stillness of the body; the second, stillness of the mind; and the third, when the yogi arrives at the void-state, absolute stillness in which there is stillness in activity, and activity in stillness (Blofeld 4: 130-139).

Accordingly, Taoism has developed three stages of Yoga: (i) breathing exercises and sexual yoga to transform energy into the essential integration of energy and awareness; (ii) the Yoga of Inner Fire, similar to the Kundalini and Tibetan Yoga of Inner Fire, to raise energy-awareness to transpersonal states of the spirit; and (iii) meditation involving the mind to transform spirit into cosmic consciousness by attaining *samadhi* and arriving at the pure void. I shall briefly describe these three stages of Taoist Yoga below.

I: Transforming Energy into the Subtle Essence

a. The posture recommended is the full or half lotus.

b. Breathe abdominally with deep, continuous, slow, gentle, and fine inhalation and exhalation until your breath becomes imperceptible. When that happens, you may feel that your breath has vanished or that you are breathing through the pores of your skin.

c. An alternate method: Close your eyes and focus attention on the abdominal center. Contract the sphincter and sex organ muscles and push upward against the abdominal center as you inhale. When you exhale, contract the abdomen and push it against the diaphragm, forcing out the impure air. Let your breath gradually become fine, inaudible, and still. This is the vase-breathing exercise similar to its Tibetan counterpart.

d. Another alternative is to start with short breaths and lengthen them gradually, without straining, as much as possible. Breathe through your nostrils slowly, gently, deeply, and inaudibly. Take the breath down to the abdomen. During meditation, pay no attention to thoughts and empty out your mind. Continue to breathe in this way outside meditation also.

e. If you feel a vibration in the abdomen or in sexual organs, inhale, visualize, and, with your "inward eye" or attention, follow the Energy going down to the base of your spine, entering the central channel and then rising up through it to the sensation center. Then stop, relax and exhale naturally. Repeat this cycle very gently and smoothly, nine times.

f. If the sensation still remains, similarly raise the energy to the next center. If it still persists, raise it to the power center. Keep concentrating on it for a while, then relax and exhale. If further work is needed, proceed in this way to the crown center. As you continue this exercise, exhale very slowly; inhale and follow the energy down to the third eye center and exhale. Do this step six times. Proceed in this way down the front to the heart region six times; from there to the navel region six times; and then back to the point of origin six times. Thus you will have a total of twenty-four exhalations. Continue this method of raising and circulating the Energy until it is stilled, that is, until a unity of attention and one-pointedness of mind is reached (Jou 132-140; Lu Kuan Yu 2: 171-175). Tsung Hwa Jou says that this is the Northern Taoist method of transforming energy. The Southern School uses sexual yoga to achieve the same goal.

Sexual Yoga

As in Hindu and Buddhist tantras, Taoist yoga offers a twofold approach to the realization of the oneness of duality: through its symbolic enactment in yourself and through ritually enacted sexual union with a partner. While the first is similar to Kundalini and Tibetan yogas, the second is similar to the *sadhana* of the Five M's, both Hindu and Buddhist.

In agreement with Buddhist and some Hindu tantras, it instructs the adept not to release his sperm, for its conservation is believed to be essential to achieving immortality. In agreement with some Hindu tantras, believing that releasing the semen brings death, it instructs the adept to overcome lustful thoughts and feelings while performing the sexual act by keeping the mind focused on and seeing the act as a union with Tao. If he is unsure of withholding emission, he is to constrict the base of his penis with an ivory or a jade ring so that he can continue the yoga all night long.

The next step for the adept is to bring his partner to repeated orgasms, and, after initially mixing his male fluid with her female fluid, to draw it back and into his abdominal center through breathing, concentration, and visualization. Then, through a continuation of the physical act involving a specific rhythm and variety of strokes, and breathing, concentration, and visualization, the blend is to be transformed into the subtle essence. As in Hindu and Buddhist tantras, this requires stilling the body, the sensations, the emotions, and the mind. As sexual energy is transformed into psychic energy, the body and the sensations become still. The focus of attention is then turned to transforming the emotions, psychic energy, and the mind, for which desiringlessness is thought to be essential. When psychic energy is transformed into spiritual energy or universal consciousness, the second barrier is crossed. For this the Yoga of Inner Fire, which is similar to Kundalini and Yoga Tantra, is taught (Blofeld 3: 132-140; 4: 117-129).

II: Transforming Subtle Essence into Spirit — Yoga of Inner Fire

As stated before, for this Yoga, unlike Kundalini and Tibetan Yoga, the body is divided into three fields. The upper field has the third eye, called the "mysterious portal," as its center. It is the focal point of the essential nature. The heart center, which is the center of the mind, is the center of the middle field. The center of the generative force and the lower field is the abdominal center. The process of awakening, raising or expanding, and transforming Energy-Awareness is accomplished through meditation based on breathing, concentration, and visualization. But the method is somewhat different from the Tibetan Yoga of Inner Fire and Kundalini Yoga. The adept aims to raise the Energy from the abdominal to the heart center, and then to the third eye. In the process Energy is transformed and consciousness destructured from the gross to the subtle level (Lu Kuan Yu 3: 31).

Unlike Hindu and Buddhist tantras, Taoist Yoga works with three major regions, seven centers, and eight channels. Moreover, unlike the West but in conformity with some Eastern views, the heart is believed to be the center of the mind and not that of the emotions. However, the mind of which it is the center is the ordinary mind, while the third eye is the seat of intuitive wisdom. The crown center is the seat of the spirit, the highest reality in human beings, out of which emerges the new, transformed, unified, and integrated universal consciousness and the archetypal self, the Child or Immortal Foetus, who alone is capable of transcending the final barrier of duality and realizing oneness with Tao. The following is one version of the steps toward this realization.

a. Instructions for Energy Yoga begin with posture. Before sitting in meditation, try to banish all thoughts. Loosen your garments and belt in order to relax and free the body from external tension. As you sit, place the left leg outside and close to the right leg. This symbolizes the positive embracing the negative. The thumb of the left hand should touch its middle finger and the right hand should be placed under it, palm up, with the thumb bent over the left palm. This symbolizes the negative embracing the positive. Hold the back straight, the head high but bent slightly forward so that the tip of the nose is in line with the navel. Hold the attention focused on the spot between the nostrils. Without straining, turn both eyes inward, to the third eye center between and behind the eyebrows. Close your mouth and touch the upper palate with the tongue in order to stop the mind and the vitality (saliva) (Lu Kuan Yu 3: 1-6).
b. As you begin to meditate, your first task is to transform sexual energy into subtle essence by raising it from the base up the central channel to the back of the head and the crown center. Then lower it to the third eye and behind the palate down to the throat center, from there to the solar plexus, and finally to the abdominal center. This is called circulation of the breath or vital energy.
c. To circulate the breath-energy through all the eight channels, stop the breath and concentrate on "the cavity of mortality" or sensation center at the root of the sexual organ, and meditate as follows:
1. While inhaling, contract the stomach and drive the breath-energy from its base into the central channel and up to the crown center and down the front of the face to the mouth. This is to be accomplished by holding the attention totally on the breath, visualizing and following it from the nostrils all the way down to the base of the spine, and making it enter and rise up the central channel to the crown center and down to the mouth.
2. As you exhale, expand the stomach, visualize your breath-energy, feel its sensation, and, with complete attention, follow it from its base in the crown

center, down the front channel (in front of the central channel) to the sensation center.
3. Inhale and push the breath-energy up—by contracting the sphincter muscle, physically pushing up, mentally visualizing the breath going up and following it with full attention—from the sensation to the abdominal center, from there to the navel. Then stop and exhale. Inhale and visualize the breath dividing and entering the belt channel (which starts from both sides of the navel and forms a belt around the waist); then exhale. Inhale and raise it up the small of the back to the shoulders, and stop.
4. Exhale and let the breath-energy flow from the shoulders along the outer sides of both arms, over the elbow, down the back of the wrists and over the back of the middle fingers, then reaching the center of the palms and stopping.
5. Inhale and lift the breath-energy from the palms and circulate it through the inner part of the arms and bring it to the chest, to a point a little above the nipple; then stop and hold the breath for as long as it is comfortable.
6. Exhale and trace the breath-energy from the two points down to the belt channel, where you visualize the two branches reuniting and then travelling inward to the abdominal center before returning to the sensation center.
7. Inhale and raise the breath up the central channel to the abdominal center and from there to the solar plexus; stop and hold the breath.
8. Exhale and press the breath down to the sensation center, where it again divides to go down the outer sides of the thighs, kneecaps, legs, ankles, the top of the feet, and through the toes to the soles of your feet.
9. Inhale and raise the breath from there up the inner sides of the thighs to the sensation center and thence to the abdominal center. Hold the breath here for as long as it is comfortable.
10. Exhale and trace the breath-awareness from the abdominal to the sensation center. Again, hold the breath here as before. Remember: All these steps are to be performed by visualizing, mentally entering into, and tracing or following the breath-awareness with complete attention and directly observing the sensation of the movement (Lu Kuan Yu 3: 23-26; Jou 150-155).

This exercise is intended to dissolve negative programming, emotional blocks and mental fixations; and to raise consciousness to higher states. Its daily practice will make the body vibrant, create a buoyant feeling for life, fill you with energy and vitality, and make your consciousness clear, fluid, tranquil, and free of problems. Physiologically, it is of great benefit to those who have a circulation problem.

Beyond these effects, the central part of the meditation is concerned with emptying the mind of thoughts and disidentifying with mental contents so that it will not be stirred by emotions, desires, or sensory stimuli, and can lead to *samadhi* and deconstruction of gross perceptual programming. It will also immobilize the senses and the generative force. This will transform sexual energy into psychic energy, which will be awakened as a result of this exercise. Once awakened, it must be raised and brought to the archetypal, universal state of awareness by destructuring ordinary consciousness. This can happen when the mind becomes still and you enter into *samadhi* with the subtle form of the meditation object.

The Method of Holding the Three Ones

In addition to the above, a fourth-century text describes a method of achieving oneness that involves the following steps:

a. At the beginning of spring (this appears to be a seasonal yoga to be performed on the first day of each season), at midnight sit upright, facing the east, exhale nine times, and swallow your saliva thirty-five times.
b. Fix your attention on the seven stars of the Big Dipper and bring them down to a position directly above your head, in an upright position, with the handle pointing forward toward the east, two stars just above the top of the head, and two stars further up.
c. Visualize the Three Ones emerging from the bowl of the Big Dipper, each accompanied by a minister.
d. Breathe very deeply three times; and each time you do so visualize one of the Three, accompanied by his minister, following with the breath and entering into you through the mouth. The first one takes his place in the third eye center, the second in the heart center, and the third in the abdominal center.
e. After you have been able to bring down and hold the Three Ones in their respective centers, meditate until they are at rest, i.e., until one-pointedness is achieved, the mind is stilled, and you experience oneness with them (Andersen 46-48).

III: Transforming Spirit into Cosmic Consciousness

The methods used for this purpose are the techniques of breathing, rolling the eyes and visualizing the breath-awareness rising, and tracing or following it with full attention along the psychic channels, from the abdominal to the heart center, and then to the third eye center. For this the following exercises are recommended:

a. Since a return to the Source is possible only in a state of "serene voidness" or absolute *samadhi,* which can be attained by stilling mind-waves, the aim of this exercise is, first, to develop concentration and then to stop the stream of consciousness or empty the mind through "outer breathing," and, through "inner" or "embryonic breathing" to raise consciousness from its lowest level, corresponding to the base of the spine, to the highest, located in the crown center.

The method of outer breathing consists in awakening and raising energy or "the fire" along the back channel to the head thirty-six times and lowering it through the front channel twenty-four times. Essential to this breathing is unifying bodily motion, breath, visualization, and attention, and raising and lowering them together as one process of awareness. This requires that you hold attention fixed on the breath, visualize it as rising, and follow it with unified attention in such a way that you experience your mind as rising and falling. In the process it will become fluid and one-pointed with the breath-energy in circulation. Complete each circulation in one breath. When inhaling, coordinate, concentrate on and unify your feeling, thought, attention, and breath; visualize them as rising while moving the breath-energy upward from the base of the spine to the solar plexus. Hold them there for a short while for cleansing, and then raise them to the crown center. When exhaling, visualize and mentally trace them down to the central channel, pause at the solar plexus, visualize them as becoming purified, and then take them down to the base of the spine.

b. When you feel a vibration in the abdominal center, inhale as above, roll your eyes from left to right, and follow the ascent by visualizing and mentally tracing it with full attention. When exhaling as above, again roll your closed eyes, from their position of looking at the crown center, from right to left so that the breath and the eyes make a complete rotation with the completion of the descent, and follow the descent with visualization and attention. Begin the rotation by directing your eyes downward and then rolling them from left to right and looking up to the crown center as you inhale and from right to left as you lower them to look down into the navel and the abdomen, thus making a full rotation.

Along with breath circulation, do the eye rotation thirty-six times for the ascent and twenty-four times for the descent. This is the inner breathing for unifying attention and making the mind one-pointed.

c. Next, you are to unite "the positive and the negative principles" or attain oneness of primal polarity by rolling your eyes until a bright light appears in the third eye center. First, draw the pupils as close to each other as possible and hold them in this position while concentrating the attention on them. Empty your mind of all thoughts and contents, and allow it to become absolutely still. Then fix your attention on the third eye center and roll your eyes, as described above, until a bright light appears in that center.

d. When it does appear, take the light down to the abdominal center and focus your attention on it there by turning the eyes inward to look into that center. Do not hold onto the light if it wavers. Just focus your bare, pure attention directly on it until the mind becomes one with it. At this point the exhalation will become subtle and the inhalation unbroken, harmonic, and restful, bringing inner harmony between the upper and the lower part of the body. While concentrating on the light, keep your mind empty of everything, void of attachment even to form or relative voidness, in order to preserve the radiant stillness. Hold the mind on the light for as long as possible. In time the center will vibrate with inner heat or Energy-Awareness.

e. When that happens, visualize and raise the Energy to the heart center and then lower it to the abdomen. Continue this ascent and descent until it suddenly slips into the abdominal center. At that point you will feel as though your eyes have fallen from your face into that center, making you feel that your body no longer exists; that is, the external form of consciousness has been destructured and *samadhi* attained with the subtle form. As this occurs, the Energy will fill your mind and the two will become one. Then vibrations will be replaced by stillness; and the inner breath will stop while the outer breath continues.

f. As this happens, practice "breathing through the heels." Concentrate on, visualize, and draw up the inhalation through the heels into and up the back channel to the crown center. Visualize and take the attention-exhalation down to the abdominal center. Circulate the breath in this way in order to raise the Energy to the crown center and free the mind from the effects of conditioning, illuminating it like a bright pearl. When this breath circulation produces "ambrosia" (saliva), gulp it down. As you do this, it will fall on and radiate the "immortal foetus" in the abdominal center. At this point your breath will nearly stop. During this exercise concentrate and keep your attention fixed on the abdominal center until the "immortal foetus" is produced or an integrated, unified, subtle, or archetypal, self emerges.

g. In order to produce it, continue to practice this method so as to unify, transform, and raise psychic energy to universal consciousness. When this happens, a golden light will appear in the white light in the third eye center and produce the foetus. Then push up and raise the foetus by driving the golden light up to the crown center in order to unite it with the primordial polarity. To bring this union, turn your eyes toward the crown center and bring the pupil of the left eye (positive spirit) together with the pupil of the right eye (negative spirit) into one conscious focus and keep the attention on it for as long as possible. By practicing this session after session, you will experience a unity with it; the sense of their separation will vanish from your mind; the essential nature will be revealed in the pervading light of vitality; and you will experience a great bliss.

h. When in the light you see "flying snow and dancing flowers," that is, when you experience *samadhi* with the archetypal or universal form, visualize yourself and mentally leap into the great Void, which will open "the heavenly gate of the sun and the moon," that is, open the doorway to transcendence of primary duality or *samadhi* with the subtle form. The leap will open the doorway on top of your head and your spirit will leave the human body and appear in the form of countless bodies in space (Lu Kuan Yu 3: 161-176; Jou 161-171). In other words, your consciousness, raised to the universal, cosmic level at the crown center will, through cultivating this *samadhi*, finally break through the limits of programming, forms, and constructs, and experience oneness with all things.

Although this return to and realizing identity with the Source is indeed the goal of Taoist Yoga, not all forms of Taoist meditation follow the above course. Some seek to bring about the same transformation through concentration, absolute stillness of mind, and *samadhi*, dispensing with the yogic techniques. Whatever the path, however, the goal remains the same. Here again Taoism is similar to other paths in providing alternative approaches to enlightenment.

Chapter 13
The Way of Kabbalah

Jewish meditation, developed by the Kabbalistic tradition, displays the same kind of diversity as the other paths. Not only does it have various concentrative and contemplative practices or insight meditation; it also uses prayer and movement for meditative purposes. The entire meditative path ranges from ethical and behavioral training to calming and purifying the mind to union, and beyond union to identity, with God (Epstein 78, 118; Idel 63-73). Thus, in common with the other paths, it clearly has the four main meditative stages of purification, illumination, union, and identity.

Preliminary Stages: Purification

In the Kabbalistic tradition, work on the path begins when an aspirant meets a *meggid* or teacher, who directs him in the awakening and unfoldment of his mind, which is ordinarily locked in a state of unawareness. This process begins with his becoming aware of the actual condition of his life. To this end, the *meggid* teaches him to observe himself neutrally, from the point of view of the higher self, the impartial witness of his thoughts, emotions, and behavior. The aim of such observations is to develop an objective view of himself. These observations range over the various states of consciousness—vegetable, animal, and ego states—that successively preoccupy the initiate throughout the day or over a longer period. A proficiency in this practice will lead to a discovery of the mechanical character of ordinary life; the limited, narrow range of the programmed mind; of emotional and habitual fixations; and of positive and negative programmings or sins. Upon such discoveries, the *meggid* prescribes practices designed to eliminate weaknesses and past sins; develop good habits; strengthen his personality; and balance and realign his life in relationship to the ultimate goal (Halevi 82-83, 91).

The initial training, as in other paths, involves both body and mind, ethical and devotional practices, and arouses a highly motivated state. Thus, as Perle

Epstein describes in detail, in the eleventh century Bahya ben Joseph Ibn Paquda prescribed ten practices or "gates," corresponding to what he believed to be the ten levels of spiritual life, through which the aspirant has to pass before beginning formal meditation. These span the physical and the spiritual realm. They include developing positive traits, such as proper worship, trust, humility, acceptance, purity, and saintliness; and working on negative ones, such as counteracting hypocrisy by developing sincerity, repenting for past sins, and abstaining according to his needs (4-9). Other masters, such as Isaac Luzzatto, add zeal, watchfulness, cleanliness, separation, fear of sin, and holiness (Epstein 27). And Moses Cordovero adopted for himself thirteen practices to "nourish the spiritual center in the heart and to cultivate the first level of mystical consciousness — Awe" (Epstein 13).

Such training is necessary before beginning formal meditation, for the path is long and its rigors may overwhelm or discourage someone who has not been properly prepared. The mental attitude to be cultivated is called *kavvanah,* which includes keeping the mind focused on the present, the aim of which is to develop present-centered consciousness. As another preparatory step, you are told to establish a regular time for practice. The preferred times are early morning, immediately after rising, and, after a short period of sleep, midnight (Hoffman 96-99). In addition, the *meggid* prepares a special time and place for group practice in order that the mind may be made receptive in a supportive environment.

Next come instructions on how to clear the mind and deal with thoughts during meditation. Several methods are recommended. One is to take the key idea in a thought that attracts the mind, project it on the *Sefirotic* Tree or the Tree of Life, and then contemplate it in order to awaken that quality within yourself. Another is to reject a thought as soon as you notice that it has arisen, and then immediately replace it with the opposite thought. A third is a familiar one — not to pay any attention to or interfere with any thought. As the mind remains indifferent to all thoughts, feelings, and images that bubble up, for a while the ego will intrude, but if you persist in paying no attention to them, in time disidentification will occur and the mind will become still (Hoffman 111-115).

Various ways of clearing emotional blocks and mental fixations are recommended. One is to meditate on one such trait at a time, facing it through self-examination, and working to dissolve it. This is, of course, a form of IAM. Along the same line, another method is to sit quietly in a dark room and focus attention on an emotion, go through your experience of it during the day, move into it, reexperience it in full awareness, and disidentify and let go of it. A third is to get rid of all repressed feelings through a "silent scream" type of technique.

This consists in imagining the sound of the scream, evoking all the repressed, pent-up feelings and letting them fill your consciousness, and then releasing them. When all the repressed feelings are thus expressed and released, you become free (Hoffman 108-111).

Another practice, very similar to Patanjali's sensory withdrawal *(pratyahara)*, is called "self-isolation" *(hitbodeduth)*. Indeed, Aryeh Kaplan considers it the most specific term for the meditative state and says that it "consists in isolating the mind from all outward sensation and then even from thought itself" (52). His description makes it clear that the term refers to sensory withdrawal as a preparatory step toward formal meditation.

Concentration and Illumination

According to Z'ev ben Shimon Halevi, there are three major types of formal meditation involving the mind: active or concentrative, devotional, and contemplative (90). The greater part of concentrative meditation and contemplation involves the use of letters of the Hebrew alphabet, divine names, and the Tree of Life *(Sefirot)*. In tantric fashion, mantra and visualization are most extensively used in the first two, while the last employs visualization and movement meditation.

Meditation Based on Letters

Like Mantra Yoga, Jewish mantra meditation is based on letters of the Hebrew alphabet, sound vibrations they produce, and their effect on consciousness. Three letters, called "mother letters" because they are said to produce primal sound vibrations that are the source of all others, form the basis of various mantra meditation. These letters are: *ALEF*, which represents silence and is used for pause; *MEM*, which is pure tone, representing harmonic state of consciousness, and producing an even wave on the oscilloscope; and *SHIN*, called "white noise," which is an amalgam of all other frequencies, producing a chaotic pattern on the oscilloscope, and representing our normal, chaotic state of consciousness (Kaplan 129-130; Sheinkin 175-176). Since sound vibrations produced by these letters relate to states of consciousness, the purpose of Kabbalistic meditation based on them is to proceed from *SHIN* to *MEM*, or from the chaos of ordinary life to wisdom *(chokmah)* and harmony with all creation, that is, becoming a cosmos yourself. The meditation goes as follows:

Exercise I: Mantra Repetition

a.   Sit comfortably with your eyes lightly closed. Your hands can rest comfortably on a table or on your lap. Fingers should not be clasped or intertwined. But if your hands are together, one should rest lightly on the other. You do not have to assume any specific posture. Just sit quietly and settle comfortably into your place. Relax (Kaplan 59-60).
b.   Breathe normally. As you exhale, make the sound "sssss" for the entire length of the exhalation. Silently inhale; and then as you exhale, make the sound "mmmmm" for the entire length of the exhalation. Then silently inhale and repeat the alternating sound for the entire meditation period.
c.   As you alternate, just be with each sound. Let it vibrate throughout your body.
d.   If the "mmmmm" sound brings you to a "new inner realm," remain in it for as long as possible, and then return to the "shin" sound (Sheinkin 176-177).

Exercise II: Mantra Repetition

a.   Maintain the same posture and breathing as in the previous exercise.
b.   Take Rabbi Nachman's mantra, *Ribbono shel Olam* (Master of the Universe) and slowly, in a very soft voice, repeat it over and over. You can either whisper or vocalize it very softly. You can also mouth it without vocalizing it.
c.   At first, you may let your mind wander freely while reciting the mantra. Or you may concentrate on the images that may appear as you repeat with your eyes closed. But as you become more advanced, you should let the words of the mantra totally occupy your attention, pushing all other thoughts to the periphery and out of the focus of attention.
d.   Generally, avoid bodily motion, since it destroys concentration. But if you find that gentle swaying eases bodily tension, you may use it.
e.   When the meditation session is over, stay in your place for about five minutes and allow the mind to absorb the effects of meditation before rising and doing other things (Kaplan 60-62).

Exercise III: Visualization of Letters

The twenty-two letters of the Hebrew alphabet and ten circles of the Tree of Life *(Sefirot)* constitute thirty-two secret paths of wisdom, ways to unite yourself with the universe, and reach the divine. When the ten circles are connected with lines, twenty-two lines are formed as pathways for the circulation of cosmic energies and raising consciousness. To each line a letter of the alphabet is assigned, very much in the fashion of Hindu Tantra. But unlike the latter, in addition to its shape and sound, to each letter a numerical value is assigned. The letters are seen as channels of the forces of creation and can awaken these forces in the meditator and unify him with the universe and with God (Sheinkin 179-180; Kaplan 81). One form of meditation with the letters proceeds as follows:

a. Close your eyes and try to picture a letter of the alphabet, say A or the Hebrew *ALEF*. Just relax and allow the thoughts and mental contents to settle down and the image of the letter to appear on your mental screen. Or you may have the letter printed on a card and set it at a comfortable distance and in line with your visual field. Then softly gaze at it until it becomes fixed in your visual field. Then close your eyes and try to see it on your mental screen.
b. As this is difficult at first, as an aid to visualization you may repeat it periodically during meditation, or you may repeat it over and over again, like a mantra. Another strategy is to write the *ALEF* on a card and contemplate it for several days before attempting to visualize it. If you find it still difficult, Kaplan recommends that you alternate between contemplation and visualization (78).
c. Once you are able to visualize the letter clearly, the next step is to "engrave" the image in your mind. This means stabilizing, fixing, and holding the image in your mind so that it does not move. No matter what other image or thought arises, it remains fixed in your mind. Others are not able to dislodge it or capture your attention.
d. The next step is to "sculpt" or "hew" it, that is, isolate it or get rid of all other images so that it alone remains in your mind. This will happen when your concentration deepens, and your attention gathers around and becomes unified with the letter until it alone remains in your consciousness.
e. In order to achieve one-pointedness of mind, you need to set the image of the letter in a pure white background. This requires you, first, to clearly visualize and stabilize the image of *ALEF*. Allow it to fill your mind. Then hew away all other images around it with white fire by visualizing or picturing white fire burning away all other images. Begin with visualizing a small spot of white fire at the top of *ALEF* burning away surrounding images. Then let the fire expand and burn away increasingly larger areas as it moves from the top to all sides until only *ALEF* is left, shimmering in a background of white fire. Now see the letters as black fire blazing on white fire (Kaplan 77-79; Sheinkin 180-182).

Meditation IV: Circle of Letters

This is a visualization that resembles Tibetan Yoga and Sufi meditation. The entire Tree of Life with its ten circles and twenty-two lines on which the Hebrew letters are projected appear like a *mandala* and can be used for the purpose of visualization. The following is a form of visualization based on letters that resemble visualization exercises in the Tibetan lower tantras and, of course, similar to the above meditation:

a. Visualize yourself in the center of a circle of letters of the Hebrew alphabet.
b. Visualize each letter as a three-dimensional figure standing before you.
c. View yourself as seeing all the letters in front of and behind you simultaneously. This means you can actually see 360 degrees.
d. When you are able to visualize this distinctly and the images are stable, visualize a connection among all the alphabets such that the letters and lines form a circle of light or energy.
e. Concentrate on this circle or *mandala* until you experience a unity with it (Sheinkin 183).

Other exercises based on the Hebrew alphabet include one similar to Tibetan yoga, in which you visualize the letters and pass them before your mind. Another is to write them down so as to form an endless chain of letters and contemplate them (Halevi 193).

Meditation Based on Divine Names

Jewish meditation on divine names, in which the focus of attention is the letters, employs the same methods as those that involve the letters of the alphabet. Of all the Hebrew names of God, the most sacred is the tetragrammaton, YHVH (YAHVEH). It is visualized as follow:

Exercise I: Visualizing the Tetragrammaton

a. Visualize, engrave and hew it in the same way as the letters.
b. Now unite the last two letters V *(vav)* and H *(heh)*. This will give you a palpable experience of God's presence. In order to unite them, focus your complete attention directly on V and H and become aware of their longing to

unite. Intensify the longing until it becomes unbearable, at which point they unite. This releases a spiritual energy which flows through your body and mind.
c.   After the union becomes prolonged and stable, visualize the sky opening and yourself ascending to the spiritual realm. Observe yourself rising through seven stages until you reach the highest.
d.   As you do so, visualize an infinite white curtain filling your mind and the entire horizon. Then visualize YHVH written on it in black.
e.   Hold your attention on the black letters and the white curtain until they intensify and appear as black fire on white fire. Let the letters fill your mind completely. A prolonged focus will make your mind and the letters one and thus you will reach *samadhi*.
f.   Now visualize the letters as solid, three-dimensional objects. When they become stable, enter into them until you experience yourself first surrounded by and then merging with them.
g.   Next, visualize the letters as living entities, like angelic beings. Then become aware of their primal force and spiritual energy, the archetypal consciousness they symbolize, and the flow of energy among them until they appear as a circle of energy. Finally, in this circle experience the primal polarity of the creative energy of the universe and the oneness between God and creation (Kaplan 79-81).

Meditation II: Visualizing Nothingness

a.   Again this meditation resembles Tibetan Yoga and Sufi meditation. Visualize YHVH.
b.   Engrave it in your mind.
c.   Hew away surrounding images and replace them with nothingness by first visualizing a small area of nothingness around Y. Then let it expand until nothingness surrounds YHVH. At this point the letters will fill your mind and nothingness will surround them.

An alternate method is to visualize a field of nothingness and see YHVH hidden behind it so that you see both simultaneously. This will bring you to the realization that God is behind nothingness and you will come closest to experiencing God's formless essence – God as "he" is in "himself" (Kaplan 90-91).

Another related exercise is to rearrange and recombine the letters involving the names of God or to form new words (Hoffman 102-103). The aim of these and similar exercises is to flood consciousness with a continuous interchange of combinations of letters so as to disrupt ordinary information processing, empty consciousness of all contents except the letters, and prevent it from translating them into the familiar world of meaning. This will not only weaken the hold of ordinary reality on your consciousness and enable it to function in a new way through evoking new associations, ideas, and insights, but will also eventually stop thought and inner dialogue, destructure consciousness, and enable you to experience transpersonal states.

Meditation Based on the Tree of Life

Before you engage in formal meditation, one of the things the *meggid* does to you is to bring you to see your true position on the Tree of Life. Like the *mandala* and the *chakra* system, the *Sefirot* symbolizes the primal forces or states of reality and consciousness emanating from and reaching all the way to the *Kether,* the crown center. As such it is the path along which consciousness must develop in order to reach universal dimensions and thus become one with the universe. Like the *mandala,* the *Sefirot* is based on the idea of the undivided wholeness of the universe and the interpenetration of all things so that when you become one with the primal forces and the states of reality and consciousness within yourself, you at the same time become one with their universal forms and thus experience oneness with the universe. To attain this unity, the *meggid* assigns various meditative exercises, such as remembering the diagram of the Tree at certain times during the day, repeating a prayer or performing the ritual of standing with your arms outstretched, first thing in the morning and before retiring, so that you can physically sense yourself and your body as the Tree and feel its energies coursing through your body. Along the same line, another practice is to invoke God by standing with arms extended in the form of the Tree (Halevi 180-181).

Another visualization in connection with the Tree is to picture a white light surrounding and filling you with its warmth and tranquility. Then visualize the light circulating upward, going through the points in your body corresponding to the points on the Tree. Thus the light simultaneously courses through the body and the Tree, awakening, expanding, and integrating the states which each represents, until it rises through the crown of your head, goes beyond, and merges with infinite, formless Light (Hoffman 107).

Another type of meditation depends on symbolic values assigned to letters and numbers. As Edward Hoffman explains, this meditation is based on the belief that the twenty-two letters and ten primary numbers represent, as in Hindu and Buddhist tantras, thirty-two primary energies that underlie the entire universe. Of these, the first letter is believed to represent the active, outward-oriented primary energy principle, while the second letter represents the receptive principle (103-105). When thus depicted and visualized, the letters and numbers become objects for contemplation. The letters may also be used to contemplate the paths on the *Sefirotic* Tree for the purpose of discerning the flow of the energies from the universe through the letters into yourself, awakening the energies within, and raising consciousness. In another type of contemplation, the letters are recited continuously while visualizing "the Lightning Flash descent of the Tree, with a triad being completed as soon as three sefirot are connected by the prime flow" (Halevi 203-207).

There is a form of walking meditation in which, while stepping to the right and to the left, you are to bring the two columns of the Tree — the column of mercy on the right and of severity on the left — to conscious unity within your own body. As the two columns of the Tree represent active and receptive modes of consciousness or the polarity of forces and states, while the middle pillar signifies their unity, in this meditation you are to be conscious of the polarity represented by your left and right sides, and their unity in the trunk of your body. And you are to achieve their unity within yourself through this meditation (Halevi 183-185).

In connection with the Tree, another meditation is to apply God's names to the pillar by associating YAHVEH with the right or merciful side and ELOHIM with the left or severe side. Use the names in the walking meditation by silently repeating the first with the right step and the second name with the left (Halevi 185-191).

Contemplation: Candle or Oil Lamp

This and the following are further examples of Jewish contemplative practices.

a.   In a dark, draftless room place a candle away from the wall so that no light is cast on it.
b.   Softly gaze at the candle and let it fill your mind.
c.   Become aware of the heat and energy radiating from the candle and try to see the energies.
d.   Become aware of white, yellow, and red colors in the flame.
e.   Now concentrate on the darkness surrounding the flame until the room becomes palpable.
f.   As you get deeper into the meditation, you will begin to see a sky-blue field around the darkness. According to the *Zohar* (a Jewish mystical work), this

sky-blue represents divine presence. You may see visions in this blue field (Kaplan 69-71).

Contemplation of YHVH

a. Since you are not allowed to pronounce this name, write it on a card or sheet of paper and place it in a well-lit room at a distance and elevation where it is easily visible when you are seated in your place of meditation.
b. Focus your gaze on the name and let the letters and the name completely fill your mind. Let the significance of the name completely occupy your heart.
c. Now see the first two letters as the primal masculine force of creation and the last two as primal feminine force of divine providence. Unify them until you become aware of and feel open to divine guidance in your life.
d. Continue to gaze at the name written on the card until the black of the letter and white of the card become very intense. Continue the practice until you are able to see the name as black fire written on white fire.
e. When the mental image of the name is formed, abandon the gross form and contemplate the subtle form until you experience oneness with it (Kaplan 72-76).

Devotional Practices

The devotional practices involve prayer with a special focus, one of which is to regard each word in a prayer as a name of God (Halevi 197-201). Other devotional practices include the use of psalms and liturgical hymns. As their main devotional practice, the Hasidic communities use music and dancing, similar to the Sufis, to induce ecstasy, which is intended to enable them to transcend separation and experience oneness with the universe and union with God. Beyond union lies the final goal of identity.

Union and Identity

To this end, one practice enjoined is called, in Sufi fashion, annihilating ego through self-surrender, which is the highest ideal of the devotional approach. As your mind becomes completely filled with God and you surrender yourself in ecstasy, the sense of separation dissolves, and you disappear in the Divine. When ego is completely surrendered, you see God everywhere and come to realize that there is nowhere where God is not and nothing that God is not. At this stage only God remains (Hoffman 100-109).

Some adepts, believing that a separate consciousness must be retained on earth to the very end, seek a permanent union (Halevi 206-207). Others, however, clearly recognize identity beyond union as the final goal of the path. Thus, some Hasidic masters, such as Shneur Zalman, his son Dov Baer, and his circle describe union as "cleaving" and identity as "merging into the Divine All" (Quoted by Epstein 133), being "swallowed up," amd becoming "one substance" (Quoted by Idel 71). Rabbi Isaac Levi, Dov Baer, and others describe the same two steps in terms of the metaphors of "cleaving," and "annihilation of [individual] existence," "dying," and poverty" (Idel 65-72).

This final transcendence occurs when union with God in *samadhi* matures. As the adept comes to experience a total deconstruction and transcendence of ego, ordinary consciousness and reality, s/he transcends duality between himself and God. At this stage, all sense of separation from God disappears, resulting in the experience of identity. This final goal of the Kabbalist path — the state of *devekut* — could be best described as an affirmation of simultaneous universality and individuality in which the individuality, far from being obliterated by identification with the Divine, is affirmed in its true state, in all its distinctiveness, as a manifestation of God on earth.

Chapter 14
Christian Meditation: The Eastern Church

As already noted, the framework of Christian meditation is similar to Hindu Bhakti Yoga, Kabbalah, Sufism, and other devotional meditative paths that generally operate within a dualistic framework. The goal of this path is union with God, conceived as a Personal Being, the Infinite Other. Upon attaining full union, the Christian mystic lives in the vibrant, loving, pulsating presence of God, who sustains and transforms him/her into "himself," resulting in a permanent union or, as the Eastern Orthodox tradition puts it, deification. Although official Christian teaching does not admit it, going beyond union, and hence the dualistic framework, many Christian mystics have attained identity with the Godhead, as their experiences clearly attest. This identity must be recognized as the final stage of the path.

The emphasis on love and relationship makes Christian meditation a path focused not primarily on the mind but on the will and emotions. The meditator works not with attention/awareness but primarily with intention and will. Since God is conceived here as the Lover and the meditator as the Beloved, as the latter's self-agency and will increasingly diminish and later drop away, God's agency (or awakening and operation of the transpersonal realm) correspondingly increases. Thus the higher stages of the path appear to be purely passive. All activity on the part of the meditator ceases while God takes the initiative to infuse "his" grace and lift him/her to the state of union.

Christian mystics generally have taken two approaches: the affirmative and the negative way. The former seeks to use images and ideas as ladders to climb toward God who lies beyond. It especially emphasizes love as the way to the goal—union with God. Believing that God is beyond name, form, image, concept, thought, and knowledge—inexpressible, unknowable, unconceptualizable—the negative way holds that it is only by emptying ourselves of all thought, image, concept, and going beyond the separate self—beyond everything that is not God — that we can experience God. It holds that when one arrives at this absolute transcendence of form and limitation, when there remains nothing in the mind to create separation from anything, one experiences one's identity with God and all that is. Although these differences between the two ways pertain to the advanced stages of meditation, in the initial stages both ways cover common grounds and prescribe similar practices.

Christian writers usually distinguish three stages in this meditative journey (although John Chirban adds two preliminary stages), corresponding to similar delineations by other paths: the purgative or the path of purification, the illuminative or the stage of insight, and the unitive stage. To these stages must now be added a fourth and final stage: identity. Various practices are assigned for each stage of the path. Although the goal remains the same, the practices of the Eastern Orthodox Church differ from those of the Western Churches.

Christian meditation was developed by hermits or solitary individuals during the fourth century of the common era in the remote regions of the Egyptian desert. Driven by the uncertainties and confusion of the times and by the desire for personal communion with God, they engaged in various practices in the isolation of the desert, free from worldly preoccupations. These practices included ascetic ones, such as fasting, silence, church rituals, vigils, that is, staying up all night in prayer; and meditative ones, such as, mantra-like verbal or silent repetition of a phrase from scripture, constant remembrance of God, and contemplation. Gradually, these hermits were drawn together to establish communities. Thus monasteries began. Rules were needed to organize and regulate life in the monasteries. In the Eastern Church, among the first to provide such rules were St. Anthony and St. Basil the Great. In the Western Church, similar rules were formulated by St. Benedict for his newly founded Order.

Meditation methods did not develop overnight. Initially, ascetic, liturgical, and sacramental practices predominated. To these practices various forms of prayer or meditation were added. One such prayer, developed and taught by Hesychius of Jerusalem, is called "The Prayer of the Heart" or "The Jesus Prayer." The essence of this practice is the invocation of the name of Jesus by means of a mantra-like repetition of the phrase from the New Testament, "Lord Jesus Christ, Son of God, have mercy on me a sinner." Like other methods, the Jesus Prayer was preceded by preliminary exercises.

Preliminary Practices: Purification

According to John Chirban, the path begins at the stage of image, which consists in a recognition of one's natural state of being created in the image and likeness of God. This recognition includes seeing your actual state, a growing realization of the true goal of life and your distance from it, and awakening longing and the motivation to reach it. Such is the meaning of Jesus' proclamation at the beginning of The Sermon on the Mount, "How blest are those who know their need of God; the kingdom of Heaven is theirs" (Matt. 5: 3). For once you learn about your true condition and your need of and distance from God, you can summon the desire, the strength, and the determination to realize what you truly are, to recover what was lost in the process of growing up.

This recognition leads to the second stage: conversion. Conversion is a reversal of the orientation of your life and consciousness from the outer focus on the world of objects to the inner world of the Spirit — the Ultimate Source and goal of existence. It is based a recognition that in our present fallen condition, we cannot *be* the divine likeness which we nevertheless truly are. A fundamental change in our consciousness, identity, and lifestyle is necessary, if we are to recover our divine image. Conversion is our conscious commitment to a total change and to follow a path that will lead to a recovery of our true Self.

Once you make the decision and seek out a community, you will be assigned various ascetic and ethical practices. Sifting through the writings of early Christian spiritual writers, you will notice that, like the early Sufis, they emphasize such practices. They do not say much about methods of prayer or meditation. They are primarily concerned with purifying oneself of sins or negative programmings and eliminating weaknesses; strengthening and developing positive traits or virtues; awakening and heightening motivation and love of God; and developing self-observation and self-knowledge.

The number of vices or negative programmings you need to uproot and the positive traits or virtues you need to cultivate are indeed formidable. Just one look at the list compiled by St. John of Damaskos, for instance, could discourage even the most redoubtable initiate. Of these, John considers unawareness, laziness, and ignorance to be the root vices of the soul; and he calls greed the "mother of vices," "the root of all evil" (Palmer et al. II: 335). In his short list St. John Cassian mentions gluttony, unchastity, greed, anger, depression, listlessness, self-esteem, and pride. All agree that pride is a root of many other vices. Perhaps no one puts it better than St. John Climacus when he says:

Pride is a denial of God, an invention of the devil, contempt for men. It is the mother of condemnation, the offspring of praise, a sign of barrenness. It is a flight from God's help, the harbinger of madness, the author of downfall. It is the cause of diabolical possession, the source of anger, the gateway to hypocrisy. It is the fortress of demons, the custodian of sins, the source of hardheartedness. It is the denial of compassion, a bitter pharisee, a cruel judge. It is the foe of God. It is the root of blasphemy. (207)

Since, as St. Theodoros says, the aim is a total conquest of the passions and vices (Palmer et al. II: 35), we can see why the virtues especially marked out for cultivation are humility, desiringlessness or dispassion, nonattachment, purity of heart, stillness of body and mind, and fasting. According to St. Isaiah the Solitary, the first virtue is detachment from every person and thing. For it produces the desire for and the stillness necessary to see God (Palmer et al. I: 27). To St. Neilos, "Detachment is the mark of a perfect soul" (Palmer et al. I: 244). According to Theodoros, "Dispassion is the wedding garment of the deiform soul" (Palmer et al. II: 26). To Abba Philemon complete stillness is the path leading to heaven (Palmer et. al. II; 349). And for St. Simeon the New Theologian, "without fasting no one was ever able to achieve any of these virtues or any others, for fasting is the beginning and foundation of every spiritual activity" (169). Similarly, St. Gregory Palamas says, "Fasting is the essence of prayer" (49).

Another group of practices especially emphasized are "guarding the heart" or controlling the senses and the mind; watchfulness or mindfulness, and self-examination. In fact, watchfulness or self-observation is regarded so essential for uprooting negative programmings and ingrained habits, and for developing virtues, and hence for a monastic life, that St. Hesychios the Priest states, "a true monk is one who has achieved watchfulness; and he who is truly watchful is a monk in his heart" (Palmer et al. I: 190). He further states, "Watchfulness is a spiritual method which, if sedulously practiced over a long period, completely frees us with God's help from impassioned thoughts, impassioned words and evil actions. It leads, insofar as this is possible, to a sure knowledge of the inapprehensible God, and helps us to penetrate the divine and hidden mysteries" (162). According to him, together with the Jesus Prayer, it is one of the essential requirements of the path.

There is a consensus among the masters of the Eastern Orthodox Church that self-observation and self-examination are to be practiced unceasingly toward everything, especially toward evil tendencies, passions, habitual inattention, and restlessness. As in other paths, the aims of all preliminary practices are the same: eliminating evil behavior and uprooting evil tendencies; purifying or simplifying life and gaining control over the senses and the mind; self-discovery, so as to eliminate the negative and enhance the positive; heightening awareness; disengaging and shifting attention from the outside and directing it inward, thus preparing the mind for formal meditation.

Formal Meditation: The Jesus Prayer

It is clear from Hesychios the Priest that mindfulness or watchfulness is more than a preliminary practice. His explicit statement indicates that, as in Buddhism, it is a form of Informal Awareness Meditation, to be practiced at all times and toward everything. This is also clear from St. Peter Damaskos, who recommends that it be practiced unceasingly, from moment to moment, for "without attentiveness and watchfulness of the intellect we cannot be saved" (Palmer et al. III: 105). More specifically, according to Hesychios, it is to be used to examine mental images; to still mind-waves; to pray and call on Jesus for help; and to keep the thought of death continually in mind (Palmer et al. I: 164-165). And he says that watchfulness and the Jesus Prayer mutually reinforce each other.

The method of the Jesus Prayer is nowhere fully described. From various descriptions in *The Philokalia*, which is an anthology of teachings of Eastern Orthodox masters written between the fourth and the fifteenth centuries, it is clear that it employs posture, breathing, and a concentrative method similar to those found in other paths. In one text the meditator is instructed, upon waking up first thing in the morning, to sit in his cell or room on a low stool, gather his mind from its wanderings among the objects of the world, and lead it into the heart, directing the attention inward and holding it focused on itself. He is then to practice breathing and to repeat the Jesus Prayer, coordinating it with the breath. The meditation session is to last an hour (Goleman 54-56).

Another text in the same anthology speaks of three "methods of attention in prayer" or concentrative meditation. According to the first, you are to stand, in Kabbalistic fashion, and, raising your hands, eyes, and mind upward, focus your attention on God. Next, like Tibetan yoga, visualize heavenly blessings, hierarchies of angels, assemblies, and dwellings of saints. Then reflect on or contemplate everything you have learned from scripture. Thus you are to arouse love of and longing for God.

The second method begins with instruction similar to Patanjali's *pratyahara* or sensory withdrawal. You are instructed to shift your attention away from external, sensory objects and guard your senses from being stimulated (to avoid giving rise to thoughts and fantasies). Next, center your thoughts and turn your attention inward so as to stop mind-wandering. With the mind turned on itself and keeping attention focused on the stream of consciousness, observe and examine its contents or what arises. Observe the words of the prayer you may utter. If your attention wanders, bring it back to focus as soon as you notice it.

Neither of these two practices, however, is considered a good form of meditation since neither is unable to dissolve negative programmings or still the mind. The third method, considered a marvelous one, is "The Prayer of the Heart." (In Eastern fashion the mind is thought to be in the heart.) With Jesus visualized as being in the heart, hold your attention there and repeat the Jesus Prayer: "Lord Jesus Christ, have mercy on me." In this way offer up prayers to God from the depth of your heart for the entire meditation period (Naranjo and Ornstein 53-54).

Other texts introduce variations on this basic form, especially by adding various types of breathing exercises. Thus, Nicophoros the Solitary instructs you to focus attention, in Theravada Buddhist fashion, on your nostrils. As you inhale, follow the breath with complete attention all the way down to the "heart" or the power center and keep it there. Nicophoros observes that at first this will be difficult, as the mind will have no interest in the practice. But if you persist and your mind becomes wholly focused on and is gripped by the prayer, that is, becomes unified and one-pointed, you will experience joy and ecstasy (Eliade 63).

Another text provides another variation on the exercise: Sit in a quiet, dark, or dimly lit room. Turn your mind away from outside and toward itself, and then, in Tantric fashion, press your chin against the chest. Compressing the inhalation and the exhalation, first slow it down and then stop the breath. As you do this, focus your eyes and attention on the power center and mentally examine the abdomen to locate your heart there. In the beginning, he says, there will be "shadows and a stubborn opacity." But practicing night and day, you will finally arrive at boundless happiness (Naranjo and Ornstein 54-55). Similarly, St. Gregory Palamas recommends that as a point of concentration, you fix your eyes on your chest or navel (46).

In another version, the Patriarch Callisotis instructs you to focus attention on your breath, follow it down to the power center, and, fixing your attention there and coordinating it with your breath, mentally repeat with the inhalation and exhalation, "Lord, Jesus Christ, Son of God, have mercy upon me." St. Gregory of Sinai adds that some of the "fathers" have taught that you should use this full form while others advised the use of the shorter form, "Lord Jesus Christ, have mercy upon me," or instructed alternating the two. But he recommends that you should not go back and forth between forms. He says further that some teachers said that the repetition should be done audibly, while others advised silent repetition. According to him, you should use both forms. You may begin with audible repetition. As the mind becomes concentrated, the repetition will become silent of its own accord. Indeed, at this stage it will be impossible to repeat it audibly (in Fleming 97-98).

To counteract the infinite distractibility of the mind, its incessant scanning the horizon for sensation, its habitual wanderings amid the object-world, and its entrapment and lostness among mental contents, Gregory recommends confession of sins, frequent and patient prayers, repentance, and uniting yourself with God. But if thoughts are too persistent or the mind gets disturbed, he recommends that you stand up and raise your arms and head until thoughts subside or the mind calms down sufficiently, and then resume the repetition (in Fleming 98-99).

With greater astuteness, St. Gregory Palamas says that in the beginning the mind has to be constantly brought back from its ceaseless wanderings. Since it is focused on the world and not on itself, it is constantly dispersed. Unless it is "recollected," that is, gathered around its object and its orientation shifted inward, it is impossible to direct the mind toward God. To stop this mind wandering, he recommends breath-control (as do other masters): At the end of each inhalation and exhalation pause, hold or stop the breath briefly, and bring your attention back to focus on the breath and the repetition. He recommends that you do this until attention becomes unified and one-pointed or remains uninterruptedly focused on the repetition. He says that this will lead to deconstruction of consciousness (44-46).

In order to achieve this reversal, or what Gregory calls "circular" direction "by which it comes to transcend itself and be united to God," and to focus the mind on itself, the masters recommend that, outside meditation periods, you make this practice your constant companion and never stop repeating it. Thus, following St. Paul's advice to pray without ceasing, Abba Philemon recommends, "Without interruption, whether asleep or awake," "eating or drinking, in company or outside your cell, or on a journey, repeat that prayer with a watchful mind and an undeflected intellect; also chant and meditate on prayers and psalms. Even when carrying out needful tasks, do not let your intellect be idle but keep it meditating inwardly and praying" (Palmer et al. II: 348).

Similarly, another text instructs you to repeat the above exercise at all times and in all activities, always repeating the same prayer, coordinating it with the rhythm of your breath and slowing it down as much as possible. If you are able to keep it going day and night "with infinite repetitions," you will, you are assured, attain all kinds of marvels and knowledge, besides finding "the heart's place there" (Goleman 56).

According to Callisotis, such constant repetitions, both in and outside formal meditation periods, will keep the mind from wandering or daydreaming and arouse love for God, who will in time become the sole object of consciousness, displacing all other thoughts and preoccupations. Eventually, the meditation will empty your mind of all other contents, shift the entire orientation of consciousness toward itself, and gather and unify attention. In time, as the Jesus Prayer first grips, then fully occupies, and finally becomes one with your mind, "abandoning the many and the varied, [you will] unite with the One, the Single and the Unifying, directly in a union that transcends reason" (Naranjo and Ornstein 54-55).

When this union or *samadhi* becomes continuous or permanent, it blossoms into what is called "transforming union" or "deification." Deification is not an identity of essence but, as Gregory Palamas tells us, an irradiation and transfiguration of the individual by and into the uncreated divine energies (57-69). As your consciousness becomes permanently united with the divine consciousness and you live continuously in the divine presence, your personality becomes steadily transformed and it becomes indissolubly joined to God.

Mystics of the Eastern Church also speak of identity. One such is Pseudo-Dionysius. According to him, as you begin the ascent to the summit, first the stage of deconstruction you experience pertains to the outer, verbal layer. As you pass beyond this stage, he says, "language falters." The next stage is deconstruction of the inner image, idea, and concept — the subtle form. Thereupon you pass beyond intellect, beyond "every divine light, every voice, every word from heaven" (*The Mystical Theology* 136), and plunge "into the truly mysterious darkness of unknowing," where the mind falls "silent completely" (139). In this state, vast emptiness and silence reigns. Out of this void state comes the experience of that supreme union which is "far beyond mind, when mind turns away from all things, even from itself, and it is made one with the dazzling rays" (109). In this state, "being neither oneself nor something else, one is supremely united by a completely unknowing inactivity of all knowledge, and knows beyond the mind by knowing nothing" (137). Since nothing remains in the mind to create any separation between oneself and God, this experience of oneness, he tells us, is direct and unmediated, and thus one of identity, in which the Godhead beyond duality reveals itself to be the ground, reality, and identity of the individual and of all that is.

Chapter 15
Christian Meditation: The Western (Catholic) Church

As it is true of the Eastern Church, it could be said that in a real sense, for the Western Church also, the meditative journey begins with the experience of conversion. It begins with seeing your actual condition the way it is, and deciding to undergo a basic change of direction in order to discover life's meaning by "following Christ," that is, by adopting a spiritual discipline that will lead to that discovery. When you make this basic decision and seek out a community where such a discipline is taught, you will be assigned various practices and observances, as in other paths, pertaining to preliminary practices of purification. These practices are designed to remove from your mind the effects of negative programming and identifications, habit-patterns, and mental and emotional obstacles that stand in the way of meditation. You will have to master your emotions and desires so that your mind may remain tranquil and your heart poised and ready; purge yourself of selfishness and surrender your will to the will of God; become attuned to the subtler forces in your life; shift the orientation of your consciousness inward and focus it on God, and begin the journey to the heart of reality.

Preliminary Practices: Purification

To attain this goal, you are enjoined various ascetic practices: repentance and fasting, not only in matters of food and drink, but also in thought, word, and deed in order to purge yourself of "sins" or negative programmings; silence and solitude (beyond mere refraining from speaking), that is, the inner stillness that opens up the discerning eye; and "custody of the eyes," or guarding the eyes from the incessant scanning that stirs up thoughts and desires, makes the mind distractible, and reinforces ordinary consciousness. Control over the senses will also purify the emotions and clear the mind of blocks, fixations, and limitations created by conditioning and habits, and will open you for further growth.

On the positive side, you will be taught to develop the virtues, not only the moral ones but especially the theological virtues of faith, hope, and love so as to overcome weaknesses and self-centered existence and to attune yourself to the will of God. You will be assigned exercises of self-awareness and self-examination to come in touch with and see yourself as you truly are. Further exercises will be enjoined to arouse the love of God.

One of the practices emphasized at this initial stage, besides other moral virtues to strengthen your character and personality, is humility. As its Latin root, *humus,* meaning "ground," indicates, humility requires you to become grounded or down to earth, to shed delusions, self-importance, self-deception, and especially to overcome pride and egotism. Humility helps you see yourself as you really are — the negative programmings that run your life and your lack of control over your thoughts, desires, wants, needs, and actions. As the author of *The Cloud of Unknowing* states, one who is humble "sees himself as he really is" — he sees "the degradation, misery, and weakness of the human condition" on the one hand, and on the other recognizes "the transcendent goodness of God" (65). This insight helps you divest yourself of illusory self-concepts, artificial needs, wants, and desires; and bring tranquility, peace, and happiness in your life. As ego begins to surrender, you begin to lose self-importance and become filled with the Spirit. You also see the need to submit to a spiritual master and be taught in the way of the Spirit.

The deepest sense of humility is expressed by Meister Eckhart. He says that humility is self-emptying, which brings self-transcendence. When one is totally empty, there remains no barrier separating oneself from God. So Eckhart says, "God and such a humble person are totally one and not two. Whatever God does, the humble person does; whatever God wants, the humble person wants; whatever God is, that the humble person is as well — one life and one being" (Fox, *Breakthrough* 167).

As in other paths, including, as we saw, the Eastern Church, a practice greatly emphasized by many mystics as necessary for the journey and to be practiced at all times is nonattachment. Thus, according to *The Cloud of Unknowing,* nonattachment, or what it calls "forgetting all the creatures God has made," is a necessary step on the path. Without it, turning off sensory awareness and shifting attention away from the external world and keeping it focused on God will be difficult and transcendence of the personal stage impossible.

Recognizing this point, St. John of the Cross says, "In order to pass from the all to the All, you have to deny yourself in all" (Peers 81). Since attachment to limited, finite objects detaches us from Reality as Such, without practicing nonattachment to all things, it is impossible to attain union with God. And underscoring its importance, Meister Eckhart seems to offer us no method except complete nonattachment as the way to a direct union with God. Since attachment to anything other than God separates you from "him," when you give up all attachments, the distance separating you from God disappears. And in a blinding flash of realization you come to see that in reality there was no separation, for what then remains is only and all that ever was and shall be.

As you progress on the path of purification and your mind becomes gradually focused on God, you turn away from the world of multiplicity, confusion, and distraction, and embrace the world of simplicity, wholeness, and clarity. To attain this state, you will need to develop, in addition, what Ruysbroeck calls "simplicity of intention," a single-minded approach to all things characteristic of a unified mind. Such wholeheartedness will enable you to cut through fantasies and illusions, and become direct and present-centered. It will awaken the love of God, who is ever-present Reality and can be found only in the present.

Concentration and Meditation

To accomplish this objective, Christian meditation begins with various methods that are essentially discursive, involving reasoning, analysis of concepts, comparisons, and reflection, as well as affection, resolution, and communion with God and the saints. Some meditative exercises involve thinking, reflection, and even visualization, in which you are instructed to picture a scene from the Bible, mentally place yourself in it and experience it in order to cultivate a specific virtue, to gain understanding of certain truths, or to purify yourself of some sin. Another objective is to arouse yourself emotionally as a preparation for contemplation. Memory, imagination, and intellect are used to arouse the will to elicit affections (Schlosser in Hanson 117).

The *Spiritual Exercises* of St. Ignatius of Loyola serve as good examples of such meditation. The *Exercises* offer a variety of methods to free you from attachments and enable you to go deeper into yourself and discover God's will concerning the direction of your life. To this end it calls for vividly picturing sins, evil tendencies, the horrors of hell, biblical scenes of faith, forgiveness, love, and so on. Next, you are instructed to reflect your own condition, resolve to overcome sin and seek God's forgiveness, cultivate the virtue with which the meditation is specifically concerned, or arouse love for God. Other objects to be used include: an image of Christ, the crucifix or scenes from the crucifixion, other events of Jesus' life, other scenes from the Bible, etc. (Egan 30-68). As you can see, these exercises resemble Kabbalistic practices and Tibetan *Kriya* and *Carya Tantras*. They aim at eliminating negative programmings; developing positive qualities; and strengthening character, personality, and motivation.

A typical *Exercise* consists of a preparatory prayer, which invokes God to help you direct your "intentions, actions, and operations" purely for "his" service. Next there are two or more "preludes" which involve imagining or visualizing the scene of the meditation and asking God to help achieve the objective of the meditation. These preliminaries are followed by several main points of the meditation. Finally, there is a "colloquy," or conversation with Christ or God, concerning what should be done. The meditation ends with a prayer. What follows is the first meditation from the *Exercise:*

Exercise I: On Sin or Negative Programming

a. Preparatory Prayer (the same for all Exercises): Ask God to help you direct all your intentions and actions for "his" praise and service.
b. First Prelude: Visualize your soul or mind in a state of bondage in this body and your whole self in a state of suffering, living in what the Kabbalah calls a vegetable and animal state ("exiled among brute beasts").
c. Second Prelude: Ask God for the ability to see your condition as it actually is—to see your shame and confusion; to observe how others have been lost for one mortal sin; and to acknowledge that many times you have deserved the same fate.
d. First Point: Recall the "first sin"—the fall of angels. Picture their state of innocence, from which they fell because of pride. Understand and reflect on the entire situation. Compare their situation to yours—how, in spite of their superior state, they fell because of only one sin, while you are not only far below, but are fallen and have committed so many sins. Then arouse your will and emotions to do something about your condition.
e. Second Point: Now consider in the same way the fall of Adam and Eve. Visualize their condition of innocence prior to the fall; the fall itself; and the consequences of separation, dislocation, conflict, and suffering. Clearly comprehend and reflect on this condition; then arouse your will and motivation to apply to your condition.
f. Third Point: Apply the same method to a particular sin for which an individual has gone to hell. Understand the nature of sin which separates us from God; then arouse your will and intention not to commit sin again.

g. Colloquy: Picture Christ before you hanging on the cross. Ask him why he died on the cross for your sins. Then look at yourself to see what you have done, are doing, and ought to do for him. Observe what arises as a result of such reflections. At one time you may ask for a favor, at another time blame yourself for your sins. Tell him about your present condition. Ask him what you should do. Then end the Exercise with a prayer: The Lord's Prayer (in Fleming 198-200).

Other masters also assign similar exercises for this initial stage of meditation. St. John of the Cross, for instance, recommends continual meditation on the life of Christ in order to turn off sensory awareness, turn the mind away from seeking external objects, from craving and self-seeking, and shift attention and will toward Christ and seek him only.

Going a step beyond, the unknown author of *The Cloud of Unknowing* recommends a concentrative, mantra-type meditation. He tells you to fix your "naked desire," or your bare intention and attention on God, stripped of all self-interest. Now choose a simple word, such as *God* or *love,* that the mind can easily retain. Gathering all your desire or intention, fix your mind on it and hold it there. As your mind remains focused on the word for prolonged periods, it will eventually become empty and God alone will remain. Such one-pointedness of mind will prepare the way for union (Johnston 94-96).

While the author of *The Cloud* does not provide any specific instruction on how the meditation should proceed, a modern form of meditation, called "Centering Prayer," has sought to remedy the lack. One of its leading exponents, Abbott Thomas Keating, describes the method as follows:

a. Choose a relatively quiet place. Assume a comfortable position that will enable you to sit still. Close your eyes.
b. Choose a word of one or two syllables that expresses your intention of opening and surrendering to God.
c. Gently place the word in your "imagination" or the center of your attention. Keep thinking the word in whatever form it arises. You are not to repeat it like a mantra but to place it in the center of your attention and place your whole being, your total intention, in it.
d. When you become aware that you are thinking some other thought, gently bring the word to the center of your attention.
e. Meditate about twenty or thirty minutes and end the session by returning to ordinary thoughts, and, for about two minutes, saying some vocal prayer, or planning the day's activities. Then open your eyes (35-37, 110).

Another version of the meditation — one that uses the chosen word as a mantra — is the following:

a. Choose a word that is meaningful to you, one that you can get into without its causing any mental resistance or conflict. I recommend that you use the word *Jesus* as a mantra, coordinating it with your attention and breath, and repeating it as follows:
b. Assume one of the postures recommended earlier. Breathe slowly, evenly, and gently in and out of your heart center. As you inhale, mentally repeat "Je-e-e...e-e" with a long, slow, smooth inhalation. As you exhale, similarly repeat "su-u-u...u-s." Make your repetition, breath, and attention one. Follow the breath with complete attention.
c. As you repeat, keeping the attention fixed on the heart center. Visualize Jesus sitting there. As you inhale, he takes on your form and fills you completely so that you become identified with him. As you exhale, visualize him contracting to the size of your heart center. Experience the sensation of this identification, expansion and contraction.
d. As the meditation deepens, the mantra will glow in your heart center and Jesus and you will become one. You will then notice that it is he who inhales and exhales. Indeed, he will become the inhalation and exhalation and everything else will drop out of your consciousness, which will then become Christ-consciousness.
e. Continue to meditate until you come to experience Jesus directly as the one who, in the words of St. Paul, "is before everything, and all things are held together in him. He is before all, in all, and is all — the complete embodiment of Godhead and your completion" (Col. 1-3).

In her book, *In God's Radiance,* Linda Sabbath describes a number of meditation exercises that I wish to reproduce here. Following is a mantra meditation which she calls "Breath Prayer":

a. Select a suitable mantra, seven syllables in length, that represents God and suits your spiritual needs. It should express such characteristics as loving, healing, and redeeming. For example, "Jesus, healer, make me whole," "Transform me into yourself," and so on.
b. Begin by first repeating it out loud, then continue in silence, repeating it in slow, regular rhythm. Coordinate it with your inhalation and exhalation as your repeat. Concentrate your whole attention on the repetition.

c. Center the mantra in your heart and then center the heart on God. Picture the prayer going into your heart as you breathe, and direct the desire of your heart toward God.
d. Meditate five to thirty minutes each day, and then continue to repeat it throughout the day as often as possible (49).

Another form of meditation, involving visualization, was practiced at least as far back as the Renaissance. Nicholas of Cusa describes it in his book, *The Vision of God*. As formulated by Linda Sabbath, it proceeds as follows:

a. If a chapel is not available, find a quiet, clean corner free of clutter, and seat yourself comfortably with the icon of your choice pasted to the wall at eye level. Sit up straight but not stiffly. Keep your hands in your lap. Breathe deeply and regularly.
b. Read a biblical passage on light, e.g., John 1: 4-5.
c. Place yourself in the presence of God by thinking that you are sitting in the presence of God, who sees and accepts you just as you are. Examine your conscience in the light of God's presence and see how you are right now, recognizing your strengths and weaknesses, and resolving to overcome the latter and develop the former. Make the sign of the cross.
d. To be in a totally relaxed and alert state of mind, briefly repeat the breath prayer.
e. Softly gaze into and beyond the icon as if you were observing a sunset or a pool of water. Just be in the presence of the icon, with no thoughts, words, or images. Let your attention remain in the center of the icon and gradually become one with it. Observe whatever arises in your mind (38).

The following is an internal visualization adapted from Father Edward Lavin. It is incorporated by Ram Dass in his book, *Journey of Awakening:*

a. Sit comfortably with your back straight in any of the recommended postures. Relax. Be alert and attentive. Breathe slowly, deeply, evenly, and normally.
b. Place yourself in the presence of God by thinking or becoming aware that you are in God's presence.
c. Picture yourself in a lush meadow. It is spring. The grass is fresh, fragrant, and green. The sun feels warm on your skin. A gentle breeze is spreading the cool, soothing freshness of spring. A feeling of joy and well-being bathes your body and mind.
d. The people around you are very still, meditating and waiting for someone. Feel the energy of their devotion.

e. On an elevation in front of you, there are people seated, surrounding a figure whose presence you immediately recognize to be Jesus. He appears radiant and enveloped in a glowing white light. Gaze upon him and feel the warmth of his love.

f. As you continue to gaze upon him, a radiant light darts out of his heart center and enters your heart center, setting you ablaze with his love, warmth, energy, and joy.

g. Now he approaches you, enters and fills your heart center, and then expands and fills you completely so that you experience yourself to be one with him. Stay in this awareness for some time.

h. Then picture yourself or your awareness rising out of the top of your head until it reaches a field of white light pulsating with vibrant Awareness, stretching from infinity to infinity. As you enter into this light, it envelops you, penetrates every cell of your body, every fiber of your being, until you feel completely one with it. Directly experience yourself as this light. No barrier, distance, gap, or separation exists between you and this light, which is God. Stay in it for as long as possible.

i. Next, visualize light from this Light shooting out in all directions, filling the universe and lighting up all things. It falls on the earth, envelops it, burns off all the darkness of unawareness, anger, hatred, violence, fear, distrust, and coldness, and fills it with warmth, joy, peace, awareness, and love.

j. Now slowly descend from this light to the earth; once more experience Jesus in your heart center; and then see him come out of it, leaving his love, warmth, joy, peace, awareness, and new life flowing through and transforming you into himself (Ram Dass 76-77).

A meditation that Linda Sabbath calls "heart-to-heart prayer" involves complete self-surrender to the radiant heart of Christ until you experience a total transformation of your heart into that of Christ. It proceeds as follows:

a. Begin with scripture reading, preferably from John's text concerning God's indwelling or Paul's text on becoming transformed in Christ's image or becoming the "New Man."

b. Center the breath prayer in the heart for a few minutes.

c. Raise sexual energy into the heart by drawing a geyser, visualizing it in your sensation center, and then seeing it rise and spill over into the heart center.

d. Seated in front of a picture of Christ and his radiant heart, visualize an inflowing of love, warmth, energy, and joy from Christ's heart into yours, setting it aglow and making it as radiant as his. Experience the current circulating between his heart and yours until the two become one and you experience ecstasy (55).

By practicing such meditations, the author of *The Cloud* says, you are to turn off memory, imagination, intellect, or the discursive mind, and its thoughts, ideas, concepts, and presuppositions, eventually emptying out its contents. In this stillness of mind, you will arrive, according to him, at a stage in which "the cloud of forgetting" is behind you and "the cloud of unknowing" is above you. Thus, at this stage, the first phase of the deconstruction of ordinary consciousness takes place. The author calls this "the death of reason" (Johnston 53-56, 92), that is, the cessation of rational, discursive thought. In Patanjali's terms, it is the first phase of stopping mind-waves. This stillness sets the stage for the dawning of insight, or "a pure, naked feeling of its own being," that is, awareness experiences itself and all things directly, prior to the triggering of mental reaction and ordinary information-processing activity.

Similarly, St. John of the Cross instructs you to go beyond conscious and unconscious states and arrive at a state of "unknowing." This is "the active night of the spirit," which consists in actively going beyond understanding, feeling, imagining, fantasizing, desiring, and thinking by placing them in a cloud of forgetting. The aim is to stop thought and inner dialogue so as to attain union with God. So he says, "He that would attain to being joined in union with God must not walk by understanding, neither lean upon experience or feeling or imagination, but...must pass beyond everything to unknowing" (Peers 75).

As a result of such exercises, your mind begins to become clear, pure, open, and illumined. Your emotions and will become disentangled, purified, aroused, active, fluid, and focused on God. Thus meditation slides into "the prayer of affective regard."

The Stage of Illumination

It is not correct to say, as does Benedict Groeschel, that the stage of illumination is what other traditions call "enlightenment" (136). Rather, it is the stage (which Patanjali calls "meditation") in which the object of meditation may appear as a stream of light. It is the beginning of insight meditation. This illumination is a consequence of a relative stilling of thoughts and emotions, of a unification and expansion of awareness, which open up intuitive understanding. Bernadette Roberts is closer to the mark when she says, from her own experience, that far from being a distinct stage, illumination occurs "throughout the passive nights and the entire unitive stage" (2: 62). Illumination becomes more pronounced as consciousness begins to be destructured; the action mode recedes; and the receptive mode becomes awakened, operative, and dominant. Traditionally, it is a transitional stage between meditation and contemplation in which sensory and mental activities decrease and you receptively place yourself in the presence of God, which is the beginning of contemplation. As the author of *The Cloud* states, "Contemplation is born when reason dies" (Colledge 174).

Contemplation, however, is of two kinds: acquired or active, and infused or passive. Corresponding to Patanjali's "meditation," the former consists of a simple, loving gaze maintained on God. Although at this stage thoughts are still present, sensory awareness, memory, imagination, and discursive activities of the mind become deactivated so that they create no interference. The orientation of consciousness shifts from the outside world, and the unified attention and will turn toward God in a simple, loving gaze.

Infused contemplation, on the other hand, begins when the mind is still and gross perceptual construction is transcended. At this stage, there is an intuitive union with God through the deepest stages of faith and love, understanding and wisdom. The death of reason of which the author of *The Cloud* speaks is especially applicable to this stage. Hence John of the Cross calls it "the passive night," since it involves no activity of ordinary consciousness. There is nothing more for the mind to do but purely *to be*—directly with the object, God, on whom it is now centered. Thus, active contemplation slides off into passive contemplation, which is pure *wu-wei*, not-doing, and very similar to *shikan-taza*. At this stage there is a cessation of striving, doing, and discursive thinking. The main meditative practice is just to open and surrender yourself completely to the action of God. In the stillness God illumines the mind and stirs the heart, and prepares them both for the final stages of the path.

At the initial stage of contemplation, called "the prayer of quiet," and still corresponding to Patanjali's "meditation," although thoughts or distractions may still linger, the discursive and other activities of the mind become still. According to the author of *The Cloud*, this should make verbal prayer fall away. However, if you do feel the urge to pray, he tells you to pay no attention to the words or their meaning, but reduce them all, in the manner of Zen Buddhism, into one word and make it the vehicle of bare intention reaching up to God—not to any concept of God but to the God beyond concepts, just as "he" is (Colledge 157). Fixing your intention wholly on God, "hold yourself continually poised and alert at the highest and most sovereign point of the spirit" (Johnston 95). This means hold your attention at the immediate point of its impact on the word *God*, or whatever you choose for contemplation, before anything arises in the mind. As he says, the mind should be so unified with the word you choose for contemplation that "surging up from the depths, it should be the expression of your whole spirit" (Johnston 96). Your whole being should be identified with it in such a way that any sense of separation disappears.

For contemplation, John of the Cross recommends three practices. One is what he calls "a simple gaze of loving faith," which consists in directly focusing your mind and will wholly on God through a pure, loving intention without any image, idea, concept or any other activity of consciousness. Like *shikan-taza,* there must be no movement of the mind. Your bare, loving intention must be directly focused on God prior to any thought about God or anything else arising in your mind. At this stage, according to John, you may experience visions and revelations, but you are not to attach any importance to them.

To cut off memory of all forms so that all thoughts and attachments to the past are erased, keep the mind wholly focused on the present, and direct and hold your desires and aspirations fixed on God at all times. For this John recommends meditation on hope. However, this is not a hope that is tied to the future but something wholly directed toward union in the here-now. Ultimately however, it is contemplative absorption or *samadhi* and the "dark nights," first of the senses and then of the soul, that will accomplish this. As John says, when contemplation deepens, you become so absorbed in God as to "forget all created things." He says further that nearing the state of union, the absorption of memory may be so great as to render you incapable of doing anything else.

To disidentify with external objects of desire, a third practice John recommends is to divest yourself of "creature-love" and put on "God-love," which consists of disidentifying with "for God's sake all that is not God." This requires the mind to be so wholly absorbed in the love of God that it displaces everything else, eventually empties out the mind and will, leaving only God as its sole object. This leads to *samadhi.* As John states, this love will cut off all attachments to creatures and open the way to a direct union with God.

The Stage of Union

As you arrive at union or *samadhi,* however, your attention/intention must penetrate the outer form of the image or concept, of which you have been simply aware, and the corresponding programming of consciousness. As St. Gregory of Nyssa states, it must cut through external associations, customary perceptions and preconceptions, and emotional associations connected with the form or idea of God in your mind. This is the function of "the dark night of the senses," which is characterized by what is called "aridity" or loss of meaning. With the mind focused wholly on God, there occurs a sensory withdrawal, a shift in its orientation, and an emptying of thought, attachment, and desire for external things. This causes a destructuring and transcendence of the perceptual and socio-cultural framework of meaning, and a purging of ego-defenses, illusions, and delusions, leaving you utterly exposed and naked (Eliade 63; Groeschel 173-174). It is this loss of meaning and of the familiar anchor to the perceptual world that constitutes the heart of this darkness.

As attention/intention passes through the dark night of the senses, it gathers around, becomes wholly absorbed, and enters into union with the form of God. This is called the "union of ecstasy" and corresponds to the onset of *savikalpa samadhi*. Ecstasy and other paranormal phenomena, such as rapture and levitation, are consequences of this direct exposure to and union with the divine form. This experience is marked by an intense certainty of God's presence, and of unity and ineffability (Groeschel 179-193). In this state, as God displaces all other mental contents from the center of attention/intention, whatever you do is accomplished in the context of God's presence. As the author of *The Cloud* states:

> [When this state grips you], it stays with you all day long so that it goes to bed with you, gets up with you the next day, follows you around all day long, whatever you may be doing, pulls you away from your usual daily exercise that comes between it and you, accompanies or follows your desire so that it seems to you either that it is all the same desire or that you do not know what it is which has altered your demeanor and made you cheerful. (Colledge 180)

However, this is not a direct experience of God but union with the gross form beyond ordinary consciousness. This is clear from the manifestation of ecstasy, rapture, and other paranormal occurrences. It is also clear from the fact that, as St. Teresa of Avila says, the experience is transitory; and it takes place through "the senses and faculties" — it is an "imaginative vision" (178). This is similar to entering *samadhi* with a koan, and the initial stages of Patanjali's *samadhi* with the "seed" or form.

As this union is still too distant — God's presence is felt and not seen — a further refinement, similar to what Patanjali and others have noted, in terms of further penetration of the form and transcendence of constructs and a corresponding stripping of the self, are necessary. This is the function of "the dark night of the soul." So the author of *The Cloud* urges: "Divest yourself of every sort of feeling of yourself, so that you are prepared to be clothed with the gracious feeling of God's own self" (Colledge 182). Benedict Groeschel explains that this dark night consists essentially in emptying the memory, the intellect and the will of their contents and programming (185). At this stage, consciousness is further destructured; and there is a corresponding transcendence of ego, as the point of observation falls away.

Distinguishing six phases of the unitive life, Bernadette Roberts says that the first phase begins with the dark night of the soul, whereas others place its beginning at simple union. According to Roberts, this first phase or dark night is a destructuring process of consciousness and programming that creates the framework of ordinary reality. She herself experienced this phase as a loss of the framework by which we create meaning and make our world familiar. Translation of the transpersonal states into the personal and familiar came to an end for her at this stage. With their removal, existence appeared to her in its true, naked state, just as it is — as pain ("the pain was all"), *dukkha,* exactly what the Buddha experienced. Along with it came the experience of ego as ego — the nothingness and impasse that is ego — as "a bottomless pit that went nowhere" (2: 29-31). As she held the focus on and penetrated further into the state, she finally reached the bottom, where she experienced stillness and silence, in which her will was at one with God. Thus the still point of existence was revealed to be the highest point of the self where union with God takes place (2: 25-50). This experience of the dark night was also associated with an opening of the third eye center, which silenced the mind and fixed and absorbed attention on itself without any object (2: 67-70).

At the second phase there is an emergence, unification or integration of a new, higher, transformed self on the transpersonal plane. As you stop identifying with anything, you transcend the ordinary sense of separation and arrive at the experience of a new, transpersonal, archetypal self. Thus, after the destructuring there is a restructuring of the self around the still point beyond ordinary consciousness. This center, where only the bare will is present, becomes the reference point for the unification of other states. They are here raised, transformed, and integrated to form what Roberts calls "the true self" or "the Christ-self." This is the emergent universal, archetypal self or state of consciousness that St. Paul called "the New Man," "the New Creation." This "New Man" is regarded by many as "the highest point of the self," where the final state of union with God takes place. St. Teresa of Avila calls it the "center of the soul" or the spirit, where God is permanently enthroned. Corresponding to Robert's next phase, it is here that full union takes place (179-182).

Upon full union, there is a shift to God-consciousness in which the object of consciousness is no longer just the self but also God, who becomes the primary object. God takes over the object-pole, while the self remains the subject-pole of consciousness. Whereas previously God's *presence* was felt, now God "himself" can be seen, though obscurely, through the filtering effects of form and primary duality. Remaining at this center, Roberts experienced a further letting go of programming, habits, and emotional life. Thereupon the initial experience of the joy and love of union gave way to a silence which, together with God, now reigned at the deepest center (2: 51-75).

Penetrating further, Roberts arrived at the third phase, which is "the highest point of the unitive life, a culmination of the transforming process and an onset of a new movement. In Eastern language, this is the full state of *savikalpa samadhi*. Traditionally it is called "transforming union" or "mystical marriage" in the West. At this stage, you are fully united with or absorbed in God in the highest part of your being or at the level of the archetypal self, which represents the primary limit of duality. Gradually consciousness and memory are absorbed. As ordinary consciousness is transcended and its usual boundaries disappear in the union, there is an experience of oneness between the archetypal self and God. A state of identification with the divine form occurs such that the two become inseparable — "there is only one will and one love, which is God's" (John of the Cross) — resulting in a permanent or indissoluble union. As St. Teresa of Avila states, "In the spiritual marriage the union is like what we have when rain falls from the sky into a river or fount; all is water, for the rain that fell from heaven cannot be divided or separated from the water of the river. Or it is like what we have when a little stream enters the sea; there is no means of separating the two" (179).

Since only God remains as the sole object of consciousness and everything else disappears, whatever you experience in this state appears as God. As awareness of God becomes the all, only the unity, only the vision, remains. In Zen this is called "the man forgotten," when union with the koan is so complete that the self is absorbed and consciousness of a self separate from the koan disappears. As this becomes a permanent state of awareness, which transforms and absorbs all aspects of the self, you arrive at transforming union or mystical marriage and live and act from the awareness and depth of this oneness.

From the depth of this completed union there arises, like Kundalini Energy, a burst of power and energy that thrusts you out beyond yourself to a life of selfless giving. Thus, after the inward movement, there is a turning point and an outward thrust. According to Roberts, the awakening and arising of this Energy marks the turning point of the unitive life and the onset of a new movement which sets the direction in which the universal self will be transcended (2: 81-111).

Robert's next three phases are not so much new stages as a process of transformation that ends in the final transcendence of the archetypal self. According to Roberts, this transcendence does not require further meditation but an active self-giving that empties out the self through disidentification and letting go. This distinction points to an essential difference between Eastern and Western approaches, partially explaining why the experience of the transcendence of duality appears relatively rare in the West. Whereas the former regards meditation as the direct path to ultimate transcendence, the latter takes the indirect route of active involvement in the world, through what Jesus and Lao-tzu called "a daily loss," or waits for it to happen. Believing that people can come to it through meditation because what is realized is not anything transcendent to one's true nature, the East has developed meditative practices and instructions applicable to this stage. Like generators producing electricity, these practices can help one come to the experience of enlightenment within a relatively short period of time. Hence it occurs more frequently in the East. On the other hand, the West believes that enlightenment can come, if at all, only from above, through divine grace, and that one can do nothing about it. As a result, relatively few have experienced it in the West, like being hit by lightning. Western dualism and theological attitudes have also contributed to its rarity.

Nevertheless, there is an essential agreement between the East and the West on one point regarding the above issue. Both agree that this transcendence cannot be caused or actively sought or brought about by the ego or by self-effort. It is purely receptive. All that the meditator can do is to maintain or remain in a state from which the breakthrough occurs. Moreover, both acknowledge that it can occur in or outside meditation, while one is engaged in daily activities in a state of *samadhi*.

In any case, Roberts has not only given an account of her own experience, which she calls "the experience of no-self," but has also delineated the steps beyond union that lead to it. These steps begin with the fourth phase, with involvement in the active life, similar to Christ's public life. This step begins with the preparation for the death of the Christ-self or the burning out of the universal self. It is a process of disidentification and letting go through selfless giving and is marked by a continuous flow of external trials that wear out the self. This process is analogous to what Meher Baba called "love from the point of failure" (Needleman 1: 97- 101). In your very inability to give an adequate or complete expression of the living flame that drives you to love and to give yourself completely, the self is exhausted and burned out.

The fifth phase is marked by a blossoming of charity, which is a further refinement of mental contents and disidentification with the organization of the world centered on oneself. Essentially, this phase involves a cessation of judging and evaluating activities of the mind and a gradual emptying out of its contents. This process lays bare the roots of the self and the primary mental construct until the primary dualistic structure is totally open and exposed.

The sixth phase represents disidentification with the archetypal self. The characteristic experience at this stage is the final transcendence of self-consciousness or the sense of separation from God. Prior to it Roberts experienced certain paranormal powers, which she considers to be a final assertion of the self similar to, I might add, Jesus's experience of temptation by the devil, or the Energy-aspect of the archetypal self, in the desert. When they were disidentified with and let go, the self also vanished. The witness-consciousness that saw the vision of God as the All and experienced union with God-as-object was transcended in an experience of identity with God, who alone remained resplendent when the self was gone. With the roots of I-consciousness thus uprooted, there remained only the All-embracing Awareness that is the Godhead, God-as-subject. The *samadhi* with the form was at last transcended in the experience of formless *samadhi,* similar to the *Heart Sutra's* "form is emptiness."

Meister Eckhart also testifies to this state of identity beyond union to which he came as a result of a breakthrough, which is similar to the experience of enlightenment described by Eastern traditions. While union is with the form of God and through what St. Teresa of Avila calls "intellectual vision," the breakthrough is transcendence of form and arrival at the prior formless and undifferentiated Ground or "isness" of God: "For in this breakthrough I discover that I and God are one" (Fox, *Breakthrough* 218). And it can take place only when all vision is also transcended. Here the mind is totally void and silent; no activity remains. Consequently, there remains in the mind no image, likeness, concept, or construct — nothing to mediate or create separation, differentiation, or distance between it and God. Thus, this breakthrough is seedless *samadhi,* in which awareness breaks free of form, content, construct, and framework, even of meditation, and arrives at the experience of identity. So Eckhart says, "Without image, without mediation, without likeness. If I am to know God in such unmediated way, then I must simply become God and God must become me. I would express it more exactly by saying that God must simply become me and I must become God — so completely one that this 'he' and this 'I' share one 'is' and in this 'isness' do one work eternally" (Fox, *Breakthrough* 179-180).

Similarly, testifying to the experience of identity, Jan Van Ruysbroeck says, "In the abyss of this darkness, in which the loving spirit has died to itself, there begins the manifestations of God and eternal life." This death of the spirit implies deconstruction and transcendence of the subtle form of reality and consciousness and the archetypal self. Upon this deconstruction, awareness arrives at the state void of every activity, content, form, and construct. This state is said to be direct and "unmediated." Beyond every duality and relative state, it is a state in which "the spirit ceaselessly becomes the very resplendence which it receives" (*The Spiritual Espousals* 147). That this resplendence is the very

All-embracing Awareness which is the formless nature of God whereby "he" is and is aware of "himself," so that in this experience the contemplator realizes his/her identity with God, is clear when he says, "To comprehend and understand God as he is in himself, above and beyond all likenesses, is to be God with God, without intermediary or any element of otherness which could constitute an obstacle or impediment" (*Espousals* 146). This realization of identity is experienced in contemplation: "Through an eternal act of gazing accomplished by means of an inborn light, they are transformed and become one with that same light with which they see and which they see" (150). The realization of this oneness requires transcendence of all forms, including the very personal form of God, and arrival at the formless essence: "Here there is a blissful crossing over and a self-transcending immersion into a state of essential bareness, where all divine names and modes and all the living ideas which are reflected in the mirror of divine truth all pass away into simple ineffability" (152).

Bernadette Roberts came to this experience, typically, as we have seen in the case of many Zen adepts, not in meditation but by a river bank, where, in an emergent smile on her face, she instantly recognized an identity of the subject, the object, and the experience. She thus came to an instantaneous recognition that the Supreme Identity of the Godhead pervades and is all and is the only thing that IS; and that a direct experience of the Godhead is always an experience of identity between yourself, the Godhead, and the experience: "the smile itself, 'that' which smiled, and that at which it smiled were identical." Roberts thereby came to realize that in the ultimate state "God is all that exists" (1: 81, 78). So, with the transcendence of relative union, there came the revelation of the Absolute, the Supreme Identity in which there remains only one Being—the Unconditioned; one Awareness—All-embracing Awareness; one life—the everlasting life of the Spirit; and one blessedness, which IS GOD.

Although many Christian mystics have undoubtedly experienced this revelation, in expressing it in personalistic terms, which is the framework of traditional Christian theology, they have invariably ignored, denied, or reduced the differences between union and identity. Nevertheless, as the experiences of mystics in both the East and the West attest, the experience of union with a personal God remains within the relative plane of archetypal consciousness. So union cannot be the final destination of the journey, which is always transpersonal and can be realized only when the relative state of union is transcended in the experience of the absolute state of identity. In spite of the experiences of a few, the pull of the tradition has led Christian mystics to express it in terms of union. Nevertheless, it remains true that at the end there remains only God, Being and manifesting "himself" in all things and at all times as That Which IS.

Chapter 16
The Way of the Sufi

The aim of the Sufi path, as is true of other paths herein discussed, is to show us a way beyond our sense of severance from everything in general and God in particular. It is a way to reconnect ourselves with the Source from which we become cut off by our programming, our separate self, our reality-construct, our way of life, and the daily dribble with which our minds are preoccupied. This reconnection requires us to go beyond everything that cuts us off and arrive at the state in which we experience no separation from anything. Such an absolute transcendence requires a shift of the center of our being and consciousness from ego to God and is called *fana*. As we transcend the self and pass into God, eventually we pass beyond union and arrive at an identity with the Godhead *(baqa)*. To live continuously in this center and from this identity is the goal of the Sufi Way. However, because in our present condition we experience ourselves to be cut off from it, we need to go through various progressive stages of awakening, transformation, and realization before we can arrive at the goal. To lead the initiate through these stages to the ultimate goal is the secret of the Sufi path.

There is no agreement among the Sufis on the number of these stages and states or the order of their progression. Al-Qushairi, for example, according to Arberry, sets down forty-five stations or stages, while al-Sarraj notes only seven (1: 75-79). One reason for this discrepancy is that, while Sufis do hold meditative practices in common, each Sufi Order has practices, approaches, and a presentation of methods peculiar to it. Another is that, since a Sufi master or sheikh introduces the seeker progressively to the various stages and techniques according to his aptitudes, needs, and place in relation to the path, the same techniques are not deemed applicable to everyone. Consequently, not every Sufi master sets down all the stages (or all in the same order), thus creating diversity and apparent inconsistency. The most useful delineation I have found is that of Sheikh Nurbakhsh, who distinguishes two stages: In the first, the initiate works to remove emotional blocks and mental fixations and to decrease ego's control so as to arrive at a state of balance, harmony, and peace. At this stage tangles are resolved, life is reordered, and the heart and mind are purified. This psychotherapeutic stage varies in length according to the psychological condition of the initiate. The master works to free him from self-centeredness and open him to the second state in which he "undergoes a process of becoming illuminated by the Divine Attributes and Divine Nature" (1: 18-19).

In general, the Sufi path has active and receptive stages, similar to those found in the Christian mystical tradition. Moreover, although many Sufis depict numerous stages, following Nurbakhsh and Christian mysticism, we may usefully divide them into four broad categories: purification, illumination, unification, and identification. As in Christian mysticism, while purification and the initial stages of illumination are active, the more advanced stages of the Sufi path are mainly receptive and depend on God's action on the person.

The Stage of Purification

The Sufi path begins, as we have seen in the case of the others, with conversion or awakening from life's slumber, becoming aware of your unawareness, turning to yourself and seeing your actual condition, and realizing that things cannot continue this way any longer. The exile must end. You must break free of everything that makes life as you experience it to be insufficient unto itself. Upon this awakening, there arises a longing for the return, for ending the separation. This awakening is conversion, which is essentially a pull from the Source to draw you back to itself. It is also, of course, as I have shown, the starting point of formal meditation. This experience is vividly portrayed by Al-Ghazali in an account of his own experience of conversion as follows:

> I looked on myself as I then was. Worldly interests encompassed me on every side. Even my work as a teacher—the best thing I was engaged in—seemed unimportant and useless in view of the life hereafter...I realized that I stood on the edge of a precipice and would fall into hell-fire unless I set about to mend my ways... Conscious of my helplessness and having surrendered my will entirely, I took refuge with God as a man in sore trouble who has no resource left. God answered my prayers and made it easy for me to turn my back on reputation and wealth and wife and children and friends. (Arberry 1: 80)

This passage brings out several important points about the very first step on the Sufi path. The starting point is dissatisfaction with the present stage and wanting something more than the usual round life provides. This first step is the same dissatisfaction, turned in on itself, that the Buddha experienced: seeing that the not-enoughness of life is not itself enough and wanting each moment of life to be sufficient unto itself. So dissatisfaction, as Arthur Deikman has noted, is the key when it is not squandered in pursuing substitute gratification in objects of desire or in finding relief in diversions and entertainment, but is used as a vantage point from which to look at life as it is ordinarily lived and to take steps to transform oneself, as did Al-Ghazali (Arberry 1: 94-96).

The next point is seeing life the way it is and discovering that it is pinned down from within and without, chained to programming and repetitive mental, emotional, and behavioral patterns, which make you think the same thoughts that come back to you in circles, which trigger the same emotional responses even though they have ceased to be satisfying, and which prompt you to do the same things automatically with clockwork regularity. In thus seeing your bondage to the Wheel of Life, what was hitherto regarded as most important loses its significance and its hold over you, as it did for Al-Ghazali. (Thomas Aquinas likewise came to see all his writings as "straw" and stopped writing.) You are then face to face with the question of fundamental change, a life-and-death decision — a choice between continuing on the present "unimportant and useless" course, which now appears for the first time as it actually is — meaningless — and embarking on a completely different course — a journey toward meaning, and beyond meaning to Being.

When the choice appears in this way, the third step, the decision to do something about it, becomes imperative. There is no more hedging, no more rationalizing, no more reluctance to be born. Al-Ghazali, as he told us, decided to take the plunge. With such a choice the instruction on the Sufi path begins.

Once you are initiated and commit yourself to the path, you undertake to clean out your act and your life. Among the practices enjoined at this stage of purification are: abstinence, poverty, purity, renunciation or nonattachment, patience, desiringlessness, solitariness, withdrawal, and contentment (Arberry 1: 74-79). Of course not everyone will be assigned all these and other similar practices, or in the same order. As Nurbakhsh points out, during this stage the sheikh will study your behavior and assign you those practices that are most necessary to purify your mind and heart of all psychological conflicts and mental fixations so that you can be open and develop into the Perfected Man (1: 18-19). For the goal of such practices at this stage, as Idries Shah also observes, is to remove the obstacles of unawareness and bondage created by conditioning, which prevent you from realizing your essential nature and thus returning, in the words of al-Junaid (who sounds very much like a Zen master or a Neo-Platonist), to your original state "in which you were before you were" (Shah 3: 309-310).

Poverty and abstinence may be assigned, for instance, to uproot possessiveness, greed, and the constant feeling of a lack or dissatisfaction with the present, and wanting something more or different from what you are now experiencing. Such practices will help awaken in you a sense of your own inner poverty on the one hand and open you to the riches of the Spirit on the other. Humility will be directed to uprooting pride, arrogance, aggression, conceit, narcissism, desire for self-enhancement, praise, and being liked or loved. Contentment will enable you to accept your life as it is, develop a conviction that life comes with everything for you to be happy here and now, and begin to change those things that need to be changed in order for you to grow. And desiringlessness is, of course, the beginning of your stepping out of the Wheel of Existence. As a contemporary Sufi from Afghanistan advises Omar Michael Burke, "You must understand that you must divorce your desire and your aspiration. That way lies truth" (105). To dislodge the other two pillars (identification and attachment) that hold up the present constructions of reality, consciousness, and self, you will be instructed to practice nonattachment. This practice will enable you to disidentify and leave behind everything that keeps you separated from your goal. It will lead you, as Idries Shah told Burke, to develop a new point of view on life and a new sense of reality (Burke 158).

Other practices, such as solitude and withdrawal, also have a similar goal. They may be enjoined by the sheikh to enable you to clarify and perfect this new point of view. You may have to withdraw for a period of time for the purpose of training but, ultimately, your place is in the world. For the solitude and withdrawal you are instructed to cultivate does not necessarily consist in withdrawing from any physical space but in creating an inner space in which the seeds of the new life can be planted and the new point of view and sense of reality germinate and grow.

The key practice designed to purify the emotions and the mind is self-examination, which I have already discussed under IAM. As Nurbakhsh points out, the Sufi is instructed to constantly search into and examine his mental states and behavior, to become aware of and observe whatever arises, positive or negative, and to eliminate the latter and expand the former. He is to simplify and balance his life, reduce complexity, and move toward unity (1: 91-99). To this end he examines what keeps him separate and disidentifies with everything to which he is attached.

In progressing through the stages of purification, you experience various states, such as fear, hope, longing, trust, love, and nearness to God. A progressive deepening of these states is a gauge of your progress on the path as you move from fear to love, which is the primary state that will lead you to union. Thus, you will need to transform fear into watchfulness and self-examination, to singleness of purpose, to longing for and constant remembrance *(dhikr)* of God. As you reach understanding, your thoughts will become clear. Light will enter and remain in your mind, replacing the prior darkness. Such an illumination will draw you near to God. Correspondingly, your remembrance of God will become intense and the love of God will enter your heart, in time transforming it, and becoming a permanent state (Arberry 1: 56).

Such purification and transformation will bring about a shift in your attention from the external to the internal domain. This will enable your mind to begin to become free of the control exercised over it by internal forces, such as programming, desire, attachment, identification, and habits; and external forces, such as society and environment. Thus you will become open to the influence of your essential nature or God, who will increasingly become the central reality in your life.

A recognition of the necessity of these factors for the path moved al-Sarraj to describe Sufism as "self-development, realizing what is relevant, concentration and contemplation, cultivation of inner experience, following the path of Search and Nearness" (Shah 2: 240). Similarly, Ansari observed, "Sufism teaches how to purify one's self, improve one's morals and build up one's inner and outer life in order to attain perpetual bliss. Its subject-matter is the purification of the soul and its end or aim is the attainment of eternal felicity and blessedness" (Shah 2: 240).

The Stage of Illumination: Meditation and Contemplation

To attain his goal, besides the above practices, the Sufi engages in various types of meditation and contemplation. Nurbakhsh defines meditation as "keeping oneself away from what is not God, both outwardly and inwardly, and concentrating one's whole being upon God" (1: 72). And according to him, "the object of contemplation is the Absolute Beloved, everything else being purged from the mind" (1: 54). Such statements make it clear that the object of both practices is to free awareness by shifting the orientation of consciousness inward, emptying it of all objects or contents so that God becomes the sole object. Thus, meditation is the path of concentration which leads to *samadhi* or union.

Sufi meditative practices range from purification of the breath, which resembles hatha yogic and tantric practices, to various concentrative practices. They may include meditation on a theme assigned by the sheikh, meditation based on a *chakra* system *(lataif)* similar to and perhaps derived from Kundalini

Yoga, and repetition of a word or a phrase (similar to Mantra Yoga) mentally, audibly, chanted or intoned, either individually or in a group. The individual practice may be accompanied, in the manner of Hindu *japa,* by the use of rosary beads. The group practice may be performed while seated or whirling. In some forms of meditation, repetition of a mantra is also accompanied by visualization, sometimes as part of a *chakra* system. Some Sufis practice longevity exercises similar to hatha and Taoist yogas. Others conduct "healing sessions" that resemble holistic medicine or therapy. Still others conduct laying on of hands — a common practice among early Christians — contacting, evoking, or arousing the mystical current, Primal Energy or grace, called *baraka* (Hebrew *baruch,* meaning "blessing") to flow through the subject (Burke 19-21). Following is a sampling of representative Sufi meditative practices.

In a publication put out by his order, Pir Vilayat Khan sets down the following exercise for purifying the breath:

a. The ideal times for the exercise are sunrise and sunset. It should be done standing, if possible, before an open window. Assume your natural rhythm of breathing, without any unusually long retention or making any movement or noise while breathing.
b. Five breaths: Earth — inhale and exhale through the nose.
c. Five breaths: Water — inhale through the nose, exhale through the mouth.
d. Five breaths: Fire — inhale through the mouth, exhale through the nose.
e. Five breaths: Air — inhale and exhale through the mouth (*The Message,* Vol. 2, No. 2, November 1976, p. 8).

Like Kundalini and other Energy yogas, the *lataif* combines a system of Energy Centers, colors, visualization, and breathing exercises. O.M. Burke mentions that the Chisti Order of Sufis in India uses posture, breathing, and a *chakra* system that parallels Kundalini Yoga. The Sufis of Kunji Zagh in Afghanistan also have a similar meditative technique. And, emphasizing the univerality of its use among the Sufis, a sheikh of the Callandar Order in India told Burke, "The illumination of the *Latayif* is the way to completion...No sage who does not teach the method of making these secret areas of the body full of power can be your guide" (74).

Unlike the seven *chakras* of Kundalini, however, and in agreement with Taoism, the *lataif* has, according to Idries Shah, only five centers. But, like Kundalini, these centers are believed to be "organs of perception" and therefore represent states of consciousness. As in Kundalini, the object of this meditation is to awaken, activate, and raise the powers especially active in these centers, and to unify and expand states of consciousness so as to produce "the New Man" in whom they are brought to completion. Idries Shah says that as each center is activated and the Sufi awakens and receives illumination from it, his consciousness correspondingly expands. He realizes a greater capacity of his mind and breaks through the automatic thinking and unawareness that make the ordinary individual captive to life (3: 332-333).

According to Shah, the five centers, arranged in accordance with their physiological, psychological, and color coordination, are:

a. Mind: located on the left side of the body. The color yellow is assigned to it.
b. Spirit: located on the right side. Red is associated with it.
c. Consciousness: located in the solar plexus. White is assigned to it.
d. Intuition: located in the forehead. Black is assigned to it.
e. Deep perception: located in the center of the chest. Green is assigned to it (3: 430).

The order of activation of these centers is also the same. The method depends, according to Shah, on the instructions given to the initiate by the sheikh. In general, the method used for awakening and raising the states of consciousness is concentration and visualization. Beyond this, however, Shah gives no indication, following the usual Sufi practice of keeping the meditation instruction secret.

The characteristic Sufi practice, however, is the *Dhikr,* which means "remembrance." In the present context, it means "remembrance of God." Thus the *Dhikr* is a remembrance having as its ultimate aim union with God through constantly keeping "him" in the center of attention until "he" floods the mind and displaces all its contents. It is a remembrance borne on the wings of love, awakened through repetition, which centers on the names of God, the main form of which is the central Islamic confession of faith—*La ilaha illa 'llah* (There is no God but the One God). Other Sufi mantras consist of other words and phrases or passages from the Quran, invocations, such as *Ya Hai* (Oh God!), and other names of God. The mantras are combined with a variety of methods, such as breathing, visualization, movement, and the like.

The *Dhikr* itself takes on a variety of forms. There is no one common form practiced by all Sufis, although all practice some form of the *Dhikr.* Developed at different centers and by various Sufi Orders, the *Dhikr* took on different forms—from a simple repetition of "the ninety-nine beautiful names of God" on a chain of rosary beads, resembling the Christian rosary and the Hindu and Buddhist *mala* and its *japa,* to the complex forms involving music, movement in unison or whirling, concentration, repetition, and visualization. The repetition is either silent, muttered under the breath, spoken aloud, or chanted. It is

Song of the Skylark II: Meditation

performed either individually or in a group. If movement is in unison or involves whirling, it is always performed in a group.

While the simplest form of *Dhikr* consists of repeating the divine names with or without a rosary, a slightly more complex form consists in assuming a seated posture, usually in a group, although it can be done alone, and repeating aloud, *La ilaha illa 'llah*. As you say aloud, *La ilaha,* throw your head to the right, draw it back, in a continuous motion, to the original position, and throw it to the left as you say, *illa 'llah*. Then bring the head back to the center and repeat. Each movement of your head to the right and the left should be on a full breath. Repeat while exhaling, so that the entire sequence of a repetition takes two full breaths. As you repeat, focus your attention wholly on the words, the breath, and the movement of the head, and make them one. Forget anything else.

A more complex form of concentrative meditation that combines posture, breathing, repetition of a mantra and concentration on Energy Centers is the following, set down by a thirteenth century Sufi, Najmeddin Daya:

a. Use an empty, dark, clean room. Burn some incense, and then sit in a cross-legged position facing the direction of Mecca.
b. Put your hands on your thighs; keep your eyes open, but do not let them wander. Keep your mind focused and attentive.
c. With deep devotion say aloud, *La ilaha illa 'llah*. As you do so, draw *La ilaha* from the root of your power or navel center and *illa 'llah* into the heart center. As you repeat, focus your complete attention on the phrases, coordinate them with and follow your inhalation and exhalation. Let your body resonate with the vibrations of the repetition.
d. While doing the above, with the mind completely focused on God, when you say *La ilaha* think, "I want nothing, seek nothing, love nothing;" and when you say *illa 'llah,* think "but God."
e. During the meditation, your mind should be in the here and now, one with the breath, the repetition, and the thought. If, during the meditation, you find that you are attached to something, let go of it as you say *La ilaha*. Uproot the desire and attachment from the center of your heart and mind, and substitute God in its place as you say *illa 'llah* (in Naranjo and Ornstein 48-49).

A *Dhikr* that resembles Tibetan Buddhism and Kabbalah and involves visualization, an experience of light, a void, and an expansion of awareness is the following, derived from the personal experience of Muhammad Alawi:

a. Invoke one word, a name of God, and visualize each of its letters until you can produce and retain the word distinctly in your mind.
b. Now expand the letters until they fill the entire horizon. Keep your attention fixed on them until they appear like pure, white light.
c. Next, let your attention go beyond the letters and into the beginningless and endless void. In this formless void, picture the universe, and the letters suspended like a bowl or a lamp.
d. Now visualize the letters, the universe, and yourself slowly dissolving until only a trace remains. Then that, too, disappears. No trace of anything is now left except the pure luminosity of the Absolute Void. Stay in this Void for as long as possible.
e. When you are no longer able to stay in this pure light of the Void, reverse the process and see the forms gradually reappear in your consciousness (in Naranjo and Ornstein 46-47).

This meditation may have been influenced by Tibetan Buddhism as it bears a striking resemblance to it. It has the same structure and intent: Purification through the experience of light; illumination and expansion of consciousness; transcendence of the limits of ego and forms; and experience of the formless void as pure light, with which the meditator seeks to become identified so s/he can arrive at the Unconditioned State.

A *Dhikr* having a structural similarity but different intent and result from the above is the following, set down by al-Ghazali:

a. Sit alone in some suitable place and assume a meditative posture. Bring your mind to a state of total nonattachment, beyond all dualities of likes and dislikes, existence and nonexistence.
b. Fix your attention wholly on God so that nothing else enters it. Keep saying aloud continuously, "Allah, Allah," keeping your attention focused on God and the repetition.
c. Keep repeating "Allah, Allah," until the motion of the tongue ceases and yet the word continues to flow; then the motion ceases altogether — only the thought remains; and finally, the word, its letters, and its shapes also disappear — only the idea remains and your mind becomes one with it.
d. Stay in this one-pointedness of mind until the reality of God is revealed to you in a realization of oneness with "him" (In Nicholson 46-47).

A *Dhikr* that combines, in tantric fashion, visualization, breathing, and stopping the breath is the following:

a. Keep your attention continuously focused on the idea of God and let your mind be filled with awe, love, and respect for God.
b. To stop mind-wandering, compress the breath and keep the mouth firmly shut, with the tongue forced against the lips.
c. Now visualize your heart shaped like the cone of a fir tree, and project your attention on it. As you mentally recite the *dhikr La ilaha illa 'llah,* draw *La* upward, *ilaha* to the right, and form the entire phrase, *La ilaha illa 'llah* on the fir cone.
d. Next, let your whole body pass through the entire frame of the fir cone. As it does so, let your body merge with it and let each part be filled with its light and warmth.
e. Continue the exercise until everything else disappears and your mind becomes one with the fir cone letters. As the *dhikr* deepens into *samadhi,* the self will eventually disappear in the Divine and separation will be transcended in the experience of Oneness (In Hewitt 168).

The *dhikr* that combines repetition, concentration, music, and movement or whirling has several different versions. This is understandable in view of the fact that it is practiced by all Sufi Orders. O.M. Burke describes one in which the dervishes first formed two circles. Outside the circles stood the sheikh, a drummer and a flute player, and two dervishes who called out the rhythm of the movement through their chant. With the dervishes and the sheikh standing, the latter intoned the opening part of each exercise. As the drums began to beat and the callers began to sing, the concentric circles began to move slowly, in opposite directions. At one point the sheikh called out, *"Ya Haadi!"* ("Oh Guide"—one of the names of God). Coordinating movement, concentration, and repetition, the participants began to move and repeat, first slowly, and then faster and faster until there was a whirl of robes.

In this meditation the attention is focused on the movement, the sound, and the repetition to the exclusion of everything else. As concentration deepens and becomes one-pointed, consciousness stops its usual operation and opens up "to produce a state of ritual ecstasy and to accelerate the contact of the Sufi's mind with the World-Mind of which he considers himself to be a part" (49-51).

The *dhikr* I attended in New York City, led by sheikh Muzafer el-Jerrahi of the Halveti-Jerrahi Order based in Turkey, began with a chant by a group of dervishes. Then the sheikh entered and took his place at the head of some sheepskin mats placed in the form of a crescent. He was followed by the dervishes, who entered, one by one kissed the sheik's hands, and took their place on the mats. Then the *dhikr* began. First came silent meditation. This was followed by mantra-repetition. And finally there was chanting, with the sheikh intoning each sequence and the dervishes repeating after him. This chanting lasted for about twenty minutes.

Then at a signal from the sheikh, everyone got up and formed two concentric circles, with the former standing in the middle. As the leader began to intone a chant, the circles began to move, first slowly, and then faster and faster, in opposite directions, with the dervishes repeating the *dhikr* and moving the head from right to left. The circles moved with the left foot leading the steps.

One of the initial repetitions was *Ya Hai* to the right and *Ya Huk* to the left, with the attention concentrated on the movement of the head, the steps, and the repetition. As the speed of the movement picked up, the repetition switched to "Allah," split into two syllables and coordinated with the movement of the head (from right to left) and of the feet. The eyes were kept closed. This sequence lasted for another twenty minutes and then, at a signal from the sheikh, it stopped. The sheikh then intoned a different chant and the dervishes began to repeat it, standing in two rows and moving their heads from right to left as before. After this sequence two circles were again formed and a different mantra was repeated. At the end of this sequence, the dervishes stopped and formed a very tightly knit circle, with arms around each other's shoulders and the sheikh standing in the middle, and repeated a different chant. Then, with the sheikh still standing in the middle, another small, tightly knit circle was formed with each dervish touching the other on the shoulder and those closest to the sheikh touching him in a gesture that seemed to signify a transmission of *baraka* or Energy. After about two hours of such alternating sequences of repetitions, the *dhikr* ended, with the dervishes filing past the sheikh, kissing his hands as before. Then the sheikh bowed to everyone and retired.

During the *dhikr* I noticed that several dervishes had a faraway look and a few appeared to be in trance. As I noticed that the dervishes had their eyes closed while moving in a circle (in spite of being in an outer circle where we were tripping over or pulling each other in an effort to keep pace with the circles of the dervishes), I, too, closed my eyes and focused the attention on the chant intoned by a dervish standing in the middle. For a brief moment I had a crystal clear perception that the sound was arising from the dervish's heart center (rather than coming from his mouth) and that the essence of the dervish was that sound. Like a tongue of flame suspended in the vast space of the cathedral, the sound appeared to arise from the void and return to it. Indeed, it appeared that the void itself was erupting in the form of the sound and returning to itself. Then I had a startling realization that the sound or the voice arising from the dervish's heart center was God "himself" manifesting "himself" in the form of the sound and returning to "his" Formless Essence.

There are other forms of *dhikr;* and besides the *dhikr,* Sufis practice other forms of meditation, such as breath-control and concentration on the breath, on a single idea, and so on. Sufi meditation has its own forms of posture, which may be formed by sitting on the heels with knees touching the ground, the easy posture, sitting cross-legged, or on a chair. In each case, the right hand is placed either on the left thigh, over the lap, or draped around the ankles of the crossed legs, with the left hand grasping the right wrist (Nurbakhsh 1: 78-87).

Like their counterparts, the initial aim of the *dhikr* and other forms of Sufi concentrative meditation is to shift the attention and orientation of consciousness away from the outside world and from thoughts and to hold them focused on God. As attention remains focused on God for prolonged periods, it gathers around "him" and becomes unified and one-pointed. As Nurbakhsh observes, "The purpose of remembering God is to create a 'unity of attention'...The remembrance of God effaces from the memory all other things, and the energy that was previously dispersed in worthless and short-term concerns now finds its proper focus in the remembrance of God" (1: 19-20).

As the mind becomes centered and one-pointed, God displaces all other thoughts and objects and becomes the central focus of attention. Pushed to the periphery, previous preoccupations, and together with them, emotional conflicts and mental fixations begin to diminish. And, with the unification of attention, as the mind becomes peaceful and tranquil, the love of God fills the heart.

Remaining focused on God for prolonged periods, the mind gradually bridges the distance separating it from "him." Cutting through name, concept and outer association, and perceptual construction, it moves closer to the subtle form of God. The Sufis call this proximity "nearness." As the mind becomes increasingly purified of its contents, thoughts, and filtering process, and as attention cuts through inner layers of construction, it gets nearer and nearer to God, who begins to wholly occupy and fill it with "his" luminous presence. As Nurbakhsh again states, "When the disciple is continually involved in the remembrance of God, his being gradually becomes liberated from egotistical and selfish qualities and illuminated by the Divine Attributes and Divine Nature" (1: 19-20). The emptier your mind, the greater is your experience of illumination in terms of insights, revelation, and expansion of awareness into the activities that were previously done in unawareness.

This illumination occurs not only when you reach *samadhi,* but also through contemplation or insight meditation. The deeper stages of contemplation grow out of the advanced stage of *dhikr* and other forms of concentrative meditation. According to sheikh Nurbakhsh, Sufi contemplation begins with IAM, and, as in the cases of insight meditation we have encountered in other paths, deepens into insight with a consideration of the Sufi's relationship with God (1: 53-65). As God comes to occupy his mind and heart continuously, gradually contemplation ripens into a sense of oneness with God and leads to ecstatic union.

The Stages of Union and Identity

Union is experienced in the state of *samadhi*. When he reaches it, as Nurbakhsh explains, the Sufi is so absorbed in God that, at the advanced stage, his attention remains continuously focused on God. This unitive path has two stages: an outward stage, in which the Sufi sees God in everything, and an inward stage, in which he sees everything as nothing other than God. The first is marked by a transcendence of separation from the outer world and of ego, which is called, as explained before, *fana*.

In the second, called *baqa*, reached through further deepening of *samadhi* and stages of insight meditation, there remains no more he, or separate self, to experience anything; there is only "the Divine meditating upon the Divine" (1: 77). As another Sufi master, Bawa Muhaiyeddeen, similarly states, "This is God knowing himself" (Hixon 163). In this final state, as Nurbakhsh observes, even the sense of meditation, with its lingering effect of duality, is lost (1: 81).

It is not surprising that, even more explicitly than their Christian counterparts, some Sufis speak of realizing the Supreme Identity beyond union, while others recoil from it and rest content with union. In any case, at the final stage of the journey, the Sufi discovers that his center has shifted from the limited to the Illimitable, from the conditioned to the Unconditioned, which is experienced as the identity of the conditioned, of that which is, and which is thus his own true identity. When he truly finds himself, then, he is beyond himself and in the heart and center of all things, of the unfathomable mystery that is God. Established in God as his identity and center, the Sufi becomes the Completed Man and experiences himself as a manifestation of God on earth.

Chapter 17
Conclusion

It is clear that each of these paths, if followed to the very end, can open the mind to the Unconditioned and bring liberation. Although at their summit these paths converge (of course, there are many paths that do not converge as they seek different summits) as pathways, they evince differences as well as similarities.

The differences are derived not only from the paths themselves, the cultures in which they evolved, and the men and women who discovered or journeyed through them, but also from the mental terrain through which the travelers trekked, the experiences they had, and the way they communicated what they found. Thus, the Western paths, particularly those that stem from Christianity, developed within a culture that emphasizes individuality, separation of the individual from others, will, and action. In a Western milieu in which self-assertion, self-will, individuality and pride tend to cause deep-seated and intractable cultural problems, these paths have come to emphasize intention, will, humility, self-surrender, and love. And consistent with the highest cultural values of individuality and personhood, they emphasize union as the highest goal.

On the other hand, the Eastern paths emerged in cultures that do not find individuality to be the highest value, but, on the contrary, the source of all deep-seated problems. As an antidote, they emphasize attention and consciousness to counteract the massive ignorance and unawareness in which the cultures have been immured; and they aim at self-transcendence as the ultimate standpoint from which to resolve cultural problems. Cultural recognition of personhood as the highest value has led Western paths to remain primarily dualistic and to aim at union, while Eastern emphasis on wholeness and totality as the highest value has led the highest Eastern paths to aim at the nondual state of identity. Correspondingly, their experiences, discoveries, and language of communication have been different.

Nevertheless, the paths not only converge at the summit, but across cultures, they also exhibit broad similarities in deep structures, stages, and practices. Thus, not only do all practice concentrative and insight meditation, but within this broad demarcation, even the preliminary, concentrative, and, to a certain extent, insight meditation practices are similar. Moreover, the paths agree that revelation cannot occur if you are closed to it, which is the case so long as you remain identified with and hold onto the separate self and try to create a world around it. They agree, too, that it is in letting go of self that you discover the truth of all beings and realize that you are directly at one with all life — that you are Being itself without any separation, differentiation, condition, or limitation.

They further agree that in discovering the mystery of all life, you leave behind an individuality characterized by separation from others and hemmed in by triviality and insignificance — "the daily dribble" of everyday life. Instead, you gain an individuality that is separated from nothing and encompasses the very universe itself in its all-embracing totality. In the process you discover that your life is not your own but the life of the universe flowing through you. When everything extraneous to Being itself is removed, the sand castles of your mind separating you from everything dissolve and disappear, and you discover that you are the ocean of Being and realize that in being your Self, you are not yourself but the "I not-I." Thus, when you are divested of everything you believed to be yourself, when you are not there to witness anything, then you awaken to Being, which emerges and shines in its splendor as your very Self and as the splendor of every being — of every person, every tree, every blade of grass, every mountain, "every wiggly little thing," as Huang Po was fond of saying. Then all there is left for you to do is to BE and manifest Being by Be-ing.

Finally, the paths agree that no one else can make the journey for you. You have to do it yourself by choosing the pathway best suited for you. In this work, I have presented an outline of the major paths, the terrain through which they course, the experiences they uncover along the way, and the final destination toward which they aim. It is now up to you to decide whether you want to pursue your destiny, choose a pathway, and make your personal journey toward realizing the purpose of existence.

Bibliography

Ajaya, Swami. *Yoga Psychology.* Honesdale, PA.: Himalayan International Institute, 1978.
Al-Ghazali. *The Faith and Practice of Al-Ghazali.* Translated by W. Montgomery Watt. Chicago: Kazi Publications, 1982.
Alper, Harvey P., ed. *Mantra.* Albany: State University of New York Press, 1989.
Andersen, Poul. *The Method of Holding the Three Ones.* London & Malmo: Curzon Press, Ltd., 1980.
Arabi, Ibn al. *The Bezels of Wisdom.* Translated by R.W.J. Austin. New York: Paulist Press, 1980.
Aranya, Swami Hariharananda. *Yoga Philosophy of Patanjali.* Translated by P.N. Mukerji. Albany: State University of New York Press, 1983.
Arberry, A.J. *Sufism.* New York: Harper & Row, 1970.
Arya, Usharbudh. *Mantra and Meditation.* Honesdale, PA: Himalayan International Institute, 1980.
_____. *Yoga Sutras of Patanjali with the Exposition of Vyasa. A Translation and Commentary.* Honesdale, PA: Himalayan International Institute, 1986.
Attar, Farid Ud-Din. *The Conference of the Birds.* Translated by Afkham Darbandhi and Dick Davis. New York: Penguin Books, 1984.
Balsekar, Ramesh S. *Pointers from Nishargadatta Maharaj.* Durham, NC: Acorn Press, 1982.
Barrett, William, ed. *Zen Buddhism.* Garden City, NY: A Doubleday Anchor Book, 1965.
Bercholz, Samuel, ed. *The Spiritual Teachings of Ramana Maharshi.* Boulder: Shambhala Publications, Inc., 1972.
Bharati, Agehananda. *The Tantric Tradition.* New York: Samuel Weiser, Inc., 1975.
Blakney, Raymond B., trans. *Meister Eckhart.* New York: Harper & Row, Publishers, Inc., 1941.
_____, trans. *The Way of Life: Tao Te Ching.* New York: New American Library, Inc., 1955.
Blofeld, John, trans. *The Zen Teaching of Huang Po.* New York: Grove Press, Inc., 1958.

_____. *The Tantric Mysticism of Tibet.* New York: E.P. Dutton Publishing Company, Inc., 1970.
_____. *The Secret and the Sublime.* New York: E.P. Dutton, 1973.
_____. *Taoism.* Boulder: Shambhala Publications, Inc., 1978.
Bromage, Bernard. *Tibetan Yoga.* Willingborough, England: The Aquarian Press, 1979.
Brown, Daniel P. "The Stages of Meditation in Cross-Cultural Perspective." In *Transformations of Consciousness.* Edited by Ken Wilber, Jack Engler, and Daniel P. Brown. Boston & London: Shambhala, 1986.
_____ and Jack Engler. "The Stages of Mindfulness Meditation: A Validation Study I-II." In *Transformations of Consciousness.*
Buddhaghosa, Bhadantacariya. *The Path of Purification. Visuddhimagga.* Translated by Bhikkhu Nanamoli. 4th ed. Kandy, Sri Lanka, 1979.
Burke, Omar Michael. *Among the Dervishes.* New York: Dutton, 1975.
Burtt, Edwin A., ed. *The Teachings of the Compassionate Buddha.* New York: New American Library, Inc., 1955.
Carrington, Patricia. *Freedom in Meditation.* Garden City, NY: A Doubleday Anchor Book, 1978.
Castaneda, Carlos. *A Separate Reality.* New York: Simon & Schuster, 1971.
_____. *Journey to Ixtlan.* New York: Simon & Schuster, 1972.
_____. *Tales of Power.* New York: Simon & Schuster, 1974.
_____. *The Fire From Within.* New York: Pocket Books, 1984.
Chan, Wing-tsit, ed. *A Source Book in Chinese Philosophy.* Princeton, NJ: Princeton University Press, 1972.
Chang (Chung-Yuan), Garma C.C. *The Practice of Zen.* New York: Harper & Row, 1970.
_____, trans. *Teachings of Tibetan Yoga.* Secaucus, NJ: The Citadel Press, 1974.
_____, trans. *Original Teachings of Ch'an Buddhism.* New York: Grove Press, Inc., 1982.
Chirban, John. "Developmental Stages in Eastern Orthodox Christianity." In *Transformations of Consciousness.* Edited by Ken Wilber, Jack Engler, and Daniel P. Brown. Boston: Shambhala, 1986.
Cleary, Thomas, trans. *The Blue Cliff Record.* Boulder: Prajna Press, 1978.
_____, trans. and ed. *The Original Face.* New York: Grove Press, 1978.
Cole, K.C. "A Theory of Everything." *The New York Times Magazine,* 18 October 1987, pp. 20-28.
Colledge, Eric, trans. *The Book of Privy Counselling.* In *Medieval Mystics of England.* Edited by David Knowles. New York: Harper & Row Publishers, 1961.

Conze, Edward et al. *Buddhist Texts Through the Ages*. New York: Harper & Row, 1954.
_____. *Buddhist Meditation*. New York: Harper & Row, 1956.
_____. *Buddhist Wisdom Books*. New York: Harper & Row, 1958.
Cozort, Daniel. *Highest Yoga Tantra*. Ithaca, NY: Snow Lion Publications, 1986.
David-Neel, Alexandra and Lama Yongden. *The Secret Oral Teaching in Tibetan Buddhist Sects*. San Francisco: City Lights Books, 1967.
De Bary, William Theodore et al., ed. *The Buddhist Tradition*. New York: Random House, Inc., 1972.
Deikman, Arthur. *Personal Freedom*. New York: Grossman Publishers, 1976.
_____. "Bimodal Consciousness." In *The Nature of Human Consciousness*. Edited by Robert Ornstein. San Francisco: W.B. Freeman Press, 1973.
_____. "Deautomatization and the Mystic Experience." In *The Nature of Human Consciousness*.
Egan, Harvey D. *Christian Mysticism*. New York: Pueblo Publishing Company, Inc., 1984.
Eliade, Mircea. *Yoga: Immortality and Freedom*. Princeton, NJ: Princeton University Press, 1969.
Embree, Ainslee T., ed. *The Hindu Tradition*. New York: Random House, Inc., 1972.
Emerson, Victor F. "Research on Meditation." In *What Is Meditation?* Edited by John White. Garden City, NY: Doubleday & Company, Inc., 1974.
Engler, Jack. "Therapeutic Aims in Psychotherapy and Meditation." In *Transformations of Consciousness*. Edited by Ken Wilber, Jack Engler, and Daniel P. Brown. Boston: Shambhala, 1986.
Evans-Wentz, Y.W., trans. *The Tibetan Book of the Great Liberation*. New York: Oxford University Press, 1968.
_____, trans. *Tibetan Yoga and Secret Doctrines*. New York: Oxford University Press, 1978.
Feuerstein, Georg. *The Essence of Yoga*. New York: Grove Press, 1976.
_____. *Yoga: The Technology of Ecstasy*. Los Angeles: Jeremy P. Tarcher, Inc., 1989.
_____. *The Yoga-Sutra of Patanjali. A New Translation and Commentary*. Rochester, Vermont: Inner Traditions International, 1989.
_____. *Encyclopedic Dictionary of Yoga*. New York: Paragon House, 1990.
Fox, Matthew. *Breakthrough. Meister Eckhart's Creation Spirituality in New Translation*. New York: Doubleday, 1980.
Free John, Da. *The Dawn Horse Testament*. San Raphael, CA: The Dawn Horse Press, 1985.
French, R.M., trans. *The Way of the Pilgrim*. New York: Seabury Press, 1965.

Fromm, Eric et al. *Zen Buddhism and Psychoanalysis*. New York: Harper & Row, 1970.
Goldstein, Joseph. *The Experience of Insight*. Santa Cruz: Unity Press, 1977.
Goldstein, Joseph and Jack Kornfield. *Seeking the Heart of Wisdom*. Boston and London: Shambhala, 1987.
Goleman, Daniel. *The Meditative Mind*. Los Angeles: Jeremy P. Tarcher, Inc., 1988.
_____. "Relaxation: Surprising Benefits Detected." *New York Times* 4, July 1986: C 1, 11.
Govinda, Lama Anagarika. *Foundations of Tibetan Mysticism*. New York: Samuel Weiser, Inc., 1973.
_____. *Creative Meditation and Multi-Dimensional Consciousness*. Wheaton, IL: Quest Books, 1976.
Groeschel, Benedict J. *Spiritual Passages*. New York: The Crossroad Publishing Company, 1984.
Gyatso, Geshe Kelsang. *Clear Light of Bliss*. Translated by Tenzing Norbu. London: Wisdom Publications, 1982.
Hahn, Thich Nhat. *The Miracle of Mindfulness*. Boston: Beacon Press, 1976.
Hakeda, Y.S., trans. *The Awakening of Faith*. New York: Columbia University Press, 1967.
Halevi, Z'ev ben Shimon. *The Way of Kabbalah*. New York: Samuel Weiser, Inc., 1976.
Hanson, Virginia, ed. *Approaches to Meditation*. Wheaton, IL: A Quest Book, 1976.
Herrigel, Eugene. *The Method of Zen*. New York: Random House, 1974.
Hewitt, James. *Meditation*. New York: David McKay & Company, 1978.
Hixon, Lex. *Coming Home*. Garden City, NY: Doubleday, 1978.
Hoffman, Edward. *The Way of Splendor*. Boulder: Shambhala, 1981.
Idel, Moshe. *Kabbalah*. New Haven and London: Yale University Press, 1988.
Johnson, Clive, ed. *Vedanta*. New York: Bantam Books, Inc., 1974.
Johnston, Charles. *The Yoga Sutras of Patanjali*. London: Robinson & Watkins Books, Ltd., 1974.
Johnston, William. *Silent Music*. San Francisco: Harper & Row, 1979.
_____, trans. and ed. *The Cloud of Unknowing*. Garden City, NY: Doubleday Image Books, 1973.
Jones, Cheslyn et al., eds. *The Study of Spirituality*. New York: Oxford University Press, 1986.
Kaplan, Aryeh. *Jewish Meditation*. New York: Schocken Books, 1985.
Kapleau, Philip. *The Three Pillars of Zen*. New York: Doubleday and Company, 1972.

Bibliography

———. *Zen: Dawn in the West*. Garden City, NY: Doubleday & Company, 1979.
Keating, Thomas. *Open Mind, Open Heart*. Warwick, NY: Amity House, Inc., 1986.
Keyes, Ken. *Handbook to Higher Consciousness*. Berkeley: Living Love Center, 1974.
———. *How to Enjoy Your Life In Spite of It All*. St. Mary's, KY: Living Love Publications, 1980.
Khana, Madhu. *Yantra: The Tantric Symbol of Cosmic Unity*. London: Thames & Hudson, Ltd., 1979.
Khantipalo, Bhikkhu. *Calm and Insight*. London and Dublin: Curzon Press, Ltd., 1987.
Koelman, Gaspar M. *Patanjala Yoga: From Related Ego to Absolute Self*. Poona, India: Papel Atheneum, 1970.
Kornfield, Jack and Breiter, Paul, comp. and ed. *A Still Forest Pool. The Insight Meditation of Achaan Chah*. Wheaton, IL: A Quest Book, 1986.
Krishnamurti, Jiddu. *The First and the Last Freedom*. New York: Harper & Row, Inc., 1954.
———. *Commentaries on the Living*. Series I-III. Wheaton, IL: A Quest Book, 1968.
———. *Think on These Things*. New York: Harper & Row, 1970.
———. *The Flight of the Eagle*. New York: Harper & Row, 1971.
———. *Talks and Dialogues*. New York: Avon Books, 1972.
———. *You Are the World*. New York: Harper & Row, 1972.
Lefort, Raphael. *The Teachers of Gurdjieff*. New York: Samuel Weiser, 1975.
Leggett, Trevor. *Sankara on Yoga Sutras*. London: Routledge & Kegan Paul, 1981.
Lerner, Eric. *Journey of Insight Meditation*. New York: Schocken Books, Inc., 1977.
LeShan, Lawrence. *How To Meditate*. New York: Bantam Books, 1975.
———. *Alternate Realities*. New York: Ballantine Books, 1976.
Levine, Stephen. *A Gradual Enlightenment*. Garden City, NY: Doubleday & Company, 1979.
Lings, Martin. *What Is Sufism?* Berkeley: University of California Press, 1976.
Lou, Tsung Hwa. *The Tao of Meditation*. Warwick, New York: Tai Chi Foundation, 1983.
Maezumi, Teizan, Roshi. "Nansen Cuts the Cat." In *On Zen Practice II*. Edited by Teizan Maezumi and Bernard Glassman. Los Angeles: Zen Center of Los Angeles, 1977.
———. "Receiving the Precepts." In *On Zen Practice II*.

Maezumi, Teizan and Glassman, Bernard T. *The Hazy Moon of Enlightenment.* Los Angeles: Zen Center of Los Angeles, 1978.
Mascaro, Juan, trans. *The Upanishads.* Baltimore: Penguin Books, 1973.
May, Gerald. *The Open Way.* New York: Paulist Press, 1977.
Merril-Wolff, Franklin. *Pathways Through to Space.* New York: Julian Press, 1973.
Merton, Thomas. *Mystics and Zen Masters.* New York: Farrar, Strauss & Giroux, 1967.
_____. *The Way of Chuang Tzu.* New York: New Directions, 1965.
Miller, Barbara S., trans. *The Bhagavad-Gita.* New York: Bantam, 1986.
Mirra, Rammurti S. *The Textbook of Yoga Psychology.* New York: The Julian Press, 1963.
Mitchell, Stephen, comp. & ed. *Dropping Ashes on the Buddha. The Teaching of Zen Master Seung Sahn.* New York: Grove Press, Inc., 1976.
Miura, Isshu and Ruth F. Sasaki. *The Zen Koan.* New York: Harvest Books, 1965.
Monks, Ramakrishna Order. *Meditation.* Hollywood: Vedanta Press, 1984.
Mountain, Marion. *The Zen Environment.* New York: Bantam Books, 1983.
Muktananda, Swami. *Meditate.* Albany: The State University of New York Press, 1980.
Murti, T.R.V. *The Central Philosophy of Buddhism.* London: George Allen & Unwin, 1960.
Muses, C.A., ed. *Esoteric Teachings of the Tibetan Tantra.* York Beach, ME: Samuel Weiser, Inc. 1982.
Namgyal, Takpo Tashi. *Mahamudra.* Translated by Lobsang P. Lhalungpa. Boston and London: Shambhala, 1986.
Naranjo, Claudio and Robert Ornstein. *On the Psychology of Meditation.* New York: Viking Press, 1973.
Narayananda, Swami. *The Primal Power in Man.* Gylling, Denmark: N.U. Yoga Trust & Ashrama, 1979.
Needleman, Jacob. *The New Religions.* New York: Pocket Books, 1972.
Neisser, Ulrich. *Cognitive Psychology.* New York: Appleton-Century-Crofts, 1966.
Nicholas of Cusa. *The Vision of God.* Translated by Emma Gurney Salter. New York: Frederick Unger Publishing Co., 1960.
Nicholson, Reynold A. *The Mystics of Islam.* London: Routledge & Kegan Paul, 1963.
Nishijima, Gudo and Langdon, Joe. *How to Practice Zazen.* Tokyo: Bukkyosha, Ltd., 1976.

Nurbakhsh, Javad. *In the Paradise of the Sufis*. New York: Khaniqahi-Nimatullahi Publications, 1979.
_____. *Sufism*. New York: Khaniqahi-Nimatullahi Publications, 1982.
Nyanaponika, Thera. *The Heart of Buddhist Meditation*. New York: Samuel Weiser, Inc., 1973.
Odier, Daniel. *Nirvana Tao*. Translated by John Mahoney. New York: Inner Tradition International, Ltd., 1986.
Ornstein, Robert, ed. *The Nature of Human Consciousness*. San Francisco: W.H. Freeman & Company, 1973.
_____. *The Psychology of Consciousness*. 2d. ed. New York: Harcourt, Brace & Jovanovich, 1977
Osaka, Koryu, Roshi. "Breathing in Zazen." In *On Zen Practice II*. Edited by Teizan Maezumi and Bernard Glassman. Los Angeles: Zen Center of Los Angeles, 1977.
_____. "Shikan-taza and Koan Practice." In *On Zen Practice II*.
Osborne, Arthur, ed. *The Teachings of Ramana Maharshi*. New York: Samuel Weiser, Inc., 1962.
Otto, Rudolf. *Mysticism East and West*. New York: Macmillan, 1972.
Palmer, G.E.H. et al., trans. *The Philokalia*. Vols. I-III. London and Boston: Faber & Faber, 1984-1986.
Prabhavananda, Swami & Christoper Isherwood, trans. *The Song of God: Bhagavad-Gita*. New York: New American Library, Inc., 1951.
_____, trans. *How to Know God: The Yoga Aphorisms of Patanjali*. New York: New American Library, 1969.
Prabhavananda, Swami and Frederick Manchester, trans. *The Upanishads: Breath of the Eternal*. New York: New American Library, 1957.
Prem, Krishna. *The Yoga of the Bhagavad Gita*. Baltimore: Penguin Books, 1973.
Pseudo-Dionysius. *The Complete Works*. Translated by Colm Luibheid. New York: Paulist Press, 1987.
Radha, Shivananda, Swami. *Kundalini Yoga for the West*. Boulder: Shambhala, 1981.
Rahman, Fazlur. *Islam*. Garden City, New York: Doubleday, 1968.
Rahula, Walpola. *What the Buddha Taught*. New York: Grove Press, 1974.
Rajneesh, B.S. *Meditation: The Art of Ecstasy*. New York: Harper & Row, 1976.
_____. *The Book of Secrets*. New York: Harper & Row, 1977.
Rama, Swami. *Lectures on Yoga*. Glenview, IL: Himalayan International Institute, 1976.
Rama, Swami et al. *Yoga and Psychotherapy*. Glenview, IL: Himalayan International Institute, 1976.
Ram Dass. *Journey of Awakening*. New York: Bantam Books, 1978.

_____. *Grist for the Mill.* New York: Bantam Books, 1979.
Reps, Paul, comp. *Zen Flesh, Zen Bones.* Garden City, NY: Doubleday Anchor, n.d.
Rieker, Hans-Ulrich. *The Secret of Meditation.* New York: Samuel Weiser, 1975.
_____. *The Yoga of Light. Hatha Yoga Pradipika.* Translated by Elsy Becherer. Middletown, CA: The Dawn Horse Press, 1978.
Rinboshay, Lati and Napier, Elizabeth. *The Mind in Tibetan Buddhism.* Valois, NY: Gabriel/Snow Lion, 1981.
Rinboshay, Lati & Locho. *Meditative States in Tibetan Buddhism.* Translated by Jeffrey Hopkins. London: Cameron Printing Co. Ltd., 1983.
Roberts, Bernadette. *The Experience of No-Self.* Boulder: Shambhala Publications, Inc., 1984.
_____. *The Path to No-Self.* Boulder: Shambhala, 1985.
Ruysbroeck, Jan Van. (John Ruusbroec). *The Spiritual Espousals and Other Works.* Translated by James A. Wiseman. New York: Paulist Press, 1985.
Sabbath, Linda. *In God's Radiance.* Warwick, NY: Amity House, Inc., 1988.
Saddhatissa, H. *The Buddha's Way.* New York: George Braziller, Inc. 1971.
St. Bonaventure. *The Soul's Journey into God.* Translated by Ewert Cousins. New York: Paulist Press, 1978.
St. Gregory Palamas. *The Triads.* Translated by Nicholas Gendle. New York: Paulist Press, 1980.
St. Gregory of Sinai. "Instructions to Hesychasts." In *The Fire and the Cloud.* Edited by David A. Fleming. New York: Paulist Press, 1978.
St. Ignatius Loyola. "The Spiritual Exercises." In *The Fire and the Cloud.* Edited by David A. Fleming. New York: Paulist Press, 1978.
St. John Climacus. *The Ladder of Divine Ascent.* Translated by Colm Luibheid and Norman Russell. New York: Paulist Press, 1982.
St. John of the Cross. *Ascent of Mount Carmel.* Translated by E. Allison Peers. Garden City, NY: Doubleday, 1958.
St. Simeon the New Theologian. *The Discourses.* Translated by C.J. de Catanzaro. New York: Paulist Press, 1980.
St. Teresa of Avila. *The Interior Castle.* Translated by Kiernan Kavanaugh and Otilio Rodriguez. New York: Paulist Press, 1979.
Satchitananda, Swami. *Integral Yoga: The Yoga Sutras of Patanjali. Translation and Commentary.* Yogaville, Virginia: Integral Yoga Publications, 1984.
Schimmel, Annemarie. *Mystical Dimensions of Islam.* Chapel Hill: University of North Carolina Press, 1975.
Schlosser, Edith. "Christian Mysticism." In *Approaches to Meditation.* Edited by Virginia Hanson. Wheaton, IL: A Quest Book, 1973.
Sekida, Katsuki. *Zen Training.* New York: John Weatherhill, Inc., 1975.

Shah, Idries. *Tales of the Dervishes*. New York: E.P. Dutton, 1970.
_____. *The Way of the Sufi*. New York: E.P. Dutton, 1970.
_____. *The Sufis*. Garden City, NY: Doubleday & Co., 1971.
Shankara. *Crest-Jewel of Discrimination*. Translated by Swami Prabhavananda and Christopher Isherwood. Hollywood: Vedanta Press, 1978.
Shapiro, Deane. *Meditation: Self-Regulation Strategy and Altered States of Consciousness*. New York: Aldine Publishing Company, 1980.
Shapiro, Deane and Roger Walsh, eds. *Meditation: Classic and Contemporary Perspectives*. New York: Aldine, 1984.
Shattock, E.M. *An Experiment in Mindfulness*. New York: Samuel Weiser, 1972.
Shaya, Leo. *The Universal Meaning of the Kabbalah*. Baltimore: Penguin Books, 1973.
Shearer, Alistair. *Effortless Being: The Yoga Sutras of Patanjali*. Winchester, MA: Allen & Unwin, Inc., 1989.
Sheinkin, David. *Path of the Kabbalah*. New York: Paragon House Publishers, 1986.
Shimano, Eido, Roshi. *Golden Wind*. Tokyo: Japan Publications, Inc., 1979.
Shivananda, Swami. *Fourteen Lessons in Raja Yoga*. Delhi: Motilal Banarsidas, 1976.
Singh, Pancham. *The Hatha Yoga Pradipika*. New York: AMS Press, Inc., 1974.
Smith, Adam. *Powers of Mind*. New York: Ballantine Books, 1975.
Snellgrove, D.L., trans. *The Hevajra Tantra*. Parts I-II. London and New York: Oxford University Press, 1980.
Sohl, Robert and Audrey Carr. *The Gospel According to Zen*. New York: New American Library, 1970.
Sopa, Lhundup and Jeffrey Hopkins. *Practice and Theory of Tibetan Buddhism*. New York: Grove Press, 1976.
Spencer, Sidney. *Mysticism in World Religion*. South Brunswick, NJ: A.S. Barner & Company, Inc., 1963.
Spiegelberg, Frederick. *Spiritual Practices of India*. New York: The Citadel Press, 1962.
Steinsaltz, Adin. *The Thirteen-Petalled Rose*. New York: Basic Books, 1980.
Suzuki, Deisetz Teitaro. *Manual of Zen Buddhism*. New York: Grove Press, 1960.
_____, trans. *The Lankavatara Sutra*. London: Routledge & Kegan Paul, 1968.
_____. *Essays in Zen Buddhism*. First Series. New York: Grove Press, Inc., 1961.
_____. *Essays in Zen Buddhism*. Second Series. London: Luzac & Company, 1933.
_____. *Essays in Zen Buddhism*. Third Series. New York: Samuel Weiser, 1971.
_____. *Mysticism, Christian and Buddhist*. New York: Harper, 1971.

Suzuki, Shunryu, Roshi. *Zen Mind, Beginner's Mind.* New York: Weatherhill, Inc., 1973.
Tart, Charles T. *States of Consciousness.* New York: Dutton, 1975.
_____, ed. *Transpersonal Psychologies.* New York: Harper, 1975.
Taimini, I. K. *The Science of Yoga: A Commentary on the Yoga-Sutras of Patanjali in the Light of Modern Thought.* Madras, India: The Theosophical Publishing House, 1965.
Trungpa, Chogyam. *Meditation in Action.* Berkeley, Shambhala, 1970.
_____. *Cutting Through Spiritual Materialism.* Berkeley: Shambhala Publications, Inc., 1973.
_____. *The Foundations of Mindfulness.* Berkeley: Shambhala, 1976.
_____. *The Myth of Freedom and the Way of Meditation.* Boulder: Shambhala Publications, Inc., 1976.
_____. *Journey Without Goal.* Boulder: Prajna Press, 1981.
Tsong-ka-pa. *Tantra in Tibet.* Vols. 1-3. Translated and edited by Jeffrey Hopkins. London: George Allen & Unwin, 1980.
Tulku, Tarthang. *Gesture of Balance.* Emeryville, CA: Dharma Publishing, 1977.
_____. *Openness Mind.* Emeryville, CA: Dharma Publishing, 1978.
Underhill, Evelyn. *Mysticism.* New York: E.P. Dutton, 1961.
Van de Wettering, Janwillem. *A Glimpse of Nothingness.* Boston: Houghton Mifflin Company, 1975.
Walker, Kenneth. *A Study of Gurdjieff's Teaching.* New York: Samuel Weiser, 1974.
Walsh, Roger. "Meditation Practice and Research." *Journal of Humanistic Psychology* 23 (1983): 18-50.
_____. "The Consciousness Discipline." *Journal of Humanistic Psychology* 23 (1983): 28-30.
_____. "Journey Beyond Belief." *Journal of Humanistic Psychology.* 24 (1984): 30-65.
Walsh, Roger and Deane Shapiro, eds. *Beyond Health and Normality.* New York: Van Norstand Reinhold Company, 1983.
Walsh, Roger and Frances Vaughan, eds. *Beyond Ego.* Los Angeles: J.P. Tarcher, Inc., 1980.
Washburn, Michael. *The Ego and the Dynamic Ground.* Albany: State University of New York Press, 1988.
Wechler, Rob. "A New Prescription: Mind Over Malady." *Discover* (February 1987): 51-61.
White, John. *Everything You Wanted to Know About TM.* New York: Pocket Books, 1976.

_____, ed. *The Highest State of Consciousness*. Garden City, NY: Doubleday Anchor, 1972.
_____, ed. *What Is Meditation?* Garden City, NY: Doubleday Anchor, 1974.
Wilber, Ken. *The Spectrum of Consciousness*. Wheaton, IL: A Quest Book, 1977.
_____. *No Boundary*. Los Angeles: Center Publications, Inc., 1979.
_____. *The Atman Project*. Wheaton, IL: A Quest Book, 1980.
_____. ed. *The Holographic Paradigm and Other Paradoxes*. Boulder: Shambhala, 1982.
_____. *Eye to Eye*. Garden City, NY: Doubleday Anchor, 1983.
_____. *A Sociable God*. New York: McGraw-Hill Book Co., 1983.
Wilber, Ken, Jack Engler, and Daniel P. Brown, eds. *Transformations of Consciousness*. Boston & London: Shambhala, 1986.
Willis, Janice D. *The Diamond Light*. New York: Simon & Schuster, 1972.
Wood, Ernest. *Concentration: An Approach to Meditation*. Wheaton, IL: A Quest Book, 1952.
_____. *Seven Schools of Yoga: An Introduction*. Wheaton, IL: A Quest Book, 1973.
Yamada, Kohun, Roshi. "Dogen Zenji and Enlightenment." In *On Zen Practice II*. Edited by Teizan Maezumi and Bernard Glassman. Los Angeles: Zen Center of Los Angeles, 1977.
Yasutani, Hakuun, Roshi. "Koan Practice and Shikan-taza." In *On Zen Practice II*.
Yu, Lu K'uan. *Chan and Zen Training*. First Series. Berkeley: Shambhala Publications, 1970.
_____. *The Secret of Chinese Meditation*. New York: Samuel Weiser, 1971.
_____. *Taoist Yoga*. New York: Weiser, 1977.
Zimmer, Heinrich. *Philosophies of India*. London: Routledge & Kegan Paul, 1969.

Index

A

Abdominal breathing, 154-155, 166
Abdominal/power center *(manipura chakra)*, 166, 124-125, 195-198, 208-216, 234
Absolute, 160, 182, 186, 204
Absolute Oneness, 47-48, 107, 114-115, 118, 130, 158, 204, 208, 264
Advaita (nondualist) Vedanta, 12, 63
Ahimsa (nonviolence), 76
Ajaya, Swami, 73-75, 106
Alawi, Muhammed (Sufi master), 262
Al-Ghazali (Sufi philosopher), 31, 256-257, 263
Al-Junaid (Sufi master), 257
All-embracing Awareness, 9-10, 47, 49, 67, 70-71, 79, 94, 100, 102, 110, 115, 119, 157, 159-161, 170, 177, 180, 182, 200, 204-205, 252
Al-Qushairi (Sufi master), 255
Al-Sarraj (Sufi master), 255, 259
Anatta, 143-144, 151
Andersen, Paoul, 208, 211
Anicca (impermanence), 134, 143, 145-146
Annihilation, 226-227
Ansari (Sufi master), 259
Aparigraha (nongreed), 77
Aranya, Swami Hariharananda, 90-91, 93-94
Arberry, A.J., 31, 255-57, 259

Archetypal Self, 46, 91-92, 181, 183, 216, 249-253
Arhant, 152
Arjuna, 73
Asamprajnata/formless/seedless *samadhi*, 47, 92, 183, 252
Asana, see posture
Asceticism, 96
Ashtanga Yoga, 72
Asteya (nonstealing), 76
Atman, 105
Attachment, 6, 37, 42, 70-74, 114, 135-136, 138, 145, 149, 199, 215, 238-239, 247-248, 258-259, 262
Attention, 5, 10, 14, 17-18, 26, 33, 37, 39, 41, 43, 47, 57, 60, 70, 78, 80-87, 89-94, 101, 104-111, 114, 116-117, 135-142, 145-150, 154-157, 168, 187, 190-192, 195-196, 198-199, 201-204, 209-210, 212-216, 218, 220, 222, 229, 233-235, 238, 241-243, 246-249, 261-267, 269, *passim*
Avalokitesvara, Bodhisattva, 179-180
Avatamsaka Sutra, 204
Aversion/Avoidance, 74, 136, 138, 149, 199
Awareness, 3-6, 8-11, 14, 17, 23, 26, 30, 40-41, 44, 47, 67, 70-71, 79, 88-90, 93, 101, 110-111, 132-136, 138, 144-145, 151-152, 159, 168-

169, 171, 179, 183, 192, 199, 200, 202, 205, 214-215, 233, 238, 241, 244-246, 250, 259, 266, *passim*

B

Baba, Meher, 251
Bandha, 116, 127, 199
Baqa, 255, 267
Baraka, 260, 266
Bare attention, 88, 133-134, 136-138, 143, 148, 198-199, 246
Bassui (Zen master), 169-171
Bawa, Guru, 267
Becoming the Source, 49
Bhajan, Yogi, 113
Bhagavad Gita, 73, 95, 107-108
Bhakti Yoga, xi, 67, 75, 106-109, 229
Bharati, Agehananda, 101, 117, 119-121, 128
Bible, 239-240
Bhikshu, Vijnana, 89
Bija-mantra/seed-syllable, 100, 117, 119-120, 178-179, 182, 191
Bindu, 118
Blofeld, John, 175, 177, 183, 186, 207-208, 210
Bohm, David, 79
Bondage, 72, 183, 240, 257
Brahmacharya, 76
Brahma, 79, 105
Brahman, 48, 63, 65, 76, 100, 105, 107, 110, 112, 115, 118
Breath-control, 82, 116, 185, 235, 266
Brown, Daniel P., 32, 41, 43-44, 79, 90-91, 93-94, 151-152, 158, 205-205
Buddha, 17, 37, 49, 52, 61-62, 85, 131, 153-154, 161-162, 164-165, 173, 181, 186, 190, 199, 200-201, 249, 259
Buddhahood, 49, 152-153, 170, 172-173, 179, 182, 184, 190, 205-206
Buddha-nature, 11, 48, 157, 162, 164-165, 167, 170, 172, 181, 182, 196
Buddhism, 11-12, 14-15, 41, 49, 131, 153, 207, 233
Burke, Omar Michael, 258, 260, 264

C

Callisotis, Patriarch, 234, 236
Capra, Fritjof, 79
Carrington, Patricia, 38-39, 99, 102
Castaneda, Carlos, 8, 19, 73, 131
Centering Prayer, 241
Cessation of suffering, 94-95
Chah, Achaan, 15, 33, 92
Chakra, 83, 116, 122, 126, 179, 185, 224, 259-260
Chandogya Upanishad, 110
Chang, Garma (Chung-Yuan), 158, 160, 163, 168, 170, 198, 200
Chao Chou/Joshu (Zen master), 158-159, 165
Ching-chin, Ku-yin (Zen master), 168
Chirban, John, 31, 230-231
Chitta-vritti (mind-waves), 8, 69
Chosen deity (ishta deva), 65, 74-75, 120
Christ/Jesus, xii, 18, 46, 49, 52, 80, 85, 153, 230, 233, 237, 239, 240, 242, 244, 251-52
Christianity, xii, 15, 269
Christ-Self, 249, 251
Christian meditation — Eastern Church, 229-236; Western (Catholic) Church, 237-254

Christian mysticism, 11, 41, 48-49, 256; affirmative way, 229; negative way, 229
Chuang Tzu, 8
Clear comprehension, 133-134
Cleaving, 226-227
Cloud of forgetting, 245, 247
Cloud of Unknowing, The, 45, 238, 241, 245-246, 248
Cole, K.C., 100
Compassion, 107, 152, 182, 187
Completed/Perfected Man, 257, 267
Completeness, 65, 77, 95, 113, 115, 118, 130, 151, 179, 182-183
Concentration, 20, 32-33, 35, 40-41, 60, 72, 75, 78, 80, 82-88, 90, 101, 106, 108, 116, 131, 139, 142-143, 147, 156-157, 186-187, 191-197, 200-201, 209-211, 215-216, 219-222, 225, 234, 239, 242, 259, 262-262, 264-266, *passim*
Concentrative exercises, 67, 84-88, 139-142, 154-157, 187-203, 208-216, 219-225, 233-236, 240-245, 259-267
Concentrative meditation, 14-15, 33, 37, 106, 139, 146, 154, 184, 186, 194, 205, 217, 219, 233, 241, 269
Conditioned existence, xii, 29, 37, 65, 67, 94-95, 139, 143-145, 151, 161-164, 168-169, 180, 185, 199-200, 203-204, 267
Consciousness, 3, 5-7, 35, 38-40, 49, 57-58, 64, 66-67, 70-71, 75, 77-82, 86, 89-91, 93, 99-102, 106-108, 110, 122, 114-123, 126, 129, 131-132, 136, 139-143, 146, 154, 156-157, 161, 163, 167, 179-183, 203-204, 208, 213-214, 217, 219-221, 223-226, 236-237, 246-247, 249-250, 255, 260-261, 263, 266, 269, *passim*
Consciousness as Such, 6, 13
Constructions of consciousness, reality, and self, 7, 89, 143, 145, 151-152, 154, 158
Contemplation, 8, 11, 40-41, 191-193, 217-219, 221, 224-226, 230, 233, 239, 245-257, 259, 266-267; acquired/active, 41, 88, 246; infused/passive, 9, 45, 47, 246
Conventional religion, 61
Conversion, 231, 237, 256
Cordovero, Moses (Kabbalist master), 218
Cosmic/universal consciousness, 45, 94, 105, 127, 169, 183, 198, 203, 207-208, 214, 216
Cross, 85, 241
Crown center *(sahasrara),* 122, 126-129, 195-199, 212-216, 224

D

Dakini, 176
Dark night of the senses, 44, 247-248
Dark night of the soul, 151, 247-248
Daya, Najmeddin (Sufi master), 262
Deautomatization, 5
Deconstruction, 4, 8, 38, 40, 69, 71, 83, 89-92, 142, 151, 164, 167, 169, 183, *passim*
of consciousness, 5, 7, 10, 38, 40, 43-44, 66, 69-71, 78, 83, 88-92, 95, 102, 111-112, 126, 129, 139, 145, 150-151, 157, 167, 169, 181, 183, 186, 198-200, 202-204, 214-216, 224, 227, 235-236, 246, 248-249, 266
of reality, 43-44, 66, 83, 88-92, 95,

112, 145, 150-151, 202, 227, 236, 249
  of self, 44, 66, 89-92, 111-112, 150-151, 227, 236, 249
Deikman, Arthur, 5, 257
Delusion, 23, 126, 134-136, 138, 248
DeMartino, Richard, 163
Dependent coarising, 151
Desire, 6, 37, 42, 65, 69-70, 73, 136, 138, 149, 238, 247-248, 259
Desiringness, 77
Desiringnessless, 210, 232, 257-258
Devekut, 227
Developing positive qualities/traits, 14, 17-19, 28, 72, 77, 217-218, 231, 233, 240
Devotion, 72, 75, 77, 107-108, 219, 243, 262
Devotional meditation, 219, 226, 229
Dharana (concentration), 75, 83-88
Dharani (*Sutra* chanting), 117
Dharma-cloud *samadhi*, 94
Dhikr, 9, 259, 261-266
Dhyana (meditation), 75, 88-89
Dhyani (meditative) Buddhas, 45, 176, 179, 181, 184
Direct experience, 96, 106, 110, 145, 157, 161, 171, 194, 204, 248
Disidentification, 6, 36, 48, 64-67, 75, 90, 92-94, 107, 110, 136, 151, 161, 184, 199, 202-203, 213, 218-219, 247, 250-252, 258
Displacement effect, 41, 83, 89, 108, 112, 247-248, 250, 261, 266
Dissatisfaction, 77, 257-258
Dissolving negative programming, 4, 20, 24-28, 136-137
Distractions, 36, 51, 59, 60-62, 84, 88, 147, 192
Dogen (Zen master), 154, 172

Don Juan, 8, 19, 73, 77
Dov Baer, Rabbi (Kabbalist master), 226-227
Dualism/duality, 12, 65-66, 152, 157, 160, 167, 169, 250, 257
Dualistic structure, 77, 88, 90, 107, 169, 229
Dualistic thinking, 7, 61, 102, 167, 169
Dukkha, 136, 143-145, 152-153, 162, 183, 194, 249

E

Eastern Orthodox Church, xii, 31, 61, 229-230, 232
Eckhart, Meister, 238-239
Effort, 51, 61-62, 72, 77, 116
Effortless Being, 61-62, 65
Egan, Harvey D., 240
Ego, 65-66, 73-75, 77, 110, 151, 157, 161, 181, 249, 255, 263, 267
Eightfold Path, 132, 139
El-Jerrahi, Sheikh Mazafer (Sufi master), 240
Eliade, Mircea, 57, 75, 78, 80, 89, 91, 95, 116, 118-119, 127-128, 180-181, 183, 234, 248
Emptiness, 77, 160, 184-187, 192-194
Emptying the mind, 44, 202-203, 213-214, 248, 259
Energy, 67, 100, 113-114, 117
Energy Principle, 116-118, 224
Engler, Jack, 39, 133, 151
Enlightenment, 11, 15, 36, 48-49, 61, 73, 92, 94, 96, 130-131, 139, 145, 152-154, 157-158, 162, 164, 172-173, 179, 181, 184-187, 190, 198, 200, 204-205, 216, 245, 251
Epstein, Pearl, 217-218, 227

Exhalation, 80-81, 86, 104-105, 116-117, 127, 140, 146, 154-156, 166, 195-196, 201-202, 209, 211-216, 220, 234, 242, 262
Experiential religion, xi, 48

F

Faith, 74, 162, 186
Fana, 255, 267
Feuerstein, Georg, 63, 65-66, 71-72, 75, 79, 90-91, 93-95
Five M's, 120, 128, 176, 179, 210
Fixations (mental and emotional), 19, 38, 118, 123, 136, 145, 180-181, 184, 186, 195, 213, 217-218, 237, 255, 266
Form is emptiness, 95, 170, 252
Formal meditation, 20, 31-49 *passim*, 139, 168, 218-219, 224, 236
Formless Essence/Ground/State, 70-71, 83, 107, 114-115, 142, 172, 182, 205, 223-224, 263, 265
Four Noble Truths, 13
Freeing natural qualities from positive programming, 28-30, 136

G

Gesture (mudra), 185-191, 195
God, 9, 11-12, 18, 25, 45-46, 48, 64-65, 76, 80, 102, 106-108, 153, 223-224, 226-227, 229-233, 237-243, 245-253, 255, 258-259, 261-267, *passim*
God-as-object, 12, 252
God-as-subject, 252
Godhead, 63, 96-97, 101, 236, 242, 252
Goldstein, Joseph, 133

Goldstein, Joseph & Kornfield, Jack, 136
Goleman, Danial, 1-2, 22, 107-109, 138, 142, 152, 233, 235
Govinda, Lama Anagarika, 7, 178-179, 183, 198
Grasping, 77, 136, 145
Greed, 24, 73, 77, 136, 152, 231, 258
St. Gregory of Nyssa, 247
St. Gregory Palamas, 232, 234-236,
St. Gregory of Sinai, 234-235
Groeschel, Benedict, 245, 248-249
Gurdjieff, G.I., 19
Guru, 52, 74, 78, 81, 83, 85, 102, 104, 106, 108, 120, 177, 181, 184, 186

H

Habits, 11, 17, 73, 152, 237-238, 250, 259
Habituation, 5, 10, 217
Hahn, Thich Nhat (Vietnamese master), 17, 156
Hakuin (Zen master), 170
Halevi, Z'ev ben Shimon, 217, 219, 222, 224-226
Han Shan (Zen master), 163
Hare Krishna Movement, 108
Hatha Yoga, 66, 259-260
Hatha Yoga Pradipika, 66
Heart center *(anahata chakra)*, 225-126, 129, 195, 197-198, 208, 211, 214-216, 244
Heart Sutra, 95, 170, 252
St. Hesychios of Jerusalem, 230, 233
St. Hesychios the Priest, 232, 233
Hewitt, James, 142, 264
Hinduism, xi, 15, 41, 45, 48-49, 61, 63, 66-67, 77, 79, 95-96, 128, 131, 207
Hitbodeduth, 219

Hixon, Lex, 267
Hoffman, Edward, 18, 218-219, 223-226
Holographic paradigm, 100
Hua Yen School of Buddhism, 204
Huang Po (Zen master), 270
Hui-neng (the sixth patriarch), 165
Human condition, 70, 162
Human paradox, 163-164
Humility, 218, 232, 238, 269

I

Ida (left channel), 122, 195-197
Idel, Moshe, 227
Identification, 5-6, 42, 65-66, 70, 90, 96, 109, 112, 114, 117-119, 126, 134, 136-138, 145, 164, 180, 183-184, 207, 209, 211-216, 220, 227, 234, 237, 242, 249-250, 255, 258-259, 263
Identity with God/Brahman/Buddha-nature/Tao, 8, 12-13, 47-48, 63-64, 107, 208, 217, 227, 229, 236, 252-5253, 255-256
St. Ignatius of Loyola, 239
Illumination, 41, 45, 217, 230, 245, 256, 259-267 passim
Illusion, 23, 46, 126, 134-135, 137-138, 144, 199, 248
Immortal foetus, 207-208, 212, 216
Impasse, 157, 161-164, 167, 249
Impermanence, 133-134, 138, 144-145, 149, 151, 193-194, 199, 204-205
Implicate-extricate order, 79
Incarnational state, 49
Incompleteness, 77, 126
Indwelling/inherence (mutual), 47, 204

Informal Awareness Meditation (IAM), 17-32, 72, 74, 76, 133, 218, 233, 258, 266
Inhalation, 80-81, 86, 104-105, 116-117, 127, 140, 146, 154-156, 166, 195-196, 201-202, 262
Initiation, 74, 78, 81, 102, 104, 119, 184, 187, 195
Insight meditation, 14-15, 33, 37, 45, 47, 131, 139, 142-152, 156, 167, 183-184, 186, 192-194, 203-206, 217, 230, 245, 266-267, 269
Insufficiency (dukkha), 138, 144, 148, 151, 256
Intention/will, 229, 240-241, 246-248, 269
Interconnected, 47, 79, 114, 127, 144, 151
Interdependence, 47, 151
Internal dialogue, 7, 44, 78, 161, 224, 245
Interpenetration, 47, 79, 93, 114, 118, 127, 151, 161, 204, 207, 224
St. Isaiah the Solitary, 232
Islam, 15

J

Jaladhara bandha, 127
Jnana Yoga, xi, 15, 67, 109-112, 116, 167
Japa, 108, 260-261
Jesus Prayer, xii, 230, 232-236, 250
St. John Cassian, 231
St. John Climacus, 231
St. John of the Cross, 46, 74, 151, 238, 241, 245-247, 250
St. John Damaskos, 231
Jou, Tsung Hwa, 209
Judaism, 15

Jung, Carl G., 69

K

Kabbalah/Kabbalistic meditation, 11, 18, 41, 48-49, 217-227, 229, 233, 240, 262
Kaivalya, 95
Kaplan, Aryeh, 58, 219-221, 223, 226
Kapleau, Philip Roshi, 59, 153-157, 162, 164, 168-171
Karma, 94-96, 151-152, 205
Karma Yoga, 17, 67, 116
Kavvanah, 218
Keating, Abbott Thomas, 39, 241
Kether, 218
Keyes, Ken, 21, 76, 127
Khan, Pir Vilayat, 260
Khana, Madhu, 117
Khechari mudra, 116
Kinhin (Zen walking meditation), 156, 172
Kingdom of God, 231
Kirtan, 108
Koan, 45, 11, 157-172, 205, 248, 250
  meaning of, 151-162
  meditation, 162-172, 205
Koelman, Gaspar, 90
Kornfield & Breiter, 140
Krishna, 73, 83, 85, 107-109
Krishnamurti, J., 17
Kriya Yoga, 72
Kundalini Yoga, 67, 120-130, 185, 194, 199, 208, 210-211, 259-260

L

La ilaha illa 'llah, 2601-262, 264
Lama, Dalai, 175, 187
Lankavatara Sutra, The, 10, 171
Lao-tzu, 250

Lataif, 259-260
Laya Yoga, 66
Lerner, Eric, 145
LeShan, Lawrence, 12-13, 87
Letting go, 250-252
Liberation, 65, 94-96, 113, 130, 134, 143, 145, 153, 183-184
Love, 99, 106-107, 229, 241, 244, 258, 269
Luzzato, Rabbi Isaac (Kabbalist master), 218

M

Madhyamika School of Buddhism, 154, 176
Mahabandha, 116, 127
Mahamudra, 116, 127
Mahamudra meditation, 200-205
Maharaj-ji, Guru, 46, 106
Mahavedha, 117, 127
Mahayana Buddhism, 176, 186
Maithuna/sexual yoga, 120-121, 208-210
Makyo, 46
Mala/rosary beads, 108-109, 190-191, 260-262
Mandala, 9, 33, 83, 85, 116, 118-120, 142, 176-178, 180-185, 200, 222, 224
Mantra, x, 9, 74, 83, 86, 99-106, 108-109, 116-120, 127, 142, 166, 176-179, 184-193, 200, 219-221, 242-243, 260-262
Mantra repetition, 116, 186-187, 190-191, 193, 234-236, 242, 262-265
Mantra Yoga, xi, 99-106, 219, 242, 259
Ma-tsu/Baso (Zen master), 171
May, Gerald, 62

Maya, 37, 199
Meditation, xi, 1-4, 6-11, 15, 20, 35-36, 41, 44, 51-55, 57-63, 67, 71-72, 80-83, 88-89, 92-94, 99, 102-105, 106-108, 112, 119, 129, 133-135, 139, 142, 145, 154, 156, 177-179, 182-184, 186-192, 195, 197-201, 203-205, 208, 213-214, 216-221, 224-226, 231, 233-235, 237, 239-246, 251-252, 256, 259-261, 267, *passim*
   nature and aims of, 1-14
   kinds of, 14-15
Meditation on *Mu,* 165-172
Meggid (teacher), 217-218, 224
Method of Holding the Three Ones, 208-210-211
Middle Path, 61, 151, 204, 206
Mindfulness, 17-18, 132-136, 143, 156, 186, 232-233
   of body, 134-135
   of feeling, 136-137
   of mind, 137-138
   of objects of mind, 138
Misra, Rammurti, 94
Moksha, 95-96
Moment-to-moment awakening/awareness, 15, 19, 24, 30, 135-136
Mudra (gesture), 58, 116-117, 176-178, 185, 187-191, 193
Muktananda, Swami, 11, 105
Mula bandha, 127
Mystical marriage, 250

N

Nachman, Rabbi (Kabbalist master), 220

Nadi (channel for circulating energy), 116
Naranjo, Claudio, 5, 75-77
Naranjo, Claudio, & Ornstein, Robert, 234, 236, 262-263
Narayananda, Swami, 115-116, 122, 127-130
Needleman, Jacob, 103, 251
Negative programming, 4, 11, 14, 17-20, 23-24, 27-28, 51, 74, 77, 117-118, 123, 125, 132, 136, 181-182, 184, 195, 213, 217-218, 231-232, 233-234, 237-238, 240
New Creation/New Man, 244, 249
New Testament, 80, 230
Nicholas of Cusa, 243
Nicholson, Reynold A., 263
Nicophoros the Solitary, 234
St. Neilos the Ascetic, 232
Nirvana, 11, 48-49, 131, 139, 145, 152, 161, 171, 176, 190, 199, 205
Nirodha (stopping), 8, 69-70, 93
Nirvikalpa samadhi, 46, 48, 107, 130
Niyama, 75, 132
Nonattachment, 6, 36, 67, 71-73, 77, 93-95, 135, 194, 203, 232, 238-239, 257-258
Nondualism/nonduality, 12, 48, 198-199, 269
Nonreturner, 152
Not-doing *(wu wei),* 9, 172, 246
Nurbakhsh, Javad, 11, 18, 255, 257-259, 266-267

O

Object-pole, 169, 249
Odier, Daniel, 181
OM, 86, 100, 101, 129
Om Mani Padme Hum, 179-180

Once returner, 152
One-pointedness of mind,33, 39, 81, 83, 88, 101, 108, 139, 142, 146, 156, 183, 186-187, 193, 197, 201-202, 209, 211, 214-216, 221, 235, 241, 263-264, 266
Ornstein, Robert, 5, 14, 78
Osaka, Koryu Roshi, 45, 155, 166-167
Ox-herding stages, 48-49, 160, 173

P

Pai-chang (Zen master), 171
Paquda, Bahya ben Joseph Ibn (Kabbalist master), 218
Paradox, 161
Paranormal powers, 46, 91, 129, 185, 248, 252
Patanjali, xi, 8, 15, 46-47, 57, 65-67, 69-96 *passim,* 116, 131, 168, 219, 233, 245-246, 248
Path-enlightenment, 48
St. Paul, 235, 244, 249
St. Peter Damaskos, 233
Philemon, Abba, 232, 235
Philokalia, The, 233
Pingala (right channel), 122, 195-197
Place (of meditation), 51-52
Positive programming, 14, 17-19, 28, 72, 77, 233
Posture, 32, 51, 57-60, 75, 78-79, 135, 154, 177, 185, 201, 212, 220, 233, 242, 266
Prabhavananda, Swami, 71-73, 91
Prakriti, 65, 92, 94
Prana/Primal Energy, 79, 80, 105, 114-115, 118-122, 127-129, 184, 209, 215-216, 250, 260
Pranayama, 75, 79-82

Pratyahara, 75, 82, 219, 233
Prayer, 217, 224, 231, 235, 240-241
Prayer of affective regard, 245
Present-centered consciousness, 18, 57, 88, 134-135, 218
Pribram, Karl, 100
Primal polarity/duality, 46, 114-115, 118, 129, 158, 178-179, 207, 215-216
(Primal Polarity of) Energy Awareness/Wisdom, 114-124, 126-128, 176, 181, 183, 185, 196-198, 211, 215-216
Primordial state/nature, 65, 93, 130, 151, 158, 204-205, 207-208
Programming, 3-5, 10, 13, 20-21, 23, 27-28, 35, 38, 42-43, 65, 69-70, 74-75, 77, 83, 89-90, 101, 106, 115, 123, 126, 132, 137-138, 145, 154, 160-161, 169, 171, 181, 193, 207 = 208, 216, 249, 255, 257, 259, *passim*
Pseudo-Dionysius, 236
Psychology, 11, 67, 69
Psychotherapy, 11
Purification/purgative stage, 31, 66, 77, 117, 217, 230-233, 237-239, 256-259, 263
Purusha, 65, 70, 92

Q

Quandary, 163
Quantum theory, 79, 100
Quiff, 19
Quran, 261

R

Rahula, Walpola, 137, 140
Rajneesh, B.S., 9, 19, 80, 113

Ram Dass, 37, 46, 106-108, 243-244
Rama, Swami, 63, 69, 73, 76, 80-81, 83, 127
Ramana Maharshi, 64, 67, 76, 107, 110-111, 167-168
Reality as Such, 9, 11-12, 20, 46, 63, 77, 96, 110, 114, 119, 126, 139, 157-158, 180, 185, 200, 205, 239
Relativity (theory of), 79
Relaxation, 1, 3-4, 51, 55-57
Reps, Paul, 3, 158-159
Restlessness, 60, 77, 232
Resurrection, 80
Return to the Source, 11, 48, 207, 214, 216
Revelation, 46, 48, 112, 118, 269
Roberts, Bernadette, 13, 44, 48, 245, 249-252
Rogers, Carl, 76
Root center (muladhara chakra), 121, 123-124, 129, 199
Ruysbroeck, Jan van, 239

S

Sabbath, Linda, 242-244
Saddhatissa, H., 132, 138, 140, 142
Sahaja Samadhi, 49, 130
Samadhi, 42, 44, 46, 66, 72, 75, 83, 89-94, 108, 119, 127-129, 131, 139, 142-143, 146, 150, 155, 158, 167, 171-173, 184-187, 197-198, 200-205, 208, 214-216, 223, 227, 236, 247, 259, 264, 266-267
Samprajnata/seed *samadhi*, 45, 90, 129, 183, 201, 248, 250, 252
  savitarka, 90
  nirvitarka, 90
  savicara, 91
  nirvicara, 91-92

Samkhya Yoga (philosophy), 65, 115
Samsara, 137, 161, 199
Satori (enlightenment), 153-154, 157, 164, 167, 169-170, 173
Satya (truthfulness), 76
Schlosser, Edith, 239
Sefirotic Tree/Tree of Life, 218-221, 224-225
Sekida, Katsuki, 155, 158
Self-examination, 18, 72, 218, 232, 238, 258
Self-observation, 17, 232
Self-realization, 48, 66-67, 69-70, 72, 83, 101, 159
Self-surrender, 67, 73, 75, 84, 107-109, 178, 187, 226, 241, 244, 269
Self-transformation, 121, 131, 200
Sensation center *(svadhisthana chakra)*, 124, 128, 209, 212-213
Separate self (ego), 44, 144, 147, 255, 267, 269
Shah, Idries, 257-261
Shakespeare, William, 99
Shakti, 115-122, 126-128, 176, 250
Shakti chalan, 128
Shattock, E.H., 147
Sheinkin, David, 219-222
Shikan-taza, 172-173, 192, 202, 205, 246-247
Shimano, Eido Roshi, 159
Shiva, 115-122, 126-128, 176
Shivananda, Swami, 82
Shneur, Rabbi Zalman (Kabbalist master), 226-227
Shostrom, Everet, 125
St. Simeon the New Theologian, 232
Skandhas, 182
Smith, Adam, 103
Soham (mantra meditation), 101

Source (Ultimate Reality as), 47, 67, 70-71, 93, 100-101, 115, 182, 203, 231, 255
Spiegelberg, Frederick, 79, 142
Spiritual Exercises, 239, 240-241
Star of David, 85
Stopping mind-waves, 64-65, 69, 214, 224, 233, 245
Stopping the world, 44, 91
Stream enterer, 152
Stream of consciousness, 57, 69-70, 84, 90, 138, 167, 188, 198, 202, 214, 234
Stress reduction, 1-2
String theory, 100
Subject-pole, 169, 249
Subtle body, 122
Subtle form/state, 47, 112, 126, 129, 142, 196, 208, 226, 236
Suchness, 100
Suffering, 77, 94-96, 240
Sufism/Sufis, xii, 18-19, 41, 48-49, 222-223, 226-227, 231, 255, 259-261, 264-267
Sufi meditation/path, 222-223, 255-267
Sunyata, 160, 170, 175-176, 181, 184, 186, 192, 194, 199, 204, 206
Supreme Identity, 48-49, 109, 123, 130, 176, 179, 252, 267
Sushumna nadi (central channel), 117, 121, 129, 195-198, 209, 212-215
Suzuki, D.T., 164-165, 167-171
Suzuki, Shunryo Roshi, 61, 172-173

T
Taimini, I.K., 94

Tantra, xi, 65-68, 80, 113-130, 142, 175-176, 178, 180, 203205, 209-210, 212, 221, 224, 259, *passim*
  right-handed path, 116, 120, 128
  left-handed path, 113, 116, 120, 128
Tao, 11, 48-49, 176, 207-208, 210, 212
Taoism, 11-12, 15, 48-49, 208, 216, 260
Taoist Yoga, xii, 11, 80, 128, 176, 185, 199, 207-216, 260
Tapas, 61, 73-74, 132
St. Teresa of Avila, 46, 248-249
Thera, Nyanaponika, 133-134
Theravada Buddhism, 17, 45, 49, 133, 152, 156, 167, 186-187, 194, 205, 234
Theravada Buddhist meditation, xii, 131-152
St. Theodoros the Great Ascetic, 232
St. Thomas Aquinas, 257
Thoreau, Henry David, 73
Throat center *(vishudha chakra),* 126, 129, 195, 197-198, 212
Tibetan Buddhism, 17, 45, 48, 58, 80, 175-176, 183, 186, 205, 222, 233, 262-263
Tibetan *Tantras*/Yogas, xii, 128, 184-206, 209-212, 222-224
  Kriya, 184, 186-192, 194, 240
  Carya, 184-186, 192-194, 240
  Yoga, 184-185, 194-200, 210
  Mahayoga, 184-185
  Anuttara, 184-185, 200-205
  Ati, 184-185
Time (of meditation), 52-54
Transcendence, 5, 8, 43, 47-48, 64-66, 71, 89-92, 94-96, 107, 114-115, 130, 139, 145, 152-153, 161-162, 164, 169, 171, 176, 181,

183, 198, 203-205, 207-208, 216, 226, 235, 238, 248-250, 252, 263-264, 267
Transcendent Unity, 160, 169
Transcendental Meditation (TM), 99-106
Transconscious state, 63-64, 70, 94, 101, 112, 114-115, 167, 185
Transformation, 22, 67, 113, 129, 132, 152-153, 177, 184, 208, 210-216, 250, 255, 259
   transforming energy into subtle essence, 208-209
   transforming subtle essence into spirit, 211-214
   transforming spirit into cosmic consciousness, 214-216
Transforming/permanent union, 226, 229, 236, 250
Transpersonal stages, 11, 44, 64, 176, 181, 249
Transpersonal states, 5, 63, 66, 80, 101-102, 116, 180, 199, 208, 224, 229, 249
Trinity, 208
True Self/nature, 10, 18, 64-65, 67, 101, 106, 112, 158, 205, 231, 249
Trungpa, Chogyam, 4, 17, 113, 118, 177, 185-186
Tsong-ka-pa (Tibetan master), 178, 187-194
Tolku, Tarthang, 4, 17-18, 73
Turiya, 49, 101, 130

U

Uddyana bandha, 127
Ultimate Reality, 12-13, 100, 167, 200
Ultimate/final/absolute transcendence, 86, 94-96, 114, 227, 250-251, 255
Unawareness, 5, 10, 17, 23, 30, 36-37, 70, 74, 81, 95, 123, 126, 132, 136, 138, 144, 148, 181, 204, 269
Unconditioned, the, xii, 10, 13, 19-20, 49, 83, 96, 114, 145, 152-153, 157-159, 161-162, 171-172, 183, 185, 199-200, 204-205, 217, 231, 244, 252, 256, 261, 267, 269
Unconditioned State, 8, 13, 46-47, 49, 63, 71, 101, 107, 118, 130, 152-153, 160-162, 173, 179, 182-184, 207, 263
Unconscious, 8, 69-70, 75, 94, 106, 111-112, 114-115, 118-119, 121, 142, 163, 167
Undifferentiated state, 110, 118-119
Undivided wholeness, 47, 93, 114, 127, 143, 151, 224
Unification of attention, 6, 33, 39-40, 83, 154-155, 209, 216-217, 235-236, 246, 266
Union with God, 8, 11-13, 45-47, 63, 66-67, 107, 217, 221, 226-227, 229, 236, 239, 245-250, 256, 258, 261, 263, 267, 269
Unitage stage, 230, 245
Upanishads, 49, 63, 110

V

Vajrayana path (Tibetan Buddhism), 175-206
Vase-breathing meditation, 195-196, 198, 202, 209
Vibration, 99-102
Vipassana, see insight meditation

Index

Visualization, 9, 14, 84, 87, 116-120, 127, 135, 141, 176-197, 199, 201-202, 210-216, 219, 221-225, 233, 239-240, 242-244, 260-264
Visuddhimagga, 142
Vivekananda, Swami, 34
Void-nature, 181, 186, 192-193, 197-199, 204
Void-state, 93, 198, 204, 216, 236
Vyasa (commentator on *Yoga Sutras*), 89, 91

W

Walking meditation, 41, 140-141, 144, 147, 156, 224-225
Walsh, Roger, 37, 43-44, 75, 77
Watchfulness, 232-233, 258
Way of the Sufi, 255-267
Wechler, Rob, 2
Wheel of Life, 257-258
White, John, 103, 105
Wilber, Ken, 6, 12-13, 44-45, 115, 163
Willis, Janice D., 180
Wisdom Principle, 116-118
Wisdom/third eye center *(ajna chakra),* 126, 129, 195-196, 208-209, 211-212, 214-216, 249
Wood, Ernest, 73

Y

Yahweh (YHVH), 222-223, 225
Yama, 75-77, 132
Yantra, 33, 83, 85, 116-118, 176, 180, 185
Yasutani Roshi, 11, 45, 153-154, 167-170, 172
Yidam, 176
Yin and *Yang,* 207, 216

Yoga, 11, 58, 63-96 *passim,* 99, 106, 113, 194, 199, 200
  meaning of, 63-66
Yoga of Inner Fire (Taoist), 210-213
Yogachara School of Buddhism, 154, 176
Yoga Sutras, xi, 15, 46, 65, 67-94 *passim,* 99, 106, 108, 116, 131-132, 142
Yogas of Naropa (six), 194-200, 202, 208, 260
  Yoga of Inner Fire, 194-199
  Yoga of Illusory Body, 199-200
  The Dream Yoga, 200
  Yoga of Clear Light, 200
  The *Bardo* (after-death state) Yoga, 200
  Transference of Consciousness Yoga, 200
Yogi, Maharishi Mahesh, 102
Yu, Lu K'uan, 209, 211-213, 216
Yuan-miao, Kao-feng (Zen master), 163
Yun, Hsu (Zen master), 170

Z

Zazen, 153-155
Zen Buddhism, xii, 3, 45-46, 48, 58-59, 111, 153-173, 175, 184, 186, 194, 205, 246, 250, 252
Zen master(s), 154, 157, 164, 166, 168, 257
Zohar, 225